A Commentary on the
Letters of John

A Commentary on the Letters of John

An Intra-Jewish Approach

by
Birger Olsson

Translated by
Richard J. Erickson

PICKWICK *Publications* · Eugene, Oregon

A COMMENTARY ON THE LETTERS OF JOHN
An Intra-Jewish Approach

Copyright © 2013 Birger Olsson. All rights reserved. Except for brief quotations in critical publications or reviews, no part of this book may be reproduced in any manner without prior written permission from the publisher. Write: Permissions, Wipf and Stock Publishers, 199 W. 8th Ave., Suite 3, Eugene, OR 97401.

Pickwick Publications
An Imprint of Wipf and Stock Publishers
199 W. 8th Ave., Suite 3
Eugene, OR 97401

www.wipfandstock.com

ISBN 13: 978-1-60899-774-9

Cataloguing-in-Publication data:

Olsson, Birger.

A commentary on the letters of John : an intra-jewish approach / Birger Olsson.

xvi + 366 pp. ; 23 cm. Includes bibliographical references.

ISBN 13: 978-1-60899-774-9

1. Bible. N.T. Epistles of John—Commentaries. I. Title.

BS2805.3 O55 2013

Manufactured in the U.S.A.

This translation is dedicated to
Shirley A. Decker-Lucke
for her encouragement
and for her kindness when it counted

Contents

Foreword – ix
Abbreviations – xi
Introduction – xiii

Third John
In or Out of the Jewish Community – 3

Second John
The Family of Truth and Love – 47

First John – 71

1. 1 John 1:1-4: Divine Life, Divine Fellowship, Divine Joy – 73
2. 1 John 1:5—2:2: A New Fellowship with God and Its Requirements – 88
3. 1 John 2:3-11: A Renewed Covenant with God and Its Consequences – 106
4. 1 John 2:12-17: Comfort and Admonition – 125
5. 1 John 2:18-27: Schism in the New Community – 139
6. 1 John 2:28—3:10: Children of God and Children of the Devil – 159
7. 1 John 3:11-24: Love One Another – 178
8. 1 John 4:1-6: Test Every Preacher – 196
9. 1 John 4:7-21: God is Love – 208
10. 1 John 5:1-12: Faith, Love, Begetting, Victory, and Eternal Life – 223
11. 1 John 5:13-21: Jesus, the True God and Eternal Life – 237
12. The Johannine Letters as a Whole – 251

Appendices

1. Hospitality – 283
2. Itinerant Brothers – 285
3. The Truth – 289

4 House Churches — 292
5 We in the Johannine Letters — 294
6 Life, Eternal Life — 296
7 Expiation and Forgiveness — 300
8 He: God, Jesus, or Both — 304
9 A Renewed Covenant — 307
10 What You Heard from the Beginning — 314
11 Begotten/Born of God — 317
12 They Cannot Sin — 323
13 Cain as the Devil's Son — 329
14 Jesus as Messiah, God's Son — 332
15 God in Them and They in God — 338
16 God is Love — 342
17 By Water and Blood — 347
18 Testify — 352
19 Sin that Leads to Death — 354

Annotated Bibliography — 357
Subject Index — 361

Foreword

THE NEED FOR COMMENTARIES arises from the biblical texts themselves and from various readers' encounters with them. A commentary is needed both by those who in one way or another read and interpret biblical texts for others and by those who for their own sake—individually or in a group—want to know more about what they find in the text. The purpose of the series in which this commentary first appeared in Swedish (Kommentar till Nya Testamentet) is simply to serve as a help for understanding the New Testament texts, and the series recommends itself to all who want to work seriously with the biblical texts.

Readers approach the biblical texts with a variety of interests. Some want to gain a grasp of the texts as wholes within their historical context; some are looking for answers regarding certain details; others want an overview of the result of biblical research as it touches on the interpretation of important themes or specific passages. Still others want help with bridging the gap between the texts' ancient situations and the present; some want to place the texts in a wider theological context; others want an idea of how the texts' content can be applied to readers today, and so on. Obviously, no one commentary can satisfy all these desires. This one is no exception, but hopefully it can provide good help in that direction—not least of all because of its arrangement.

The commentary assumes no knowledge of the Bible's original languages. Of course, it builds on detailed work with the Greek text, but the presentation proceeds from an English rendering. In its character it is a text-oriented commentary. That is, its primary goal is to clarify and explain the content of the texts. Consequently, it makes no extensive effort to trace the texts' origins or to apply the texts to readers and situations today.

The internal arrangement corresponds to this focus on the text and its proclamation. Each biblical book is viewed first as a whole, a coherent self-standing unit—even though for practical reasons it must be treated in smaller paragraphs in the process of interpretation. These smaller passages are handled in four sections. First, the text or section of text is arranged analytically in "Translation displays." Then, the "Notes" throw light on individual details needing clarification. This can involve peculiarities in the underlying Greek text or concepts, persons, names, and situations that are obviously not familiar today. In "Analysis," questions are taken up that are important for understanding the interpretation of a passage as a whole: context, structure, genre,

Foreword

literary features, etc. The section "Interpretation" gives the interpretive results as a whole. This final section can be read independently of the previous two sections. This arrangement gives the readers help in working first-hand with the biblical text and lets them follow the commentator's work step by step.

Separate interpretive problems are handled in smaller investigations (appendices) gathered at the end of the commentary. The standard questions about the biblical book's origin and situation are found in a special final chapter. By virtue of its arrangement, the volume becomes both a commentary and something of a handbook.

It is our hope and prayer to God that this commentary, and the series in which it originated, will go on enriching people's involvement with the Bible and lead to a better and deeper understanding of the biblical texts.

LarsOlov Eriksson
Birger Olsson
Mikael Winninge

Abbreviations

THROUGHOUT THE TEXT OF the commentary abbreviations conform to the standard lists in Patrick H. Alexander et al., eds., *The SBL Handbook of Style: For Ancient Near Eastern, Biblical, and Early Christian Studies* (Peabody, MA: Hendrickson, 1999). The two exceptions are the following:

Gkt refers to "the Greek text" of a given passage.
TOB refers to *Traduction Oecuménique de la Bible* (1972)

Introduction

"Are you the one who is to come, or are we to wait for another?" (Matt 11:3)

John the Baptist and many other Jews of the first century posed this very question. The answers they received eventually shaped the history of the entire Western world. This Messiah Jesus, the Prophet who was to come—is he sent by God to save the world or is he not? The answers have consequences even for people living today.

The New Testament's Johannine literature to a very great degree focuses on this question about Jesus of Nazareth. The Gospel of John is written "so that you may believe that Jesus is the Christ, the Son of God, and that believing you may have life in his name" (John 20:31). The way the original is worded implies that the Gospel is aimed primarily not at awakening faith, as if it were a missionary text, but rather at strengthening and deepening faith in Jesus as Messiah, the son of God. It is a text of edification. The Letter of First John—also primarily a text of edification—is written "to you who believe in the name of the Son of God, so that you may know that you have eternal life" (1 John 5:13). In a difficult situation, the author wants to encourage and support those who believe in Jesus as Messiah, son of God; and at an early stage of things those who believed in Jesus were Jews—he wants to confirm and deepen their faith. In both documents the concern is eternal life, being united with God himself both now and eternally.

Who is this Jesus from Nazareth? From the beginning, the question is a Jewish question, that is, it presupposes the tradition we find in the Hebrew Bible and in Jewish faith of two thousand years ago. In one sense, the Gospel of John is the most Jewish of the New Testament writings. Even the Johannine letters can be read from an intra-Jewish perspective. A great deal of evidence suggests that during the closing decades of the first century, Jews who confessed Jesus as Messiah, God's son, were exposed to external pressures to abandon their faith. (In the following commentary, whenever these Jewish believers can be connected with the Johannine documents I will refer to them as Johannine Christians.)

Following the tragic defeats of the 70s, Jews strove to strengthen Jewish solidarity and to secure a Jewish identity; the consequence was that those who deviated found themselves forced to leave the Jewish community. Meanwhile within Roman society it had become necessary to distinguish between who was and who was not

Introduction

a Jew. Far too many non-Jews had affiliated with the new messianic movement. As worship of Caesar became prevalent, one could more clearly tell who was Jewish and who was not. Jews were not required to worship Caesar. But what was to be done with the Christians? Where did Jews who followed Jesus fit in? It was in this situation, so increasingly difficult for Jesus-believing Jews, that the Johannine teaching was eventually written down.

The Letters of John can be read from various perspectives. Since the end of the first century it has been normal to approach them from the interpreter's current situation, that is, from a *general Christian perspective*. I refer to it that way because in large measure it has dominated the entire history of the church. From this point of view, the first two letters especially are taken as powerfully addressing Christian teachers and Gnostic preachers who had a heretical—docetic, Gnostic—understanding of Jesus. Some Christians had lapsed from pure, correct doctrine. Thus, at the base of an interpretation from this perspective lies *an apostasy hypothesis*.

In the last thirty years, not least of all after Raymond E. Brown's massive commentary of 1982, many scholars have chosen to interpret the letters from a *Johannine community perspective*: the particular form of Christian faith found in the Johannine writings, with its so-called high Christology, had been further developed by some Johannine Christians to such a degree that it was no longer acceptable to the leading teacher within the movement. Foundational to an interpretation from a perspective like this is *a progression hypothesis*, that is, a hypothesis that some believers—probably many—overstepped their own faith tradition and broke away from the Johannine community. It is a phenomenon we recognize from later epochs in the church's history.

These two perspectives, together with their accompanying hypotheses, will appear within my commentary, but I will place the primary weight on *an intra-Jewish perspective*. Those who are referred to in the two first letters as antichrists and false prophets—that is, those who have broken away from the Johannine community—are Jews who have abandoned their faith in Jesus as Messiah, the son of God, and gone back to their previous faith, probably as a result of external pressure. This approach to the Johannine letters proceeds therefore from *a regression hypothesis*. John the Baptist's question, quoted above, thus becomes primary. The various alternatives are treated in more detail in point 4 of the commentary's conclusion, chapter 12. One can find legitimate support in the text for all three perspectives. I choose to pursue the regression alternative mostly because it has seldom been used in reading the letters of John, but also because I believe this alternative provides the simplest explanation for the formulations in all three documents.

If, then, Jesus of Nazareth is the promised Messiah, the one who was to come, sent by God himself, what does that mean in terms of Jewish ways of thinking? These letters verbally formulate the implications of such a Messianic faith and employ those formulas in their arguments: to live in the light, to live as Jesus lived, to love one's fellow believers, to be pure from sin, to know God, to be born of God, to be God's

Introduction

children, to be closely united with God, to have the Spirit, to be confident in the face of final judgment, to have eternal life here and now, and so on. There were in Jesus' day many conceptualizations of the messianic time. I will pay special attention to promises connected with the renewed covenant of Jeremiah 31, Ezekiel 36, and various Qumran texts: purification from all sin, a new close union with God (knowing God), lack of need for teachers, a new heart, a new spirit, God's spirit given as a gift, a new life in accordance with the will of God. In terms of a tradition such as this, it is easy to understand that Johannine Christians saw themselves as a renewed Israel, as a new family, fully characterized by the truth and the love that flowed out from God himself.

I have been studying the letters of John for a long time. In the early 1960s, Professor Harald Riesenfeld conducted seminars at Uppsala University on 1 John, with special reference to Rudolf Schnackenburg's large commentary, which had just come out in a revised edition. Harald Riesenfeld had the ability to inspire his students with enthusiasm, and I therefore dedicate this commentary to him in appreciation for the instructive, encouraging, and challenging years at Uppsala.

At the end of the 1970s, I began to write a commentary on the Letters of John, but I had to give it up. It was too difficult to understand and interpret all the antitheses, the stark either-or argumentation, the constant framing of things in black and white. That kind of thinking may be perfectly satisfying during one's college years, but not two decades later. Change of perspective and an emphasis on the robust anchoring of the letters in history have made it easier now to explain these letters, which are so unique in the Christian canon.

No one knows in what order the three letters were written. There is, however, something to be said for the view that 3 John reflects a situation predating the great schism within the Johannine community. Although we know so little about these three letters, the order I have chosen to follow can also provide a greater coherence among them.

Each chapter of the commentary is supplied with a table that reproduces the text in smaller pieces; the connections among these pieces are indicated by means of indentations. This text presentation provides a translation that communicates more information about the form of the original, while simultaneously creating a more precise system of reference than the traditional verse divisions do.

The Johannine letters, particularly 1 John, are typically among those texts read first by students of the New Testament in Greek. I have therefore offered a little more information about linguistic issues in the notes to 1 John. In the portion of the work dedicated to the other two letters, I have tried for pedagogical reasons to model important questions one must ask of the text in the process of interpreting an ancient letter. All this has meant that the commentary is somewhat longer than I had at first anticipated.

The Gospel of John records that many Jews who have become disciples of Jesus leave him when in the synagogue he teaches them who he is. At last there are twelve left and Jesus asks them, "You don't want to go away, too, do you?" They answered him, "Lord, to whom shall we go? You have the words of eternal life. We have come to believe and to know that you are the Holy One of God" (John 6:67–69).

Readers wanting immediate access to my interpretation of the Letters of John would do well to read first what I have written in the "Interpretation" sections for each letter. Alternative interpretations and a defense of my own can be found in the "Notes" and "Analysis," as well in the appendices.

Third John

Third John: In or Out of the Jewish Community

Translation Display

1a	From the Elder to Gaius
1b	the beloved
1c	whom I love in truth.
2a	Beloved
2b	I pray
2c	that in everything you do well and are in good health
2d	just as your soul does well.
3a	For I was very glad
3b	when brothers came and testified to your truth
3c	just as you walk in the truth.
4a	Greater joy I do not have than this
4b	that I hear
4c	that my children walk in the truth.
5a	Beloved
5b	you faithfully do
5c	whatever you do for the brothers, for strangers
6a	who have testified to your love before the congregation
6b	whom you do well to send on worthily of God.
7a	For it is for the Name's sake that they have gone out
7b	and they accept no support from the non-Jews.
8a	Therefore, it is we who ought to give hospitality to such men
8b	so that we may become co-workers with the truth.
9a	I have written something to the congregation
9b	but the one who likes to put himself in charge of them
9c	Diotrephes
9d	he does not welcome us.
10a	Therefore, if I come

Third John

10b	I will call attention to the things he is doing
10c	in speaking evil things against us.
10d	And not satisfied with doing these things
10e	he refuses to welcome the brothers
10f	and he even hinders those who want to do so
10g	and drives them out of the congregation.
11a	Beloved,
11b	do not imitate what is evil, but what is good.
11c	Whoever does good is from God.
11d	Whoever does evil has not seen God.
12a	Demetrius has been testified to favorably by all
12b	and by the truth itself.
12c	We also testify regarding him
12d	and you know that our testimony is true.
13a	I have many things to write to you
13b	but I do not want to write to you with ink and pen.
14a	I hope to see you soon
14b	and we will talk face to face.
15a	Peace to you.
15b	The friends send you greetings.
15c	Greet the friends by name.

Notes

1. the Elder. Gkt *ho presbyteros*, sometimes rendered "the Presbyter." There are no other Christian examples from the period of this absolute usage of *ho presbyteros*, where it is not followed by a personal name. The expression thus functions as a name: the Elder or the Presbyter. I use both forms in this commentary. I see him as bearer and guarantor for the Johannine proclamation with its roots extending back to Jesus himself; he is certainly an older man of Jewish origin, a Christ-believing Jew in the second Christian generation. See further chap. 12, point 2.

Third John has the usual form of ancient epistolary introduction: the sender is stated in the nominative and the recipients in the dative. On the letter's form and special character, see Analysis, point 2.

Gaius is known to us only through 3 John. His name is a typical Latin one, especially associated with the imperial family in Rome. The name may indicate that either he or his father or grandfather was a manumitted Jewish slave from Rome. He probably owned a large house, since he was able to accommodate and support itinerant Jews and presumably also to receive Johannine Christians in his home. In this way he is similar to his namesake in Corinth, who according to Paul "is host to me and to the whole church" (Rom 16:23; 1 Cor 1:14). In Gaius' circle of friends in Corinth there were persons with Roman names (Tertius, Quartus) and persons of higher social standing (city treasurer Erastus). Two of Paul's traveling companions during the 50s, probably Jewish Christians of the Diaspora, were also named Gaius (Acts 19:29; 20:4).

The Gaius in 3 John was likely a Christ-believing Diaspora Jew well established in the Roman world. He obviously belonged to the Johannine Christians. According to a tradition from the fourth century, he was installed as bishop of Pergamum by the Apostle John.

the beloved. Gkt *tōi agapētōi*, from the verb *agapan*. The word "beloved" (*agapētos*) does not belong to the usual vocabulary used at the beginning of ancient letters, contrary to our word "dear." It should therefore be seen as characteristically Christian, even more so as a Johannine idiom. It is used six times as a vocative in 1 John and three times in 3 John. See note on "Beloved" in 1 John 2:7.

The Christians are God's beloved (1 Thess 1:4; John 16:27) and they love one another (John 13:34; 1 John 3:23; 2 John 5). In a Johannine context, this idiom emphasizes unity and solidarity within the Johannine community.

whom I love in truth. This description, found also in the opening of 2 John, is annoyingly ambiguous. It has few parallels in Greek. There are two main alternatives:

a. "Whom I really love." The phrase "in truth" modifies the word "love." So NAB, "indeed," and TEV, "truly." As a linguistic parallel, one usually refers to the Greek epistolary phrase, "to love sincerely" (*philein pros alētheian*; Fayyum papyri 118.26; 119.26–27) and to the exhortation in 1 John 3:18 to "love in truth and action."

b. "Whom I love in (the) truth." (According to CEV, "because we follow the truth.") The word "truth" can have either definite or indefinite form with no great difference in meaning. See the Note "live in the truth," v. 4 below. The phrase "in truth" thus takes on a greater weight and leads one's thoughts to the concept of "truth" in the Johannine writings and to such biblical formulations as "all who love the Lord God in truth and righteousness" (Tob 14:7), and "they who love him [the Lord] in truth" (*Pss. Sol.* 10:3; 14:1). According to this alternative, both love and truth express a close relationship between the Elder and Gaius. See further Appendix 3, The Truth.

The words "whom I love in the truth" are a clear reinforcement of the word "beloved" immediately preceding. The verb "to love," in the Johannine writings, is first of all a strong expression for unity, belonging, and solidarity. Love and truth bind the believers together as Jesus' true disciples and distinguish "we" from "they" in the world. In a Johannine context these final words of v. 1 take on a richer meaning than is often given them in translation.

Third John

If a choice must be made between the two alternatives, I choose the latter. It is possible that the author alters an epistolary phrase here right at the start in order to open the way to two important concepts in his unfolding argument. For several examples of this, see the Analysis, point 2.

2. Beloved. Gkt *agapēte*. For the third time the author uses the word "love," here as a vocative, similarly in vv. 5 and 11. It has an appealing, intimate tone; within a letter it can emphasize something already mentioned, move on to something new, or introduce a special instruction. Based on the form of the letter, it is unexpected here. See the Analysis, point 2. Already here in the introduction the author is setting things up for his subject.

With the word "beloved," Gaius is addressed as a member of God's own people on the earth. "Beloved" (*agapētos*)—which in the LXX can render both the Hebrew *jāchīd* ("exclusively loved, unique") and *jᵉdīd* ("friend")—is a frequent description of God's people (Jer 6:26; Ps 60:7; 127:2; cf. Rom 1:7). In Exod 19:5 it is stated that those who enter into the covenant with God are to be his own possession above all other nations. The word for "possession" (*sᵉgullā*) is rendered in an Aramaic translation (targum) with "a nation of beloved ones." Thus, this seemingly normal epistolary phrase has a special, biblical Christian background. See also the note on "beloved" in v. 1.

I pray that in everything you do well and are in good health. In Gkt the verb "I pray" is followed by the sentence structure of the accusative + infinitive type—literally, "you to prosper and to be healthy." Many letters of the period have similar phrases at just this point and with the same verbs: "I pray" (*euchomai*), and "be healthy" (*hygiainein*). See examples in the Analysis, point 3. Third John is the only letter in the NT that has such an ordinary wish for good health. Yet, this usual formulation has been altered in a couple of ways. See the Analysis, point 2. The addition of the verb "do well" to the traditional phrase "be in good health" prepares the way for the next clause, *just as your soul does well*—literally, "as (*kathōs*) your soul prospers." Clearly this is the fact the author wants to emphasize in v. 2, and not simply a wish for good health. The "just as" sentence is followed later by the same construction in v. 3—literally, "just as you walk in the truth."

As a rule, the Greek conjunction *kathōs* introduces a comparison ("just as") or sometimes a rationale ("since"); in the Gospels it is often used with reference to a proof text, in the Johannine writings with regard to the relations between Father, Son, and disciples. Here, a comparison is the probable choice, but the comparison is not completed in v. 2. *Kathōs* most likely modifies the assertion in the sentence, so that its validity is left somewhat open. The recipient is invited to confirm what is being said. See the Analysis, points 2 and 4.

soul. The word in Gkt, *psychē*, is used in the Gospel of John as almost synonymous with life (John 12:25). Here the word refers to Gaius as a whole person, including his relationship to God.

3. For I was very glad. Gkt *echarēn gar lian* ("for I rejoiced very much") is also a typical phrase in letters. See the Analysis, point 2. The same sentence occurs in 2 John 4 and in the letter of Polycarp to the Philippians, 1:1. Cf. 1 John 1:4.

The question is whether the aorist form *echarēn* is to be translated "I was overjoyed" (on this particular occasion), or "I became happy" (ingressive), or "I am happy" (epistolary aorist). The formal expression in Gkt makes it difficult to insist on one particular nuance. In the context, v. 3 is part of an appreciative praise of Gaius, something which is important for the argument. It is reminiscent of many instances of "I rejoice over you" in Paul's letters (Rom 16:19; 1 Cor 16:17; 2 Cor 2:3; 7:7, 9, 13, 16).

Verse 3 is connected to the foregoing in Gkt by *gar* ("for"), which lacks a corresponding expression in some translations (NRSV, e.g.). But the author is forming an argument. See the Analysis, point 2.

when brothers came. Gkt uses the genitive absolute with the verb "come" (*erchesthai*), in the present, likely indicating repeated visits. According to v. 3, both the Presbyter and Gaius were used to "brothers" from other places arriving for a visit, only to travel on again almost immediately. These itinerant brothers were able to meet people in synagogues, in house-churches, and in homes; they were able to witness to their faith and give instruction; they could give and receive information from their fellow believers; they received economic support for their continued journeys. See Appendix 1, Hospitality, and Appendix 2, Itinerant Brothers.

testified. The verb "testify" (*martyrein*)—occurring here with the dative of interest (*dativus commodi*), to the advantage of; cf. John 5:33; 18:37; Acts 14:3—belongs among the most important Johannine words. See Appendix 18, Testify.

your truth. Literally, the same construction as in "your soul" in v. 2 and "your love" in v. 6. "Your" is emphasized in Gkt by being placed in front of the word it modifies.

The word "truth" (*alētheia*), runs like a crimson thread throughout the letter: 3 John 1, 3 (twice), 4, 8, 12. In v. 1 it is connected with "love"; in v. 6 it is further defined as "your love." The same combination and the same heaping up of related words occur at the beginning of 2 John. The context shows that the author focuses on Gaius' manner of conducting himself toward the visiting brothers (vv. 5–8), referred to here, however, as "Gaius' truth." See further Appendix 3, The Truth.

just as. Gkt *kathōs*, i.e., the same construction as in v. 2d. In translations it has been used for introducing a comparison, "as you always" (TEV); a rationale marked by "since you"; an example or further defining of what has just been said, "how you" (NIV, NRSV); or a positive affirmation and reinforcement from the author's side: "you who" (TOB). In Gkt the "you" is emphasized in the sentence through the use of the personal pronoun. The last named translation alternative probably does most justice to the argument in the section and to the use of *kathōs* in v. 2. See the Analysis, point 2.

walk in the truth. A literal representation of Gkt; the reference is to how Gaius conducts himself. See the note on "walk" in 1 John 1:6. The present tense in this concluding, affirming sentence contributes to reinforcing the positive image of Gaius that the Elder is careful to draw before he gets down to the letter's main business.

4. Greater joy I do not have than this. Word for word: "Greater than these not have I joy." Form and content in v. 4 are clearly connected with v. 3, a repetition that strengthens and generalizes what was just said, while simultaneously rounding off a paragraph in the presentation. To read *charin*, with Codex Vaticanus and some early translations (bo, lat—"grace/favor"), in place of *charan* ("joy"), can be supported from introductions to several Pauline letters (Rom 1:5; 1 Cor 1:3), but it is contradicted by the entire introduction in 3 John, as well as by the majority of manuscripts.

Gkt begins with "greater than these (things)" (*meizoteran toutōn*). The double comparative form *meizoteran*—simple form, *meizona*, in the parallel construction in John 15:13—presumably carries no special nuance. Possibly v. 4 as a whole receives a greater weight and roundedness with this longer form together with the plural of "this" (*toutōn*—referring both to the previously mentioned report of the brothers and to the following "that"-sentence), and with the word-order ("greater" in first position in the sentence and "joy" in final position). The author is generous in his positive comments about Gaius.

that I hear. Gkt *hina akouō*, which can also be rendered "when I hear." This *hina*-clause gives content to "these" at the beginning of v. 4. In similar formulations—plural of *touto* plus *hina*-clause—the pronoun usually refers backward and *hina* indicates purpose. See John 5:34; 15:11; 16:4, 33. The singular of *touto* would be the natural choice.

my children. The expression marks both a close solidarity and a distinct difference between the author and the Johannine Christians he has in mind. The Johannine use of the word "children" is described in notes on 1 John 2:1 and 3:1.

When the Elder here in 3 John speaks of "my children" with the more common *tekna* (and not the diminutive form *teknia*), and in 2 John describes the members of the two congregations in question there as "the elect lady's children" and "your elect sister's children" (2 John 1, 4, 13), we should hear the Johannine context in the background. This formulation testifies indirectly to the strong sense of belonging within the Johannine fellowship. It works well, besides, with the epithet "the Elder."

The idea that "my children" implies "people whom I have led to Christian faith," an idea found in Paul (Gal 4:19; 1 Cor 4:14–15; Phlm 10), finds no support in the Johannine contexts and is contradicted to a certain degree by the Johannine emphasis on God as the one who gives birth (John 1:12–13; 1 John 5:1, 4, 18).

walk in the truth. See the note to v. 3 above. The same phrase is found in 2 John 4, but without the definite article in front of "truth." See also John 17:17, 19. This implies that the use of the article with the concept of "truth," familiar to the author and the recipient, can vary without a difference in meaning.

5. you faithfully do. Literal rendering of Gkt *piston poieis,* implying that Gaius shows himself faithful. The word "faithfully" (*piston*) is adverbial or a predicate adjective modifying the following relative clause, "whatever you do." After the laudatory introduction in vv. 1–4, Gaius could have expected here a request of some sort, opening with the words "you will do well if." This very phrase occurs in v. 6, but here in v. 5 the author continues praising Gaius, doing so with words reminiscent of a request. See the Analysis, point 2.

The word for "faithful/dependable/loyal," *pistos,* is related to "truth" (*alētheia*), in the preceding text, and in a Christian context it can also bring to mind the thought of faithful stewards (Luke 12:42). With the verbs *poiein* and (in the next sentence) *ergazethai*—both meaning do/accomplish—the focus now is directed to what Gaius does. Making his faith real through action is how he lives in the truth.

whatever you do. Gkt *ho ean ergasēi.* This relative clause functions as the object of the verb "do" that precedes it. The subjunctive plus *ean* expresses commonly recurring circumstances: "every time that." The aorist form *ergasēi*—and not the present, which we might have expected based on the preceding sentence—is constative, that is, a number of acts are taken as a whole. It refers to what Gaius has done, is doing, and will do.

The verb *ergazesthai* ("labor/work/accomplish") is used in John especially with regard to the divine work that Jesus or the believers carry out (John 5:17; 9:4; 6:28–29). The related noun *ergon* is frequently used of activity in the congregation (1 Thess 5:12–13; Titus 3:13–14).

for the brothers. The word "brothers" renders Greek *adelphous* and has in view Jewish-Christian itinerant preachers. See Appendix 2, Itinerant Brothers.

for strangers. Literally, "and this, strangers" (*kai touto xenous*). The same construction occurs in 1 Cor 6:6. The three words in Gkt further describe "the brothers" and emphasize that they are strangers to Gaius. As such they have no right to expect privileges in the locality where Gaius lives. They were outcasts in dire need of someone to show them hospitality. Their status with someone in the vicinity needed to be changed from stranger to guest. Gaius clearly does not know these brothers, since they need letters of recommendation as they arrive (vv. 9, 12). See Appendix 1, Hospitality.

6. Gkt here has two relative clauses. Various translations, including NIV and NRSV, render them as two independent sentences, with the brothers as subject in one and object in the other; this makes the syntactical construction of vv. 5–6 somewhat awkward. The first sentence, which takes up the word "testify" from v. 3, is more

Third John

parenthetical; the other, regarding Gaius' relationship to the "brothers," is more of a continuation of v. 5.

have testified. The verb is in the aorist, which indicates a particular instance of testimony or more likely a series of such instances (a parallel to *ergasēi* in v. 5). In v. 3 the present is used. The letter presupposes a certain traffic of "strange brothers" between the two places where the Presbyter and Gaius live.

your love. The word makes more precise "your [faithfulness to the] truth" in v. 3. Truth and love belong very closely together (2 John 3). Love incarnates truth. Some late mss in fact have "your truth and love."

before the congregation. Or the more general "before Jewish congregations" (Gkt has an indefinite form of *ekklēsia*). Gkt uses the so-called improper preposition *enōpion* ("before one's eyes")—common in the LXX as a rendering of Hebrew *lifnē*—plus *ekklēsia* ("gathering/congregation"), without the article. In Greek the use of the article can vary with known concepts or in prepositional phrases without significant difference in meaning. The combination *enōpion* + *ekklēsia* (with the article) occurs also in the LXX (1 Sam 8:22; 1 Chr 29:10; Neh 8:2).

The word *ekklēsia*, mostly through Paul's letters, came to be a typical designation for a Christian gathering, most often for Christians in a particular place, although sometimes in a large area (Acts 9:31) and sometimes regarding all Christians (Col 1:17–18, 24; 2:10). Via the Latin *ecclesia* it then became the standard Christian word for church, congregation. This probably explains the fact that almost all interpreters, so far as I know, assume that *ekklēsia* in 3 John refers to Christian communities.

However, at the time 3 John was written, the word had a significantly wider use. It is very common in the language of politics, for example, as a technical term for a public gathering, often a gathering of free men with voting rights. Through its use in the LXX, mostly as a translation of the Hebrew *qāhāl*, the word acquired a cultic flavor, referring to a meeting assembled for worship. The new thing within Judaism was that "congregation" incorporated even women and children, and that people assembled not to make laws but to listen to the law that God had given them (Neh 8:2, 17). In the book of Sirach the word *ekklēsia* is used of gatherings of Jews in cities and towns with functions suggestive of the synagogue of the first century (Sir 21:17; 23:24; 31:11; 33:19; 39:10; 44:15). In Philo it can refer to some form of synagogue fellowship (*Deus* 108; *Virt.* 111). In the book *Liber antiquitatum biblicarum*, dating from the beginning of our era or earlier, we hear that on the Sabbath the Lord is praised "in the assembly [*ecclesia*] of the elders." Cf. Sir 24:23 and *Ps. Sol.* 10:7, which speak of similar assemblies (*synagōgai*), and also Jas 5:14, "the elders of the congregation [*ekklēsia*]."

The word *ekklēsia* occurs also in vv. 9 and 10. On the basis of an intra-Jewish perspective, I have interpreted it as referring to the Jewish community in the locality where the Johannine Christians also were. This interpretation simplifies the relationships between the persons and groups named in 3 John. The Elder uses other words for his fellow Christians: "the friends" (3 John 15); "beloved" or "(my) children" (often in 1 John); "brothers" (1 John 3:16–17); "the elect lady and her children" (2 John 1); "your elect sister's children" (2 John 13). *Ekklēsia* in v. 6, then, would be the Jewish congregation located where the Elder lived, a congregation that also included Johannine Christians. Sometimes I use the word "synagogue" for this fellowship, even if we do not know anything of the building where these Jews gathered. The general Christian apostasy hypothesis and the intra-Johannine progression hypothesis—with its later dating of the letter—both proceed on the assumption that *ekklēsia* refers to a Christian congregation.

whom you do well. The words in Gkt are an epistolary phrase that often introduces a moderate and respectful request or an extremely mild and carefully worded exhortation: "it would be good if." See the note on v. 5 above. One of the standard phrases uses the future followed by an aorist participle, precisely as here. See examples in the Analysis, point 3. Not just the formulation itself, but even the entire clause-structure in vv. 5–6, serves to ameliorate the indirect exhortation (the phrase is part of a relative clause coming at the end of the sentence). The reader is thus left unsure about whether the letter's main purpose is found here or comes later on in vv. 11–12. The balance between assertions and desires in 3 John is troublesome for those who prefer to have definitive answers. Several translations have rendered the later portion of v. 6 as an independent command (TEV, JerB).

to send on. Gkt has the verb *propempein*, which seems to have a nearly technical sense in the NT: to equip missionaries for traveling to their next destination. It is used most often of Paul and his fellow workers (Rom 15:24; 1 Cor 16:6, 11; 2 Cor 1:16; Acts 16:3). The jurist Zenas (and Apollos) in Titus 3:13—who clearly delivered the letter of Titus to its addressees—do not need to be missionaries. Travel was a pervasive reality in the early church and not least for itinerant preachers lacking their own means and dependent on support and help. See Appendix 1, Hospitality.

worthily of God. This literal rendering of the formulation in Gkt—*axiōs tou theou*—is difficult to define as to its content. It probably expresses not so much the shape of Gaius' activity as its context and motivation: to equip these Christ-believing Jews for their continued travels is part of a godly context. That is, the context's exclusive focus on God is decisive here. Paul exhorts the Christians in Rome to receive the sister Phoebe in a manner "fitting [in Greek *axiōs*] for the saints" (Rom 16:2).

7. For. Gkt, *gar*. The word can be taken as support for reading the end of v. 6 as an exhortation that is now further rationalized in v. 7.

it is for the Name's sake that they have gone out. Literally, "for the name's sake they went out." According to Bengel, they did so either as exiles or as proclaimers of the

Third John

gospel. These two alternatives are still discussed today, even though they could be combined in the hypothesis regarding Jewish Christ-believing itinerant preachers who because of conditions in the east were forced to make their way westward. See further, Appendix 2, Itinerant Brothers. The words in this verse do not give us much help in describing the brothers. The verb *exerchesthai*, rendered in the NRSV as "began their journey," is used of itinerant teachers in the *Didache* and, e.g., Matt 10:11; 13:13, 49, and of Paul and Silas in Acts 15:40. According to 1 John, antichrists "went out from us" (1 John 2:19)—indeed, many false prophets "have gone out into the world" (1 John 4:1; 2 John 7).

The formula "for the Name's sake"—or more literally as in the NRSV footnote, "for the sake of the name"—supports such an interpretation. It can refer either to God or to Jesus. Linguistic patterns in the NT speak in favor of the latter.

  a. To *suffer* "for the Name's sake" as Jesus' disciples (Acts 5:41). Other texts indicate that the name of Jesus Christ is in view (Acts 9:16; 21:13; 1 Pet 4:14; cf. Phil 1:29; 2 Cor 12:10). Paul and Barnabas risked their lives "for the sake of [the name of] our Lord Jesus Christ" (Acts 15:26).
  b. To *leave one's house and family* "for my name's sake," i.e., for the sake of one's Christian faith (Matt 19:29).
  c. To *bring about the obedience of faith among all the Gentiles* "for the sake of his [Jesus Christ's] name" (Rom 1:5). See also the use of "name" in John 1:12; 1 John 2:12; 3:23; and 5:13.

Neither the name Jesus nor the name Christ occurs in 3 John, which can be explained on the basis of the letter's Jewish context. In 1 John there is a significant tendency to avoid always using "Jesus" or "Christ," and instead to use the personal pronoun or "this one" (*ekeinos*) of Jesus. See the note on "he" for 1 John 2:6 and Appendix 8, He: God, Jesus, or both.

These brothers have set out on their journey as Jesus-believers, either of their own free will or compelled by external circumstances, in order to proclaim Jesus in word and deed. Homelessness, suffering, and mission can be combined here in certain cases. See Appendix 2, Itinerant Brothers. In the 110s, Ignatius praises the Christians in Ephesus because they "live according to the truth, and . . . do not listen to any one other than to those speaking of Jesus Christ in truth. For some are in the habit of carrying about the Name in wicked guile, while yet they practice things unworthy of God [*anaxia theou*], whom you must avoid as you would wild beasts" (Ign. *Eph.* 6:2—7:1).

and they accept no support from the non-Jews. Literally, "nothing receiving from the non-Jews," in Gkt *mēden lambanontes apo tōn ethnikōn*. The word choice in Gkt—*mēden* and not *ouden* for "nothing"—presumably gives the verb a modal aspect: they do not wish to accept anything/they should not accept anything.

There is a great distance between these brothers and the non-Jews. The author reinforces the distance by choosing the word *ethnikoi* rather than the usual *ethnē* for "the non-Jews." The word *ethnikos* in this verse emphasizes the qualitatively other. The perspective is intra-Jewish. See also Gal 2:14.

The fact that the itinerant brothers receive nothing from the non-Jews, then, probably involves more than just a refusal to accept payment from non-Jewish audiences (or from newly converted non-Jews); it is a mark of their belonging to the Jewish community, within which there were also Jesus-believing Jews (Johannine Christians).

8. Therefore it is we who ought. Gkt has three words, *hymeis oun opheilomen* ("therefore we ourselves are obliged to"), a formula that sounds Johannine in several ways. See 1 John 3:16; 4:11; as well as 1 John 2:6; John 13:14. At the forefront stands an emphatic "we" (*hymeis*), i.e., we Jews in contrast to the non-Jews named in v. 7, or more likely we Johannine Christians, represented in this context by the letter's author and recipient. Then comes the conjunction *oun*—very common in John (200 times, but only here in the Johannine letters), which sometimes marks a conclusion: so then, therefore. Finally, the verb *opheilein*—meaning, to owe, to be obligated—followed by an infinitive. See the note on "ought" in 1 John 2:6.

These three words become a Johannine way of delivering a powerful indirect exhortation, even though here they form part of a wider argument. See the Analysis, point 4. That Jews should welcome other Jews can seem self-evident. In crisis situations, to welcome Jews of peculiar traditions and lifestyles can be more difficult.

to give hospitality. Gkt *hypolambanein*. The JerB has "welcome," the TEV has "help," and the NIV "show hospitality." See further Appendix 1, Hospitality.

such men. Gkt, *toioutous*, which can be used in the NT without particular emphasis, e.g., 2 Cor 2:6–7. Here the point is more qualified: we are obligated to open our homes to such people as these! The word *toioutos* occurs with emphasis also in John 4:23 and 9:16.

so that we may become co-workers with the truth. Gkt *hina synergoi ginometha tēi alētheiai*. The last two Greek words might also be rendered "for the benefit of the truth."

This clause, which clearly reinforces the indirect exhortation in the beginning of the verse, can be translated in two ways, depending on how one interprets the idea of "truth" at the end of the clause and its dative form. Gkt has a typical *hina*-clause, which normally expresses purpose (final clause) or result (consecutive clause). The verb used here indicates a process: to become something more and more. The same verb is used in John 15:8.

This leaves the words *synergoi* and *tēi alētheiai*, placed at the beginning and the end of the clause for emphasis. The word *synergos*—as it and the corresponding verb are used by Paul—often has a technical sense of fellow laborer in God's mission work on the earth (1 Cor 3:9; Rom 16:3, 9, 21; 1 Thess 3:2), but it can also have a more general sense (Rom 8:28; Jas 2:22). Taken together with the dative phrase *tēi alētheiai*, it offers two translation alternatives:

a. To become fellow workers (with the brothers) for the benefit of the truth (dative of interest or advantage, *dativus commodi*), i.e., the interpretation found in most translations (JerB, NIV, CEV, TEV). It is taken for granted then that the brothers are missionaries and that the truth is synonymous with the message of Jesus Christ, the gospel. The CEV renders the clause as "so that we can take part in what they are doing to spread the truth."

b. To become fellow workers with the truth (the dative prompted by *syn* in *synergoi ginometha*), something that the brothers are also presumed to be. This type of construction normally requires a personal noun, but the truth is personified in the letter. The truth is said to testify favorably for one of these brothers (3 John 12). See also John 8:32 and the construction in Jas 2:22. Rhetoricians call this phenomenon *personificatio*.

The latter alternative, followed in the NRSV, has the advantage of giving a more Johannine sense to the concept of "truth"—see the note above on v. 3—and it does not interpret the formula from a Pauline linguistic form. The truth had come into the world with Jesus and those who believed in him, and it is being increasingly made real (1 John 2:9–11). Receiving these brothers in love is a link in the process of manifesting the truth.

9. I have written something. To judge from the context, this phrase refers to a letter that took up what has just been discussed: the duty to welcome such brothers (v. 8). According to the author's own words it was a very short letter—Gkt has merely *ti*, "something"—presumably some form of a letter of recommendation. See the Analysis, point 3. Since nothing in the other Johannine letters fits this description, the reference is to a letter that has been lost.

to the congregation. Gkt has the word *ekklēsia* in the definite form and dative case. The reference is to the congregation where Diotrephes wished to be the leader. The formula can reasonably be taken to imply that the congregation was well known to Gaius. At the same time, the author relates to Gaius what had taken place in this congregation. I have previously interpreted *ekklēsia* in 3 John as the local Jewish fellowship. It included also some Johannine Christians. It was there that the itinerant brothers sought to come. Paul likewise sought his first audiences in the synagogues. See the note on "before the congregation" in v. 6, above. Most commentators place 3 John in a later period and view the *ekklēsia* as the local Christian congregation. See chap. 12, point 4. In what follows, "the congregation" is replaced with "them," an expression that also places Gaius a bit outside the congregation.

the one who likes to put himself in charge of them. Gkt can also be translated "who likes to be their leader" (TEV) or "their would-be leader" (NEB). Gkt uses the verb *philoprōteuein*, attested only in 3 John and in Christian literature dependent on the letter. It is formed by compounding two words, the very common stem *phil-* ("love") and *prōteuein* ("be the first"/"have the first position," from *prōtos* ["first"]). Compounds with *philein* occur frequently in Greek: *philo-sophia* ("love-wisdom"), *philo-theos* ("love-God") *philo-timeisthai* ("love-to-be-honored"), etc. The word's individual parts thus give the idea of loving to be the first. Diotrephes, the person in question (see next note), is in some sense a leader, or strives to be, which the Elder (judging by the way he expresses the matter) does not fully want to accept. The following text shows that it is Diotrephes who decides who may and may not have a place in the local Jewish congregation.

Diotrephes. The name comes from Greek *Dio-trephes,* which means nurtured/cherished by Zeus. It is a genuinely Greek name, connected with heroes and leaders from Greek literature (*Iliad* 2:196; Diodorus Siculus 15.14.1). It does not occur in the LXX or in Josephus, and I have not seen it used of Jews. This can possibly be taken as proof the Diotrephes belonged to the "Greeks," i.e., non-Jews who used to attend Diaspora synagogues as proselytes, God-fearers, or sympathizers. Some of them could have an important function in the Jewish community. Clearly, Diotrephes had earlier taken in itinerant brothers, which indicates that for a time he had been positive toward the Jesus-believers, but afterward he had become more and more doubtful about their confession that Jesus was the Messiah, God's son.

he does not welcome us. Gkt has the verb *epidechesthai*, which in v. 10 has its usual meaning of welcoming guests. Everything points to its having the same meaning here. In recommendation letters of the time, there are often exhortations to receive the recommended bearers (or bearer) as if they were actually the author. See the Analysis, point 3. Refusing to receive the brothers was the same as refusing to receive the Presbyter. Therefore, many translations have "does not support us," or, as in the NRSV, "does not acknowledge our authority." The Presbyter's honor and position were thus called into question. The use of the present tense in Gkt indicates that this was more a general pattern of behavior than an isolated occurrence.

The Presbyter uses here the word "us" rather than "me," even though in vv. 9–10 he speaks of himself in the first-person singular. This is not likely a mere stylistic variation. "We" stands for the Presbyter and others in his circle, i.e., a group of those who hand on the tradition. See the Interpretation, vv. 1, 13–15.

10. if I come. In TEV and TOB, the clause is introduced with "when"; in CEV, NIV, JerB, and NRSV, with "if." The Greek construction *ean* + subjunctive normally bears a certain level of uncertainty, either with regard to an action, as in "if I should come," or with regard to the time of an action, as in "whenever I come."

call attention to. The verb in Gkt, *hypomimnēskein*, means to remind someone of something. In the Johannine writings, it is used otherwise only of the Paraclete, the Spirit of Truth (John 14:26). When the subject of discussion is something negative, it takes on a nuance of warning and censure (Wis 12:2; 2 Tim 2:14). Unfortunately, the text gives no clear answer to the question regarding whom the Presbyter intends to remind of these things, whether he intends to do so before the entire congregation, or with what effect.

the things he is doing. Literally, "his acts that he is doing," a formula that undeniably puts the emphasis on Diotrephes' actions and not on his teaching. We met a similar focus on the deeds of Gaius in v. 5. In a Johannine perspective, the actions of a disciple of Jesus are in some sense divine, since they are the result of the disciple's being united with the Father and the Son (John 13–17).

in speaking evil things against us. Literally, "disparaging (*phlyarōn*) us with evil words." With this participial construction, the author begins to describe the deeds of Diotrephes while simultaneously explaining, at least in part, his earlier words that Diotrephes "does not welcome us" (v. 9). In both cases, the behavior of Diotrephes is directed against "us," i.e., against those responsible for the tradition or against the Johannine Christians more broadly.

Nevertheless, the description of Diotrephes' actions is quite general. The verb *phlyarein*—a *hapax legomenon* in the NT—means to talk rubbish, to babble, to gossip, or to spread empty, groundless rumor. The corresponding adjective describes the young widows in 1 Tim 5:13. In 3 John, the verb is strengthened with an instrumental dative: "with evil words." The book of Acts relates that even unbelieving Jews libel and speak ill of the believers (Acts 13:45; 18:6; cf. Luke 6:22). The formula does not hint at any particular doctrinal disputes.

And not satisfied with doing these things. Word for word, the text roughly reads, "and not being satisfied (*arkoumenos*) with these things." With yet another participle, the author continues his description of Diotrephes' actions, now as a mounting introduction to three clauses (neatly connected by means of the combination *oute . . . kai . . . kai*, unusual in Greek). All five verbs in this compact presentation of Diotrephes are in the present tense, which suggests repeated acts, at least as the Presbyter views things. The author's manner of describing the deeds of Diotrephes—and of Gaius—has a certain standardized feel to it, suggesting a clear preparation for what he is about to say in v. 11.

welcome. Gkt uses a technical term for welcoming people as guests. See notes to vv. 8 and 9, above.

and even hinders. The verb in Gkt, *kolyein*, means to prevent someone by word or deed from doing something, to hinder, to forbid. It is in the present tense, a form that some interpreters want to read as conative, i.e., he *tries to* hinder them. But the close correlation with the surrounding clauses makes that reading less likely.

those who want to do so, i.e., to welcome brothers. According to 2 John 10–11, to receive itinerant preachers is to participate in their work.

drives. The word in Gkt, *ekballein,* means to force out and is used also in John 9:34–35 (to expel from the Jewish community?) and in Josephus, *J. W.* 2.143 (to exclude from the Essene community). It is difficult to know whether the issue is one of exclusion from the Jewish community or one of being shut out of Diotrephes' house, where Jews and Johannine Christians had been in the habit of gathering, or of other measures that isolated and opposed those who wanted to welcome brothers. Forms of church discipline are treated in Matt 18 and 1 Cor 5. See Appendix 4, House Churches, and chap. 12, point 4.

11. Beloved. See the note on v. 2, above.

do not imitate. Gkt *mē mimou.* This is the only imperative in the letter and it is embedded in a general ethical rule. The verb means to emulate, to follow, to imitate. In the NT it is always used in a positive sense and most often with a person as the example (1 Thess 1:6; 2 Thess 3:6–9; 1 Cor 1:11).

what is evil . . . what is good. In the context of the letter these phrases are clearly illustrated by the actions of Diotrephes and Gaius (vv. 9–10 and 5–8, resp.).

Using the Greek terms *kakos* and *agathos* to speak of what is evil and what is good is not Johannine practice, but it is certainly biblical (Ps 37:27; 1 Pet 3:12–13). In v. 11 this conceptual pair is used in a chiasm: evil—good—good—evil. The author clearly begins his "final appeal" with a common rule—maxims form an important part of Johannine argumentation—and applies it to the current situation before he comes to his actual purpose: urging Gaius to welcome one of the brothers (v. 12).

Whoever does good is from God. Whoever does evil has not seen God. The beginnings of these two sentences connect to the general clause in v. 11a with words that otherwise do not occur in the Johannine writings: "do good" (*agathopoiein*), and "do evil" (*kakopoiein*). But cf. John 5:29; 18:30. These two verbs express an ethical norm in concrete situations (Mark 3:4 par) and are used in 1 Pet 2:13–17 as controlling terms in that letter's ethic for how Christians should relate to other people.

The endings of the two sentences have a Johannine form: "is from God" and "has not seen God." The phrase "to be from (*einai ek*) someone" occurs fifty-five times in the Johannine writings, compared to twenty-eight times in the rest of the NT; it expresses both origin and belonging. Whoever "is from God" is born of God and belongs to God (1 John 3:10; 4:7, 20). See further Appendix 11, Begotten/Born of God.

The phrase "not to see God" is parallel to "not to know God" and can be predicated of all humanity (John 1:18; 5:37; 6:46; 1 John 4:20). By the same token, it can be said that whoever has seen the Son has seen the Father (John 14:9). But whoever commits sin has never seen him nor come to know him (1 John 3:6). According to the Presbyter's way of reasoning, being united with God through Jesus Christ implies fellowship and solidarity with the brothers.

12. Demetrius. Gkt has only the name Demetrius in the dative, placed at the beginning of the sentence, where he is introduced into the text without further ado. There is not even a grammatical particle in the Greek to function as a transition between the clauses (it thus forms a so-called asyndeton). He appears to be unknown to Gaius, since he needs to be recommended. At the same time, he is introduced as someone already known. This is best explained by Demetrius' being the person delivering the letter to Gaius.

Demetrius, like Diotrephes, is a genuinely Greek name. It means "belonging to Demeter" and is often attested in texts and inscriptions, even in the LXX (1–2 Maccabees) and in Josephus. See also Acts 19:24. According to Josephus, Seleucid kings and other leaders in the Jewish environment bore this name, including a representative for the Alexandrian Jews (*Ant.* 20.147). According to a later tradition, from the end of the fourth century, the apostle John is believed to have installed Demetrius as bishop in Philadelphia. The entire fabric of the letter clearly demonstrates that Demetrius belongs to the group the author refers to as "the brothers." As such, according to an intra-Jewish perspective, he would be a Christ-believing Jew. The Greek name is no fool-proof indicator of his origin.

has been testified to favorably by all. Gkt uses the passive voice, which makes it possible to place Demetrius first in the sentence, contrary to the NRSV rendering. This fronted positioning of Demetrius marks the emphasis and the change of personal focus. Moreover, putting Demetrius in the dative (dative of advantage)—the nominative would also have been possible (Acts 16:2)—stresses the positive aspect of the testimony: "for the benefit of Demetrius."

It is not clear who the "all" are who bear witness about Demetrius. The following text suggests that it is a wider circle than the Elder and his children. It can refer to all Jews who confess Jesus or all Jesus-confessors he has met or—in this rhetorical letter—it can be merely an exaggerated expression, a hyperbole.

and by the truth itself. The author uses a personification of the truth, a not unusual stylistic feature of the Johannine writings. The use of the concept "truth" in 3 John makes it difficult to interpret this phrase as merely an assurance that what has just been said is completely true or as a reference to Demetrius' teaching. See the notes on vv. 3 and 8. The idea of "truth" is connected also in the *Didache* to the wandering preachers. See Appendix 2, Itinerant Brothers.

We also testify regarding him, and you know that our testimony is true. The formula is reminiscent of similar formal attestations in John's Gospel (NRSV): "He who saw this has testified ... His testimony is true, and he knows that he tells the truth" (19:35); "and we know that his testimony is true" (21:24). There exists an affinity extending from Jesus by way of the Beloved Disciple to a group "we." These parallels and the use of "we" in 3 John 9–10 suggest that "we" is not synonymous with "I." Last in the series of witnesses come the Elder and others who with him are responsible for the preservation of "what was from the beginning." See Appendix 5, We in the Johannine Letters.

Three witnesses establish a testimony, an *amplificatio* according to textbook rhetoric. According to Jewish custom, a matter must be judged on the authority of two or three witnesses.

13. I have many things to write to you. Gkt has the imperfect plus aorist infinitive, while the corresponding phrase in 2 John 12 has the present participle plus present infinitive. Presumably this is merely a stylistic variation. The imperfect can nonetheless express necessity, obligation, or possibility: *must/ought to / could* have much to say to you (as in certain translations). The Elder says that he has much more that he ought to write to Gaius. An interpretation of this sort binds the sender and receiver more closely together in 3 John than in 2 John, a fact which corresponds to the letter's character as a whole.

but I do not want to write to you with ink and pen. The Greek formulation in v. 13 deviates from the corresponding verse in 2 John. It is more detailed, more balanced; it reads "ink and pen," rather than "paper and ink"; the words "write to you" are repeated. This shows that we are not dealing with a fixed formula. The words are natural at the end of a letter, but I have not come across any good parallels in the literature of the period.

14. to see you. The expression is perhaps more personal than "to come to you" in 2 John 12. Here, too, 3 John is more well-turned than 2 John.

and we will talk face to face. Literally "and we shall talk mouth to mouth." The phrase "mouth to mouth" is not unusual in biblical and secular texts. Cf. "face to face" in Exod 33:11; 1 Cor 13:12.

15. Peace to you. Jewish and Christian letters often have a wish for peace at the beginning. Cf. 2 John 3. As a rule, Paul has at the end of his letters "grace to you all," sometimes with a peace-greeting as well (Gal 5:16; see also Eph 6:23–24; 1 Pet 5:14).

"Peace" (*shālōm* in Hebrew) sometimes extended with "to you," is used by Jews as a greeting both on arriving and on leaving. In John the words are especially associated with the Risen One's meeting his disciples (John 20:19, 26). "Peace to you" should probably be read more as a statement of fact than as a wish.

The friends. The term in Gkt, *philoi,* is in the definite form. It is one of the many names referring to the first Christians (Acts 27:3; Luke 12:4; John 11:11). Presumably it was often used in Johannine groups. The Jesus-believers are "friends" because Jesus has given them knowledge of God (John 15:15). Cf. Wis 7:27, where wisdom is said to make people into "God's friends and prophets." They are "friends of Jesus" when they accept and follow his commands (John 15:14–15). Slaves must obey whether they understand or not; friends understand and obey.

In a Johannine perspective, "friend" (*philos*), and "beloved" (*agapētos*), are synonymous. See the note on v. 1 above. The emphasis lies on the fact that they are both friends of God/Jesus and friends to one another. The Elder has a group of Johannine Christians around him who send greetings to Gaius. Presumably this does not imply that Gaius was known to all of them in the community. In Gnostic circles the word "friends" was used of the spiritually elite. Nothing points toward such a usage within the Johannine fellowship.

by name. The phrase in Gkt, *kat' onoma* ("by name"), surely means "each and every one specifically." When Ignatius uses the same expression in his letter to the Christians in Smyrna, he greets those whom he has not mentioned by name (13:2). Thus, "the friends" in Gaius' community do not need to be understood as personally known to the Elder.

Analysis

1. A Communication

We can approach a text in many ways. Sometimes what engages us are certain concepts, ideas, or philosophical systems. Sometimes it is other interests: historical situations, linguistic peculiarities, psychological events, group processes, social relationships, etc. We can read a text for our own enjoyment, for our spiritual edification, in search of models for our own actions and for those of others, etc. We could go on listing other examples for some time. We always approach a text with something of ourselves. And a text can be used for many purposes.

In the following I regard 3 John first of all as an event, a communication of a message from one person to another. A perspective like this embraces many of the dimensions of a text I have just listed, but at the same time it directs attention to the text's function(s) in a definite communication situation. Someone has chosen to communicate something to someone else in a particular situation, with a particular purpose, by means of a certain medium and with the help of certain linguistic tools.

Approaching the letter's message and function in a historical way like this makes certain questions about the text more interesting than others. Is it possible to reconstruct the letter's communication situation (sender, recipient, current linguistic conventions, relevant actions, and so on)? Third John is a very short, anonymous text, and contemporary information about it is lacking. Nonetheless it is necessary to give certain answers to this main question in order to be able to determine the letter's content and function more closely. What medium—oral/written—does the author choose for his message? What sort of text? Does he have a special strategy for his writing? Can the letter's language and ideological world be more precisely described? What general interpretive frameworks have been recommended for the letter? The following analysis must attempt to answer these questions. Doing so provides a better foundation from which to be able to choose among the many possibilities offered by the text's words and clauses, and this will enable me later, in the Interpretation section, to suggest a reading of the letter as a whole.

2. A Private Letter?

Anyone who has a specific message for another person or other persons, if he wants to get across successfully what he has to say, must choose a medium that functions in the current circumstance. The choice is made on the basis of media available in a society at a particular point in time and on the basis of the conditions prevailing at the moment of communication: the sender's abilities, the recipient's knowledge, accessibility, costs, linguistic conventions, and other concerns.

The author of 3 John chose to *write*, i.e., to use an indirect form of communication. In spite of what he says in vv. 9–10 and 13–14, he does not seem at this time to be very "mobile." The words in v. 10—"if I come"—express something that only possibly may happen in the future. The closing verses indicate distance between sender and recipient. The word "write" is used twice, set in opposition to the more personal "see, meet," and "speak." The indirect medium the author has chosen does not seem to be the most expedient and natural for communication between these parties, but under the circumstances it is necessary.

The content of the two final verses also binds the sender and recipient together. These two persons have much to say to one another, at least according to the author. Possibly the choice of verb tense—imperfect—implies a certain caution on the author's side: "I have much to write to you." See the note to v. 13.

Of course, the words in vv. 13–14 also indicate that the reader has arrived at the end of the letter. And they give a special weight to what has been said earlier. The letter's message could not be delayed. The written form had to be used precisely because this message, more than anything else the author had to say, needed to reach the recipient.

The author furthermore chose to write to *an individual person*. Only Gaius is named as recipient (the comparable letter to Philemon names several persons) and he is requested to greet other fellow Christians, the so-called friends, each "by name." See the note to v. 15. Third John is to be regarded above all as a private letter, the only one in the New Testament, other than the Pastoral Letters. It is evidently not intended as one letter in a longer correspondence. The author expects only the wished-for action. The letter's argument should thus be analyzed as a means for getting Gaius to act in a certain way.

Third John

In v. 12, Demetrius is named at the beginning of the sentence without any introduction whatsoever. He needs recommendations, but clearly does not need to be introduced to Gaius. The best explanation for this unexpected feature of the text is that Demetrius is there when Gaius reads the letter, either bodily or in Gaius' thoughts. Demetrius is the bearer of the letter, and the author—as he formulates his letter—can assume that Demetrius will be present with Gaius.

What all this means is that the author chose to write *a letter*. Thus, the form available to him was largely predetermined. The ancient letter consisted of four parts:

1. *Opening formulas.* First, the sender's name, sometimes with a descriptor and possibly mention of co-senders; then, the recipient's name, sometimes also with a short description. Then follows a short word of greeting, expanded in Paul's letters to include words of grace and peace and occasionally a wish for good health. "I hope you are well," or something similar. This wish can also come at the end of the letter.

2. *Thanksgiving.* The writer of the letter offers a prayer or thanks to the gods: "I pray for you before the gods of this place . . . ," or "Having been saved by God out of grave dangers, we thank him greatly" (2 Macc 1:11). In Paul's letters this part becomes quite long; he thanks God whenever he thinks of the recipient and often indicates somehow what his letter will deal with. A clause like "It gives me much joy . . ." can replace various forms of thanksgiving.

3. *Main body.* This portion varies widely in its form, depending on what sort of letter it belongs to. Nonetheless, its opening and closing can be quite formalized. In the beginning the sender often creates a close connection with the recipient through positive comments and phrases such as "I want you to know . . . ," "Do not believe that . . . ," "I was surprised when . . . ," and "I rejoiced that . . ." In the closing words of the main section, what has been said earlier is often repeated and reinforced more precisely and clearly.

4. *Closing formulas.* Greetings are often found here once again, as well as some concrete detail and final words like "Be well!" In Christian letters there is frequently a wish for grace and peace.

Third John has been described as the most profane letter in the New Testament (Robert W. Funk), i.e., it is most like the many letters that have survived from antiquity. The fifteen verses would have fitted on a sheet of papyrus. The format is thus the usual one, containing many phrases typical of letters: "I pray that you . . . may be in good health," "I was overjoyed," "that all may go well with you," and others. See notes to vv. 2, 3, 5, and 6. Yet, 3 John also contains a number of deviations from the form of ancient—and early Christian—letters, which is of considerable importance for understanding this one.

- The sender does not use his name at the beginning of the letter, but only the

Third John: In or Out of the Jewish Community

words "the Elder" (*ho presbyteros*). This phrase functions almost as a name and is presumably a title for one who is responsible for the tradition in the Johannine community. See chapter 12, point 2. This very unusual opening implies that the recipient is to be understood as knowing the sender well and that because of his age and his role, the latter has a certain superior status in relation to the recipient. Everything points to their both being members of the Johannine fellowship within the early church.

- The sender emphasizes in v. 1 his positive relationship with the recipient through two weighty phrases that are not completely required by epistolary protocol: first a post-positioned attribute of Gaius, "the beloved"; then a relative clause about Gaius, "whom I love in truth." Short characterizations do occur—they are common in New Testament letters—but seldom in the form of entire clauses. In a letter of recommendation there is a tendency at the beginning to say something positive about the recipient.

- The use of a vocative—"beloved"—before the traditional wish for good health is very unusual. With this word, the author has already at the start, in a threefold way, characterized his relationship to the recipient with the word "love." At the same time, also right from the beginning, a tone of appeal is perceptible on the sender's part.

- The usual wish for prosperity in such letters has the form "above all I hope that you are in good health" (*pro pantōn euchomai se hygiainein*). However, the author of 3 John writes, "in everything" (*peri pantōn*), in place of "above all" (*pro pantōn*), and adds yet another verb, "do well" (*euodousthai*). Both formulations point forward to the last clause in v. 2, where the latter verb is repeated and where "in everything" is understood to include the soul. This ending to the verse—see the note on v. 2—does not belong to epistolary convention. The wish for prosperity in this letter embraces not only health and strength, but the soul as well.

The same syntactical pattern reappears then in v. 3 with a new clause of the same type as the one that ends v. 2. These two matched clauses, by means of repetition in the text and deviation from standard epistolary form, assume a marked place in the letter's introduction and for that reason deserve careful attention in the interpretation. It can be noted that the author does not say, "I know that," "I am convinced that," or something similar, which would come across as a clear assertion by the author, something like saying, "your soul is healthy" or "you walk in the truth." Instead he chooses two comparative clauses, formulations that appear to invite the recipient to confirm in some way what the sender says about him: "just as it is well with your soul, right?" and "just as you walk in the truth, as far as I know."

- The words of thanksgiving in v. 3 "I was very glad" (*echaren lian*), are a standard letter phrase. In 3 John, this clause is supplied with a "for," *gar*, which gives the text the character of argumentation. The phrase reappears in modified form in v. 4, reinforcing what has just been said. The author thus uses typical epistolary phrases, while clearly incorporating them into his own argument.

- After the long introduction in vv. 1–4, which praises the recipient in several ways, we would expect in this kind of letter that after the vocative "beloved" in v. 5 there would come a request of some sort, which in many cases is formulated with the phrase "you would do well" (*kalōs (an) poiēseis* plus an aorist participle). See notes on vv. 5 and 6. Instead we find an unusual but similarly formulated "you faithfully do" (*piston poieis*); additional background material is then supplied before the actual request is formulated in v. 6 with a normal but well embedded epistolary phrase.

- If we read 3 John as a letter of recommendation, then the content of v. 12 also becomes rather noticeable. There is no explicit recommendation and no description of the relation between the author and the one who is being recommended, elements that otherwise are characteristic of such letters. See below, point 3.

- There are parallels in other letters to the content of vv. 13–14, but I have not found good parallels to the form of the ending of this letter.

The letter of 3 John is therefore in terms of its form not only the most private letter in the New Testament, but also the most secular in terms of its use of current epistolary conventions. At the same time, there are many small deviations—consciously devised?—that indicate what the author is angling for. Third John is more than a private letter; it is concerned with truth and love in the first Christian fellowship.

3. A Letter of Recommendation?

In antiquity, as today, there were many diverse kinds of letters: letters between friends, letters of comfort, letters of complaint, business letters, official letters, letters of instruction, fictional letters, letters of recommendation, etc. They are described in surviving manuals with concrete examples of how they should be framed. Instruction in writing letters was important in Roman society, especially for professional scribes.

The classification of letters could vary. In a manual attributed to Pseudo-Demetrius from around the time of the New Testament, titled "Types of Letters," there are twenty-one forms mentioned. A later author, Pseudo-Libanius (or Proclus), provides forty-one examples. The following is what is said there about the so-called recommendation letter:

> The recommending type (*ho systatikos* with an implicit *typos*), which we write to someone on behalf of someone else, contains words of praise, since we are making unacquainted persons acquainted with one another. An example:

NN, who delivers this letter to you, is a man whom we have tested and whom we love because of his trustworthiness. Kindly be hospitable toward him (*kalōs poiēseis . . . axiosas*) both for my sake and his, and actually for your own sake as well. You will not be disappointed if you depend on him in word and deed for any confidential matter you might wish. When you have learned how useful he can be in all respects, you yourself will sing his praises to others.

The most important parts of a letter of recommendation show up here clearly and plainly: a positive introduction of the person in question and a concrete request with motivation both fore and aft.

A couple concrete examples can further illuminate the form. The first has to do with a father visiting his son in the Egyptian army, dated January 4, 254 BCE (Michigan Papyrus no. 33):

> From Aleximachos to Zenon. Greetings.
>
> Nikanor, who brings this letter to you, is a friend of ours. He has come to see you because his son belongs to the recruits who are currently stationed at Arsinoïte. Kindly take him in (*kalōs an oun poiēseis*) and give him whatever he needs. For (*gar*) you will do me a great service in this. Write back to us, if this is something you would like to do.
>
> Farewell.

The second example dates from around 25 BCE, addressed to a highly placed finance official in Egypt (Oxyrhynchus Papyrus 292):

> From Theon to his most honored Tyrannos. Many greetings.
>
> Heraclides, who brings you this letter, is my brother. Therefore, I implore you with everything in my power to take him under your protection. I have also asked your brother Hermias to inform you about him. And you would be doing me the greatest service of all if you allow him to enjoy your approval. Above all I hope you are well (*pro de pantōn hygiainein se euchomai*), untouched by evil powers and prosperous in your work.
>
> Farewell.

Based on these examples, three main parts of a letter of recommendation can be descriptively summarized:

1. Introduction of the person in question. The author often describes the recommended person in terms of family relationships or degree of nearness, in the hope that the addressee will receive him as if he were the author himself. The presentation, with its various forms of praise, prepares for and motivates a favorable response to the request the author wishes to make.

2. A concrete request. This is the kernel of the letter, often broached with the polite phrase, "you would do well" (*kalōs an poiēseis*). For other forms of request, see

the Analysis of 2 John, point 2.

3. Expression of satisfaction if the request is granted. This gives further support to the request put forth.

The main purpose of a letter of recommendation is of course to ask for something, and it leads naturally to a certain structuring of the content. The most stereotypical formulations have to do with the request itself, while the supportive background material can be arranged and formulated in more varied ways. In the Roman world people often traveled by foot and the need for such letters of recommendation was considerable. Many such letters have been preserved down to our own day.

The custom of recommendation letters is well documented in the New Testament (Acts 9:2; 18:27; 22:5; 1 Cor 16:3). Recommendations also appear here and there in the Pauline letters (1 Cor 16:15–16, 17–18; Phil 2:29–30; 1 Thess 5:12–13). Only Galatians and 2 Corinthians lack them altogether. The most common term for a letter of recommendation, *epistolē systatikē*—see the quotation from "Types of letters," above—also occurs in the New Testament (2 Cor 3:1–2).

The main components of a letter of recommendation, mentioned above, can therefore also be traced out in the New Testament material, e.g., Rom 16:1–2.

> I commend to you our sister Phoebe,
> a deacon of the church at Cenchreae,
> so that you may welcome her in the Lord, as is fitting for the saints,
> and help her in whatever she may require from you,
> for she has been a benefactor of many and of myself as well.

At the center stands the request and motivating factors, with background material bookending it before and after. The last words can be taken to imply satisfaction for the letter's author if the recipients do what he wants them to do. The argument here is somewhat different, however, in that the author refers to a family relationship and the fellowship of the people of God—"the saints"—which embraces all interested parties.

The letter to Philemon has its own particular place among letters of this type. It is a recommendation, formulated with tremendous skill, made on behalf of a fugitive slave to his master and owner. After a letter such as this one had been read out to Philemon, in the midst of the house church and presumably with the slave himself present, there was only one sensible alternative for Philemon: to do what the letter's author wanted him to do. Cf. also Antiochus' petition to the Jews in 2 Macc 9:19–27.

The letter to Philemon begins by setting its purpose within a powerful context of personal relationships, well marked with words like "brother," "sister," "beloved," "fellow worker," "fellow soldier," "house" (vv. 1–2). Paul presents himself as a prisoner (v. 1), as an old man who has no wish to take advantage of his status vis-à-vis Philemon (vv. 8–9).

Then, with this well-crafted introduction to the letter's aim in mind, Paul continues with a series of good words about Philemon (vv. 4–7) regarding his Christian faith and love, especially the latter. In several repeated ways, he thus prepares the ground in the first part of the letter before he comes with his request: first with a completely ordinary "I appeal," "I appeal for Onesimus" (vv. 9–10), and then at the end of the letter quite clearly with "welcome him as you would welcome me" (v. 17). He does a lot of beating around the bush before he gets to his point!

Verses 10–21 in the letter to Philemon are reminiscent of the ancient recommendation letter. The person in question is introduced; his relationship to the interested parties—not least of all to Paul—is expressed with the greatest eloquence. Paul spares no effort to get Philemon to accept his runaway slave, who has now become a Christian. To do so is to do something for Paul himself. At the end Paul writes as if the request were already fulfilled, and the not uncommon announcement of an impending visit functions almost as a threat for poor Philemon (v. 22).

The letter to Philemon is no ordinary letter of recommendation. It deals with a fugitive slave. His return as a Christian becomes an example for how one ought to practice "love toward all the saints" (Phlm 5, 7, 8, 12, 20). Paul proceeds on the basis of the idea that they are all brothers and sisters in a new fellowship.

Third John contains recommendations, but they are well embedded within a larger argument and are partly indirect (vv. 5–6, 12). Some features are reminiscent of recommendation letters, especially vv. 6–8 and 12, but the letter can scarcely be characterized as a typical letter of recommendation. It has much more in common with the letter to Philemon, just analyzed. The only explicit exhortation in the letter, at v. 11, has a very general form and is introduced very well by the double example of Gaius and Diotrephes. The issue here, from the author's point of view, has eternal consequences (v. 11). The author of 3 John argues for a practical solidarity with the itinerant brothers: welcome them and equip them for their continued journey. Demetrius is one of these brothers (v. 12). The letter thus recommends a person or a group of people without fully using the normal form of a recommendation letter. The most common ground of inducement—one's own position, one's honor, one's own advantage—is conspicuous by its absence, unless we take a continued close fellowship in truth and love as precisely that. The request to welcome "the brothers" in a tangible way is connected to the question whether one has continued fellowship with God or not.

4. Strategy in the Letter

Dividing 3 John into smaller discrete paragraphs is difficult, whether it is attempted on the basis of the form that generally applies to a letter—see point 2 above—or on the basis of thematic connections, or on the basis of certain verbal repetitions, e.g., of the word "beloved" (vv. 2, 5, 11). See the Translation Display and its structuring of the letter as a whole. Many people have tried to carry out this analysis, but without success. Should v. 2 be attached to v. 1 or to vv. 3–4? Do vv. 3–4 belong better together with vv. 1–2 or with vv. 5–8? And how should v. 11 be described? As a conclusion to

vv. 9–10? As a transition to v. 12? As the point in the letter to which everything else tends? Exegetes give various answers to these questions.

Perhaps for this kind of text it is more fruitful to concentrate our attention on what is going on between the sender and the recipient. What is the author doing in order to get the recipient to act as he wants him to? How does the author make use of the linguistic conventions we have highlighted in the foregoing? For the sake of summarizing, I will take the text verse by verse.

Verse 1. Attention, good will, and mutuality are established. The sender binds the recipient to himself from the very first with the words "beloved" and "whom I love." This love-relationship recurs throughout the letter (vv. 2, 5, 11, as well as in v. 15 indirectly in the words "the friends"). The word choice should be understood to imply that both sender and recipient belong to the Johannine group of Christians. See further, point 5 below.

This close union is strengthened by the sender's manner of presenting himself: "the Elder" or "the Presbyter." His self-description is further reinforced later on with the words "my children" in v. 4. In my view, the Elder is the link back to the Johannine community's beginning; he is responsible for the Johannine tradition, for "what was from the beginning." See further, chapter 12, point 3.

The love-relationship is also strengthened through the phrase "in truth." The phrase gives a special quality to this love with emphasis on divine unity, fellowship, and solidarity. Already in the opening formula the author announces the two most important frameworks for his message: love and truth. The latter word, moreover, recurs at crucial points in the argumentation (vv. 3, 4, 8, and 12).

Verse 2. Here, right up front, and in very subtle terms, comes a clause implying that the recipient will do what the author asks: "just as it is well with your soul, right?" A healthy soul can function in only one way. This is most likely an assertion on the sender's part, but the way he frames it invites confirmation from the recipient. See the note on v. 2.

Verse 3. Attention is shifted here from the more general "your soul" to the more specific "your truth." The clause "how you walk in the truth" has almost the same function as "just as it is well with your soul" in v. 2. It is now no longer only the author who testifies about Gaius (vv. 1–2), but also "brothers" who come and go among the congregations.

Verse 4. We meet now for the first time a mild exhortation from the Presbyter, put forth in a very indirect manner: If you wish to belong to "my children," you must continue to walk in the truth. If you walk in the truth, you will make me happy.

Verse 5. Already at this point the recipient is described as demonstrating "his truth," or his "faithfulness to the truth," when he welcomes brothers who are traveling through. Not only the sender (v. 2) and the brothers (v. 3) but also the congregation can bear witness about him. The phrases "your soul" and "your truth" are here further refined as "your love" (v. 6).

Verse 6. At the end of this verse comes a traditionally, but very carefully worded request: "you will do well to . . ." As an appeal it is well incorporated into the context, in terms of both form and content.

Verse 7. The request in v. 6 is provided with a further motivation: it was for the sake of "the Name" that the brothers had set out in their traveling, and they have spurned all support from non-Jews.

Verse 8. The request in v. 6 is repeated here, but in *we*-form and *ought*-form, rather than in the imperative. With regard to the recipient, the exhortation is truly indirect: you and I, folks like us (= Johannine Christians), should help such people. To this is added a further argument in v. 8c: it is a matter of being co-workers with the truth.

Verses 9–10 reinforce—and motivate—what has been said, doing so by adducing a contrary example, Diotrephes, who by his actions demonstrates that he is not a co-worker with the truth. His misdeeds are piled up on one another in the text: he does not obey the Elder and his fellow workers, he does not welcome the brothers, he hinders those who would like to welcome them, and he expels people from the congregation. Rhetoricians call this heaping-up technique an *accumulatio*.

Verse 11 issues a clear command: "do not imitate." It is the sole imperative in the entire argument. The summary of the foregoing (Gaius and Diotrephes as two examples), the linguistic structure (chiasm, antitheses, word repetitions, and more), and the content of the motivation (fellowship with God or not) give this verse an enormous weight within the letter. On this basis, Gaius should be able to draw his own conclusions in the matter of what attitude to take toward the brothers.

Verse 12 can be read as the clearest concretization of the letter's errand, as v. 17 does in the letter to Philemon: Welcome the itinerant brother Demetrius! Yet the author does not put it quite so directly. The case of Demetrius is at most an example of what has just been said. The main thing is that the recipient should continue to welcome these brothers and help them in their further travels.

Verses 13–15 primarily function to bring the letter to an end, but they also contribute to the argument. Expressed here once again is the closeness between the author and the recipient (much to talk about, the desire to visit). The content is connected to the love-relationship that marked the introduction to the letter. The concern with the act of writing itself also gives weight to what has in fact been written. The letter and its message could not wait; the situation was that urgent.

5. A Johannine Letter?

The letter to Gaius is titled in our Bibles as 3 John, and that would seem to answer the question heading this section. But this title is not original.

The New Testament writings did not get their names until the second century. Conclusions were drawn then from whatever information about the authors was available in the texts themselves, from content and form of the various writings, and from inherited traditions. Still, many documents remained anonymous. In the great manuscripts of the fourth century—Vaticanus, Sinaiticus—this letter is called "John's Third Letter." And it is not until the fourth century that this letter is mentioned explicitly. Eusebius (d. 339) refers to Origen, who had said that not everyone acknowledged 3 John as genuine. Eusebius himself places the two smaller Johannine letters among the disputed writings. Thus, the current title is no guarantee that our letter was written by the disciple John or that it was his third letter.

Nevertheless there can be scarcely any doubt that 3 John belongs to the anonymous New Testament writings we have traditionally called Johannine. Third John must have the same author as 2 John. See the Analysis on 2 John, point 1. And in terms of its content, 2 John comes very close to 1 John, which in its turn is connected to the Gospel of John. There are also numerous typical Johannine words, such as love, truth, testimony, and joy.

On the other hand, 3 John is the most un-Johannine of the Johannine writings. For example, in relation to 2 John it has nearly double the number of words peculiar to itself and fewer of the typical Johannine words. There are assuredly several contributors behind the Johannine literature, but they were closely associated with each other. See further chapter 12, points 2 and 3. In the interpretation of 3 John it is important to establish the principle that the closest parallels, both linguistic and ideological, should be sought within the Johannine writings.

The sequence among the three letters, in terms of both chronology and material, is no more assured by the current titles than their authorship is. The traditional arrangement is based on size and importance and on nearness to 1 John. As is well known, something similar prevails in the canonical arrangement of Paul's letters. Among exegetes of the Johannine letters, nearly all possible arrangements are defended: 1–2–3; 1–3–2; 2–3–1; and 3–2–1.

The choice among the various alternatives depends to a great degree on how one reconstructs the historical situation behind the Johannine writings. See further chapter 12, point 4. In the first letter, the serious crisis is resolved through theological analysis and instruction; in the two other letters things are handled through certain practical measures. As I read them, the two smaller letters reflect an earlier stage of the Johannine development. The congregational situation presupposed in them is less resolved. The author of 1 John, meanwhile, looks *back* to the tragic schism and assures his readers that in their faithfulness to "that which was from the beginning" they have eternal life fully and completely (1 John 5:13; 2:12–14; 1:1–4). We may also be dealing with quite different localities in the various letters.

In any case, the three letters likely are chronologically close to one another and reflect various situations in the Johannine community's rise and fall. See further chapter 12, points 3 and 4.

6. Various Interpretive Frameworks

To this point, I have defined the interpretive task and more generally characterized the text, its genre, its rhetorical strategy, and the most relevant aspects of its conceptual world. But even this is insufficient for attaining a clear grasp of the letter's content and function. The text remains multivalent, not least because of uncertainty about its external situation. Needful information is lacking. In what context was 3 John meant to function? What were the problems it was intended to solve? In this regard the history of interpretation shows that what is said in the text can be construed variously. Five alternative ways of filling in the context lead to five different scenarios for the problem in 3 John.

1. *A pastoral problem.* A younger congregational leader exercises his office in an improper way, so that an older leader, the aged apostle John, is obliged to step in.

    John, son of Zebedee, had been active in Ephesus for thirty years before he died around the year 100. On the basis of his life with Jesus, his experience, character and age, he had greater authority than anyone else in Asia Minor and could effectively intervene against a person like Diotrephes. There was no fitting official title for this unique person, but he had attained the honorary title of the Elder, the Presbyter.

    This person-centered interpretive framework can probably be labeled the traditional one—it occurs already in Irenaeus (d. 202)—and finds advocates even in our own time (Zahn, Michaelis, to a degree also Schnackenburg). It is not difficult to critique it. Is John to be taken as the sole author of the Johannine writings, including the book of Revelation? Are the actions of Diotrephes depicted as a one-man rebellion? How are we to explain the letter's cautious tone?

2. *An organizational, ecclesiastical-legal problem.* An older form of organization or an older view of congregations and official positions comes into conflict with a newer one.

    An interpretive basis of this sort for 3 John was presented with great skill by Adolf von Harnack in 1898. The Presbyter John, not to be confused with the apostle John, functioned as "over-bishop" in Ephesus; through his own travels and through missionaries, emissaries, and supervisors whom he sent out, he conducted an extensive mission in Asia Minor. This patriarchal, provincially focused mission organization gradually came in for criticism. Local congregations began setting up boundaries for themselves externally, while internally gathering themselves around their own leaders. Diotrephes is an example of such a leader, the first monarchical bishop known to us by name. His exclusionary policies toward the Presbyter John and John's missionaries awakened sharp mistrust among some people. The Presbyter thus sought contact with the friends he still had in Diotrephes' district. Thus we see him fighting here on behalf of something that

Third John

was already on the way out. The form of organization represented by Diotrephes would eventually win the day.

This framework, with its assumption of competing views about congregations and official positions, has had numerous supporters in recent research, even if not of von Harnack's stature. Howard Marshall locates 3 John within a trajectory from the apostles' more overarching mission activity to a greater local self-governance with overseers as leaders. The Presbyter becomes a parallel to Timothy and Titus. This latter view is also supported by Karl Donfried. The Presbyter has official functions similar to the *m^{e}baqqer* in the Qumran material. Klaus Wengst speaks of a conflict between Johannine, non-hierarchical church order and a monarchical-episcopal order. Raymond Brown finds the church's need for a fixed office confirmed in the development of the Johannine community, evidenced most clearly in 3 John. With his official actions and church discipline, Diotrephes regarded himself as more clear-sighted in the current situation than the Presbyter. The connection to a special problem in the Catholic Church is obvious here. It can also be seen in the work of Hans-Josef Klauck.

Von Harnack's well developed hypothesis has rightly been criticized: there is no trace in the letter of general distrust on the author's part; there is likewise nothing to support a patriarchal, provincially focused mission in Asia Minor, and there is no clear mention in the letter of any mission activity promoted by the Presbyter. Even for later exegetes operating on the basis of a related interpretation, the notion of the itinerant brothers in 3 John is decisive. I find it hard to see them as the Presbyter's "contra-missionaries" (Brown, Klauck) in the difficult conflict with the secessionists in the Johannine group. See Appendix 2, Itinerant Brothers.

3. *A theological, dogmatic problem.* Third John describes a clash between true and false teaching that has parallels in the development of the early church.

    In his book *Rechtgläubigkeit und Ketzerei im ältesten Christentum*, Walter Bauer sought to show that what later became heresy began as normal Christian faith. The heretics regarded themselves as Christians. In many localities, the heretics outnumbered the orthodox. Especially the regions of the Pauline mission, including Asia Minor, were strongly influenced by Gnostic thinking. Jewish Christians compelled to flee Palestine came to Asia Minor and attached themselves to the orthodox believers in the vicinity of Ephesus. Thus a struggle arose between old faith and new, a struggle over the Pauline heritage. In this conflict the orthodox gradually pulled away and isolated themselves in order to preserve their faith (1 and 2 John), while the heretics, Diotrephes among others, replied by doing likewise (3 John). In this way, 3 John becomes a testimony to sharply opposing theological views.

    But Bauer's general thesis does not hold up. Nothing is said about Diotrephes' heresy in 3 John. The mere use of the concept "truth" does not demonstrate that Diotrephes was promoting a Gnostic Christianity. The fact that on assuming

Bauer's professorial chair at Göttingen in 1951, Ernst Käsemann turned his predecessor's thesis on its head does not help to make it more convincing. According to Käsemann, the Elder in 3 John had been one of Diotrephes' presbyters (elder brothers), a Gnostic Christian who had been excommunicated by Diotrephes because of his teaching. The author of 3 John had thus carried out a two-pronged campaign, partly in opposition to his "orthodox" bishop, and partly against a general gnosis. This form of theological context for interpreting the letter is even more difficult to confirm from the text itself.

4. *A practical, social problem.* The lack of hospitality destroys the Christian fellowship. Hospitality among Christians is something both natural and necessary.

   Hospitality, according to Abraham J. Malherbe (1977), is the main theme of 3 John. In some heavily populated place, otherwise unknown, there were at least two house churches. The one gathered at the home of Gaius, the other at the home of Diotrephes. The Elder sent a letter of recommendation to all Christians of this place: Welcome these itinerant brothers (3 John 5–10). The letter had a double effect: Gaius welcomed them into his house; Diotrephes refused. Diotrephes wanted nothing to do with the Elder; indeed, he reviled him and forbade "his people" to concern themselves with these brothers. In response to this situation, the Elder sent a second letter, 3 John, addressed only to Gaius and his friends, with a request that they continue welcoming these Christians, and particularly Demetrius.

   This sociological perspective is important for understanding 3 John, but scarcely sufficient. Hospitality is part of a larger context, in which the Johannine Christians' place within the Jewish community is beginning to be called into question. The formulation "I have written something to the congregation" conforms poorly with a picture of two churches, both of whom are sent this one letter. Was hospitality such an important issue that it completely determined one's fellowship with God (3 John 11)? And how should we view the relationship between 3 John and 2 John?

5. *A problem of belonging, religiously, socially, economically, and politically.* Whether the Christ-confessing Jews and the Johannine Christians truly belonged to the Jewish community begins to be questioned, and they are at risk of being "put out of the synagogue."

   In an intra-Jewish perspective, the question of what is meant by the term *ekklēsia* in 3 John becomes important. If the word is taken to stand for the Jewish community in the locality where Johannine Christians and other Christ-confessing Jews are also living, the relations among the people mentioned in the letter becomes simpler. The itinerant brothers are Jesus-believing Jews who in word and deed proclaim Jesus as Messiah and by virtue of that a new messianic era in God's salvation act as well. We also meet these evangelists, e.g., in Matthew

10 and the *Didache*. They affirm "that which was from the beginning," just as the Elder and his fellow workers do. Any who ally themselves with these Jesus-believing Jews and the Elder risk being excluded from the congregation, that is, from the Jewish fellowship. They find themselves "without a synagogue" and must form their own "synagogue." See further, chapter 12, point 4.

I have chosen this final interpretive framework for my exposition, although I also include a few notes based on other frameworks. I do so fully conscious of the fact that there can be reasons for choosing another situational context to guide the reading. This last interpretive framework undeniably has most in common with the other Johannine writings and with the way they present the Johannine Christians. Thus the Johannine writings give us the most important background material for interpreting 3 John.

Interpretation

1. The Elder and his children (vv. 1, 13–15)

Third John is the smallest book among the New Testament's twenty-seven documents; in fact it is not a book at all, but a short, apparently private letter originally occupying no more than a single sheet of papyrus. In spite of its limited size it mentions a bewildering number of persons, most of them nameless and for today's readers completely unknown. Only three of them bear names: Gaius, Diotrephes, and Demetrius; none of them turns up anywhere else in general biblical lore. We can list the following persons:

- *I*, i.e., the Elder, the Presbyter, who speaks as the letter's sender.
- *You*, i.e., Gaius, the letter's addressee. A plural "you" never occurs in the letter. Gaius is included in "my children" (3 John 4), in "we" (3 John 8, 14), and in "whoever does good" (3 John 11).
- *He*, i.e., Diotrephes, who sometime earlier had received a short letter from the Presbyter, directed to his congregation (3 John 9–10).
- *They*, i.e., the brothers, itinerant preachers requiring backing and support from others (3 John 3, 5–10).
- *Demetrius*, i.e., one of the brothers, probably the one who delivered this letter to Gaius (3 John 12).
- *My children*, i.e., the Elder's children in an extended meaning, the Johannine Christians. Among them is Gaius, and possibly for a time Diotrephes as well (3 John 4).
- *We*, to be understood in several senses. It can refer to the Elder and Gaius (3 John 14), but also to these two persons together with other Christians, probably those belonging to the Johannine community (3 John 8). In a couple instances, "we"

has in view a smaller group, probably the Elder and others who have the same function he does (3 John 9–10, 12). See Appendix 5, We in the Johannine Letters.

- *Non-Jews*, in many translations rendered by "Gentiles," i.e., people of non-Jewish origin belonging to an entirely different faith (3 John 7).
- *The congregation* (or the church, as in the NRSV), i.e., local Jewish communities where the Elder, Gaius, and other Johannine Christians also find themselves (3 John 6, 9, 10).
- *Everyone*, i.e., all those whom the itinerant brothers met in the Jewish and Johannine communities (3 John 12).
- *The friends*, i.e., Johannine Christians, some of whom are where the Elder is and others in the place where Gaius lives (v. 15).

The letter's sender, the Elder or the Presbyter, as I alternatively call him based on the underlying text, stands out most clearly against the background of this varied flock. He is also the author of 2 John and—in my view—responsible for the content of 1 John. If we combine the information about him that we can gather from these three documents, the following picture emerges.

The Johannine documents presuppose a small group of prophetic teachers who transmit and explain instruction both from and about Jesus Christ. Their roots reach back to Jesus himself, especially through the disciple whom Jesus loved. This is why the "Johannine school," as it is sometimes called, was able to pass along "what was from the beginning" (1 John 1:1–4) and assure its continuity all the way back to the origins of the Johannine community.

The Elder in 3 John is one of these teachers; indeed he is the primary teacher in the Johannine community during the latter part of the first century. He was presumably a second generation Christian with close connections to the first disciples of Jesus. Thus he represents the tradition from Jesus and functions as a guarantor of the message that comes from him (1 John 1:5). He belongs to the "fathers" of the Johannine community, which gives him a definite function and status, as well as a special authority. See further, chap. 12, point 3.

The Johannine writings presuppose not only a continuous small college of teachers descending from Jesus himself, but also—as already presupposed in the foregoing—a group of Christians typically and variously called the Johannine group, community, congregation, church, or movement, among other things. I most often refer to them as Johannine Christians. They have their own particular Jesus traditions, a specific language and history of their own, clearly preserved in the Johannine documents. Unfortunately, we have very little knowledge of this branch of the early church. They lived for a long time within the framework of the Jewish synagogue. Some of them appear to have migrated from Palestine, perhaps northward first to Syria, and then in some form to Asia Minor where there were already many Jews (3 John 4).

Third John

When the Elder speaks of "my children," it is precisely these Johannine Christians that are in view. See further, chap. 12, point 2.

The close inner fellowship among the Johannine Christians is expressed in many ways. It is already there in such terms as "the Elder" and "my children." And this inward love recurs frequently in the author's descriptions of these persons, even in 3 John: "the beloved Gaius, whom I love in truth" (3 John 1), "beloved" (3 John 2, 5, 11) and "the friends" (3 John 15). What is typically Johannine in these terms is taken up in the Notes on the relevant verses.

The Johannine friends together form a community of love with a special commandment from Jesus to love one another as he had loved them (John 13:34). The Elder and Gaius have much to talk over with each other (3 John 13). The ability to speak face to face, person to person, rather than the exchange of written communiqués, is the normal, preferred form of intercourse (3 John 14). See the Analysis, point 2. Gaius quite obviously belongs to this Johannine group, as also perhaps Diotrephes, who had earlier received a letter from the Elder and who now can expect a visit from him (3 John 9–10). Demetrius on the other hand (3 John 12), like the itinerant brothers, does not seem to belong to the category of "my children." See Appendix 2, Itinerant Brothers. Nonetheless it is the duty of the Johannine Christians to support these preachers and to provide for them when they come to visit (3 John 8).

A motivation for this hospitality is "the truth" (3 John 8). The fellowship among Johannine Christians is strongly determined by "the truth" (3 John 1; likewise 3 John 3, 4, 8, 12). In Johannine perspective, the truth is the revelation of God that took shape in the words and life of Jesus. It is the life-form and life-style birthed forth from this revelation. See further Appendix 3, The Truth. Nothing gives the Elder joy like hearing that his children live in the truth (3 John 4). A truth received in obedience, realized in love and solidarity, binds the Elder's children together in a unique way. The word "truth" is defined as "love" (3 John 6). The serious and decisive issue in 3 John is that this life-giving fellowship with God and with one another is now being torn apart, among other things through various attitudes toward the itinerant teachers. This lack of unity is exemplified in the letter through the difference between what Gaius and Diotrephes are doing (3 John 2–8 and 9–10, resp.).

The situation requires immediate intervention on the part of the Elder, which results in his writing this letter to Gaius. In accordance with then-current practice, both sender and addressee are found at the beginning (3 John 1) and the hopes for a personal visit, for peace and good health at the end (3 John 13–15). See the Analysis, point 2. In terms of its form, 3 John has been characterized as the most secularized letter in the NT. But the author skillfully uses typical letter formulae to achieve his purpose. That purpose is to safeguard in Gaius a positive relationship with the traveling teachers and thus indirectly with the Elder and the faith and community he represents, all of them anchored in Jesus himself.

2. Gaius and the Brothers (vv. 2–8)

Gaius is in view throughout the entire letter, but 3 John 8 closes the first section regarding him. It ends with a tactful exhortation to Gaius to receive the itinerant teachers and to supply what they need for their continued travels.

It is not easy to know who these brothers were. Jewish refugees? Persecuted Christians? Christ-believing Jews? Johannine Christians? Missionaries of various kinds? Emissaries from the Elder in his struggle against false teachers? In Appendix 2, Itinerant Brothers, I have given reasons for regarding them most likely as wandering Jewish-Christian preachers from the vicinity of Palestine and Syria. In common with the Elder they represent, connections reaching back to the historical Jesus. In their way of life, they looked like genuine followers of Jesus: no house, no established place of residence, no family, no resources of their own. Presumably they too were able to speak about what Jesus had said and taught. In certain respects they were transmitters, "tradents" of the Jesus traditions. It is possible that they also preserved in a special way Jesus' teaching about the kingdom of God and its imminent fulfillment, and that they lived in an intense longing for Jesus' imminent return. In anticipation of this stupendous future they traveled around teaching God's kingdom in both word and deed. There is reason to suppose that they had developed a Jewish Messianic faith in line with that of wandering charismatic preachers of Jewish descent, a faith with similarities to the Johannine Christians' confession of Jesus as Messiah. And as we have said, both groups regarded themselves as responsible for the tradition from Jesus. The stance one took toward these wandering preachers thus entailed taking a position with regard to the development of the Johannine teaching, such that for some members of the community, the connection with "what was from the beginning" (1 John 1:1) was at risk of being broken.

The Johannine community appears to have gradually split into two groups. See chap. 12, points 2 and 4. In 1 John, this schism is taken as a given and beyond repair. The author turns to the "faithful remnant" who above all else seem unsure of their own standing and identity. The Elder wishes to strengthen them in their faith. This situation is not as obvious in the two smaller letters, which points to their being earlier than the first letter. The Johannine Christians in 3 John are still part of the Jewish community. The Elder does not charge Diotrephes with false teaching, but only with wrongly treating the brothers and thus indirectly the Elder himself and what he stands for.

We only know of Gaius through 3 John. He has a common Latin name, one otherwise connected with the imperial family in Rome. It is possible that at one time either he or his father had been a Jewish slave in Rome. He may well have been rather rich, owning his own large house, since he was able to shelter and support the itinerant brothers, and presumably took in other friends as well. He also has an independent standing with respect to Diotrephes, who wanted to be in charge of the local Jewish community. In this way he somewhat resembles Gaius in Corinth, who according to

Third John

Paul "is host to me and to the whole church" (Rom 16:23; cf. 1 Cor 1:14). It was in the latter Gaius' house that Paul wrote his letter to Rome.

There is nothing in the letter of 3 John to indicate that Gaius was a congregational leader in the usual sense, though he may later have become one. The letter is directed solely to him, and some have therefore wanted to draw the conclusion that the Christians used to gather in his house, constituting a house church similar to the one Philemon had (Phlm 1–2). But this surely was not the case when Gaius received the letter from the Elder. The situation is different in 2 John and in the letter to Philemon. See further Appendix 4, House Churches. The best guess would likely be that Gaius is a rather well-fixed Christian with his own house, a Johannine Christian who, from my perspective, was probably a Western-minded, Christ-believing diaspora Jew. He lived somewhere in Asia Minor and had the means to receive and support other Jews who trusted in Jesus. Hospitality of this sort implies in its own right a certain status, especially a social-economic status, but sometimes a spiritual one as well.

Gaius' relationship to the Elder can be partly inferred from the text of 3 John. They both belong to the Johannine community. The Elder does not need to introduce himself to Gaius, and Gaius is well known to the Elder, primarily from the testimony of the itinerant brothers. It is unclear, however, whether the two had ever personally met. In the opening lines of the letter, the Elder brings up only positive characteristics of Gaius: the healthy state of his soul, his life in the truth, his faithfulness and love. See the Analysis, point 4.

Gaius' relationship to Diotrephes is much more difficult to discern. The letter does not provide many clues about it. Gaius and Diotrephes are probably both related to the Johannine community, and one phrase in the letter indicates that in some way they belong to the same "congregation," i.e., the local Jewish community (3 John 9). If it was a larger town, the Johannine Christians would have been able to gather in homes, while at the same time also constituting a part of the synagogue. Diotrephes exercises the most authority in the Jewish community, perhaps because it was his house that functioned as the synagogue, or because in various ways he had contributed to the building and the activities of the synagogue. The Elder seems unwilling to accept Diotrephes' role in the congregation. Since Gaius and the friends are connected to Diotrephes and his congregation, the Elder fears that Diotrephes' attitude toward the brothers will influence them.

At the same time, there is a certain distance between Gaius and Diotrephes. Gaius does not seem to see himself as one who could easily be excluded from Diotrephes' congregation. And the Elder speaks of the letter to Diotrephes and its reception as if Gaius did not know about it. The information we have in 3 John is in fact difficult to synthesize into any clear picture of the relationship between Gaius and Diotrephes. Perhaps this is because the letter seems to have a double purpose. On the one hand, a more limited purpose would be to encourage Gaius to receive Demetrius and to equip him for his continued journeys; on the other hand, a more general purpose would be to present Gaius as a good example and Diotrephes a bad example in the matter of proper treatment of the brothers (3 John 11–12). In reality, the issue has to do with having fellowship with God or not.

The Elder begins his argument with describing Gaius as his "beloved Gaius" and his relationship to him with the words "whom I love in truth" (3 John 1). This description is echoed in the direct address "beloved" in 3 John 2 and 5, which divides the paragraph into two parts. In the Analysis, points 2 and 4 above, I have sought to describe the line of thought in these verses, the author's manner of convincing Gaius of his point, and his way of using words and phrases that are typical of a letter. Here, however, we can sort out the various means the Presbyter uses to attain his goal.

- He binds Gaius to himself in several ways: directly through words like "beloved," "I love you" (3 John 1); indirectly through including Gaius in "my children" (3 John 4), and through his claim to know a good deal about Gaius (3 John 2–3). Later he also includes Gaius in the "we" who are obliged to help the brothers (3 John 8).

- He praises Gaius in a number of ways: his soul is healthy (3 John 2); he lives in the truth (3 John 3); he shows himself to be faithful (3 John 5); his love is widely known—by the Presbyter, the itinerant brothers, and by the "congregation" (3 John 6). Gaius is presented as a good model for continued behavior.

- He describes Gaius and the brothers in 3 John 5–8, but unfortunately not enough to permit a clear identification of the latter. The brothers set out on their travels "for the sake of Christ"—or as the Greek text has it, "for the Name's sake" (see the note to 3 John 7)—and they have refused to accept support in their journeys from non-Jews. For these two reasons, the Presbyter, Gaius, and the Johannine Christians—the "we" of 3 John 6—are duty-bound to provide them with board, room, and expenses for their travels.

- He refers to the truth, in fact to "co-working" with the truth (3 John 8). This is the closing—and the weightiest— argument in 3 John 2–8. The word "truth" has already occurred several times (3 John 1, 3 [twice], 4), as has the related term "faithfully" (3 John 5). The formulation as it appears in the Greek text does not speak of co-working with the brothers, but with the truth itself. See the note to 3 John 8. In some way these traveling preachers manifest the truth, in their lives and in their message, perhaps not least in the former. About Demetrius it is said a bit later on (3 John 12) that the truth bears witness in his favor. Receiving these brothers in love and sending them on their way makes the truth a reality.

This consciously crafted and powerful argument leads to urgings that surprise a present-day reader by their prudent caution. "You will do well to send them on" (3 John 6); "we ought to support such people" (3 John 8). The Presbyter issues no direct command to Gaius to do this service. He appeals to him. He would like Gaius himself to be convinced of what is right. In spite of his age and status, he puts himself on the

Third John

same level with Gaius. At root, they are both Jesus' friends, both loved by Jesus, both members of the greater Johannine community.

3. Diotrephes and the Brothers (vv. 9–10)

Diotrephes is presented here as a counter-example to Gaius, as one who "does evil" (3 John 11). This paragraph thus constitutes part of the argument while simultaneously casting light on why the letter was written in the first place. As an argument, it works well; as information on the situation behind the letter, less so.

Diotrephes remains a puzzling personage in the New Testament. He has a certain, independent position of leadership within the Jewish congregation: he can, like Gaius, receive and equip itinerant brothers; he is the one who receives letters written by the Presbyter recommending these brothers (3 John 9); he can neglect what the Presbyter and his co-workers say; he can reject brothers; he can interfere with members of his congregation. Even if it is expressed a bit darkly—"who likes to put himself first"—it is clear that he already functions in a leadership role of some kind.

But how is his position to be further described? He is a significant person within the local Jewish community, perhaps because he has made his house available for these Jews or because he had contributed to the building and operation of the synagogue. His name indicates that he is a diaspora Jew from the western part of the known world, possibly a proselyte or a God-fearer, that is, a non-Jew who has converted to Judaism or who in many ways lives and believes like a Jew. It is likewise possible that he has demonstrated sympathy for the Johannine Christians and their faith in Jesus. His position makes it possible for him to exclude members from the congregation and leave them without a synagogue. Thus he serves as an early example of how Jews at the local level may have excluded Christ-believing Jews from the synagogue assemblies, forcing them to form their own (house) churches outside the Jewish community. Nothing in the letter explains why he has now changed his tune and will no longer have anything to do with Jesus-believing Jews who travel around preaching the kingdom of God.

If we read 3 John from a general Christian perspective, the picture of Diotrephes looks rather different. He can be seen as the first so-called monarchical bishop, the primary leader and pastor of a Christian congregation, like Ignatius was in Antioch, c. 100 CE. From an ultra-Johannine perspective, Diotrephes appears as a wealthy, respected home-owner, host to a group of Johannine Christians, or as one of the secessionists from the Johannine group (1 John 2:19). He could also, like the Presbyter, have fought against these secessionists, but in a more radical, forceful way than the Presbyter did. In the exercise of his office he witnesses to what would become a necessary discipline for the church. There are thus many varying descriptions of Diotrephes; the most we can say is that we cannot know with any assurance who he really was. Yet we must envision him somehow in order to understand the letter of 3 John. For other possible interpretations, see the Analysis, point 6.

The Presbyter, as we have seen, wrote a letter to Diotrephes (3 John 9); it was clearly a short letter of recommendation for one or more wandering preachers. Diotrephes had refused to accept these people and thus had refused to follow the Presbyter's recommendation. The Presbyter's honor and status were challenged, which required countermeasures. The situation is presented in particular way now in vv. 9–10.

The emphasis is placed on Diotrephes' way of behaving, on "the deeds which he is doing," as the Greek text has it (3 John 10). The same thing applies to Gaius (3 John 5): the one man opens the door to the wandering preachers; the other does not. And opening the door in this context presumably implies giving these teachers the opportunity to teach. The one man promotes the activity of these preachers; the other man does not. This means that Diotrephes' deeds are directed not against just one category of people but against three, which enlarges the problem to something more than a mere breach of hospitality toward Christians.

- Diotrephes "does not welcome us" (3 John 9); he is "speaking evil things against *us*" (3 John 10). It is hardly likely that in this private, very personal letter the word "us" would be synonymous with "me." In Johannine literature, the first-person plural pronoun "we" could also refer to the tradents and expositors of the tradition in the Johannine community. "We" here includes the Presbyter and others who have the same function he has; it highlights precisely their role as prophetic teachers with roots in Jesus' teaching. The behavior of Diotrephes, as the Presbyter views it, challenges the tradition and teaching he stands for. The verb in 3 John 9 has the same meaning in this context as it has in 3 John 10: "to receive as one's guests." Declining to receive the brothers implies in fact declining to receive the Presbyter who recommended them. See the note on 3 John 9. Through his actions Diotrephes refuses at least indirectly to accept the authority and role of the Presbyter, and this applies to every instance of taking this attitude toward the wandering preachers. Clearly, Diotrephes' assault is aimed more at the Presbyter's role and function than at the man himself.

The fact that we are dealing here with an actual attack from Diotrephes is obvious from the content of 3 John 10. At any rate, that is how the Presbyter takes it. Diotrephes is speaking rubbish about us, he says; the man is spreading empty and groundless accusations. The verb form in the Greek text indicates that this behavior is typical and ongoing. Diotrephes is circulating nasty and unreliable talk about the Presbyter and his colleagues, thereby undermining their status and exposing them to disgrace. He finds it easier then to ignore their letters of recommendation and refuse to receive wandering preachers who probably had functions somewhat similar to the Presbyter's. See Appendix 2, Itinerant Brothers.

- Diotrephes refuses to receive *the brothers* (3 John 10), that is, wandering preachers who came to his congregation. To "receive" in this context means to "receive as a guest," to offer board and room for a few days and then to help these guests continue their journey. Itinerant prophets and teachers were part of the early church. They made an essential contribution to the first mission, but at the same time they were the cause of many local conflicts, e.g., in Galatia and Corinth (Galatians, 2 Corinthians). For the situation in Syria, see Appendix 2, Itinerant Brothers.

In 3 John it is strongly argued that one should open the doors, in 2 John that one should shut them—in the latter case because of the itinerants' perversion of the teaching about the Messiah. Both postures can be seen as an attempt on the Presbyter's part to defend "what was from the beginning" (1 John 1:1), the proclamation about Christ that birthed the Johannine community.

- Diotrephes prevents *other people* from receiving the wandering preachers, even to the point of expelling them from the Jewish community (3 John 10). The conflict encompassed not only Diotrephes, the Presbyter and his colleagues, and the wandering preachers. Other local believers became involved as well. This situation hints at the beginning of the schism described in 1 John (1 John 2:19). Even if Diotrephes was not reckoned among the "secessionists" in the state of affairs presumed by 3 John, his behavior could have quickly led to a much more serious situation, where the roots connecting the congregation to the Johannine community were cut off.

The letter gives no answer to the question about why Diotrephes was acting in this way. If the other Johannine writings are taken into consideration as supplemental material, along with what is known about the situation among Jews and Christians at the end of the first century, this nascent schism can be explained in several ways.

Its background may have been the Jewish uprising against the Roman occupation in the 60s and its tragic outcome in the fall of Jerusalem and the temple in the year 70. This event made it obvious that the Jews were in no way united against the Roman domination. It led to a process of reorganization in which it became important to strengthen Jewish identity and unity. Who is a Jew? Can Greeks and Jesus-believers be Jews? The pressure on Johannine Christians to choose sides became severe.

The schism may also have arisen from the fact that following the Jewish defeat, the Roman Caesar instituted a special tax on every adult Jew. This would have required determining who was a Jew and who was not. At the same time, the Caesar cult was growing in strength. Jews were exempt from it, but could the same be said of the Christian Jews who had formed separate communities alongside the synagogues? Here too one was forced to choose: to offer sacrifices or not to offer them. This became an especially pressing issue for wealthy, respected and influential people.

Diotrephes can be thought of as belonging to this latter category. In these circumstances he chose not to have relations any longer with Jews who confessed Jesus as Messiah, the coming one, sent by God as a human being of flesh and blood. It was for this reason he was unwilling to receive the itinerant brothers. So runs one explanation. Other readers prefer to view the letters completely within a Christian perspective and thus look to differences regarding doctrines or official functions or in questions of organization. Such matters can have been of significance, but as a whole, the Johannine writings point mostly in another direction. Not until the end of the second century, with the church's intense internal conflicts, do we see changes in the premises for interpreting the Johannine letters.

4. A Test Case: The Brother Demetrius (vv. 11–12)

With the vocative "beloved" (3 John 11), the author returns to the earlier line of argument and directs now a clear word of instruction to Gaius: "do not imitate what is evil," that is, do not act like Diotrephes. The comparison is not made explicit, but it is reasonably the conclusion Gaius should come to. Even here at the end of the letter, the Elder expects Gaius to draw his own positive conclusions from what has been said between the lines.

The content of 3 John 11 operates to a significant degree as a summation. That which is evil, as exemplified by the behavior of Diotrephes (3 John 9–10), is mentioned first, since it has just been under discussion. Then comes what is good, as exemplified by Gaius' behavior (3 John 2–8). In the latter half of the verse, both the evil and the good appear again, but in reversed order. Motivation follows instruction. The whole verse is carefully formulated, both with regard to what has been said earlier in the letter and with regard to the verse in and of itself. See the notes on 3 John 11.

The motivation is the strongest imaginable: those who do as Gaius does belong to God; those who do as Diotrephes does have no communion with God. Severing connections both with the Elder and what he stands for and with the wandering preachers implies a withdrawal from confessing Jesus as Messiah, God's son, and thereby from Jesus Christ himself. And without him, no one can see God, no one can know God.

The next verse provides an example of what has been stated with such seriousness in 3 John 11. Demetrius, one of these wandering preachers, is brought forward onto the scene. It was presumably he who came to Gaius with the letter. And now the question is whether Gaius will welcome this wandering preacher and help him on his way. Will Gaius continue in his previous path or not? We do not know what Gaius did, but since 3 John has been preserved, he surely complied with the Elder's wishes and thereby safeguarded communion with the Johannine "school."

In order to further assure correct action on Gaius' part, yet another argument is added at this point for what Gaius should do. Yet there is no explicit instruction; rather the author simply puts heavy stress on motivations for doing the good thing. No directive is given here, but the Elder looks instead to Gaius' own ability to weigh the issues and to come to an inner conviction about them.

Third John

Three witnesses can now be called forth on Demetrius' behalf. First, *everyone*, which we may reasonably take as a reference to all those Demetrius has met in Jewish and Christian circles in the course of his travels. Even if the author has reason to express himself as positively as possible, Demetrius' reputation must have been as good as the Elder judges it to be. In addition, the *truth* itself bears witness, which in this context probably refers to Demetrius' message and lifestyle. According to the *Didache*, an early Christian writing, wandering preachers were to be tested first of all on the basis of their way of life, whether they lived in accordance with their own teaching, whether they shared the Lord's manner of living (*Did.* 11–15). See Appendix 2, Itinerant Brothers. The truth that was revealed and brought to reality through Jesus and was now formed in this wandering preacher's life bore witness on his behalf.

To these two testimonies is added a third: "We also testify for him, and you know that our testimony is true." Even the Elder—responsible as he was for the message that came from Jesus Christ—puts in a word for Demetrius, and he does so with the full weight of his dignity behind it: "you know that our testimony is true." The same thing is said in the Gospel of John about the eyewitness to the consummation of Jesus' works (19:35) and at the end of the same Gospel (21:24) about the testimony of the disciple whom Jesus loved. The Elder is conscious of his place in the chain of living witnesses: Jesus—the Beloved Disciple—"we" (among others, the Elder)—"you." It is in this perspective that he recommends a continued fellowship with the wandering preachers.

Under the combined effect of the powerfully personalized argument directed at Gaius (3 John 2–8), the appalling negative example of Diotrephes (3 John 9–10), the broad exhortation in 3 John 11 with its generalized motivation, as well as the three testimonies in 3 John 12, Gaius could do only one thing in response to this letter. To him it was obvious, even though the author has not said straight out what it is he wants Gaius to do. This is the Johannine style of argumentation.

Third John thus shows itself to be something more than a simple private letter between Christians. It deals with hospitality, but this hospitality toward the brothers is set within a much wider context. According to the Elder, the question has to do with having fellowship with God or not having it—nothing more and nothing less. In the Johannine writings this issue is further connected with the confession of Jesus as Messiah, the son of God. Diotrephes no longer wants anything to do with this confession, at least not publically, and thus he excludes himself from the renewed fellowship with God. Whoever has the Son has the Father. Whoever does not have the Son does not have the Father (2 John 9).

When the Johannine Christians left the Jewish community, they had little choice but to form their own congregations. Having been rendered "synagogue-less," they established new "synagogues," mostly in the form of house-churches. This is the situation in 2 John.

Second John

Second John: The Family of Truth and Love

Translation Display

1a	From the Presbyter to the elect lady and her children
1b	whom I love in truth
1c	and not only I, but also all who have come to know the truth,
2a	because of the truth
2b	which remains in us and will be with us forever.
3a	Grace, mercy, and peace from God the Father and from Jesus Christ, the Father's Son, will be with us in truth and love.
4a	I was very glad
4b	to find some of your children walking in the truth
4c	as we received a commandment from the Father.
5a	And now I ask you, dear lady,
5b	—not as if I were writing to you [sg.] a new commandment, but the one we have had from the beginning—
5c	that we should love one another.
6a	And this is love:
6b	that we should walk according to his commandments.
6c	This is the commandment
6d	as you [pl.] heard from the beginning:
6e	that you [pl.] should walk in it.
7a	For many deceivers have gone out into the world,
7b	those who do not confess
7c	that Jesus is the Messiah coming in human form.
7d	This one is the deceiver and the Anti-messiah.
8a	See to it that you [pl.] do not lose what we have worked for, but receive a full reward.
9a	Everyone who goes beyond and does not remain in the teaching of the Messiah does not have God.

Second John

9b	Everyone who remains in his teaching has both the Father and the Son.
10a	If anyone comes to you [pl.] and does not bring this teaching,
10b	do not receive him into the house or welcome him.
11a	For the one who welcomes him shares in his evil deeds.
12a	Although I have much to write to you [pl.],
12b	I would rather not use paper and ink,
12c	but I hope to come to you [pl.] and speak with you face to face,
12d	so that our joy may be complete.
13a	The children of your [sg.] elect sister greet you [sg.].

Notes

1. the Presbyter. The words in Gkt can also be rendered as "the Elder." See note on 3 John 1.

to the elect lady and her children, Gkt *eklektēi kyriai kai tois teknois autēs*. This description of the letter's recipients is unique. Early Christian letters—like ancient letters generally—normally have a name at this point, or they refer to the recipients as the church, God's church, the saints, or the elect in a given location. This cryptic formulation in 2 John early on led to other suggested translations: "to the lady (of the house) Eklekta and her children," attested in the third century and after; "to the chosen Kyria and her children," fourth century and after; "to the charming lady and her children."

The Greek word *eklektos* means chosen, exquisite, excellent, and *kyria* means lady (of the house), mistress. Neither of these two words is known to have been a name, which speaks against the interpretations Eklekta and Kyria. A collective sense of the term *kyria* is most likely: the word "lady" indicates a local (house-)church, and her children are its individual members. Biblical linguistic patterns, the vacillation between you-singular and you-plural in the letter, the qualifier "elect," and the fondness for the collective aspect of Jesus' disciples in the Johannine writings, speaks in favor of this reading. See further, the Interpretation.

The fact that specifically *kyria* is used, rather than, e.g., *gynē* ("woman"), can be explained according to some people in terms of its associations with *Kyrios* "Lord." *Kyria* is the feminine form of *Kyrios*.

whom I love in truth. The phrase can also be translated, "whom I truly love," or "whom I love in the truth." The implication is that the truth gives birth to, fosters and defines the love that the Elder has toward the recipient church. See the note on 3 John 1, where the same phrase occurs.

all those who have come to know the truth. This general formulation echoes other Johannine statements (John 8:32; 1 John 2:21). To know the truth is to know the True

One (John 17:3; 1 John 5:20). On knowing God, see the note on 1 John 2:3 and Appendix 9, A Renewed Covenant.

The verb "to know" (*ginōskein*), is used in the Johannine writings as a parallel to the expressions "to love," "to remain in," "to be with/of," and "to have"; here it denotes a very close relationship between the truth and the persons named in v. 1. The truth binds them together in a unity. See further Appendix 15, God in Them and They in God.

2. because of the truth. If we take the preceding words—"and not only I, but also all those who have come to know the truth"—as a parenthesis, this phrase, "because of the truth," becomes most closely connected to "whom I love in truth." The Elder loves the elect lady in the truth, for the truth's sake.

which remains in us and will be with us forever. To the words "know the truth" at the end of v. 1—cast in the perfect tense, implying a past event with current effect—the author now adds two related verbs, "remains in" and "will be with," using the present and future tenses, respectively. The union between the truth and those implied in the "we" is total, in terms of both its content and its permanence. The words "to be with" express both presence and support.

3. The usual epistolary greeting has been reshaped into a covenant promise. See the Analysis, point 2, as well as the Interpretation.

4. I was very glad. See the note on 3 John 3, where the same epistolary phrase occurs.

to find some of your children. Gkt uses the perfect tense of the usual word for "to find" (*heuriskein*), with its object in the form of a prepositional phrase—"(some) of" (*ek*, plus the noun "children"). Using prepositional phrases as subject or object is not uncommon in the Johannine writings (John 16:17). The verb *heuriskein* in John 1:41, 43, 45, etc., means to meet or come across someone without intentional searching. So here as well. How the Elder came by this information we do not know. Verse 4 functions as a transition and introduction to what follows. The content should probably be taken in a rather general sense: I was happy to hear that some in your fellowship were living in the truth.

walking in the truth. See the note on 3 John 3 and the note on "to walk" in 1 John 1:6.
as we received a commandment from the Father. This clause is connected to v. 3 (the word "we" and the expression "from the Father") and introduces what follows with the word "commandment" (*entolē*), which also means both message and order. The conjunction *kathōs* ("just as") can introduce both a comparison and a rationale. See the notes on 3 John 2 and 3.

In the Johannine writings both the singular and plural forms of the word "commandment" (*entolē*), are used. This may be a way of attaining stylistic variation. But in general the singular form is used when the commandment is seen as coming from the Father, and the plural form is used when the point is a person's obedience toward this revealed will of God. In the latter case, the noun is combined with verbs like

Second John

"keep," "do," and "walk according to." The commandment/message from the Father is synonymous with "the word that we have heard from the beginning" (1 John 2:7; 2 John 7). It includes more than the love command and comes close to the Johannine concept of "truth." See the Analysis of 1 John 2:3–11, point 2.

5. And now. The main function of these words is to provide a transition to the request that follows. They form part of the contemporary way of making a request. An intentional marking of the temporal aspect "now" is not likely, but it is possible here: past time in v. 4, present time or a reference to the prevailing situation in v. 5, described later in vv. 7–11.

ask. Gkt has the verb *erōtan*, the most familiar of the four usual expressions for "ask for" in the letters of the time. See the Analysis, point 2.

dear lady. Gkt has "lady" (*kyria*), as a vocative. The author has in mind the church as a whole. A vocative often occurs at this point in letters making a request. See the Analysis, point 2. The personal, collective address, the parenthetical modification that precedes the request itself, and the first-person plural form of the exhortation softens what the author now wants to say.

not as if I were writing to you a new commandment, but one we have had from the beginning. The parenthetical comment, as just mentioned, softens the request, but it also justifies it by referring to something old and well-known, and it connects it with the situation that prompted the letter (vv. 7–9). Holding fast to what was from the beginning is decisive in this circumstance. There is no need here, as there is in 1 John 2:7–11, to emphasize as well what is new in the old commandment.

The words "from the beginning" point here to the time when the Johannine Christians first heard the message about Jesus and put their faith in what God had said and done through him. See Appendix 10, What you Heard From the Beginning.

that we should love one another. Gkt uses a *hina*-clause. This construction occurs again twice in v. 6: "that we should walk according to his commandments" and "that you should walk in it," that is, in the commandment we have had from the beginning. The words "that we should love one another" complement both "I ask you" and "a new commandment." For an example of the latter sort of construction, see 1 John 3:11.

In Jesus' mouth, the love-command naturally has the you-plural form (John 13:34; 15:12, 17); in 1 John on the other hand, we always have the first-person plural form, as here (1 John 3:23; 4:7, 11, 12). In 2 John, the words are first of all a prayer that "we" and "you" (plural) would remain together, something that ensures the church's union with "what was from the beginning." Not until the end of v. 6 does the author shift to the second-person plural form.

6. The content in this verse is a somewhat detailed commentary on or explanation of the exhortation "that we should love one another." It begins with an ordinary

Johannine definition-formula of the type "and this is" (1 John 1:5; 2:22; 3:23; 5:4, 11, 14). The formula signals a further development of something in the foregoing text, in this case the word "love," and is followed by a *that*-clause (*hoti*-clause or *hina*-clause in Greek). The introductory word "and" (*kai*), has approximately the same function as "for" in 1 John 3:11 (*hoti*) and 5:3 (*gar*). See similar introductory phrases in John 3:19; 15:12; 17:3. First comes a comment on "love," and then on "commandment," and the result is an embellishment of and powerful emphasis on love as the core of the commandment from the Father.

As a whole, v. 6 consists of a series of short, simple clauses, rendered fairly literally above. But their interrelationship is somewhat unclear. Should the lines 6c and 6e (if one leaves out 6d, "as you heard from the beginning") be read as repeating the content of lines 6a and 6b? The constructions are very much alike. Only v. 6d disrupts the symmetry. Many translations construe "it" at the end of 6e as a repetition of what comes before. Such translations thus render v. 6e something like "that you should walk in love."

It is worth considering, however, whether the last three clauses of v. 6 are more loosely attached to the foregoing text than this. They repeat, corroborate, and finish out the theme found in vv. 4–6. What in fact is new is merely the transition to the you-plural form in v. 6e, and maybe also the emphasis on obedience to the message from the Father.

The clause in v. 6c rounds off the paragraph in vv. 4–6 with the closing words "This is the commandment/message," i.e., what these verses focus on and describe. The word "this" should then primarily be seen to point backwards; there is no connecting "and" here as there is in v. 6a. Then the reference to "what was from the beginning" is repeated, this time as a statement about the recipients: "as you have heard from the beginning." The argument in the letter's later portion is clearly tied to the letter's recipients. Finally comes a repetition of the main point: to walk, i.e., to live in word and deed, in accordance with the commandment/message the author is speaking of.

Lastly, the Gkt for v. 6 has a word—"it"—that by its form can refer to the truth in v. 4, love in v. 6a, or the commandment in v. 6c. In terms of syntax, the last of these options is the most natural one. As a whole, v. 6 issues in the command they received from the beginning, here concretized by the love-command. The formulations in the TEV ("that you must all live in love") and the JerB ("to live a life of love") are thereby mainly correct. But the somewhat clumsy, pleonastic formulation in the original is awkward: "This is the commandment/message—which *you* heard from the beginning—*you* must walk in it." The commandment includes both believing and loving (1 John 3:23). What follows deals with believing.

7. For. Gkt begins with *hoti*. The word binds vv. 7–11 together with the preceding text, even though these verses present new content. In Johannine texts, subordinating conjunctions like *hoti* can introduce a new paragraph. See, e.g., 1 John 3:11. Verses

Second John

7–9 give a clarifying background both to the general request in vv. 5–6 and to the specific warning in v. 10.

Many deceivers have gone out into the world. This formulation in v. 7 reminds one of statements in 1 John: "They went out from us" (1 John 2:19); "many false prophets have gone out into the world" (1 John 4:1); "many antichrists have come" (1 John 2:18). See the note on 1 John 4:1. From an intra-Jewish perspective therefore, the concern is with Jesus-believing Jews who have reverted to their former faith.

those who do not confess that Jesus is the Messiah coming in human form. Word for word, Gkt runs as follows: "those not confessing Jesus Christ coming in flesh." We could also translate it "those who do not confess Jesus as Messiah coming in the flesh." The use of the present tense for "coming" probably depends on the description of Messiah as "the coming one/the one who is coming" (John 6:14; 11:27; Matt 3:11; 11:3; Ps 118:26). See note on 1 John 4:2. The *Letter of Barnabas* (6:9, 14) emphasizes that Messiah is coming "in flesh" and quotes Ezek 36:26: "Because he was to be manifested in flesh, and to sojourn among us."

The word "confess" (*homologein*) is used in the Johannine letters in two ways: to confess Jesus as Messiah (1 John 2:22; 4:2–3; 5:1, 5; 2 John 7) and to confess one's sins (1 John 1:9). Gkt here has the present participle, "confessing," which indicates the continuous, ongoing character of the action.

This one is the deceiver and the Anti-messiah. Literally, "antichrist." The false prophets are seen as a collective—likewise in 1 John 2:18 we find a shifting between singular and plural—and they are joined together in this way with the personified evil in the great end time. The word in Gkt, *antichristos,* is found only here and in 1 John in the NT, and it has no clear corresponding form in Hebrew or Aramaic. Conceptions of an enemy of God in the end-times struggles is nonetheless common in both Jewish and Christian sources. That the words "deceiver" and "antichrist" occur here in definite form can be interpreted to imply that they introduce into the text concepts already familiar to the recipients. See the note on "lawlessness" in 1 John 3:4.

8. See to it, Gkt *blepete heautous,* is a phrase with apocalyptic overtones (Mark 13:5, 9, 22–23; Eph 5:5; Col 2:8; Heb 10:25). The style in v. 8 is more apocalyptically colored than the rest of the letter. The author and the recipient congregation clearly have both a present and a future eschatology: the kingdom of God has been realized in the present, but its full manifestation is yet to come.

The words "see to it" constitute the first clear exhortation to the recipients and set the stage for the imperative in v. 10. The situation that the author has just described compels him to focus his attention on the recipients, which he now does in what follows.

that you do not lose what we have worked for, but receive a full reward. Gkt has three finite verbs here: "lose" (*apollynai*), "work for" (*ergazesthai*), and "receive" (*apolambanein*). The three verbs all have varying subjects in the surviving manuscripts. Some manuscripts, e.g., Codex Vaticanus, have the combination you-we-you ("you" being plural in both cases), while most others have the more consistent alternative you-you-you (all plurals; among others, Codex Sinaiticus and early translations) or we-we-we (the great mass of later manuscripts). Choosing among these alternatives is not easy. The first of them has the advantage of explaining the origin of the other two. Additionally, it is the most difficult reading and it is supported to a certain degree by the dominance of the we-form up through v. 6. With some scholarly editions, as well as with the NRSV, I prefer the we-form for the second verb.

The verb *ergazethai* means to work, labor, especially with the result in mind. In a Johannine context, the phrase "what we have worked for" takes on the sense of faith in Jesus Christ. See, e.g., John 6:27, where the same verb is used. On "work" as a missionary term, see the note on 3 John 5. On the "deeds" of the disciples, see John 14:12, a text that, among other things, presupposes the Paraclete's ongoing revelation of who Jesus Christ is. The words "what we have worked for" thus come quite near to the expression "the teaching of Christ," which is mentioned immediately now in v. 9.

9. **Everyone who goes beyond and does not remain in the teaching of the Messiah.** More literally, "everyone (*pas*) who goes further (*proagōn*) and does not remain in (*menōn en*) the teaching of Christ." By means of two present participles, *proagōn* and *menōn*, both governed by a common determiner *pas* ("everyone"), Gkt binds the two actions into one, which explains the rearrangement found in the NRSV. Otherwise, by itself the verb *proagein* means to go ahead (in a temporal sense) and to go forward (in a spatial sense); in a more extended meaning, it refers to going further, advancing, making progress. The context here in 2 John gives the word a negative, ironic connotation: they have gone too far and have thus left the teaching of Christ.

the teaching of the Messiah. In order to understand Johannine texts it is important sometimes to translate "Christ" (*Christos*) as "Messiah." Such is the case here, as earlier in v. 7. Cf. the explanatory comment supplied to readers in John's Gospel: "We have found the Messiah (which is translated Anointed [Christ])" (John 1:41). The Gospel has been written so that people will believe "that Jesus is the Messiah, the Son of God" (John 20:31). For this reason, I rather often translate the word *Christos* as Messiah in this commentary, so as not to lose sight of the sense the word had in a Jewish milieu, even among the Johannine Christians.

The Greek construction "teaching of Messiah" can of course be understood as "teaching about Messiah" (objective genitive) or as "teaching from Messiah" (subjective genitive). The use of the word *Christos*, rather than Jesus, and the confessional formulation in v. 7 speak in favor of the first alternative, as in certain NT parallels (1 John 3:23; Eph 4:20–21; Heb 6:12). On the other hand the use of the word "teach/instruct" in John's Gospel with Jesus as subject (John 7:16–17; 18:19; Rev 2:14–15) and the immediate context can speak in favor of the second alternative. The emphasis placed on the commandment's being "from the beginning" has also been adduced as an argument for the second alternative.

This interpretation is certain if we describe the situation behind the Johannine letters as an inappropriately "advanced" development of Johannine ideas, that is, if we choose an ultra-Johannine perspective. In that case likewise, the verb *proagein* (see the preceding note) is well suited to the meaning "advance," "make progress." However, on the basis of an intra-Jewish perspective (a regression hypothesis), I choose the first alternative. The Johannine Christians referred to here—described as deceivers in the last times—have changed and have not retained their faith in Jesus as Messiah, the son of God. They have overstepped the bounds of the teaching about Messiah. But in Johannine thinking, the two alternatives are probably not mutually exclusive. The instruction from Jesus and the instruction about Jesus as Messiah are indissolubly united with one another.

does not have God. To have God expresses a close covenant fellowship between God and human beings. See the Interpretation, as well as Appendix 9, A Renewed Covenant.

remains in his teaching. There are similar formulations in covenant contexts: a curse on "anyone who does not uphold the words of this law by observing them" (Deut 27:26); "for they did not continue in my covenant" (Jer 31:31–34; Heb 8:9). See Appendix 15, God in Them and They in God. The "teaching" is most readily to be understood here as implying a subjective genitive, in the sense that it is the teaching that comes from him.

has both the Father and the Son. Whoever holds fast to the teaching about Jesus as Messiah has fellowship with the Son and thus also with the Father (1 John 1:1–3). See further the Interpretation.

10. If anyone comes to you. The construction in Greek—"if anyone comes to you," *ei* ("if") plus indicative—implies that what is reported here is a present fact: whenever any of these itinerants comes to you.

and does not bring this teaching. Gkt has the usual word for "bring/have with one" (*pherein*). Does this mean not proclaiming the teaching *about* Messiah as mentioned in v. 7, or not communicating (handing on) the teaching that comes *from* Jesus? Support has been offered for both alternatives. They can very easily be combined in a teaching that comes from Jesus and says that Jesus is Messiah.

do not receive him into the house or welcome anyone. There are reasons for interpreting this double formulation as a single act: to refuse to welcome into the house church any evangelist who does not confess Jesus as Messiah (see following notes).

The author of 2 John uses double expressions rather often: "abides in us *and* will be with us forever" (v. 2); "from God the Father *and* from Jesus Christ, the Father's son" (v. 3); "in truth *and* love" (v. 3); "anyone who does not remain . . . *but* goes beyond" (v. 9); "if anyone comes to you *and* does not bring this teaching" (v. 10); and of course "the Deceiver *and* the Antichrist" (v. 7). The closest parallel is v. 9 with two coordinated words mentioned first, followed then by just one of them. When the thought expressed in v. 10 is repeated in v. 11, only the latter of the two verbs is used to refer to the same act. Therefore all of v. 10b should be regarded as a single event.

Gkt has two imperatives: do not receive . . . [do not] welcome. These are the only concrete exhortations in the letter, other than the indirect formulations in vv. 5–6 and the general, preparatory admonition in v. 8. As such, they take on a special weight, strengthened by their double form and by their place at the end of the letter.

The phrase "to receive someone into a house" (*eis oikian*) can in fact imply receiving someone privately into one's home—as in the NIV and other translations—or receiving someone into the house where one gathers for worship. Based on the letter as a whole, and on its purpose and argument, as well as on the fact that the recipients of the letter likely constituted a house church, I prefer the latter alternative.

or welcome anyone. More literally, "and do not say to him, 'Greetings!'" The last word, in Greek *chairein,* is a typical word of greeting used both when someone arrives—i.e., something like "Good afternoon, and welcome!"—and when someone departs—i.e., something like "Farewell! See you soon!" The elder warns them not to receive or to welcome anti-Messianic teachers into the congregation.

11. shares in his evil deeds. The actions of the visiting preachers are described in the same way as Cain's are, and Cain "belonged to the evil one" (1 John 3:11–12). The verb in Gkt for "share in" (*koinōnein*), corresponds to the noun "fellowship" (*koinōnia*), which is used frequently in the beginning of 1 John. For a similar harsh admonition, see Ign. *Smyrn.* 4:1; 7:1.

12. Extended segments of the formulations in this verse agree with those in 3 John 13–14. See the Analysis on 2 John, point 1, and notes on 3 John 13–14.

so that our joy may be complete. Some manuscripts have "our joy" (among others, Codex Sinaiticus); others have "your joy" (among others, Codex Vaticanus). Current scholarship remains uncertain about what originally stood in the text. Those who prefer "your joy" believe that later scribes have altered the text under the influence of 1 John 1:4, "to make our joy complete." Those who choose "our joy" claim that scribes have been influenced by "you" as it is used in the context or by the more expected form for the closing of a letter, where one as a rule is thinking about the recipients.

The alternative "our joy" is the more difficult reading and in my opinion ought to be given preference. The author returns to his typical we-form that has dominated the entire first part of the letter: in vv. 2–3 of the introduction; in v. 4, "as we have received a commandment from the Father"; in v. 8, "what we have worked for." The word "we" as used here does not mean "I," nor does it mean "we bearers of the tradition"; rather it

Second John

means "you and I," or more likely—as in vv. 2–3—we Johannine Christians. The entire letter deals with the internal fellowship of the Johannine community. The alternative "our joy" also has good support in the Johannine way of thinking. See the interpretation of 1 John 1:4.

13. The children of your elect sister. The words point to the Johannine fellowship in the locality where the Elder finds himself. See the note on v. 1. Some late manuscripts have "your sister church" in place of "your elect sister," which is a correct interpretation of the Johannine phrase.

In some manuscripts the letter ends with an "amen," sometimes preceded with the words "peace be with you," which is also found in various Pauline letters.

Analysis

1. A Genuine Letter?

The Second Letter of John does not contain much that is not also found in 1 John, and it shares the same epistolary form as well as certain phrases with 3 John. Some scholars have therefore described 2 John as a literary imitation of the two other letters, one that lacks a particular epistolary "occasion." Second John would then have been a fictive letter that could be sent to any congregation.

The similarities with 3 John both at the beginning and at the end are undeniably striking:

2 John	3 John
From the Elder to . . .	From the Elder to . . .
. . . whom I love in truth.	. . . whom I love in truth.
For I was very glad . . .	I was very glad. . .
. . . to find some of your children walking in the truth.	. . . that my children walk in the truth.
I have much to write to you	I have many things to write to you
But I would rather not use paper and ink	but I do not want to write to you with pen and ink
but I hope to come to you	I hope to see you soon
and speak with you face to face	and we will talk face to face
. . . greet you	. . . send you greetings

The phrases at the beginning are almost completely identical, while the formulations at the end vary quite a bit in details; they are thoroughly treated in the notes on 3 John 13–15. The structures of the two letters are likewise similar:

1. The introduction consists of a striking description of the recipient (and sender).
2. A form of thanksgiving supplies the transition to the letter's main body.

3. Typical epistolary phrases for the request have an important function in the beginning of the main body.

4. The later portion of the letter's corpus issues in a warning that contains the letter's primary purpose.

These many similarities—in part determined by the genre of the letter—I interpret as evidence that the same writer/author is responsible for both letters. Each letter has its own clear strategy that can reasonably be associated with a definite situation. See the Analysis, point 3, and the Analysis for 3 John, point 4. In addition there are surprising variations in relation to 3 John that cannot easily be explained on the basis of a theory of imitation. The word "we" in the sense of "we bearers of the tradition," important in both 1 and 3 John, is noticeably absent in 2 John. And there are other formulations that occur only in 2 John (vv. 2, 3, and 8).

Second John is therefore best read as a genuine letter. And it ought to be allowed to stand on its own two feet, even though it must be interpreted within a general Johannine framework. See further the Analysis for 3 John, point 4.

2. Greek, Jewish, and Johannine Elements

Second John—like large portions of the Johannine literature—displays a peculiar blend of typically Greek, Jewish, or Johannine elements.

The letter has the form of a traditional Greek letter, most obvious in the beginning and the ending, as well as in a phrase such as "I was very glad" (v. 4). See further the Analysis for 3 John, point 2. The form of the request found in the letter's first part also has many parallels in ancient epistolary literature. There we usually find three main elements:

1. *A laying out of background rapport* so as to enable the recipients of the letter to respond positively. In 2 John this includes primarily the many expressions of solidarity in vv. 1–3, the statement of praise in v. 4, and the reference to "the commandment we have received from the Father" (v. 4), a commandment that had been there from the beginning (v. 5). All this lays the groundwork for the request "let us love one another" (v. 5).

2. *A verb meaning "ask,"* always in the first-person, present. Generally speaking, Greek offers four alternatives: the verb *axioun*, which is the most formal and official expression (Acts 28:21–22); the verb *deisthai*, which also expresses a rather formal, polite request (e.g., Acts 21:39; 24:2–3); the verb *erōtan*, which conveys a nuance of familiarity between social equals (Luke 14:18–19; 1 Thess 5:12); the verb *parakalein*, the most personal form, and also the most common in the New Testament.

Second John

It is the third alternative that is used in 2 John. Thus the request is personal, but with a clear tone of appeal. The author is not issuing a command, nor does he direct his request to his social superiors; rather both sender and recipients stand on the same level, a conclusion we can base on the pattern typical of Greek letters.

3. *The letter's main concern:* let us love one another. Here of course one would expect "you" as the subject, and not "we." But to begin with, the request includes the sender as well.

In addition to these three main elements there is sometimes a vocative as well: a name, a title, a status word or a mere pronoun. In 2 John we have "lady" (*kyria*), in the vocative case. Some ancient letters combine "(my) lady" (*kyria*), or "(my) lord" (*kyrie*), with the verb *erōtan* for "ask," not least of all, letters between family members. The first part of 2 John, especially v. 5, thus follows a known Greek model.

However, like 3 John, 2 John also demonstrates many deviations from the contemporary letter form (see the Analysis for 3 John, point 2) as well as elements associated with a Jewish and/or Johannine milieu. The opening of the letter provides examples:

- No names are mentioned, whether of persons or of places. The sender is described in the same way as in 3 John. See the note there. The recipients are called "the elect lady and her children" (v. 1). Referring to a group of people as "lady" has Greek parallels, but the addition of "the elect" is more reminiscent of Old Testament-Jewish speech patterns. See further the Interpretation. The same metaphor appears in the last verse: the children of the elect sister (v. 13). Here, in addition to those from Greek and Jewish culture, we have a Johannine feature: the emphasizing of close fellowship between Christians through words that have to do with family: children, brother, sister, bride, lady, the Elder.

- A boldly expanded description of the recipients in vv. 1–2, accomplished by means of several Johannine terms: love, truth, know, remain in, be together with. The description covers not only the recipients, but all Johannine Christians as well. We-statements dominate the end of the letter's introduction.

- The expected peace-wish uses a future-tense verb that turns its entire meaning into one of reassurance or even of promise: "Grace, mercy, and peace . . . will be with us" (v. 3).

- The peace-wish does not read "with you," as in most New Testament letters, but "with us," further emphasizing the fellowship.

- Instead of "grace and peace," three words are used: "grace, mercy, and peace," something that 2 John has in common with the two letters to Timothy and the letter of Jude. The background is Jewish. The combination "mercy and peace" appears in the Aaronic blessing (Num 6:25–26), in the opening of the letter in *2 Baruch (Syriac Apocalypse)* 78:2, and in the greeting in Gal 6:16. Even a manuscript of Tobit has this double phrase at Tob 7:12. This phrase, together with the usual formula in the New Testament, yields three words. They are all Old Testament covenant terms that describe the relationship between God and his people. Here they are taken to describe the divine relationship within the Johannine community. See Appendix 9, A Renewed Covenant.

- Verse 3 reads "from Jesus Christ, the Father's Son," rather than the usual "from our Lord Jesus Christ." The use of "the Father" for God and "the Father's Son" for Jesus in the opening of the letter brings to the fore in a Johannine way important relationships within the Christian fellowship: the Father–the Son–we, in a renewed covenant, marked by grace, mercy, and peace.

- The phrase "in truth and love" at the end of the letter's opening is loosely attached to the foregoing and seems mostly reminiscent of the most important aspect of that opening. The expression echoes the words in the beginning—"whom I love in truth" and "because of the truth" (vv. 1–2)—and thus functions as a kind of bookending framework (*inclusio*), while simultaneously preparing for the letter's message in vv. 4–11. Of course I need scarcely mention that the phrase is Johannine.

Thus the opening of 2 John provides good examples of a blend of Greek, Jewish, and Johannine elements. A Jewish background also lies behind the apocalyptic language in vv. 7–8—deceivers, Antichrist, be on your guard, lose, receive a reward—and it is not difficult to list Johannine elements: love, truth, know, remain in, love one another, commandment from the Father, not a new command, confess Jesus Christ come in the flesh, and so on. These features of the letter show that the Johannine community was anchored in both Jewish and Greek milieus and that above all it had developed its own way of speaking.

3. Structure and Argument

Second John is on the surface a normal ancient letter—it would have fit on a typical sheet of papyrus—and its structure is determined among other things by general models of letter writing:

1. *The opening of the letter* with sender, recipients, and greeting (vv. 1–3).
2. *The body of the letter* with v. 4 as transition and introduction—"I was very glad..."—and v. 12 as conclusion and transition to the actual ending. The author notes that he has more to write, that he hopes soon to visit them, and that they then may share complete joy (vv. 4–12).
3. *The end of the letter,* consisting only of greetings (v. 13).

The ancient letter form is discussed in the Analysis for 3 John, point 2. But there, as here, it is apparent that the author uses this form in his own way, especially in the beginning of the letter. See point 2, above. He has a serious message: Keep away from itinerant preachers who deny that Jesus is Messiah (vv. 10–11). And quite purposefully—but very carefully just the same—he aims to reach his goal. From the point of view of its argument, the letter can be described in the following way:

- *A shared point of departure:* the close fellowship between "all who know the truth," here no doubt primarily among Johannine Christians (vv. 1–3). The author uses many words from the sphere of family relations—the Elder, lady, children, father, son, and (in v. 12) sister—and terms that lead to thoughts of a fellowship characterized by covenant: love, know, remain in, be with, elect, grace, mercy, peace. See further the Interpretation. The sender and the recipients are bound together above all by *truth* and *love,* words heaped up in the beginning of the letter (five times and four times, resp.). The covenant unity with God and Jesus Christ is expressed in v. 9 with the powerful words "to have the Father and the Son," as well as with those anchored in covenant terminology. This fundamental "fellowship," *koinōnia*—the corresponding verb is used in v. 11—among those most closely concerned in the letter is reinforced by the content of the letter's final two verses: much more to say, hope for a visit, converse face to face, experience of full and mutual joy, greetings from "your elect sister's children," (vv. 12–13). This impressive, thematic *inclusio*—the close solidarity—is the basis for the remainder of what is said in the letter.

- *A request* in we-form: let us love one another (vv. 4–6). Truth and love, which so completely determine the status of the recipients and the sender, must come to expression in action, in their manner of living. The author begins with a few words of praise (v. 4) and refers then to what he and his readers have in common, what is old and original, what was there from the beginning (vv. 4–5). This prepares the way for a rather moderate plea that first includes the author (we-form in v. 5) and then limits itself in more general terms to the recipients (you-form in v. 6): you must walk in it, that is, in the commandment.

- *A rationale* for this request that the recipients have heard reasonably often and have themselves understood as natural and taken for granted: a serious risk that their solidarity could be destroyed, that they could lose what they now have and forfeit their future reward, i.e., eternal life (vv. 7–9). The danger arises from itinerant preachers who have lost contact with the teaching about Jesus as God's Messiah, and with it have lost contact with God himself (v. 9).

- *A concrete warning:* do not receive these traveling preachers into your fellowship (v. 10). Opening the door to them makes the letter's recipients partakers in their evil and destructive activity (v. 11). The fellowship of truth and love on earth is disrupted and the new fellowship with God comes to an end.

Interpretation

1. The Family of Truth and Love (vv. 1–3, 12–13)

The persons mentioned in 2 John bear no names, but they are all described with words that clearly indicate where they belong. On the one hand there is a family of Christ-believing Jews: the Elder, the elect lady and her children, the elect sister's children, in fact all those who have learned the truth and remain in it. This is the Johannine family in the early Christian church, the Johannine Christians who have not forsaken the teaching about Jesus as Messiah. The author frequently refers to these people as "we" (2 John 2, 3, 12; see also vv. 4, 5, 6, 8). On the other hand, there are the many "deceivers," itinerant "anti-messianic teachers," who are likely to visit the Johannine Christians to whom the letter of 2 John is directed. The upcoming encounter with these deniers of the Messiah is the reason for this letter. From 1 John we gather that they had once belonged to the Johannine community, but now had left it because they no longer wished to confess Jesus as Messiah (1 John 2:18–27; 4:1–6). See further, chap. 12, point 4.

The letter is addressed to "the elect lady and her children" (2 John 1), and it ends with a greeting from her "elect sister's children" (2 John 13). These formulas are unique, although they do have counterparts in that milieu. In antiquity, a group of people, such as a city, could be referred to as "lady," *kyria*. In Old Testament and Jewish writings, God's people on earth—or parts of God's people—are called "daughter of Zion" (Zeph 3:14) or "virgin Israel" (Jer 31:21). The Samaritans are "Jerusalem's sister" (Ezek 16:46; 23:4). The people are God's bride, an image that occurs again in the New Testament, for example in John's Gospel (John 3:29), where all those who become Jesus' disciples are seen as a bride. The covenant is portrayed as a marriage (Hosea 1–3; Ezekiel 16). Since many of the terms occurring in the letter's introduction are associated with covenant thought, this background of female-oriented linguistic imagery is entirely appropriate. See further Appendix 9, A Renewed Covenant.

The book of Revelation should also be mentioned here, not so much because it uses the image of the bride, but more because of its description of "the woman and her child." In Revelation we hear how the prophet sees the Ark of the Covenant in the heavenly temple (Rev 11:19), and what follows is nothing less than a vision of the story of the covenant people (Revelation 12). The woman represents the people of God as a whole, including both their Old Testament and their New Testament dimensions. The expression "her children" (Greek: "her seed," Rev 12:17) is a term designating the people of God. Just as "the woman and her 'seed'" can be understood as a renewed people of God, in the same way "the elect lady and her children" in 2 John can be seen as a local community within this people of God.

The elect woman in 2 John thus represents a part of God's people on earth, a specific Johannine community, probably a house church. See Appendix 4, House Churches. The nearest linguistic parallel to this is found in 1 Pet 5:13, where "she who is in Babylon, chosen together with you"—that is, a congregation in Rome—greets "the chosen" who are named in the letter's introduction (1 Pet 1:1). The idea of God's people is dominant in this letter as well. The congregation in 2 John is addressed as "dear lady" (2 John 5), and the individual members of the congregation are referred to as "her children" (2 John 1). This double description of the letter's addressees corresponds to the alternation in the letter between the singular (2 John 1, 13) and plural (2 John 1, 12) forms of the second person pronoun "you." See also 2 John 4, 5 for the singular and vv. 6, 8, 10 for the plural.

It is precisely the collective aspect, the local (house-based) congregation as a unified whole, that stands out in this particular use of language. In addition, the fact that the author speaks of both the "elect" lady and her "elect" sister (2 John 1, 13) confirms what has just been said, since the word "elect" is readily employed of the people of God as a whole or of individual members of this people. The congregation is chosen by God/Jesus (1 Pet 1:1; Rom 8:33; Col 3:12) and is therefore dependent on him. The way the words of the introduction are associated with family and marriage, perhaps also with "the Lord" (*kyrios*), strongly emphasizes the solidarity within the group and the collective aspect. The local Christian congregation here is not only a number of separate individuals, but a well-integrated whole, a flock of God with Jesus as the shepherd (John 10), one of God's vines, that is, Jesus the vine with his disciples as the branches (John 15).

There are therefore two Johannine (house) churches in 2 John—and no mention of a Jewish community. They find themselves at a considerable distance from each other, since it is necessary to communicate by letter (2 John 12). The link between them is the Presbyter, the Elder, who lives in the one place, although we do not know where. Perhaps it is in Syria, perhaps in Asia Minor. A part of the Johannine community's history points to the recipients as living in Asia Minor. See further, chap. 12, point 4.

The Elder has either met or heard of some of the members of the recipient congregation (2 John 4), and he knows something of what is about to happen to it (2 John 7–11). He holds a certain position in relationship to the addressees, since he is able to write to the congregation—which, as a group, he clearly does not know personally—to warn and admonish them. Still, he cultivates a certain restraint in his argumentation. See the Analysis, point 3. I see in the Presbyter an older person, highly revered within the Johannine community, who together with a few others was responsible for guaranteeing the continuity of the tradition all the way back to Jesus, as well as for imparting and presumably interpreting its significance regarding him. See chap. 12, point 3.

Almost all of the many deviations from contemporary letter openings (see the Analysis, point 2) emphasize the fundamental unity within the Johannine community, characterized as it is by union with God the Father, through Jesus Christ the Son. In the first three verses, the author uses numerous expressions having to do with covenant.

- *To love in the truth, because of the truth,* 2 John 1–3. The word "love" here expresses principally a close bond between two parties, in the Johannine writings mostly determined by the close relationship between the Father and the Son in word and deed. See Appendix 16, God is Love. Truth and love are what most effectively hold these people together. The two concepts clearly frame the entire presentation in the opening of the letter.

- *To know the truth, that the truth will abide in them, and that the truth will be with them forever,* 2 John 1–2. In a doubly three-fold way, the author depicts the total union between the truth and "us," namely, "us" the Johannine Christians. Three very closely related concepts from the Gospel of John are used here: "to know," "to abide in," and "shall be with." These formulations are strongly reminiscent of the way the Gospel describes the relationship between the Paraclete (the Advocate) and Jesus' disciples, the Spirit of the truth who shall lead them into all truth (John 14:16). Jesus is the truth, but this truth can only be communicated in its fullness through the Paraclete (John 14:6; 16:12–15). Expressions like "abide in" and "be with" presumably have their roots in covenant language. See Appendix 15, God in Them and They in God.

- *Grace, mercy, and peace will be with them,* 2 John 3. These features are especially characteristic of God in God's covenantal acts toward God's people (Exod 34:6–9). God's covenant is a covenant of peace (Isa 54:10; Ezek 34:25), a peace brought about by the risen and glorified one (Rom 5:1; John 14:27; 20:21, 26). Grace and truth are brought together also in the prologue to John's Gospel. The law was given through Moses when the covenant was established at Sinai; through Jesus Christ, "grace and truth" are found in a renewed covenant (John 1:14, 16). And in both cases, love is the source of God's covenant action (Deut 7:6–8; John 3:16; 1 John 4:10).

    Love, truth, grace, mercy, and peace stand as characteristics of the covenant with God. The usual epistolary greeting (see the Analysis, point 2) has been reformulated in 2 John as a covenant promise.

- *God the Father and Jesus Christ, the Father's Son,* 2 John 3. In the Johannine literature, the new fellowship with God is completely conditioned by the close relationship between the Father and the Son. Whoever has seen the Son has seen the Father (John 14:7–9) and whoever knows the Son knows the Father (1 John 2:23), for the two are one. This is why the relationship to the Son and his revelation of God is so crucial (2 John 9). One may well wonder whether the closing phrase of the introduction—"in truth and love"—is meant to indicate the condition for the new covenant for the close union with God. The covenant is valid if the people hold fast to the truth, if they live in love.

Thus these people who are presented to us in the letter's beginning and ending form a fellowship of love grounded in the truth, a family of God who share a mutual

Second John

joy when they meet at last (2 John 12), a perfect joy because it has its source in God and is eternal. Yet the full reward is still to come (2 John 8).

2. Truth and Love: A Commandment That Was There from the Beginning (vv. 4–6)

Using a typical epistolary phrase, the author introduces the main section of the letter and a new stage of his argument. See the Analysis, point 3. Three new concepts or motifs recur constantly in this short section: "walk," three times (2 John 4, 6); "command," five times (2 John 4, 5, 6); and a command they have had "from the beginning," two times (2 John 5, 6). Actually, the presentation with its many repetitions almost turns to gibberish by the end, and readers today do not quite know how to tie all the threads together. See notes on v. 6. These three motifs lead into three more or less direct instructions: "let us love one another," we must "walk according to his commandment," and "you must walk in it [his commandment]."

Truth and love are regarded in this new paragraph as something requiring obedience and action on the part of the recipients. These people have received a message, a commandment. The emphasis falls no longer on their fellowship with God, but on their way of life. They are to *walk*—to live—in the truth, that is, to put the new fellowship with God into practical action in the serious situation that has now arisen.

The author is happy that some in the congregation have demonstrated that they are "walking" in the truth (2 John 4). Whether he has only heard about these people or has met them himself is unknown. He does not seem to have personally known the congregation as such. In the design of the letter, the content of v. 4 primarily sets the stage for the instructions that follow. See the Analysis, point 3.

Love is then defined as a way of living in obedience to God; it is to "walk" according to his commandments (2 John 5). And the entire paragraph issues in the instruction that they must "walk" in the commandment they have received (2 John 6). In this way, 2 John 4–6 is held together by the thought of a practical application of the truth and love that unites the people in this letter into a chosen family.

The commandment occurs right away in 2 John 4: "as we have been commanded by the Father." See Notes. In point 2 of the Analysis for 1 John 2:3–11, I have argued that the commandment from the Father has a broader meaning than the commandment to love one another. It includes as well faith in Jesus as Messiah, the Son of God. Faith and love constitute the double commandment of the renewed covenant (1 John 3:23). The readers received it from the Father (2 John 4); they have had it from the beginning (2 John 5), and they have heard it from the beginning (2 John 6). If this is the case, then one wonders why the author must remind them of it—and must do so not just once in this short paragraph, but three times! The best explanation is that there were Christ-believing Jews who challenged the necessity of this commandment.

They had "gone beyond" and left behind them the teaching about the Messiah and about mutual love (2 John 9). See chap. 12, points 3 and 4.

The core of this text contains an instruction to the recipients, but remarkably enough, it is formulated in the first-person plural: "we." The inclusive use of the *we*-form (2 John 4, 5, and 6; see also vv. 2, 3) shows that the concern is for unity not only within the recipients' congregation, but also within the entire Johannine community. The author fights for oneness and solidarity among these Johannine Christians, because in his eyes it comes down to a matter of fellowship with God or of no fellowship with God. Without obedience to the double commandment of the covenant (1 John 3:23), there can be no fellowship with the Father. The second half of the commandment—love—is handled in 2 John 4–6; the first half—faith— is treated in what now follows.

3. Beware That No One Leads You Astray (vv. 7–9)

The title for this section is taken from the so-called apocalyptic discourse in the Gospel of Mark (Mark 13). Jesus describes there the coming end time terrors and warns against rampant delusion and backsliding. This is why terms like "beware" (Mark 13:5, 9) and "be alert" (Mark 13:23) are used; they represent the same Greek phrase as occurs in 2 John 8, rendered "see to it." The situation facing the Johannine Christians is so serious that they risk losing what they already have and losing out on what awaits them. That is, they risk losing the most fundamental element of their faith, that Jesus is the Messiah, the Son of God, a faith that gives eternal life.

In this context, the author uses more apocalyptic language than he typically does: deceivers, Antichrist, beware, lose or receive a reward. This difficult crisis situation can only be understood in an apocalyptic perspective. The last hour has arrived (1 John 2:18). The phrase, "see to it," or "be on your guard," in 2 John 8 is the first clear instruction in the letter, and it prepares the readers for the instructions coming in the next section (2 John 10). The prevailing situation forces the author to direct his attention to the recipients in particular. At the end of 2 John 7, he switches to you-plural forms and with a few exceptions does not deviate from them throughout the remainder of the letter.

"See to it that you do not lose what we have worked for" (2 John 8). Regarding the use of "we" in place of "you," see the Notes. The word "lose" here means to miss out on something one has already achieved, to discover that one is missing what one once had (1 Cor 1:19). It is sometimes used with reference to eternal life (John 3:15–16; 10:27–28). The phrase "what we have worked for," in Johannine perspective, most likely entails our faith in Jesus as Messiah. The "work" God looks for in human beings is that they believe in the one whom he has sent (John 6:27). And the true confession of Christ is something belonging to the entire Johannine community, and not only to the recipients' congregation. Thus, the we-form appears at this point.

Second John

Even the expression "to receive a full reward" fits in among apocalyptically colored remarks. In Jesus' teaching, the word "reward" refers to eternal life: "your reward is great in heaven" (Matt 5:12) and "none of these will lose their reward" (Matt 10:42). According to Hebrews, Moses "was looking ahead to the reward" (Heb 11:26). In this context, the expression "full reward" comes close to the Johannine concepts of "complete joy" (1 John 1:4; 2 John 12; John 15:11, 16:24) and "perfect love" (1 John 2:5; 4:12, 17–18). Even though the addressees already have eternal, divine life, they are waiting for this life to come in full measure. This will be possible only when they are completely united with the Father and the Son. The situation behind the letter is one of great risk that this goal will not be reached because of severed contact with the teaching from Jesus Christ. The last times are here: "See, I am coming soon; my reward is with me, to repay according to everyone's work" (Rev 22:12).

As is clear from its opening word in the Greek text, *hoti* ("because," "for"), this paragraph functions as an explanation and motivation for the instructions just given (2 John 4–6). Since the command in the previous paragraph includes both love and faith, the new theme in vv. 7–9 is to be expected. The terse instruction in 2 John, however, must somehow be supplemented with what is said about the deceivers and antichrists in 1 John. But how these deceivers are visualized today depends on the interpreter's chosen perspective on the larger context.

In 2 John 9 the author employs a verb with the extended meaning of going further, advancing, making progress. See Notes. This fits in well with an ultra-Johannine perspective (progression hypothesis). Those who now are traveling around and leading the Johannine Christians astray are "progressivists." From this perspective, the Johannine way of thinking involves a built-in program of renewal, a continuous dynamic between old and new, through envisioning the Spirit as the Advocate, the Paraclete (John 16:12–15; 14:16–17). All individual members in the Johannine family are bearers of this spirit; they have an anointing from the Holy One, who teaches them and leads them further on (1 John 2:20, 27).

In this constantly ongoing process of old and new, there are according to the Presbyter two secure reference points: *the Paraclete,* the Spirit of truth, and *a chain of witnesses,* i.e., several people within the Johannine community who pass on and confirm the tradition from the earthly Jesus. In the view of the Presbyter, who has responsibility for the tradition, the progressivists in 2 John have gone too far and have lost the vitally necessary contact with Christ and the teaching that has come down from him. In the author's eyes, this makes them antichrists, i.e., manifestations of Satan's work amidst the difficulties of the last times. In all their spirituality and in all their renewal and advanced faith, they are in fact *anti* Christ—against Christ—and deserve no other title than that of "the Deceiver" (2 John 7).

This is how the text reads from the ultra-Johannine perspective. From a general Christian perspective (apostasy hypothesis), the false teachers are seen as coming from outside the community and preaching a gnostic-colored Christology. See further, chap.

12, point 4. The problem with both these depictions of the situation is that they require a very complicated and advanced form of Christology. The limited information provided in 2 John can more easily be understood from an intra-Jewish perspective (regression hypothesis). The deceivers do not confess Jesus as Messiah, come in human form. They no longer believe in him. See the notes on 2 John 7. They have abandoned the teaching about the Messiah and no longer partake of the teaching that has its roots in Jesus himself. See the notes on 2 John 9. The result, in the opinion of the Presbyter, is devastating: they no longer have fellowship with God, a fellowship described in v. 9 with the particularly covenantal terminology "to have God" or "not to have God."

The phrase "to have God" occurs several times in the Johannine writings. Very likely it has its roots in the description of the relationship between God and the people of God in the Old Testament. In *2 Clement* the Jews are called precisely those "who seem to have God" (*2 Clem.* 2:3). Israel had once become God's own treasured possession through the covenant at Sinai (Exod 19:5). This led to a mutual possession: "I will be your God and you shall be my people," says the Lord (Lev 26:12). This mutual relationship would be intensified in the new covenant (Jer 31:31–34).

The phrase thus expresses a very close fellowship between God and his people— cf. the expressions "to have a wife" and "to have a husband"—similar to the related words "to know God," "to have fellowship with God," and "to be/remain in God." They are all tied to the covenant-oriented description of the addressees at the beginning of the letter. According to the Gospel of John, those who have God have God's life (John 3:16), God's love (5:42), God's message (5:38), God's light (8:12), God's peace (16:33) and God's joy (17:13). They "have" God in the sense of the word's actual meaning. But this is possible only through the Son (1 John 2:25; 5:11–13). That is why the relationship to Jesus Christ—both the earthly and the exalted Christ—is so decisive. The itinerant preachers, who were shortly expected to come to the letter's addressees and who had at one time belonged to the Johannine community and needed no introduction among the Johannine Christians, denied that the Messiah "has come in the flesh," i.e., that he is the earthly Messiah whom God, in accordance with his promises, had sent to the Jewish people. Consequently, even the message, the commandment that they have had from the beginning, loses its significance. The content of 2 John 7–9 can indeed function as an effective motivation for the instruction contained in the preceding paragraph, that their lives should bring to reality the message/commandment from the Father (2 John 4–6).

4. Do Not Receive Them Into Your Congregation (vv. 10–11)

With this paragraph, the author has reached the goal of his argument. In five stages he has led the recipients to where he wants them:

1. Through truth and love, we are one with each other and with the Father and the

Son (2 John 1–3).

2. We are to live in truth and love, i.e., in the commandment from the Father (through the Son), which we have had from the very beginning (2 John 4–6ab).

3. You must live in the commandment that you received from the beginning (2 John 6cde).

4. Beware the risk of losing what we have attained. The danger comes from certain people within the Johannine community who have departed from what was there from the beginning, from the instruction that Jesus gave. They have not remained in the teaching about Jesus as Messiah (2 John 7–9).

5. Do not receive these deceivers in your congregation! If you do, you destroy the fellowship you have with God and you participate in the devil's work (2 John 10–11).

These final verses of the letter's main section provide direct and indirect insight into the Johannine house churches' situation at this time.

- The Johannine Christians were used to itinerant teachers, prophets, and others who were dependent on the hospitality of these churches for survival and for continuing their work. See Appendix 1, Hospitality.

- Among these itinerants there were also Johannine Christians and clearly, judging from the letter of 2 John, the addressees needed no letters of recommendation for them. The situation in 3 John is different, since there the traveling teachers are not known to the addressees and others in the congregation, and thus they do need such letters.

- Johannine communities were bound together by these traveling brothers (among other things) and gradually formed a separate community within the early church. Only in this way can we understand the Presbyter's role and the fact that he had excellent information about what was happening within the Johannine community, even though in some cases the distances between congregations was considerable.

- A serious division within the Johannine community had occurred (1 John 2:19). As the Presbyter saw it, it constituted secession. Some of the itinerant teachers had consequently come to the point of joining or sympathizing with the secessionists. The congregation to which 2 John is addressed does not seem to be well informed about what has taken place, since those the Elder expected would soon visit the group would not be recognized as false teachers. This leaves the congregation vulnerable.

- The characteristic identifying these secessionists is primarily christological in nature. They no longer confess Jesus as the Messiah, coming in the flesh, they have not remained in the teaching about the Messiah, and—according to the regression hypothesis—they have returned to their previous Jewish faith.

In this circumstance the author offers merely a threefold recommendation: do not receive them into your fellowship; give them neither food nor shelter; make no provision for their continued travels. In this way these last-day deceivers would have no possibility of influencing the congregation with their teaching. This is the most likely meaning of the words "do not receive him" and "do not welcome him" (v. 10). See the Notes. This radical instruction from the Presbyter is motivated by the serious consequences that this new teaching could have: an end to faith in Jesus as Messiah and with it no fellowship with God, no renewed covenant with God. How then are the addressees to know who belongs to this secessionist group and who does not? The text provides no answer to the question. Some form of test may have been used, judging by the exhortation in the latter half of 1 John (1 John 4:1). The criterion there, as in 2 John, is a confession of Jesus as Messiah, as the One who was to come in flesh. We can perhaps get some sense of how the congregation was to proceed in this by considering a number of quotations from the *Didache,* a writing contemporaneous with 2 John.

> If anyone comes and teaches you what has been said above, you are to receive him. But if he who teaches has turned to another doctrine and teaches it in order to destroy, you are not to listen to him. But if anyone teaches so as to increase righteousness and the knowledge of the Lord, you are to receive him as if he were the Lord himself. [. . .] Not everyone who speaks in the spirit is a prophet, but only he who lives as the Lord lived. By their manner of life are the false prophet and the true prophet to be known. [. . .] Every prophet who teaches the truth, but does not live according to it, is a false prophet. [. . .] Everyone who comes in the name of the Lord is to be received. Then, however, you are to test him in order to know him. For you are to have insight both right and left. (*Did.* 11:1–2, 8, 10; 12:1)

Itinerant preachers and Christians certainly had a unifying effect in the early church. But at the same time, they also provided an occasion for opposition and division, as the New Testament letters testify. In general, the Presbyter was positive toward itinerant brothers, but in 2 John he wants to warn against those who no longer bring with them the instruction from Jesus and the teaching about him as Messiah. Without Jesus Christ there can be no fellowship with God, and no renewed covenant. Thus the Presbyter issues his categorical word: Do not receive them in your congregation!

First John

1

1 John 1:1–4: Divine Life, Divine Fellowship, Divine Joy

Translation Display

1a	What was there from the beginning
1b	what we have heard
1c	what we have seen with our eyes
1d	what we have looked at and touched with our hands
1e	concerning the word of life—
2a	and the life was revealed
2b	and we have seen it and bear witness to it
2c	and we declare to you the eternal life
2d	that was with the Father
2e	and was revealed to us—
3a	what we have seen and heard
3b	we declare also to you
3c	so that you also may have fellowship with us
3d	and our fellowship is with the Father and with his Son Jesus Messiah.
4a	And these things we write
4b	that our joy may be complete.

Notes

1:1. What. The first four clauses are introduced with "what"—literally, "that which" (neuter of the relative pronoun, *ho*)—and not with the masculine "him who" (*ton*), as in 1 John 2:13. The latter of course points to the person of Jesus, while "that which," or "what," is more general and open. Some of the verbs in these clauses—see, know—imply that the object is a person, while others—hear, proclaim—imply that it is a message. In the Gospel of John, the neuter can be used to refer to persons of a certain type or quality. See, e.g., John 6:37. Thus, here in 1 John it is Jesus who is in view, with all that Jesus is and stands for, his being, his person, his words and deeds, i.e., Jesus as the revealed God and the divine life (1 John 5:20). The four relative clauses cover the entirety of his earthly life, although not until the end of the introduction (1 John 1:3) is Jesus mentioned by name, as in the prologue to the Gospel of John. The word "what" can be explained as well as a reference to the sweeping experience, enjoyed by Jesus' witnesses, of the Life revealed on earth.

was there. Gkt has the imperfect of the verb "be" (*ēn*), i.e., the same word used in John 1:1. It can be interpreted as an existence before all time, but here it primarily functions as a parallel to the words "have heard," "have seen," "have looked at," and "have touched," which speaks in favor of Jesus' earthly life being in view.

from the beginning. The Greek expression *ap' archēs* gives chronological precision to "what was," but it is not clear which time-period the writer has in mind: from time before all time (John 1:1); from the beginning of the history of salvation (John 8:44); from the beginning of Jesus' ministry (John 15:27); from the beginning of the proclamation about Jesus (1 John 2:7, 24). Similarities with John 1 make possible the meaning "before creation," while the formulation itself—"from the beginning" and not "in the beginning"—and what comes after it point rather in the direction of Jesus' life, from his birth to his death and resurrection, and its place in the proclamation. See further Appendix 10, What you Heard From the Beginning.

we, i.e., the Johannine eyewitnesses and bearers of the tradition. See Appendix 5, We in the Johannine Letters.

have heard ... have seen ... have looked at and touched. The piling up of four verbs of perception—four often being a number standing for completeness—yields first of all a stylistic and rhetorical effect. The two first verbs are in the perfect, the latter two in the aorist. The variation can be merely stylistic or it can express the aspects that these two verb-forms have: an event with ongoing effect in the present (perfect), and an event as such (aorist). The perfect can also characterize the we-group's role as eyewitnesses, while the aorist can function to give precision to the two preceding verbs. The verbs "see" and "hear" are often found in the perfect tense in the Johannine writings.

In the Gospel of John and in 1–3 John, there occur five various verbs for "see" without significant difference in meaning; here we have *horaō* and *theaomai*. See, e.g., 1 John 4:12 and John 1:18. According to some readers, the latter probably means "look at," "observe," "regard." The Greek verb for "touch" is also used in Luke 24:39.

with our eyes ... with our hands. Gkt has "with the eyes" (instrumental dative) in v. 1c and "our hands" as a substitute for "we" in v. 1d. The construction is beautifully balanced. Both expressions can indicate the we-group's role as eyewitnesses through physical contact with Jesus, but it is not certain that the expressions should be interpreted that concretely. See chap. 12, point 3.

concerning the word of life. In Gkt *peri tou logou tēs zōēs,* a phrase that can be understood in several ways.

The preposition "concerning" (*peri*), is often used to indicate the theme for a paragraph or a text, something that can be translated as "we declare to you" (NRSV) or "we write to you about" (TEV). The phrase does not fit well with the verbs in v. 1 and v. 3. The introductory syntax is thus disrupted by this phrase; grammarians call such a construction an anacoluthon. The heaping up of parallel clauses in the beginning of the letter is made all the more pronounced by this construction.

Based on its use in John 1, the word *logos* in Gkt can be interpreted as the Word. Some translations capitalize it in this way (TEV, JerB, TOB). But the term's most common meaning in John and the context in 1 John (an emphasis on "the life" in what follows, and the word "message" [*angelia*], v. 5, as a parallel) speak in favor of the sense "word," "message." See, e.g., Matt 13:19 and 1 Cor 1:18. The situation in 1 John is reminiscent of John 6:60–71 and the confession of the Twelve: "You have the words of eternal life" (John 6:68). Already by the end of the second century, Tertullian translated the phrase "word of life" as *sermo vitae* ("the speech about life").

The word "life" (*zōē*) belongs to the commonly used words in the Johannine writings—49 times, of which 23 occur with the adjective "eternal"—and it has a central place in the letter (1 John 1:2; 2:25; 3:14–15; 5:11–12, 16, 20). As a rule it refers to real, genuine life, a life of divine quality, synonymous with "eternal life" (1 John 1:1–2; 5:13, 20). See further Appendix 6, Life, Eternal Life.

The genitive construction "the word of life" can be explained in several ways: the Word, namely, Life (explanatory genitive); the life-giving word (qualitative genitive; cf. the expressions "bread of life" and "water of life"); the word about life (objective genitive). If the expression is not dependent on John 1, then the last alternative becomes the most likely one. The entire phrase can then be rendered, "it has to do with the message about the Life." Nevertheless, the ambiguous nature of the formulations in the letter's introduction justifies the view that one alternative does not exclude another.

2. and the life was revealed. Gkt begins v. 2 with "and" (*kai*), introducing an explanatory parenthesis about the Life mentioned at the end of v. 1. The word "and" often introduces clauses in 1 John and can thus express both a close connection with the foregoing thought and a development of it. "And" introduces additional commentary and defining clauses in, e.g., 1 John 1:3d; 2:1d, 2a, 17; 3:4b, 5a, 12d, 15b, 24b; 4:21a; 5:6d, 14a, 17b, and 20d. The word can thus be translated "for," but is often omitted in modern translations, such as here in the NRSV.

"The life" refers to the life just mentioned at the end of v. 1. The definite article in Gkt functions as a demonstrative pronoun.

The verb in Gkt, *phaneroun,* means to make the unknown known, to make the invisible visible. It is used both of Christ (1 John 2:28; 3:5, 8) and more generally (1 John 3:10; 4:9). The personification of the life can justify capitalizing the word: the Life became visible.

and we have seen it and bear witness to it. In Gkt the perfect and the present are combined with no indication of object. The implied object could be the life, Jesus Christ, or "that which"—the clauses in v. 1. On the use of the perfect, see the note "have heard . . ." on v. 1, above. See further Appendix 18, Testify.

declare. The verb in Gkt, *apangellein,* belongs to a family of words with the stem *angell-* with or without *ap-, an-, ep-* as prefix (1 John 1:2, 3, 5; 2:25, and 3:11). They are often semantically interchangeable. These words have a background in the Scripture where the psalmist or the prophet declares what God has done or will do (Ps 71:17–18; Mic 3:8; and especially in Second Isaiah 44:8; 57:12 [LXX]). See also Note on 1 John 1:5, "the message we . . . proclaim."

the eternal life. The Greek word for "eternal" (*aiōnion*) suggests more a quality than a measure of time: almost "of divine character," "belonging to another world." Being eternal is a characteristic belonging to God. Only here and in 1 John 2:25 does the definite article appear with both "life" and "eternal," which gives the phrase a special weight. I will often use the words "divine life" for Johannine texts, in order to avoid the usual meaning of "eternal life." Eternal life, according to the Johannine writings, can only be mediated through the Son. By its placement at both the beginning and the end of the letter, the concept "the eternal life" provides a strongly eschatological dimension to the entire epistle. See further the Interpretation and Appendix 6, Life, Eternal Life.

that. The word introduces the two last clauses in v. 2, both of which say something important about the idea of "eternal life." Gkt has the less common form, *hētis,* which can be translated as "of the sort that."

was with the Father. Many take this phrase as indicating the Life's preexistence, but the context points more in the direction of the Life's divine character.

and was revealed to us. This clause repeats the beginning of v. 2 and thereby binds together the verse's parenthesis into a unit, a so-called *inclusio.* The word itself and its double use indicate that it is the divine life's incarnation that is central here and not its existence before the creation of the world.

3. what we have seen and heard. These words, which in Gkt have the same form as in the first clauses of the letter, take up the thread from v. 1. The primary verbs there are used here in reverse order. Possibly this is to emphasize the act of seeing, or it may be a stylistic finesse.

we declare also to you. This main full sentence makes the five "that which" clauses objects of the verb "declare."

Gkt has "and/also" (*kai*), preceding "to you," which indicates a definite distinction between "we" and "you" (pl.). It can be rendered "in turn"—implying a sequential order—but in certain translations there is nothing corresponding to it. To interpret "we" as the author and all believers/the Christian church, as is sometimes suggested, is contradicted by the reference to two Christian groups in this verse.

may have fellowship with us. Fellowship with God and with one another is a central theme in 1 John. The word "fellowship" (*koinōnia*) is reminiscent of fixed forms of fellowship in the world of that day and includes within it participation, association, fellowship and oneness. It is also reminiscent of a Qumran term for the fellowship there, *yaḥad,* and of the Johannine phrase to "be one" (John 17:11, 21–23).

and our fellowship is. The entire clause provides a more exact defining of "fellowship" in the foregoing. 1 John contains many "defining clauses" introduced with "and." See the note "and the life was revealed" for v. 2, above. The expression for "our," a postpositive *hēmetera,* normally carries special emphasis. But it can also be a stylistic word choice. See 1 John 2:2.

with the Father and with his Son Jesus Messiah. Gkt formulation "with A and with B" indicates that we are dealing with two entities. The fellowship with God/the Father is mentioned first and is a basic motif in 1 John. According to John 1:41, Christ is the same as Messiah, for the Johannine community. See further Appendix 14, Jesus as Messiah, Son of God.

4. And these things. "And" ties together the two verbs in the letter's introduction: "we declare" and "we write." The phrase "these things" points backward to vv. 1–3 (anaphoric function), but because of its place in the introduction, it can also have in view the entire letter. Cf. "these things" in 1 John 5:13.

we. Gkt's use of "we" (*hēmeis*), and placing it last in the clause, give the word emphasis: "we ourselves." One would have expected instead "to you" (*hymin*), at the end, as in v. 3. Many later manuscripts and versions have "to you" in place of "we."

write. See chap. 12, point 3.

our joy. Many readers expect "your joy" here. Cf. John 16:24. Later manuscripts as a rule do in fact have "your" (pl.), but "our"—the more difficult reading—is certainly the original. The words for "our" and "your" were early on pronounced in the same way.

The letter's introduction is "we"-focused from start to finish. Here the phrase "our joy" most likely means our common joy. In the Johannine writings, unity, fellowship, solidarity, mutual love, joy and life, i.e., the consequences of Jesus' life and ministry, belong closely together. See, e.g., John 15:1–17.

First John

Analysis

1. An Open, General Introduction

Those listening to the beginning of 1 John do not get much guidance regarding what sort of text they are dealing with. The short, similarly formed clauses—see the Translation Display—invite a slow, careful reading. Thought for thought, ideas are piled upon one another and repeated in various forms until we hear in v. 3b the words, "we declare also to you." Verse 3 gives structure to the many short clauses that introduce the letter.

The listeners are effectively drawn into what is being read aloud. This drawing-in occurs through repetitions and many vague, open, and positive words—that which, from the beginning, the word of life, the life, the Father, fellowship, joy—and not least through the many open we-formulations and the heaping up of verbs of perception: hear, see with our eyes, look at, touch with our hands. See further the Notes.

1 John begins as if it were a solemn, serious, meditative speech, and it could be taken that way were it not for the term "write" in v. 4, which indicates that it is a written document. By proven means the author builds up a confidence and an expectation among his hearers, not least in terms of emotion. The continuation in v. 5 makes it clear that the first four verses stand as a self-contained introductory paragraph, as a prologue that in several ways reminds us of the prologue in the Gospel of John.

2. Structure

Many of those who study the introduction to 1 John focus on the syntax in vv. 1–3, i.e., on the way in which the author ties his clauses together. Frequently the beginning of a text is linguistically well-formed and not so difficult to read. See, e.g., Luke 1:1–4; Heb 1:1–4; Rom 1:1–7. That is certainly not the case with 1 John. Judged by the rules of grammarians, the introduction is hardly attractive.

The introduction is made up of two main sentences that are constructed in the same way: "we declare [these things] to you, so that . . ." (vv. 1–3), and "we write these things, so that . . ." (v. 4). In several ways, however, the first sentence is impressively overloaded. This is quite obvious from the Translation Display. The first four segments break off in v. 1e with the phrase "concerning the word of life." See the note. Then follows a long parenthesis (v. 2), before the first four clauses are taken up again in v. 3a. These five parallel utterances thus become the object of "we declare" in v. 3b. The first purpose clause (v. 3c) is completed—in familiar Johannine style—with a definition clause (v. 3d).

Likely, stylistic and rhetorical aims have most heavily influenced the form of the introduction. For this reason it is not so easy to describe more precisely the semantic relations between the different clauses. The interpretation I offer is built among other things on the following observations:

- Verses 1a, 1e, 2a, 2e, and 2d taken together can yield a thought pattern that would comply well with a general Christian apostasy perspective. The Life, i.e., the Word according to the prologue to John, came into being at the beginning of time with God, but became visible to human beings, "to us" as the text has it. The verbs in vv. 1a and 2d are in the imperfect, and those in vv. 2a and 2e are in the aorist. From an intra-Jewish regression perspective, however, great weight is laid on that which was from the beginning (v. 1a), i.e., Jesus' life and ministry and the proclamation about him as the source of the fellowship with God enjoyed by the letter's recipients.

- Verses 1b–d, 2b, and 3a appear to treat the same thing: some persons' experience of the Life (or the Word?) that became visible. They *saw* it (mentioned four times) and they *heard* it (mentioned twice). The piling up of words of perception—see the note on v. 1—surely cannot be interpreted otherwise than to imply that this is something very important to the author. The parenthesis (v. 2) deals precisely with the Life, eternal life, who, according to 1 John 5:20, is God's son, Jesus Christ. Because that life took on earthly form, human beings can bear witness to it and convey it to others.

- Verses 2b–c, 3b and 4a emphasize the relationship between "we" and "you" (pl.). We bear witness to you; we declare to you (mentioned twice); we write (to you). All these verbs are in the present. The experience of the Life becomes a testimony; the testimony becomes a proclamation; the proclamation becomes a special writing.

- Verses 3c and 4b give a double formulation of the writing's aim: close fellowship with "us" and full mutual joy.

- Verse 3d stands alone without parallels. Here for the first time is mentioned what the Life (and the Word?) primarily refers to: God's son, Jesus the Messiah. This full christological formula is found only here in the beginning of the letter (v. 3), in the middle (1 John 3:23), and at the end (1 John 5:20). It is Jesus who unites humanity and God.

3. A Commentary on John 1:1–18?

First John has a great deal in common with the Gospel of John in terms of vocabulary and thought, not least with John 13–17, even though there are numerous striking shifts in the meaning of particular words and in longer sections of text. There are several similarities even in the structure of the two texts. Both begin with an elevated prologue (1 John 1:1–4 and John 1:1–18). Both conclude with a similar formulation that states the aim (1 John 5:13 and John 20:30–31), followed by a somewhat unexpected continuation (1 John 5:14–21 and John 21:1–25). See further chap. 12, point 5. To this we can add that each writing as a whole evidences a two-part division: 1:1—3:10 and 3:11—5:21 in the letter, and 1–12 and 13–21 in the Gospel.

These observations have led no one less than Raymond Brown to conclude that 1 John should be interpreted as a commentary—"a comment"—on the Gospel. The letter is primarily a reading guide for the use of the Gospel; indeed, it is actually what rescued the Gospel for the Christian church. The rubric that Brown places over the paragraph 1 John 1:1–4, therefore, is "Reflections on the Prologue of the Fourth Gospel."

There are reasons to seek help from the Gospel of John in the interpretation of 1 John. But the close connection that Brown sees is not convincing. It builds too much on certain formal similarities and does not, e.g., take into account the strategy found in the letter. See the various Analyses and chap. 12, point 6. The shared external pattern possibly indicates that both writings in their present form are the result of an editorial process, either such that someone edited the one document on the basis of the other, or such that the same writer stands behind the two writings. See chap. 12, point 3.

With regard to the two writings' introductions we can note the following. Both avoid mentioning Jesus by name at the outset. The Gospel speaks of the Word, and 1 John speaks of that which was there from the beginning, of the Life. Not until the end of each prologue is Jesus Christ named (John 1:17 and 1 John 1:3). And there are several similarities:

1 John	Gospel of John
What came into being/was there from the beginning	In the beginning was the Word
what we have seen	No one has seen God, but. . .
what we looked at	We beheld his glory
the word of life	In it [the Word] was life
and the life was revealed	And the Word became flesh
and we bear witness	to bear witness of the light
which was with the Father	and the Word was with God

If the texts are read in their entirety, however, there are numerous differences. The prologue in the Gospel of John—which is significantly longer—has, not unexpectedly, a broader range. The divine, preexistent Word is active at the creation. It is described as the light of humanity, and humanity's manner of receiving the Word is significantly featured: his own did not receive it, others received him, those who believed in Jesus Christ's name, those who are born of God (John 1:12–13). This is the core of the Johannine prologue. Moses and Jesus are placed side by side at the end. Through the Son, the true revealer of the Father, there is a renewed covenant, characterized by grace and truth (John 1:16–18). Almost the entire history of salvation is found in John 1:1–18.

In 1 John, the prologue is concentrated almost totally on what is expressed in John 1:1 and 14: the Word was with God; the Word became flesh; we saw its glory. This

1 John 1:1–4: Divine Life, Divine Fellowship, Divine Joy

can be seen in the comparison above. At the same time, the interest is shifted from the images of the Word and its reception to the concept of Life (1 John 1:2), its mediation through "us," and its expression in fellowship and joy. The concern is to convince believers of what they have in Jesus Christ. The author wants to show them that they already have eternal life now when they hold fast to the confession of Jesus as Messiah, God's son (1 John 1:3; 3:23; 5:13, 18–20). The emphasis lies therefore on the fellowship with "us," i.e., with the Johannine eyewitnesses and bearers of the tradition, and thus with God himself. See also the Interpretations of 2 and 3 John.

4. A Handbook, a Testament, a Pastoral Letter?

The beginning of 1 John does not say much about the sender, the recipients, or text genre. The text does not begin as ancient letters usually do, even though that standard text form is well known within the Johannine community. See the Analysis of 3 John, points 2 and 3. Here there is no wish for well-being and no greetings at the end. Of the related texts in the New Testament, the letter of James at least has a standard letter opening and the letter to the Hebrews a form of letter closing. If the word "write" were removed from 1 John, it would hardly be called a letter any longer.

The letter's genre is treated in more detail in chap. 12, point 5. In what follows, I will refer to 1 John as a letter, even though in long stretches it resembles more a presentation of the Presbyter's teaching in consequence of the secession (1 John 2:19), or a handbook, a sort of compendium of his guidance for this difficult intra-Jewish or intra-Christian or intra-Johannine crisis.

Nonetheless there are some distinguishing characteristics of a letter in 1 John: a relation of friendship between the sender and the recipients, a form of being present when one is not present, a form of conversation. Perhaps the letter can be called a pastoral letter. It has a clear pastoral, admonishing character. There is both nearness and distance between sender and recipients, indeed a certain flavor of a testament. The closest parallels in the Gospel of John occur also in Jesus' farewell discourse (John 13–17). What we call a pastoral letter does not need to have the outward form of a letter, even if it is sent to certain recipients in written form. In an extended meaning, it is indeed a letter that we meet in the first four verses of 1 John.

Interpretation

1. These Things We Declare to You (1:1–4)

First John begins in a surprising way. The style is both elevated and meditative. It requires a slow, thoughtful reading, clause by clause. See the Translation Display above. The formulations are simple, abrupt, and open in a way that requires an additional effort on the hearers' part so that they can make sense of what they are hearing. The

First John

entire structure of the introduction demands considerable attention and ability to take the various statements together. Presumably the first listeners also had difficulty at first getting a grasp on just what sort of text (genre) they were dealing with. See chap. 12, point 6. The introduction to this letter, which of course does not sound letter-like at all, is unique. The closest parallel is probably the beginning of the Gospel of John. Undeniably, both documents have well-defined introductions, so-called prologues, with a good deal of common form and content. See the Analysis, point 3.

"What we have seen and heard we declare also to you" (v. 3ab). The formulation gives the impression that what follows is a speech of some kind. In fact, the letter could well be described as a speech, were it not for the word "write": "These things we write" (v. 4a). See also 2:1, 8, 12–14, 21, 26; and 5:13. It is a written document intended to be read aloud to a group of people who are addressed in the letter with words like "my little children," "beloved," and "brothers and sisters." There is clearly a close relationship between the sender and the recipients. Who are these persons to whom the writer refers in the introduction as "we" and "you"?

The word "we," as always, invites several possible interpretations. See Appendix 5, We in the letters of John. I have taken it to refer to a rather small group related to the tradition about Jesus, responsible both for passing on this tradition and for interpreting it, therefore tradents and teachers within the Johannine community. The chief person in the group during the later portion of the first century is presumably the one who stands behind the two smaller Johannine letters, namely the Elder or the Presbyter. Within the group, then, there may still have been eyewitnesses. Certainly the Elder had at least had contact with those who had been eyewitnesses. But the linguistic conventions of the time do not require the formulations in v. 1 to imply that "we" are eyewitnesses in a concrete sense. See further chap. 12, point 3. But they constitute a link, completely essential for life itself, between "what was there from the beginning" and the people being addressed. The Elder and the bearers of the tradition who are around him can reasonably be said to have great authority in this community, but he does not appeal to it in his manner of argumentation, as Paul, e.g., does when he writes to Philemon and the Christians who gather at Philemon's house (Phlm 8–21).

The word "you" (pl.) stands for the community where the Elder and his co-workers had their ministry; they were a people who at the end of the first century were clearly spread over a rather large geographic area, since it required letters to stay in contact with them. Writing down the Elder's message also made it possible to communicate with other groups. These people were Jews—and possibly some who were not Jewish born—who confessed Jesus as Messiah, God's son. From 2:18–27 we see that a portion of them had cast over their Messiah faith and left the community. The writing therefore is directed to the Jews who remained faithful to their confession; it is intended to encourage and strengthen them in their faith in Jesus as Messiah, the son of God, and especially to underscore that through this faith they have a part in eternal life (5:13). The purpose then is almost the same as the one we find in the Gospel of

1 John 1:1–4: Divine Life, Divine Fellowship, Divine Joy

John (20:30–31). In the following discussion, I will often refer to these Jesus-believing Jews, associated as they are with the Gospel of John and the Johannine epistles, as Johannine Christians. See further chap. 12, point 2.

2. What Was There from the Beginning (1:1)

A significant place in these introductory lines is given to the content of the proclamation that the Elder wants to convey to those who are listening to his written message being read aloud. First it is described with an interpretation of "what was there from the beginning" (v. 1), then with a presentation of "eternal life" (v. 2), and finally in 1:5 as "God is light" with what that entails. It is a message about the Life, a life that gets its content from the master and lord of life, God himself. And the message is also God's own testimony regarding his son (5:9–12). Thus the letter has to do with the Son and with the Life. The letter's beginning and its end (1:1–5 and 5:9–21) need to be interpreted in the light of each other. The beginning and the end normally have an important function in understanding a text as a whole.

In a separate appendix I have argued that the first line of the letter, "what was there from the beginning" (v. 1a), is primarily a reference to the first stage of the Johannine Christians' history. It embraces Jesus' words and deeds as well as the proclamation of Jesus as Messiah that led to their faith. In this early proclamation, Jesus' earthly ministry was an indispensible part of the content. See Appendix 10, What you Heard From the Beginning. It has to do with the foundation of their faith, the revelation of God that became a reality when Jesus Messiah, God's son, came forth in word and deed. This revelation can be referred to in other parts of the letter as "the word" or "God's word," as "the message" or "the truth" (2:4–5, 7–8, 20–21; 3:23, etc.). The event was interpreted among other things as a renewal of God's covenant with his people and, as a consequence, a new fellowship with God and a new mutual belonging. Even the pious Jews who went out to Qumran in the second century BCE could regard themselves as a new covenant, based on a reinterpretation of the Law of Moses, and thus as a group separated from the rest of Israel. See Appendix 9, A Renewed Covenant.

According the Elder, the proclamation regarding Jesus Messiah, God's son, which the letter's recipients had heard in the beginning when they came to faith, was grounded upon absolutely certain events. In v. 1bcd, four simple verbs of perception are used to express the experience of these events: hear, see, look at, and feel, in two cases reinforced by the word "eyes" and the word "hands," respectively. Two of these words, "see" and "hear," are repeated then in v. 3a. The word "see" dominates, being used four times (if we include v. 2b), followed by "hear," which is used twice. What people had seen was important for ancient historians and was valued more than written sources. Even when the covenant was established at Sinai, it is said that the people "saw" the voice (Exod 20:18); the Greek translation of the Old Testament, the

Septuagint, also renders it that way: "All the people saw the voice." It was similar on the first Pentecost day (Acts 2:2–4). That day coincided with the Jewish festival, which was celebrated by some Jews as a covenant renewal feast, involved both seeing and hearing. The Jewish theologian Philo, a contemporary of Jesus, says that the words at Sinai were so clear and obvious that the people appeared to see them rather than to hear them. "The voice of men is calculated to be heard; but that of God to be really and truly seen. Why is this? Because all that God says are not words, but actions which the eyes determine on before the ears" (*Decal.* 47). What the letter's recipients first heard rests on a firm ground. The Elder and his co-workers can guarantee it.

3. A Divine Life (1:2)

The second description of the proclamation's content is given in the long parenthesis in v. 2, anticipated by the phrase, "concerning the word of life" in v. 1e. The word and the life are bound together here, which is important for the letter's argument as a whole (2:23–24; 5:9–13, 20). But how are the word and the life related to one another? The formulation is open to several interpretations. See the note on 1:1, "concerning the word of life." I read "the word" as primarily referring to the proclamation that the listeners had encountered when they came to faith, as well as its content: Jesus as Messiah, God's son. This message was either a message about the life, or a message that leads to life. It is not so easy to choose between these two alternatives. Probably both are in view. At the end, God's son is presented as "eternal life," and thus union with him by faith gives eternal life (5:20).

Judging by what follows, the emphasis here lies on the life and not on the word. This is one of the arguments against the view that the author is primarily thinking of the Word (*Logos*), something that existed with God before the creation of the world and that can itself be described as God (John 1:1). The Life, capitalized because of its personification in the text, is presented in a limited way by the words "was revealed," i.e., became visible. What is heavenly became visible on the earth. Humanity saw it, they can bear witness to it, indeed the Elder passes it on to the recipients of the letter. Here we see the same chain of communication in v. 1 and v. 3. God's testimony becomes the testimony of human beings.

The Life is further defined as "the eternal life," one of the central concepts in 1 John, the Gospel of John, and the Revelation of John (sixty-six times of 135 in the entire New Testament). In today's speech, "eternal life" is nearly always understood as life after death, often synonymous with heaven. The word "eternal" in English primarily refers to time measurement. But this does not correspond to the concept's use in 1 John and the Gospel of John. There it is more an expression of quality, implying that this life is of divine character. The word for "eternal" in the original language, *aiōnion*, comes from a word that means "time, age, aeon."

In Jewish conceptions of "this age" and "the age to come," eternal life belongs to the new age. According to the Elder, that age has already broken in (2:7–8; 3:1–2). The Johannine movement is a "five minutes to midnight" movement—the last hour is here—something that is reinforced by the content given to "the life eternal" in the letter's beginning and end. The qualifier "that was with the Father" (v. 2d) marks the life's close connection with God. God alone has life in himself (John 5:26); God is the living Father (John 6:57). God's great intention in sending God's son to the earth was that humanity would share in this divine life. Thus eternal life is already present here and now, even if in its connection to God it exists both before and after humanity's time on the earth. See further Appendix 6, Life, Eternal Life. In what follows I will use "eternal life" and "divine life" as interchangeable concepts.

4. Divine Fellowship (1:3)

The purpose of the Elder's writing, like the content of his message, is expressed in a double fashion: that we should have fellowship with each other (v. 3) and that we should have complete joy (v. 4). This fellowship is defined as a fellowship with God and his son and thus it takes on a divine character. The shared joy is also divine, since in the Johannine writings it is presented as a consequence of union with God through his son (John 15:1–17).

The mutual fellowship between "us" and "you" is mentioned first: "so that you also may have fellowship with us" (v. 3c). It corresponds to the unexpected formulation in v. 7c, "we have fellowship with one another," where anyone hearing read aloud the text following v. 6a would have expected "fellowship with God." The fact that this fellowship is mentioned first is certainly connected with what had happened within the Johannine community. Some of the Jesus-believing Jews had left their faith in the Messiah and broken away from the congregation (2:18–27; 4:1–6). The family of love and truth was threatened from within and from without (2 John). The Elder had clearly been forced to experience the pain of seeing those who had been positive toward him now turning their backs on him (3 John). Hence this constant admonishment in the letters that we must love one another. The mutual fellowship is not only theological, a firm commitment to what they had heard from the beginning, but it is also personal and social. If their association with the Elder and what he stands for is broken, the consequences are reciprocal. Those who have left are thus no longer partakers in the divine life that had become theirs though union with Jesus Messiah, God's son.

This fellowship is then defined as a fellowship "with the Father and with his son Jesus Messiah" (v. 3d). This is why in the title for this section I speak of a divine fellowship. This close union with God is described later in several various ways: to know God, to be born of God, to be of God, to be or remain in God, etc. See Appendix 11, Begotten/Born of God, and Appendix 15, God in Them and They in God. For a

First John

description of Jesus as Jesus Messiah, God's son, a phrase occurring in three passages in the letter (1:3; 2:23; 5:20), see Appendix 14, Jesus as Messiah, God's Son.

5. Divine Joy (1:4)

The second formulation of the purpose of the Elder's writing has a somewhat unexpected form. It is referred to as "our joy," where we might have expected "your joy." "Our joy" is most easily understood here as "our joy and yours," i.e., our shared joy. We find the same phrase in 2 John 12. In Jesus' farewell discourse in the Gospel of John he speaks several times about the joy that awaits the disciples once he has returned to the Father (John 15:11; 16:20-24; 17:13). This same joy and peace are present also on Easter (20:20-21). The final evening with Jesus in the Gospel of John contains primarily instruction on the consequences that Jesus' departure will have for the disciples: cleansing, the Spirit, insight, fellowship, mutual love, peace, eternal life, etc. And to these is also added joy. This complete joy therefore has to do with the renewed fellowship with God. It too has a divine character. The recipients of the letter can, like the recipients of 1 Peter, rejoice in unutterable, heavenly joy (1 Pet 1:3-9). The long introduction to 1 Peter (1:1—2:10) also has many formulations reminiscent of a renewal of the covenant with God. Finally, this new life results in their becoming like God (1 John 3:2). Yet even now they already have a part in God through his son, Jesus Messiah, the son of God.

6. 1 John 1:1-4 from Other Perspectives

To this point, I have been reading the introduction to 1 John from an intra-Jewish perspective, i.e., as a communication between Jews who confessed Jesus as Messiah, God's son, a group in the early church whom I refer to as Johannine Christians. See chap. 12, point 3. At some distance now from the letter's actual situation there lies an earlier traumatic experience in which several of these Jews no longer wished to confess their Messiah faith openly and therefore left the Johannine community (2:18-27; 4:1-6). See chap. 12, point 4, where I have presented two other perspectives: a so-called general Christian perspective (Gnostic apostasy hypothesis) and a so-called ultra-Johannine perspective (progression hypothesis).

In a general Christian perspective, which became especially common once 1 John gained a place in the Christian canon, the letter is read mostly as a communication between God and Christians. The emphasis is placed on Christology, i.e., on the question how a true confession of Jesus Christ should be formulated. The letter became part of the christological debates in the early church. At the end of the second century, e.g., the church father Irenaeus read the letter in terms of the battle the church was then having with the so-called Gnostics. It was largely a matter of how to conceive of Jesus Christ. Thus, in the prologue of the letter, the emphasis on the incarnation, i.e., on God's becoming a human being, became significantly more important. The description in 1:1–2 is read in terms of John 1, so that "the word" in v. 1e becomes the same thing as the Word (*Logos*), and the numerous verbs of experience are meant to assure us that the Word actually did become a human being. By identifying the author with the disciple John, the son of Zebedee, Irenaeus is able to forge an unbroken historical connection with both the Gospel of John and 1 John. 1 John 1:1–4 thereby contributed powerfully to the traditional conception that the Gospel and the letter are testimonies of an eyewitness. This interpretive tradition is still an important one, within both the church and the academy.

In an ultra-Johannine perspective, the reading of the letter becomes more related to theological, ecumenical problems where questions about the role of tradition and authority and of the unity of the church stand at the center. Ecclesiology (the doctrine of the church) becomes more important than Christology (the doctrine of Christ). The entire letter is thus read in terms of what happened with the special tradition we have in the Johannine writings. In Raymond Brown's major commentary of 1982, e.g., the letter's introduction is characterized as "reflections on the prologue of the Fourth Gospel." See the Analysis, point 3. In place of the traditional stages (God—Jesus Christ/Logos—we/God's children) we have a four-link chain of communication in the letter's introduction: God—Jesus Christ—we/bearers of the tradition—you/the rest of God's children. Jesus' earthly ministry is an indispensible part of the proclamation. Therefore fellowship with the Johannine tradition-bearers, something the secessionists despised, is completely necessary. "[E]ven in the Johannine Community where the role of the Paraclete was dominant as the teacher of all things . . . , there is place for a human chain of tradition-bearers" (p. 184), i.e., in the church's later history there is a firm authority. Brown then interprets the content of the letter's introduction in terms of these four links, as well as in terms of the letter's purpose of binding together the recipients and these tradition-bearers.

2

1 John 1:5—2:2: A New Fellowship with God and Its Requirements

Translation Display

5a	And this is the message
5b	we have heard from him and proclaim to you:
5c	God is light,
5d	and in him there is no darkness at all.

6a   If we say, "We have fellowship with him,"
6b   and walk in the darkness,
6c   then we lie
6d   and do not do the truth.

7a   But if we walk in the light
7b   as he is in the light,
7c   then we have fellowship with one another,
7d   and the blood of Jesus, his Son, cleanses us from all sin.

8a   If we say, "We do not have sin,"
8b   then we deceive ourselves
8c   and the truth is not in us.

9a   If we confess our sins,
9b   then he is faithful and just,
9c   so that he forgives us these sins
9d   and cleanses us from every wrongdoing

10a   If we say, "We have not sinned,"
10b   then we make him a liar
10c   and his word is not in us.

1a	My little children,
1b	these things I am writing to you
1c	in order that you may not sin.
1d	But if anyone does sin,
1e	then we have an advocate with the Father,
1f	Jesus Messiah,
1g	a righteous one,
2a	and he is the offering for our sins,
2b	and not only for ours, but also for the sins of the whole world.

Notes

1:5. And this is. The formula is typical in 1 John where the word "this" almost always refers to what follows (cataphoric usage; 1 John 2:25; 3:23; 4:21; 5:4, 11, 14, as well as 2 John 6). The introductory word "and" (*kai* in Gkt) can also be rendered "for" (1 John 3:11; 5:9 [*hoti*]; 5:3 [*gar*]). It can both make a connection with what precedes and introduce a new paragraph. Thus, e.g., in John 1:19; 1 John 2:3 and 3:11 (here with "for" [*hoti*]). See the note "and the life was revealed," on 1 John 1:2.

the message we ... proclaim. Gkt has two words here that belong to the same word-family: *angelia ... anangellomen*, something like "a proclamation that we ... proclaim," "an announcement that we ... announce" (a so-called *figura etymologica*). See the note on 1 John 1:2. In John these Greek words are mostly used with regard to the Spirit as interpreter and teacher (John 16:13–15). The meaning approximates "reveal" (John 4:26). The word for "message" (*angelia*), is found only here and in 1 John 3:11 in the New Testament and can be said in a sense to substitute for the term "gospel" in other New Testament books. 1 John 1:2–3 has a related word, *apangellein*. See the note "declare," on 1 John 1:2.

from him, i.e., from Jesus Messiah, God's son, and therefore from God.

God is light. Gkt uses the term *hoti* ("that") here in the sense of a so-called *hoti recitativum*, which can introduce both direct and indirect speech; i.e., it can be translated with "that" or, e.g., with a colon, as is done here. The same construction occurs in vv. 6, 8, and 10.

There are three statements of this kind in the Johannine writings: "God is light," "God is love" (1 John 4:8), and "God is spirit" (John 4:24). They express more what God does (God's actions) than what God is (God's essence). The statements proceed from a perception of God as a person. See the Interpretation and Appendix 16, God is Love.

in him there is. Gkt has the usual word for "be" with the preposition "in" (*einai en*). The same phrase is found in vv. 8 and 10 and in numerous other passages in 1 John. See further Appendix 15, God in Them and They in God.

no . . . at all. Gkt has two negative expressions here: "not . . . none." The two negations reinforce each other, yielding something like "and in him there is no darkness at all," or "no darkness whatsoever." In an antithetical construction, such as we have in v. 5cd, the emphasis lies on the second clause. This is not an uncommon form of expression in biblical texts (Deut 32:4; Ps 92:15).

darkness. Gkt has the usual word for "darkness" in Johannine texts, *skotia*. The change to *skotos* in the following verse is most likely a stylistic variation. *Skotos* is also used in John 3:19.

6. If we say . . . then we lie. The formulation in Gkt is conditional, where the if-clause has the subjunctive and the then-clause the present indicative. The construction dominates this section of the letter (1 John 1:7, 8, 9, 10; 2:1). "We say" means "as we often say" (the so-called iterative use). "We" in this section is probably a rhetorical way of saying "anyone of us/you." See Appendix 5, We in the Johannine Letters.

The construction functions as an indirect warning: Do not claim to have fellowship with God if you continue to walk in the darkness! Similarly in the remaining verses of chap. 1, where the same construction occurs. The form is reminiscent of Old Testament covenant reasoning, where certain conclusions are drawn on the basis of certain laws.

and. The Greek *kai* ("and") can often be translated as "but," or with the NRSV as "while." Syntactically, however, it is way of stringing together coordinate clauses.

walk. The Greek present tense expresses ongoing action: be engaged in walking, continue to walk. The word "walk" (*peripatein*), is used in biblical and Jewish texts with respect to people's way of life: "let us walk in the light of the Lord" (Isa 2:5); "I walk in the way of righteousness" (Prov 8:20); "[God] created humankind to rule over the world, appointing for them two spirits in which to walk until the time ordained for His visitation. These are the spirits of truth and falsehood" (1QS 3:17–19). See also Rom 14:15; Eph 5:2, 8. Compare expressions such as "*way* of life." To walk in this sense occurs frequently in the Johannine letters: walk in the truth (2 John 4; 3 John 3 and 4); walk in the commandment/in love (2 John 6); walk as Jesus walked (1 John 2:6); walk in light/darkness (1 John 1:6, 7; 2:11). See also John 8:12; 11:9–10; 12:35, and Rev 21:24.

lie. According to the letter, lying is a typical characteristic of the secessionists. See the note "many false prophets have gone out into the world," on 1 John 4:1.

do the truth. An expression influenced by Hebrew. The word "do" in this type of construction means to practice, to live by, to realize. This applies as well to the phrases "do God's will" (1 John 2:17); "do righteousness" (2:29; 3:7, 10); "do sin" (3:4, 8–9); and "do lawlessness" (3:4). See further Appendix 3, The Truth.

7. he. The word in Gkt is a personal pronoun, *autos*. To judge from the context, it refers to God. The pronouns he, him, and his in 1 John 1:5c–10 are most naturally understood to refer to God, as is expressly stated in v. 5c.

However, the letter's expression "as he" with a different pronoun, *ekeinos*, refers to Jesus (1 John 2:6; 3:3, 7; 4:17). "As he is" in 3:2 (without any pronoun) could also be understood to refer to God. See Appendix 8, He: God or Jesus or Both.

with one another. In some mss, the phrase has been altered to the expected "with him." The original expression "with one another" focuses, like 1 John 1:3–4, on the fellowship within the Johannine movement and especially on the fellowship between "us" and "you" (pl.) mentioned in vv. 1–5.

and. The content of v. 7d (unexpected for this context) creates uncertainty about what the function of "and" is here. Either the word binds vv. 7c and 7d together into two parallel consequences of what is said in v. 7a, therefore "if we walk in the light . . . then the blood of Jesus his son cleanses us from all sin." Or "and" introduces a consequence of the preceding line (v. 7c), i.e., "then we have fellowship with one another, and as a consequence the blood of Jesus his son cleanses us from all sin." Both alternatives give us a workable meaning. See the Interpretation. But one could also say that "and" marks a rather loose attachment to what precedes it. The content of v. 7d would then simply move the argument further along (1 John 1:8—2:2).

the blood of Jesus. These words are reminiscent of the Old Testament sacrificial institution, where the blood itself was used when sacrifices were made for sins committed. Of the 362 passages where blood is mentioned in the OT, 103 refer to blood sacrifice. It was the blood that cleansed, not the death of the sacrificial victim. See further Appendix 7, Expiation and Forgiveness.

8. we do not have sin. Gkt uses the usual word for "have" (*echein*), plus "sin" (*hamartia*). The formulation is attested only in Johannine texts (John 9:41; 15:22, 24; 19:11; 1 John 1:8). The word *hamartia* has the sense of offense, sin, transgression in relation to God, with an emphasis on culpability.

deceive. In the letter, to deceive (*planan*) especially characterizes the so-called secessionists. See the note "many false prophets have gone out into the world," on 1 John 4:1.

9. confess our sins. The verb used here is the standard verb for "confess" (*homologein*; John 1:20; 9:22; 12:42). What is said about confession of sins in other contexts of the early church (Mark 1:5; Matt 3:6; Acts 19:18; Jas 5:16 and *Did.* 4:14) demonstrates that it is here very likely a matter of a public confession of sins. The plural form, "our sins," suggests the possibility that individual, concrete sins are meant rather than sin in general. Confession of sins was also part of the ritual for the covenant renewal in Qumran. See the Interpretation and Appendix 9, A Renewed Covenant.

faithful and just. This description of God is somewhat unexpected in the context—"gracious and merciful" would certainly fit better. The reference is to God's covenant and renewal of the covenant. See the Interpretation and Appendix 9, A Renewed Covenant.

so that he forgives. Gkt has a *hina*-clause here, although some translations, such as the NRSV, use the simple future. The word *hina* carries consecutive meaning. It can also be translated "in order that" or merely "that." At the same time, the clause functions in an explanatory way, i.e., as a clarification of God's faithfulness and justice.

these sins. Gkt "the sins" (*tas hamartias*). The definite article in Greek, here *tas*, can function as a demonstrative pronoun, i.e., these sins that we have confessed.

every wrongdoing. In Gkt the word for "wrongdoing," *adikia*, is often in biblical terminology a synonym for the word "sin." It has probably been chosen here to correspond to the word "righteous," characterizing God (1 John 1:9) and Jesus (2:1).

The expression "every wrongdoing" can also be rendered "all unrighteousness" or "every misdeed," as in parallel with "our sins" in v. 9a and "these sins" in v. 9c. This would underscore the fact that the issue throughout v. 9 concerns individual sins, which becomes even more obvious in 2:1. See also the clause of definition in 1 John 5:17: "every wrongdoing (*adikia*) is sin."

10. We have not sinned. It is not clear whether this is merely a stylistic variation on "we do not have sin" in v. 8, or whether it is intended to indicate concrete sinful actions. In the Interpretation I have taken it in the latter sense. See further Appendix 12, They Cannot Sin.

liar, one of the letter's names for the secessionists (1 John 2:22). See also the note "deceive" on v. 8 above.

his word, i.e., God's word/command/message, which they had received from God through Jesus (1 John 1:5). See the Analysis of 1 John 2:3–11, point 2.

is not in us. The meaning is something like this: "we do not accept the message we have received from God," or "we do not accept what God has said." The sense is largely the same as "the truth is not in us" (v. 8). See Appendix 15, God in Them and They in God.

2:1 My little children. Gkt has the word *teknia* (with the possessive pronoun "my"), i.e., the diminutive form of the usual word for "child" (*teknon*). It is the most common vocative in the letter (1 John 2:1, 12, 28; 3:7, 18; 4:4; 5:21). Greek diminutives (like German *-chen* or *-lein*) express emotional closeness and intimacy.

Especially in the Johannine fellowship, "(my) children"—"my" is expressly used only in 2:1 in 1 John—seems to have been a standard designation. In John the vocative *teknia* is used when Jesus takes leave of "his own" and bids them love one another (John 13:33). When Jesus reveals himself to the disciples for the last time, the synonymous term *paidia* is used (John 21:5). As they often do elsewhere, these two diminutive forms—from *teknon* and *pais*, respectively—express a close togetherness among the persons involved. They occur nine times in 1 John and then are not used again in Christian texts until the third century.

Addressing persons—and speaking about them—with the word "child" (not the diminutive form) occurs often in instructional situations, e.g., in Jewish wisdom literature (Sirach, Tobit, Proverbs, Qumran texts, rabbinic texts), as well as in the NT (Mark 10:21). In such situations there are as a rule differences in age and a marked distance between teacher and disciple. Togetherness is created through repeatedly being together and through common understanding. See the note on 3 John 4. In the Johannine literature the use of the vocative "(dear) children" is also certainly connected with the concept of Jesus' followers as being born of God. See Appendix 11, Begotten/Born of God.

these things. The Greek word *tauta* points back to the content of 1 John 1:5–10 (anaphoric reference), but because of its proximity to 1 John 1:4, it may even have in mind the entire letter.

I am writing. See the note on 1 John 2:12 and chap. 12, point 3.

in order that. Gkt *hina*, which can be translated by "that" (content), "so that" (consequence) or "in order that" (purpose).

sin. Gkt here uses the aorist tense, which can indicate that we are dealing with the act as such or with a particular instance of it (to commit a sin), rather than long practice of sinning over time (to sin over and over again). The same tense is used in the next clause. See Appendix 12, They Cannot Sin.

But. Gkt has "and" (*kai*). See the note "and the life was revealed," on 1 John 1:2 and the note "and," on 1:6.

anyone, i.e., anyone of you, a meaning that was earlier implied in the use of "we" in 1 John 1:6–10.

advocate. Gkt *paraklētos*, which is used in John of the Spirit, often translated as "the Helper," or "the Comforter." It can have many senses: defender, advocate, spokesperson, intercessor. Some translations use a circumlocution, as in the TEV: "someone who pleads."

The word *paraklētos* has a basic meaning of one who is called to another's side. It is used here in an active form: one who comes to someone's side, one who comes to help, an attorney. In the Gospel the concern is mostly to render help by teaching and admonishing; in the letter it is more about speaking on behalf of someone, of representing someone, or of praying for someone. The high priest functioned as a representative, on the Day of Atonement for example, and *paraklētos* can be used in relation to the ideas of sacrificial offerings in 1 John 1:7 and 2:2. But there are other backgrounds as well, e.g., Moses as the great intercessor. See Appendix 7, Expiation and Forgiveness.

a righteous one. Gkt has only the word "righteous" (*dikaios*). It works as a further defining of the representative and/or of Jesus Christ; placed as it is after its head term and at the end of the clause, it receives marked status. It can be read attributively as an apposition to Jesus Christ, "a righteous one," "one who is righteous," or predicatively as modifying the verbal activity, "one who as a righteous one speaks on our behalf." "Righteous" means "without sin." See 1 John 3:4–8.

2. and he. Gkt *kai autos*, indicating that the description of the representative continues with yet another clause. See the note "and the life was revealed" on 1 John 1:2. The use of the personal pronoun *autos* gives "he" special emphasis. Cf. the note "and our fellowship is," on 1 John 1:3.

the offering. Literally, "the atonement." Gkt has one word, *hilasmos*, which can also mean expiation, atonement, cleansing, forgiveness. See further Appendix 7, Expiation and Forgiveness.

of the whole world, i.e., of all humanity. See also the note on 1 John 2:15.

Analysis

1. Textual Boundaries

The boundaries for the section 1 John 1:5—2:2 are well defined and the text is well constructed. The beginning, v. 5ab, repeats and summarizes very clearly a line of thinking in what precedes: a message from Jesus Christ through us to you. Even though the section begins with "and"—as is the case in 1 John 2:3 and 2:28—v. 5ab, with its forward-pointing "this," has an introductory function.

The ending of the section is more disputed. Some are of the opinion that 1 John 2:1 begins a new paragraph marked by a number of features: asyndeton (no transitional conjunction at the beginning of the clause), the first instance of a vocative, "this" as a backward-pointing and summarizing term, the recurrence of word "write," "I" used for the first time, and an indirect injunction. However, the entire section is marked by asyndeta, and vocatives are used for other purposes than merely to introduce new sections. See, e.g., 1 John 3:2 and 3:21. There is a "this" also at the end of the first section, 1 John 1:1–4, and indirect injunctions have already occurred before 1 John 2:1. See below, point 3.

The beginning of 1 John 2:1 highlights the relationship between sender and recipients and sounds like the means of preparing the way for something not so pleasant, giving added weight to what follows. The entire verse is somewhat parallel to 1 John 1:4, although there the subject is joy, while here it is something more troubling, namely, the fact that believers sometimes do sin. The latter part of 1 John 2:1—viewed as a continuation of 1 John 1:10—can be seen as parallel to 1 John 1:7 and 9, and 1 John 2:2 can be seen as parallel to 1:7d and 9cd. By means of the introductory words at the beginning and the expansion at the end of 1 John 2:1-2, the communication is tightened up and given a final intensification and deepening. Since a new theme is taken up beginning with 1 John 2:3, there is good reason to read the section 1 John 1:5—2:2 as a unit.

2. Structure

The translation above for 1 John 1:5—2:2 clearly shows how the section is constructed. First, v. 5 gives a foundational summary of the message, and then follows a reasoned exposition in three stages: vv. 6-7, 8-9, and 1:10—2:2. Not only the first two stages, but the third as well (if we put v. 10 together with v. 1defg), display parallel structures in four parts:

> If we say . . .
>
> then we lie and . . .
>
> But if we . . .
>
> then . . .

The second of these four parts has a reinforced form in that the same thing is said twice (vv. 6cd, 8bc, and 10bc). The fourth part is also expressed in double fashion (vv. 7cd, 9bcd, and 2:1d-2b).

As mentioned already, the third stage of the exposition (1:10—2:2) is expanded with regard to both the actual communication and the content, foreshadowed in v. 7d and v. 9. Truth and falsehood form a consistent theme throughout. In the first stage (1:6-7) the issues are fellowship, light and darkness; in the two latter stages, the issues are sin, cleansing, forgiveness, and expiation. The shift at v. 7d can seem unexpected in the context, but in a Johannine perspective God's light shines brightest in Jesus' great moment, i.e., when he dies and goes to the Father (John 13:31-32). Sin constitutes the most serious hindrance to fellowship with God.

It should be pointed out that these three similarly formed stages relate to what precedes them in such a way that they could be introduced with the word "therefore." God is light and there is no darkness in him. *Therefore:* If we say that we have fellowship with him and walk in the darkness, we are being inconsistent (v. 5cd + vv. 6-7). God's light, i.e., his action in the world, culminates in the death of Jesus and in the cleansing from sin that his death brings. The light makes sin fully obvious. *Therefore:* If we say that we do not have sin, we lie, etc. (v. 7d + vv. 8-9). God's light also uncovers individual sins in people's lives, and that leads to confessions of sin. *Therefore:* If we say that we have not sinned, we are fooling ourselves (1 John 1:9 + 1:10—2:2). See further the Interpretation.

First John

It is ethics, the way people live, and not Christology, that in general terms is taken up in the beginning of the letter. At the same time, Jesus' act of reconciliation has a central place in the opening argument. Not least through 2:1abc, with its focus on communication, the question of sin becomes the most prominent one in this first paragraph of the body of the letter. If anyone in God's new fellowship sins, what then? No true fellowship with God? Denial of the sin? Public confession of the sin? Forgiveness?

3. Hortatory Features in the Text

First John is a "we"-text. We-formulas are found in more than half of the verses. This personal pronoun is probably one of the more ambiguous words in the language. Hearers need to fill in possible and intended referents for themselves. In 1 John 1:5—2:2 "we" can be thought to stand for Johannine tradition bearers, Johannine Christians, the secessionists, all Christians, you and I, some of you. See further Appendix 5, We in the Johannine Letters.

Since there are always numerous possibilities for interpretation, the use of "we" is an effective rhetorical tool. Listeners are included, but to some degree only as they themselves determine. Verses 6–10 are dominated by the phrase "if we say," mostly in the sense of "if anyone of us says," or more likely, "if anyone of you says." In fact, in 2:1 the very word "anyone (of you)" is used, and in the next section the phrase "the one who says" is used three times in the same way. This is a highly circumspect way to include the listeners and to do so with formulations that indirectly convey an injunction: You must not walk in the darkness! You must acknowledge sin! You must confess your sins! You must not sin! The text has a hortatory (admonitory) character.

Veiled admonitions are threaded throughout the entire letter. Content-laden injunctions in a direct form—imperatives in second-person plural—actually occur only six times: 1 John 2:17, 27, 28; 4:1 (twice), and 5:21. Other imperatives are found in 1 John 2:24, 29, and 3:7, 13. The hortatory subjunctive—"let us love"—occurs in 1 John 3:18 and 4:7. In addition to these forms of injunction, we also find the following:

- Constructions with "ought to" (1 John 2:6; 3:16; and 4:11)
- Constructions with "commandment" plus a content clause (e.g., 1 John 3:23)
- Clauses introduced with "so that/in order that/that," *hina* (1 John 2:1, 28; 4:17; 5:3; 16).
- If/then-constructions of various kinds, as in 1 John 1:6–10.
- Participial constructions that correspond in terms of content to an alternative structure (1 John 2:28—3:10).

Taken together, these linguistic features give a particularly hortatory (admonitory) character to the entire letter, and this is already visible in 1 John 1:5—2:2, although in a subtle form.

The Elder wants to lead and direct his children with love and consideration, so that—if they examine their lives on the basis of his direct and indirect instructions—they will clearly grasp that eternal life is already operative here and now through faith in Jesus as Messiah, God's son, the true God and eternal life (1 John 5:13, 20).

Interpretation

1. God Is Light (1:5)

Following the letter's introduction there is a longer section held together by the words "light" and "darkness" (1:5—2:11). These words occur only here in the letter. They are used figuratively, as they often are in religious texts, and not least of all in the Johannine texts (John 1:4-9; 3:19-21; 5:35; 8:12; 9:5; 11:9-10; 12:35-36, 45-46). The section is clearly divided into two parts, 1:5—2:2 and 2:3-11, and these two parts are structured in the same way. In fact, even 2:12-17 could be included in this longer section. The comment about the letter's recipients in 2:12, "your sins have been forgiven on account of his name," is clearly connected to the first part, 1:5—2:2, and the further remark in 2:14, "you know the Father," is reminiscent of the theme in the second part, 2:3-11. My reason for taking 2:12-17 separately has to do with its special form and function.

First John 1:5—2:2 opens with a thematic verse dominated by the words "God is light." As we shall see, these words could just as well be taken as a title for the larger section, 1:5—2:11. Then come three short paragraphs, all of which are introduced with the phrase "if we say," most likely in the sense, "if anyone of us/you says." See Appendix 5, We in the Johannine Letters. The sequel in each paragraph has often been taken as a quotation or a slogan: "We have fellowship with him" (v. 6a), "We do not have sin" (v. 8a), and "We have not sinned" (v. 10a). I read these sentences more as a part of the author's rhetoric. The three paragraphs are quite similar in their argumentation. The last of them is expanded, however, and thus takes on a marked place in the section. The presentation is marked in many places by an Old Testament, Jewish manner of speaking. See the Translation Display above and the commentary on it in the Notes.

The thematic verse (v. 5) connects to the introduction by mentioning again the various parties in the communication, highlighting the passing on of the message, and once again describing the message's content. Since the text is designed to be heard, it requires the means of indicating transitions from one section to another. Often then what has just been heard is repeated, but with new formulations. Here, as already mentioned, the three parties in the communication chain are once more identified: Jesus Messiah, God's son; the Elder and his coworkers; and the letter's recipients. The author chooses a new word for "message," which is also used one more time in 3:11, "This is the message we have heard from the beginning." The content in this message that is being passed along is not something new, but rather something that belongs to "what was there from the beginning" (v. 1a).

First John

If the phrase "God is light" is a summary of Jesus' message—the word "gospel" is not used in the Johannine texts—or a summary of the early proclamation of Jesus, one would expect to find the words in other New Testament writings as well, but that is not the case. The closest to it is Jesus' own proclamation in John 8:12, "I am the light of the world." The formulation "God is light" is more reminiscent of Old Testament and Jewish texts. "The Lord will be a light to me" (Mic 7:8); "The Lord will be your everlasting light" (Isa 60:20); "Let the light of your face shine on us, O Lord!" (Ps 4:6); "For with you is the fountain of life; in your light we see light" (Ps 36:9); "The Lord is my light and my salvation" (Ps 27:1).

This figurative use of light and darkness in Old Testament, Jewish texts could be summarized under three points:

1. *Light stands for enlightenment, knowledge, insight.* Compare the expressions "a bright young lady" and "the light dawned on him." We need light in order to see. God "dwells in unapproachable light" (1 Tim 6:16), but the light surrounding him, indeed God himself, has come to the world of human beings through various forms of revelation: the Law, the commandments, God's word, wisdom, etc. These are described as light for humanity (Prov 6:23; Isa 51:4; Ps 119:105, 130; Wis 7:6). Israel is to be "a light of the nations" (Isa 49:6); the disciples are to be a light for the world (Matt 5:14). When Moses ascended the mountain of revelation, Sinai, and received revelations from God, his face began to shine, so that he had to put a veil over it when he met the people at the foot of the mountain (Exodus 34). According to Paul, the brilliance of the revelation shines even more intensely through Christ and those who preach him (2 Corinthians 3–4). Already in Old Testament texts it is said that God will shine most powerfully in the messianic time (Isa 40:1–11; Jer 31:31–34; Joel 2:28–29).

   Jesus is the light of the world (John 8:12), the one who reveals to the world who God is (John 1:18). "God is light" as a summation of the message from and about Jesus is not primarily a description of God's nature, but a statement about God as active among humanity. See Appendix 16, God is Love. In the context of the letter, "God is light" means that God has revealed himself to some people in Galilee and Judea and that this revelation has now been brought to the letter's recipients. Thus "God is light" approximates the description of the message in the introduction, "the life was revealed," i.e., the life that has God as its origin and sole source. In the Old Testament the light, more than anything else, represents life (Job 3:20; Ps 56:13). See further Appendix 6, Life, Eternal Life.

2. *Light stands for help, deliverance, life, liberation and salvation.* We need light in order find our way, so as not to stumble and fall. There are many examples of this use of light in the Old Testament (e.g., Isa 9:1; 45:7; 60:1–5, 19–20). Thus, light and darkness often stand as parallels to life and death. Here, too, there are statements that God will shine most brightly in the coming messianic age. In the context of the

letter, then, "God is light" means that God has begun to save the world (4:14); God has sent God's son as the offering for the sins of all humanity (2:2; 4:10).

3. *Light stands for what is good, pure and holy, and darkness stands for the opposite* (Job 24:13–17; Isa 5:20). Thus the words "light" and "darkness" also occur in ethical texts. We hear of the deeds of the light, fruit of the light, walking in the light, sons/children of light (John 12:36; Eph 5:8–9; 1QM). God is light, i.e., God is good and holy, and fellowship with him has consequences for how people live.

These three possibilities for interpreting the metaphor of light are all applicable to 1 John, but it is not always easy to distinguish among them in the text. What precedes v. 5 clearly takes up the revelatory aspect in "God is light," while what follows, focused on cleansing from sin and atonement, brings out the salvation aspect. To follow God's commandment and to live as Jesus lived (2:3–6) belongs in the sphere of ethics. Even the heavy emphasis on the fact that there is no darkness at all in God (see the note) prepares us for ethical conclusions. At the same time, in 1 John these three dimensions include one another: the revelation includes the salvation, which in turn includes guidance for living in the world. In the section 1:5—2:11, as I see it, light as *revelation* is dominant in 1:6–7 and in the closing words in 2:11; light as *salvation* through Jesus' sacrificial death dominates in 1:8—2:2; and light as *a way of life*, i.e., keeping God's commandments, dominates in 2:3–11. Thus the last dimension receives the greatest space. The death of Jesus as a cleansing of humanity's sin and the life of Jesus as an exposition of God's commandments will be seen as central in the new revelation of God that was manifested through Jesus the Messiah, the Son of God.

Even though the words "God is light" are not found in the Gospel of John, the Gospel's use of light in various constructions is important for understanding 1 John 1:5—2:2. This is especially true of the use of light in the summary of the Johannine message in 3:16–21 and in the interpretation of Jesus' words in 8:12, "I am the light of the world," which reaches forward all the way to and includes the waking of Lazarus from the dead. See John 9:3–5 and 11:9–10. Most interesting with regard to 1 John 1:5—2:2 is the narrative of the man born blind (John 9:1—10:21), and not least of all the transition in 9:39–41 to the parabolic discourse on the Good Shepherd. In this narrative, Jesus as the light of the world reveals the works of God (9:3–5).

The story of the man born blind closes with Jesus' commentary: "I came into this world for judgment so that those who do not see may see, and those who do see may become blind" (John 9:39). We might well have expected something along the lines of Jesus' having come to the world in order to save and to give life and health. But his words are mostly directed toward some Pharisees who are standing there. These persons are described with the words "those who do see," while the man born blind is an example of a different group of people, "those who do not see." Those who see become blind and those who do not see begin to see.

First John

The Pharisees who heard what Jesus said reacted angrily, which gave Jesus an opportunity to explain himself. They had insisted that they could see, i.e., that they had insight, they had Moses and the law, they were Moses' disciples; they knew that Jesus was a sinner, ignorant as they were of his origin. Therefore they were not open to the light when it came into the world, with the result that they become blind. The light revealed their sin, i.e., that they did not believe in Jesus as the one whom God had sent. Sin is failure to believe in Jesus as the Messiah, the Son of God (John 16:9). The double effect of the light's having come into this world—of the fact that God is light—is developed further in John 3:16–21. God's love, i.e., Jesus the son of God as a gift to human beings, leads to salvation and eternal life for those who believe, but to judgment and eternal destruction for those who do not believe. The metaphor of light becomes part of a dualistic way of speaking. Even the narrative of the man born blind resulted in a division, a *schisma* among the Jews who heard Jesus' message (10:21). This double effect of "God is light" dominates all of 1 John.

2. Walking in the Light of the Revelation (1:6–7)

The first paragraph of the argument is connected to the introduction by the words "we have fellowship with him" (vv. 3cd and 6a). Presumably, among Johannine Christians, this is an inherited formulation in which God is called "him." We should perhaps write "him" with a capital H. Compare "We know Him" in 2:3. Many commentators interpret "we" as a reference to the opponents in the letter (2:18–27), whereas from an intra-Jewish perspective, I read "we" more rhetorically as "anyone of us/you," i.e., primarily with reference to the Johannine Christians, the "we" and "you" in the first part of the letter. See Appendix 5, We in the Johannine Letters. Lying behind the letter as a whole, and thus also serving as background to 1:5—2:11, is a division within the Johannine community that comes to expression in 2:18–27 and 4:1–6. There is, however, some distance between this division and the epistolary situation in 1 John.

The Elder often argues on the basis of oppositions, here with the help of the words "light" or "darkness" and "truth" or "lie." To these oppositional pairs we could add having fellowship with God or not having fellowship with God, to have sin or to be pure from sin. In three applications of the argument he draws conclusions from the theme "God is light and in him there is no darkness at all." The parallel structure of the three segments invites a comparison among them and an interpretation in which all three relate to one another. The three "quotations" (vv. 6a, 8a, and 10a) must be read together; the truth (vv. 6d and 8c) and God's word (v. 10c) stand for the same thing; fellowship with God and the question of sin belong closely together, etc. The section 1:6—2:2, as well as 2:3–11 besides, must be interpreted as an overall exposition of "God is light and in him is no darkness at all" (v. 5).

Fellowship with God and walking in the darkness are mutually exclusive, according to v. 6abc, since God is light and there is no darkness at all in him. To walk in the darkness then is to refuse to accept that God is light, i.e., that God has revealed himself in Jesus the Messiah, the Son of God, the one who is the light of the world (John 8:12). The use of the word "walk" (see the note) opens the way as well for the ethical consequences of a life lived in this divine light, but the content of "walking in the darkness" is mainly the same as failing to "do the truth" (v. 6d), i.e., failing to live a life determined by the truth about God that has been revealed with Jesus Christ (John 1:17).

Walking in the light (v. 7), then, is the opposite of this; it is to live in this truth. But the author couples this phrase together with certain other formulations. First, he gives an explanatory refinement with the words "as he is in the light." Why not "as he is light"? The context requires that "he" is the same as God. However, similar comparisons usually refer to Jesus: "as he lived" (2:6), or "as he is pure" (3:3), or "as he is" (4:17). But in these latter passages, "he" is marked by a special pronoun. See the note "he," on 2:6. If we maintain that "he" in v. 7 refers to God, then what is meant by saying that "God is in the light"? The formulation is biblical (Dan 2:22; Isa 2:5; 1 Tim 6:15–16), and it can be understood as a variation on "God is light." But since in the Johannine writings God's light is mediated through Jesus Christ, the expression can also serve as a way to include him. God is in the light that reached the Elder and others in and through Jesus Christ. It is God's deeds that are revealed in the deeds of Jesus.

Secondly, the consequence of walking in the light is not expressed in terms of our living in the truth or of our having fellowship with God, but with an unexpected "we have fellowship with one another" (v. 7c). Usually this is interpreted to refer to the intra-Johannine fellowship or to Christian fellowship in general. But the proximity to v. 5 and v. 3 makes it more likely that the text refers to fellowship between the "we" and the "you," i.e., between the Elder and his coworkers on the one hand and the recipients of the letter on the other. To walk in the light then becomes receiving and accepting the message that the Elder delivers, namely "what was there from the beginning," along with its implications.

Thirdly, there is a sentence that appears to have no connection at all to the foregoing: "and the blood of Jesus, his son, cleanses us from all sin" (v. 7d). Some scholars claim that this line, too, is a later interpolation. But in fact it provides a transition to what dominates the remainder of this section, namely sin and cleansing from sin. Linking texts with "and" can be interpreted in numerous ways (see the note). The line of thought one follows depends on how one interprets the words "walk in the light." If it is only an ethical comment about our actions, it becomes difficult on the basis of the other Johannine writings to claim that the cleansing from sin is a result of good deeds. But if we interpret "walking in the light" more generally, as accepting the revelation implied in "God is light," understood from the introduction's communication of a message that was there from the beginning, then neither conclusion (v. 7c or 7d) is so unexpected. Those who hold fast to the message, the revelation of God, which the Elder delivers, have fellowship with him and his fellow workers—they have fellowship with each other—and by receiving the message they also have cleansing from sin—Jesus' blood cleanses all their sin. A decisive point in the new revelation is precisely Jesus' death and "the blood" that cleanses from all sin (2:2; 4:16; 5:6). Through the renewed covenant with God, those who believed God's testimony regarding his son received a share in divine life (5:9–13). See Appendix 9, A Renewed Covenant, and Appendix 7, Expiation and Forgiveness.

With the words "Jesus' blood cleanses from all sin," the death of Jesus is interpreted on the basis of contemporary conceptions of blood-sacrifice. Such sacrifices were brought forward in the Jewish temple every day, according to Leviticus 4, in order to atone for unintentional sins. "For, as life, it is the blood that makes atonement" (Lev 17:11). This sacrificial ceremony was intensified on the Day of Atonement. "For on this day atonement shall be made for you, to cleanse you; from all your sins you shall be clean before the Lord" (Lev 16:30). How exactly the cleansing through Jesus' blood was understood to occur cannot be discerned from the formulations in v. 7. See further 2:2 and Appendix 7, Expiation and Forgiveness. Purification from sin is a presupposition for the renewed covenant. See Appendix 9, A Renewed Covenant.

3. Acknowledge Sin and God's Forgiveness Through Jesus' Blood (1:8–9)

Cleansing from all sin through Jesus' blood could reasonably lead to avowing that we now have no sin. But in v. 8 such an avowal is labeled a lie, indeed as deception and absence of the truth (v. 8bc). This has led scholars to propose many definitions of "sin" in this statement (temptation to sin, inherited sin, conscious sin, etc.) and to various translations: "We have no guilt, because we have never sinned," i.e., an expression of a so-called perfectionist view according to which Christians have reached such maturity that they sin no longer. Or: "We have no guilt, although we have sinned," i.e., a so-called libertine view in which Christians are free to use their bodies any way they wish, since it is only the spirit that counts for anything. Raymond Brown renders this text, "We are free from the guilt of sin."

If we read the words "We have no sin" in close connection with what we already said regarding the sense of "God is light" and interpret the truth as the revelation that came to reality through Jesus Christ, the words could be understood to mean a repudiation of the cleansing through Jesus' blood. Anyone who does not acknowledge sin has no need of such cleansing. The argument resembles Paul's in Gal 2:21: "if justification comes through the law, then Christ died for nothing." The death of Jesus implies that humanity is in need of justification. Jesus' words and Jesus' death imply that humanity is sinful. "If I had not come and spoken to them, they would not have sin," says Jesus in John 15:22. Compare what was said above regarding John 9:39–41. The same logic is applied with reference to Jesus' deeds in John 15:24. The words in v. 8, "we have no sin," are then a way of saying that we have no interest in the revelation through Jesus Christ (God is light) and especially not in his atoning death, which is mentioned in the preceding line (v. 7d). An attitude of this sort rejects "the new covenant in the blood of Jesus" (Luke 22:20; 1 Cor 11:25).

The proper attitude is to see and to acknowledge sin, to confess it and receive forgiveness (v. 9). The words regarding confession of sin and forgiveness in this verse, like the description of God as faithful and just, remind us of the covenant with God and its renewal. The new covenant in the prophecy of Jeremiah rests on God's forgiving the people their sins and iniquities (Jer 31:34). Cleansing and forgiveness also have a central role in other texts related to renewal of the covenant. See Appendix 9, A Renewed Covenant. In 1 John it is presumably a matter of a public confession of sins, as with the covenant renewal at Qumran. See the note "confess our sins," on 1:9. The words in v. 9 can be interpreted as a foundational confession of sins that took place when recipients of the letter were converted and baptized. The formulations, however, are such that they also allow for a confession of particular sins at one of the gatherings of the faithful. It is sins like these that threaten the believers' part in eternal life and that can be the subject of fellow Christians' intercession.

On the basis of biblical speech patterns, it is easy to speak of God's being "gracious and merciful" as a basis for God's forgiveness. These words occur first in God's self-introduction when God reestablishes the covenant in Exodus 34 and then in a number of similar texts (Joel 2:13; Jonah 4:2; Ps 86:15; 103:8; 145:8–9; Neh 9:17). See Appendix 9, A Renewed Covenant. The covenant rests exclusively on God's mercy and grace. But there are several relevant words used in Exod 34:6–7, among them a reference to God's faithfulness, and in the Greek translation also to God's righteousness. The word for "faithful love" in covenant texts can likewise be rendered in the Septuagint as "righteousness" (Exod 15:13; 34:7). The Lord God is "the faithful God who maintains covenant loyalty with those who love him and keep his commandments, to a thousand generations" (Deut 7:9). The faithful God has called human beings into fellowship with God's son (1 Cor 1:9; 2 Tim 2:13). At the covenant feast in Qumran, the priests rehearse God's righteousness and God's many wonderful deeds, reminding the congregation of God's love and God's faithful acts toward Israel (1QS 1:21–22). God is "true and righteous" in God's covenant acts (1QS 1:26), God's faithfulness and mercy endure forever (1QS 2:1). Even Clement of Rome (90s CE) speaks of God as "faithful in His promises, and just in His judgments" (*1 Clem.* 27:1; 60:1). Thus, a biblical, Jewish way of speaking appears to lie behind the description of forgiveness as anchored in God's covenant, a covenant that expresses God's faithfulness and God's righteousness toward God's covenant people.

4. But if Anyone Does Sin (1:10—2:2)

Judging by 2:1, the third stage of this section appears to deal with specific sins that the believers might commit. "If anyone does sin," what happens then? It is a delicate question in the letter. Every individual sin is dangerous, because it threatens life (5:14–17). The world and all that is in it constitute a continual temptation to fall away from God (2:15–17). The struggle against the Evil One is still a live issue (4:4; 5:4–5). This is especially pertinent to the younger generation. The word that Jesus proclaimed had made his disciples clean, but the pruning of the vine and its branches continues (John 15:3). The foot-washing, in the Gospel of John a symbol for the death of Jesus and its effects, made the disciples clean through and through. But they still had to wash their feet (John 13:10). Does the same argumentation apply also in 1 John? To walk in the light is to acknowledge sins and to know that there is forgiveness for them. This is why the believer can never say, "We have not sinned." See further Appendix 12, They Cannot Sin.

If, then, sin, confession of sin, and forgiveness of sin occur even in a renewed fellowship with God, it is not surprising that the Elder comes now with a further defining of what he means in the closing of the section. He writes not so that they should sin, but that they should not sin (2:1). See the note "sin," on 2:1. He prepares the way for these words with a special vocative form and with a more personal "I write" in place of "we write." The relationships in this written communication become clear once again. He addresses them with a word that could be translated "dear children," here reinforced with "my." It is the most common vocative in the letter. See the note "My little children," on 2:1. Even Jesus used this form of address to his disciples on the occasion of his departure and in the final story of the Gospel (John 13:33; 21:5). The Elder speaks as one who communicates what was there from the beginning and thus imitates Jesus' way of speaking to his own at the Last Supper. The authority he has is based on the fact that he is one who bears the Jesus tradition.

At the beginning of chapter 2 the continued exposition of the cleansing through the blood of Jesus (vv. 7d and 9) testifies that it is important for the author to show that there is forgiveness for a believer who commits a sin. Thus he strengthens the possibility of forgiveness through referring in part to Jesus as an intercessor and defender and in part to Jesus as an offering for sin. Both concepts can be connected to the ideas of the Jewish Day of Atonement when the high priest functioned as intercessor for the people as a whole and offered sacrifices (sprinkled blood on the mercy seat in the Holy of Holies) as expiation for the people's sins, thus creating reconciliation between God and the people and between members of God's people.

Still, it is difficult to know how much of these ideas of sacrifice is echoed in the Johannine expressions. In the letter, concepts of a new covenant dominate. That new covenant also rests on God's forgiveness, but it is not connected with the sacrificial institution. See Appendix 7, Expiation and Forgiveness. It is strongly emphasized that the one who before God prays for those who have committed a sin or who before God defends them—both meanings apply to the word in the Greek text, *paraklētos*—is himself without sin, here expressed with the word "righteous." See the note, "a righteous one," on 2:1. When it is said in 3:5b that Jesus came into the world "to take away sins," it is also observed that in him there is no sin, and immediately following that we hear that he is righteous (3:7d). It is completely clear that Jesus' expiatory work in 1 John has its origin and its source in God's love and that it embraces all of humanity (2:2; 4:14). We may compare this with what is said in John 3:16–21.

1 John 1:5—2:2: A New Fellowship with God and Its Requirements

5. An Interpretation in Terms of the Opponents' Theology (1:5—2:2)

The most common way of relating the three paragraphs in 1:5—2:2 is to claim that they represent a dispute with the opponents, i.e., the secessionists (2:18ff.). The latter are said to have arrogantly claimed: "We have fellowship with him" (i.e., with God), "We do not have sin," and "We have not sinned." At the same time, their manner of life—they do not love their fellow believers—shows that they no longer have a part in the renewed fellowship with God that became a reality through Jesus the Messiah, God's son. Into the bargain they claim that they are without sin, in fact that they have not sinned. Therefore Jesus' death, his cleansing blood, his intercession and atoning sacrifice, are of no importance for them (5:6). This reading functions best in an ultra-Johannine perspective (progression hypothesis), and even in a general Christian perspective (apostasy hypothesis). But an intra-Jewish perspective (regression hypothesis) opens the door for another interpretation in which the letter's recipients come more to the fore. It focuses on their need to know that through their faith in the renewed revelation of God through Jesus the Messiah, God's son, they have fellowship with God and thereby have a part in divine life here and now (5:13). The interpretation above proceeds on the basis of an intra-Jewish perspective.

One of the more influential attempts to interpret this section from an ultra-Johannine hypothesis is Raymond Brown's. He sums up his reading in the following way: (1) The Elder fears that the recipients of the letter will be led astray by the way the secessionists interpret the Gospel of John's comment on the disciples' purity; they claim that one's lifestyle after the purification from sin has no significance for salvation. God dwells within them. They have fellowship with God, although they walk in the darkness, i.e., although they live a life of unrighteousness (1:6). According to the Elder, this is an impossible position. (2) Those who have been influenced by the secessionists can then object that sin as guilt exists only with those who do not believe. They themselves are free from the guilt of sin (1:8). The Elder insists that when believers sin, they must not deny their own guilt, but should confess their sins and receive forgiveness. (3) The believers may go one step further and claim with the opponents that they never sin. Those who believe in Jesus will never come under judgment (John 3:18; 5:24). No one can convict God's son or a child of God of any sin (John 20:23). The Elder continues then to press the possibility of sin's forgiveness by insisting on Jesus as an advocate with God and on Jesus as expiation for humanity's sins, as God's lamb who takes away the sins of the world (John 1:29).

This interpretation, in my opinion, is more complicated than the one I have given above based on the Elder's desire to attempt leading, admonishing, and comforting his children. Nevertheless, an earlier experience of schism within the Johannine fellowship (the regression of some to their earlier faith) is important for understanding the letter as a whole.

3

1 John 2:3–11: A Renewed Covenant with God and its Consequences

Translation Display

3a	And by this we know that we have come to know him
3b	if we keep his commandments.
4a	Whoever says, "I have come to know him,"
4b	and does not keep his commandments
4c	he is a liar
4d	and the truth is not in this person.
5a	But whoever obeys his word
5b	truly in this person the love of God has reached perfection.
5c	By this we know that we are in him.
6a	Whoever says that he abides in him
6b	he ought himself to walk
6c	just as he walked.
7a	Beloved,
7b	a new commandment I do not write to you
7c	but an old commandment that you had from the beginning.
7d	The old commandment is the word that you heard.
8a	Yet I do write to you a new commandment
8b	which is true in him and in you
8c	because the darkness is passing away
8d	and the true light is already shining.
9a	Whoever says that he is in the light
9b	and hates his brother

9c	he is still in the darkness.
10a	Whoever loves his brother
10b	he remains in the light
10c	and in him there is no cause for stumbling.
11a	But whoever hates his brother
11b	he is in the darkness
11c	and he walks in the darkness
11d	and he does not know where he is going
11e	because the darkness has blinded his eyes.

Notes

2:3. And. Gkt *kai*. Here, similarly to 1 John 1:5, "and" introduces a new paragraph. See the note there.

by this we know. The words in Gkt for "by this" (*en toutōi*) form an important Johannine phrase (1 John 2:3, 5c, 3:10, 16, 19, 24; 4:2, 9, 10, 13, 17; 5:2). Altogether the phrase occurs twelve times in the letter, eight times followed by the verb "know" (*ginōskein*). Often there is also a subordinate clause that provides the content of the word "this," mostly introduced with "that" (*hoti*), but also with "(so) that" (*hina*; 1 John 4:17), "when" (*hotan*; 5:2), or—as here—"if" (*ean*). In 1 John 3:10 and 4:2 the text continues with main clauses. As a formula, the construction varies in several ways, a not uncommon stylistic feature in 1 John.

The question is whether the word "this" in the formula points backward (anaphoric) or forward (cataphoric), or both backward and forward. It is difficult to go with just one of these alternatives; every passage must be evaluated individually. A cataphoric function is dominant, however, as here in v. 3. In 1 John 2:5c; 3:19; and 4:17, on the contrary, the reference is backward. This is not to say that there cannot be found a consistent nuance of double reference in this formula. It contributes to emphasizing what the author wants to say.

we have come to know. Gkt has the perfect tense of *ginōskein* ("know, be acquainted with, understand"), a verb that occurs twenty-five times in 1 John and once in 2 John. Another verb for "know" (*eidenai*) occurs fifteen times in 1 John and once in 3 John. Knowledge, insight, and wisdom constitute fundamental themes in the letter. Some scholars wish to interpret the first verb as knowledge or insight based on actual experiences, and the other as knowledge or wisdom acquired through authoritative assurances. But it is difficult to make a sharp distinction in meaning between the two verbs. See, e.g., John 8:19 and 14:7. In v. 3, the verb *ginōskein* is used twice. To know God is a mark of the new covenant. See Appendix 9, A Renewed Covenant.

him, i.e., God, as in the parallel statement, "we have fellowship with him" (1 John 1:6). See Appendix 8, He: God or Jesus or Both. Knowing God is a very central concept in this section and is examined in more detail in Appendix 9, A Renewed Covenant.

if, Gkt *ean,* marks the hypothetical aspect in the clause more than would be the case with the usual "that" (*hoti*). Or perhaps the author only wanted to avoid repeating "that," which he had just used. The if-clause supplies the content of the word "this" in the foregoing. See the earlier note.

keep his commandments. 1 John is almost unique in using this Old Testament phrase, but see "keep the commandments" (Matt 19:17); "keep the Father's commandments" (John 15:10); and "keep the commandments of God" (Rev 12:17; 14:12). In the Gospel of John, one hears mostly of keeping Jesus' commands or Jesus' words (singular or plural). Here "his" refers to God.

The word in Gkt for "commandment" (*entolē*) is the usual term for "commandment" in the Johannine letters. Here it occurs in the plural. See further the Analysis, point 2.

4. Whoever says. Literally, "the one who says." Gkt has a present participle with definite article, *ho legōn,* a formulation that often has a conditional function in 1 John: if anyone says. In v. 5a, a conditional relative clause is used as a variation. "The one who says" occurs in v. 4, v. 6, and v. 9 and corresponds to "if we say" in 1 John 1:6, 8, and 10. In all six cases, the construction "if . . . then" expresses an indirect exhortation.

have come to know. Gkt uses the same tense of the verb as in v. 3—"have learned to know"—to indicate an event in the past having continued effect in the present. Some translations use the present "know."

is not. The words have the sense of "does not exist," as in 1:8.

5. whoever obeys his word, truly in this person. The manner of expression in Gkt—"the one who obeys his word, in him"—is an example of a typical Johannine form of anacoluthon (change in sentence structure) called *casus pendens,* where part of a clause—in this case "the one who obeys his word," in the nominative—is placed first in a projected sentence in order to be then taken up in a new sentence through the words "in him."

obeys. Gkt uses the word *tērein,* which is naturally translated "keep," but here—as in v. 4b—it is rendered "obey." It has a very broad application: pay attention to, observe, watch over, protect, take responsibility for, keep, obey, and notice. In the LXX, almost all cases of the expression "keep the commandments" use another verb, *phylassein.* But see *tērein* in Sir 29:1; Tob 14:9, and later in Acts 15:5 and Jas 2:10.

his word. Gkt has "word" (*logos*) in the singular, i.e., God's word, God's message through Jesus, in Johannine writings often termed the truth. See the Analysis, point 2.

truly. Because of its connection with the concept of "truth" in the Johannine letters, the expression here in Gkt probably means more than just "really." See further the note on 3 John 1.

the love of God. We meet the word "love" (*agapē*) here for the first time in the letter. More than a fifth of all love-words in the NT are found in the letters of John, a reminder that love is a primary concept in these texts. See Appendix 16, God is Love.

The phrase "the love of God" or "the love of the Father" (1 John 2:5, 15; 3:17; 4:9, 12; 5:3) can have numerous meanings in Greek usage: love for God, i.e., someone loves God (objective genitive); God's love, i.e., God loves someone (subjective genitive); divine love (qualitative genitive); or various combinations of these three possibilities (so-called semantic condensing). Translators and commentators have many different ideas about what is meant in the various passages.

There are several reasons for the various possibilities, especially for the first two. In the OT, loving God can be a parallel to keeping God's commandments (Exod 20:6). And human love for God is certainly something that can be continually developed, is it not? However, in the Johannine writings, love is primarily God's love for human beings (1 John 4:7–21). It is a love that must come to expression in people's love for others and thus something that can be en route to a much greater completeness. 1 John 4:12 is not least among texts that speak in favor of the translation "God's love." The Johannine concept of love seems to me to be such that God's love (subjective genitive) is the point in all texts where *agapē* is used, even where the immediate context may indicate a love for God (objective genitive). See further the Interpretation, the commentary on 1 John 4:7–21, and Appendix 16, God is Love.

has reached perfection. Gkt has the perfect passive of the verb *teleioun* ("fulfill, make complete"). It is used of Jesus' ministry in John 4:34; 5:36; and 17:4, and of God's love in 1 John 2:5; 4:12, 17, 18. "Perfect (complete: Greek *teleia*) love casts out fear" (1 John 4:18).

By this. The same phrase as in v. 3, which can easily be interpreted as a rounding off of what has been said in vv. 3–5.

are in him, i.e., in God. The phrase is a close parallel to "have come to know him" (v. 3). See Appendix 9, A Renewed Covenant, and Appendix 15, God in Them and They in God.

6. that he abides in him. Gkt uses indirect speech in an abbreviated clause (accusative + infinitive, where the accusative is unstated because it is the same as the subject of the foregoing clause; see the Translation Display). The same is true of v. 9a. In earlier corresponding clauses, direct speech is used (1 John 1:6, 8, 10; 2:4). For "abide in him," see Appendix 15, God in Them and They in God.

ought to. The verb in Gkt, *opheilein,* means to be obliged to, to be duty-bound to. This verb, followed by an infinitive and often with an expressly emphasized subject sounds particularly Johannine (1 John 3:16; 4:11; 3 John 8; and John 13:14). It is an indirect form of a stern exhortation.

walk just as he walked. Gkt has a somewhat awkward sentence structure that lays the emphasis on "he": "as he walked, also you yourselves walk so." It would have been enough with just "also," or "so." See 1 John 2:18; 4:17.

walk . . . walked. That is, "live . . . lived." See the note "walk," on 1 John 1:6.

he, i.e., Jesus. Gkt has a demonstrative pronoun instead of a personal pronoun: "this one/this person" (*ekeinos*), which in 1 John clearly refers to Christ, the earthly and the exalted (1 John 2:6; 3:3, 5, 7, 16; 4:17). Some translations make the reference explicit, either as Jesus or Christ or as Jesus Christ; others use a capital letter: "He." See Appendix 8, He: God or Jesus or Both.

7. Beloved, in Gkt, *agapētoi* from the Johannine verb *agapaō* ("love"). Together with "my little children"—see the note on 1 John 2:1—it is the most common vocative term in the letter (1 John 2:7; 3:2, 21; 4:1, 7, 11). Latin translations have the literal *dilectissimi* ("greatly loved"). Jesus is God's beloved son (Mark 1:11); Israel is God's beloved (a covenant term; Jer 31:20; Ps 127:2); the Christians are God's beloved (Rom 1:7); and the Johannine fellowship has a special relationship to "the disciple whom Jesus loved." The author has many reasons for addressing his Johannine Christians as "beloved," not least of all in sections that deal with their being expected to love one another. See further the notes "the beloved" and "Beloved" on 3 John 1 and 2.

that you had from the beginning. Gkt has the imperfect, which can also be rendered "that you have had from the beginning," i.e., from Jesus' own day or from the time they came to faith. See Appendix 10, What you Heard From the Beginning.

the word, i.e., God's word/message, the same as in v. 5a and in 1 John 1:10; 2:14. See the Analysis, point 2.

heard. Gkt has the aorist tense, which here has a function similar to the perfect in 1 John 1:1, 3, 5. See also Appendix 10, What you Heard From the Beginning.

8. Yet. The word in Gkt, *palin,* is the usual word for "again." Here it has the "logical" function of introducing a new thought about what has already been said.

new, i.e., new in a qualitative sense, as "new" in the expressions "new covenant," "a new creature," "a new Jerusalem," "new heavens and a new earth," all of them referring to God's transformational work at the end-time. See the Analysis, point 2, and Appendix 9, A Renewed Covenant. In v. 7, "new" is contrasted to "old" and means "new" in the sense that they have not heard it before.

which is true in him and in you. Or "that is true both through him and through you." Some mss read "in himself" in place of "in him."

The word in Gkt for "true" (*alēthes*), which belongs to a typically Johannine word-family, is best translated "made true," "verified," "realized," "manifested." The introductory "that" (*ho*), which is in the neuter nominative, has no corresponding neuter word as its antecedent in the previous clause. It probably refers to the attribute "new" in the phrase "a new commandment" and could thus be rendered with "something that." A smoother translation might be "that is demonstrated," as in "demonstrated in him and in you," or "that both his life and yours demonstrate." The word "him" refers to Jesus.

is passing away. The present tense in Gkt implies that the darkness is in the process of passing away. In 1 John 2:17 the same verb is used with regard to the world and its desire.

the true light. Here is used the typical Johannine word *alēthinos*—meaning true, genuine, real—and not *alēthes* as in v. 8b. See Appendix 3, The Truth.

9. Whoever . . . The verse opens with the same kind of construction as in v. 6.

says . . . and hates. Literally, "the one saying . . . and hating." Some translations (e.g., NRSV) read "while hating"; the saying and the hating are envisioned as occurring simultaneously. A common definite article governing both participles binds them together into one expression.

The word "hate" is an opposite (antonym) of the word "love." See especially 1 John 4:20. To hate would then mostly mean to lack love, and not so much to have feelings of hatred or enmity. Love then comes close to the attributes of unity and solidarity. To hate is to fail to be in solidarity (1 John 3:16–17). See the Interpretation on v. 9 and Appendix 16, God is Love.

his brother. The word stands for any fellow Christian, a fellow believer. This was a usual meaning of the word "brother" in the early church. Judging by the Gospel of John, women had a prominent role in the Johannine community.

The word "brother" is used 16 times in the letters of John, six times with "love" and four times with "hate." Only once—and then in a special context—is it used as a term of address (1 John 3:13). With the exception of the phrase "to love/hate one's brother," the word seems not to have been very common in the Johannine fellowship, except possibly during an early stage of its history. According to John 20:17, Jesus refers to the disciples as "his brothers," and the rumor about the beloved disciple spread "among the brothers" (John 21:23). See further chap. 12, point 2.

10. and in him there is no cause for stumbling. More literally in Gkt: "and a snare/trap (*skandalon*) is not found in it/him."

The meaning of the clause is unclear, to say the least. The question is what *skandalon* means here. The concrete meaning is a snare or a trap, but the word is also used in the LXX, NT, and papyri more generally of something that leads to a fall, something that causes a person to stumble, also in extended meaning (Lev 19:14; Matt 16:23; 18:7). It is often translated "stumbling block," "hindrance," or "offense" (cf. 1 Cor 1:23; Gal 5:11). In John 16:1 the corresponding verb in the passive voice means to be tripped up, to stumble, in the sense of to fall away from one's faith. The English term "scandal" comes from this Greek word.

Where is this *skandalon* to be found, or rather where is it not found? Is it lacking in the light mentioned immediately before, or is it lacking in the one who loves his brother? The letter's use of the phrase "to be in" regarding persons (1 John 1:8, 10; 2:4) speaks in favor of the latter alternative.

Who then is it that can be caused to fall, i.e., to fall away from the truth and the fellowship with what was from the beginning? Is it the person(s) being addressed or other persons? The latter is the typical sense when *skandalon* is used. But in 1 John, one's love toward fellow Christians ensures one's belonging to the truth (1 John 3:18–19), something that supports the first alternative. Moreover, there are several parallels to such an interpretation: Ps 119:165; Hos 4:17 (LXX); and Jdt 5:20. The book of *Jubilees* reads, "create in them a clean heart and a holy spirit, and let them not be ensnared in their sins" (*Jub.* 1:21). I therefore follow this same interpretation. Love for fellow believers stands in opposition to falling away from the faith. In the renewal of the covenant at Qumran, the "stumbling stone" is linked with "sin" and "idols." See Appendix 9, A Renewed Covenant.

11. has blinded his eyes. Gkt has a so-called complexive (or constative) aorist, which describes the result of a longer process, "made him blind." The lack of love for fellow believers has led to the inability to receive the light and the truth.

Analysis

1. Delimitations and Structure

With 1 John 2:3–11 comes a new stage of the argument, which in its three-fold form resembles the preceding section, 1 John 1:5—2:2. See the Translation Display above and compare it with the Translation Display for that preceding section.

With v. 3 a new theme is introduced: to know God and to keep his commandments. Knowing God, in the context of a renewed covenant, is closely related to fellowship with God and to cleansing from sin, which were mentioned prior to v. 3. See Appendix 9, A Renewed Covenant. What follows next is a reasoned exposition in three steps: vv. 4–5, 6–8, and 9–11. Each one of them begins with "Whoever says" and in terms of content is connected to what comes immediately before it: knowing God in the first paragraph, being in God in the second paragraph, and being in the light in the third. See the Translation Display. Each part is formed in its own way, which means that we are not dealing with the same, consistent structure for all three, as was the case in 1 John 1:5—2:2.

1 John 2:3-11: A Renewed Covenant with God and its Consequences

The first paragraph, vv. 4–5, which has a clear, antithetical structure like the separate paragraphs of 1 John 1:5—2:2, is rounded off in v. 5c with a clause whose content refers to the beginning of the paragraph while at the same time advancing the discussion and preparing for what follows. This is a typical way in which the author links paragraphs to each other (1 John 3:10, 24). See also the note "By this," on v. 5.

The second paragraph, vv. 6–8, lacks an antithesis and indirectly expresses a clear exhortation: live as Jesus lived. This increased level of earnestness and severity is softened somewhat with the word "Beloved" in v. 7, with a reminder of the relationship between the sender and the receivers in this communication act, and a discussion of the old new commandment. The words "him" in v. 8b and "he" in 6c—see the note on these verses—both refer to Jesus, which binds vv. 6–8 into a coherent paragraph.

The third paragraph is antithetical in a double sense. The first member of the antithetical parallelism in vv. 9–10, concerning "the one who hates his brother," is repeated and expanded in v. 11, something that shows where the emphasis lies in the presentation. The entire section ends with "darkness," a word repeated three times in v. 11, with its devastating effects among human beings.

Thus the letter begins with two triads, 1 John 1:6—2:2 and 2:4–11, each with its own introductory thematic verse. They make it natural to let 2:3–11 constitute a section unto itself, set off from the rest. The continuation in 1 John 2:12-17 has a different character, which is best explained on the basis of a rhetorical strategy in the letter—see the Analysis for that section—even though the ending in v. 17, "the one who does God's will," is connected to the introduction in 1 John 2:3–11. For this reason some expositors wish to see 1 John 2:3–17 as a unit. In any case, with 1 John 2:18 we come to a new theme only hinted at in the foregoing.

2. God's Commandments and the New Commandment

My interpretation of 1 John 2:3–11 very much depends on my intra-Jewish perspective with its openness towards ideas of a renewed covenant as an important key to the understanding of the letter. See Appendix 9, A Renewed Covenant. Therefore, I include here an analysis of the concept of "commandment" in the Johannine letters.

In the history of their interpretation, the words "a new commandment" in 1 John 1:7–8 have been consistently understood as referring to Jesus' words, "A new commandment I give to you, that you love one another" (John 13:34). This meaning is appropriate here, but probably "commandment" stands for something beyond this, namely, for God's commandment in the covenant renewed through Jesus, most clearly formulated in 1 John 3:23.

If the author is taken as expressing himself in terms of "beginnings language," i.e., in terms of ideas about a renewed covenant paired with a certain sort of dualism, there is good reason to review what he says about the law and the commandments. We meet the word for "commandment" for the first time in 1 John 2:3, and it is used in this section both in the singular and the plural. The question is why. How many commandments are there according to the Johannine tradition? And is "keeping his commandments" (in the plural) the same as "keeping/guarding his word" (in the singular) in vv. 3–5? "The word" is also mentioned in v. 7.

The Greek word for "commandment," *entolē*, can mean commandment, order, word, rule, law, and even message, or charge. In the Old Testament (LXX) it is often used of God's will as it is found in the Law of Moses. In the Johannine tradition it gets its meaning through Jesus Christ. The word stands for the Father's charge to the Son (parallel with the word "work"; John 10:18; 15:10), for the Father's message through the Son (1 John 2:23), and for Jesus' message to his disciples (John 13:34 [singular]; 14:15 and 21 [plural]). The use of *entolē* is therefore connected to the revelation of God in Jesus Christ, to the qualitative new covenant between the Father, the Son, and the disciples. The new commandment established a new fellowship (John 13:34), and this effect was there as an indispensible aspect from the very beginning.

If we limit the analysis to the letters of John, the material on *entolē* yields the following:

- The most common phrase is "keep his commandments" (1 John 2:3, 4; 3:22, 23, 24; 5:2 [substituting "do" for "keep"], and 5:3). In 2 John 6 the phrase varies to "walk according to his commandments." In all cases the word is in the plural—"keep his rules"—and "his" is with the greatest likelihood the same as "God's." See Appendix 8, He: God or Jesus or Both. It expresses a general requirement to do what God demands (communicated through Jesus Christ), corresponding to "the will of God" in 1 John 2:17 and to "what pleases him" in 3:22. We hear in 1 John 5:3 that these commandments "are not burdensome." The yoke of Christ—i.e., God's requirement that comes to expression in Christ—is easy and his burden is light (Matt 11:30).

- "His [i.e., God's] commandment" in the singular occurs in 1 John 3:23. In the same verse we hear about "a commandment that he gave us," in 1 John 4:21 about "this commandment that we have from him," and in 2 John 4 about "a commandment that we have received from the Father." In the last case (see the note on that verse), as in 1 John 3:23, it is clear that it is not only a matter of the commandment to love one another. God's commandment is to "walk in the truth," i.e., to allow God's work in Jesus Christ to be imprinted on one's life. This includes as well to "believe in the name of his Son Jesus Christ." The word *entolē* is used here in a wider meaning.

- With this background, we can now go to 1 John 2:7–8 and to what is said there about the old new commandment. Usually it is interpreted only in terms of 1 John 2:10, regarding loving one's brother, and John 13:34, regarding Jesus' new commandment, rather than in terms of the immediate context and the Johannine letters as a whole. In John 13–15, "commandment" and "word" (singular or

1 John 2:3-11: A Renewed Covenant with God and its Consequences

plural) seem to be generally interchangeable. From the perspective of the context in 1 John 2, the commandment is old, because it was there when the letter's recipients came to faith (v. 7c). It is the message that they heard at that time (v. 7d). At the same time it is new, since it is continually being realized in Jesus and in the recipients of the letter (v. 8b). In addition, the new is more generally described through the words about the darkness that is in the process of passing away and through the words about the true light that is now already shining. The commandment in the Johannine letters is said to be a commandment from the Father and not from Jesus. Against this background, then, I interpret the commandment in 2 John 6c as the commandment from the Father that is mentioned in v. 4c, i.e., a commandment to shape one's entire life on the basis of the truth.

- This more general sense of *entolē* in 1 John 2:7–8, almost a message of binding character effective in the new covenant, is reinforced by the definition found in the text: "the old commandment is the word that you have heard" (v. 7d). "The word" (*ho logos*), is used in a more definitive meaning in 1 John 1:1, 10; 2:5, 7, 14, clearly identified in the last passage as "God's word." I therefore interpret "his word" in 1 John 1:10 and 2:5 as "God's word." The formulations in 1 John 1:10c and 2:14g are almost identical. Both the choice of the word *logos* in the original text and the qualifier, "which you heard," in v. 7d convince me, unlike most readers, not to interpret "his word" in 1 John 2:5c as synonymous with "his commandments" (plural) in 1 John 2:3b and 4b. To keep his word (1 John 2:5c) has a more precise meaning: to guard the message that God conveyed through his son Jesus Christ, the message that is mentioned at the beginning of the letter.

- The question of how this message of God (*entolē, logos*) is closely connected to Jesus forms the theme in the introductions to John and 1 John. In the letter, the words "message," *angelia* (1 John 1:5; 3:11), "promise" (*epangelia*; 1 John 2:25), and "testimony" (*martyria*; 1 John 5:9–11) stand for nearly the same thing, although from differing perspectives. Several of the words are exceptionally appropriate to the sphere of covenant thinking.

Closer study of 1 John 3:22–24, which strategically holds the whole letter together, can give us an answer to what this new concord between God and humanity implies according to the letters of John. The content of this text is shaped into a double chiasm. In a somewhat paraphrased form it has the following six members:

a	God answers our prayers, because we keep the commandments
b	And this is his commandment:
c	we are to believe in the name of his son Jesus Christ
c'	and we are to love one another
b'	as he gave us a commandment.
a'	We are in God, and God is in us, when we keep the commandments.

The general condition of keeping God's commandments (in the plural)—lines a and a'—frames this paragraph. Fulfilling this condition leads to rich blessing: full audience and close union with God. In the summarization of the commandments that then follows in lines b and c, the text can be read so as to yield two commandments: bc constitutes the first commandment, and b'c' constitutes the second (synonymous with Jesus' commandment in John 13:34). Jesus becomes then the subject in b'. Another possibility is to let b and b' express the same thing. Lines c and c' would then give the content of God's covenantal demand. This seems to me to be the simpler reading, corresponding to the place God has in the context and consistent with 2 John 4–6 as well.

The foundational agreement between God and human beings in the new covenant would then consist of two articles: to believe in Jesus as Messiah, God's son, and to love one's fellow believers. If this is compared with the so-called double love commandment that characterized the covenant God established with Israel at Sinai, then "love God" has been has been refined to "believe in Jesus the Messiah, God's son," and "love your neighbor (fellow Jew)" has been restricted to "love your fellow believers." See further the Interpretation of 1 John 3:11–24. In the letter's historical situation, the new fellowship is grounded in a two-part covenant commandment. In the Johannine letters this duality is often connected with the words "truth" and "love." The recipients in these letters can be described as a family of the truth and love. See especially the Interpretation of 2 John 1–3, 12–13.

This particular formulation of the essence of Johannine Christian faith is motivated by the situation of the letter's recipients. At this moment in their history, true or false faith could be determined on the basis of these two points. In the latter half of 1 John 3:24, the Spirit is also introduced as a criterion. Some Johannine Christians were perhaps claiming that God's spirit within people was insufficient as a guide without obedience to God's commandments as they were fleshed out in Jesus Christ, i.e., without the practice of the truth and love. What follows in 1 John 4:1–6, however, as we shall see, shows that it was not so simple merely to claim the authority of the Spirit.

Interpretation

1. Knowing God and Keeping His Commandments (2:3)

The section 2:3–11 deals with the recipients as a new fellowship of brothers and sisters and their way of living (ethics), i.e., the third possible area of meaning in "God is light." The arrangement of the text is the same as in the section 1:5—2:2. Employing repetitions with variations was a sound rhetorical rule in the ancient world. See the Analysis for 2:12–17, point 2. The section 2:3–11 should therefore be read together with 1:5—2:2.

First there is a thematic verse, 1:5 and 2:3. Then the theme is worked out in a reasoned way in three steps. Compare the Translation Displays of 1 John 1:5—2:2

1 John 2:3-11: A Renewed Covenant with God and its Consequences

and 1 John 2:3-11, as well as the commentaries on them. Each part in this three-fold presentation is connected to the preceding part. One part in each of the two sections is drawn out, first 1:10—2:2 and then 2:6-8. In both cases the expanded text is introduced with an appealing form of address, "my little children" and "beloved." See the Notes on these expressions in 2:1 and 2:7. The new fellowship's foundations (revelation and salvation) are handled in 1:5—2:2 and the new covenant's results (ethics) in 2:3-11. We can also say that the basic summary of the message from Jesus, "God is light and in him there is no darkness at all" (1:5), is unpacked in a six-fold way in 1:6—2:11. The words "to walk/be in the light/darkness" in 1:6-7 and 2:9-11 clearly bind together this part of the letter.

The formulation of the theme in this section, to know God and keep his commandments (2:3), has a natural background in conceptions of the renewed covenant, especially as it is presented in Jeremiah 31 and Ezekiel 36. This is reinforced by the letter as a whole. See Appendix 9, A Renewed Covenant. The covenant with Israel at Sinai rests on promises made by both parties: God promises in his own name to make Israel his own people; Israel promises to obey God with their whole heart (Exodus 19-24; 32-34). It is God who takes the initiative; his choice of Israel in particular rests solely on his love; it is his faithful grace that keeps the covenant alive. The covenant with Israel rests on God's grace and God's righteousness (Exod 34:8-9). These two words are used as parallel expressions, e.g., in Ps 36:6-7, 11; 143:1, 11-12. At the same time demands are placed on Israel to love God and to keep his commandments (Exod 20:1-6; Deut 5-6; 10:12—11:25). The covenant is sometimes described in terms of a marriage, with the considerable inequality that was normal between a husband and wife at that time (Hos 1-2). The word "love" in covenant texts in Deuteronomy presumably has a background in contracts between vassal kings and their overlords: vassals are to love their lord, i.e., be in solidarity with him and obey him in all things.

When God renews the covenant with his people, according to Jeremiah 31, he will place his law within them, write it on their heart, with the result that they will all "know the Lord." They will all know what the Lord wants and can therefore realize his will, i.e., keep his commandments. According to Ezekiel 36 God gives his people a new heart, a new spirit, in fact a share in his own spirit, so that they can walk according to his commandments and keep his statutes and act in accordance with them (Ezek 36:25-28). This new manner of knowing the Lord has its foundation in forgiveness and cleansing (Jer 31:34; Ezek 36:25), which were dealt with in the preceding section (1 John 1:5—2:2). A Jesus-believing Jew would scarcely have said "know YHWH" (YHWH as the Hebrew name of God), since he would not wish to speak God's name; he would instead replace it with "know the Lord" or "know Him." It seems as if the phrases "have fellowship with Him" (1:6) and "know Him" were stable expressions within the Johannine community.

To know the God of the covenant implies knowledge and insight about God. In a renewed covenant no one will any longer need to say, "Know the Lord." They all have insight; there is no need of a teacher (Jer 31:34). The Elder reemphasizes this for the sake of the letter's recipients in 2:20–21, 27. They know the truth. It is now just a matter of doing the truth. The latter therefore becomes a criterion as to whether they know God. It is precisely what is stated in the theme verse: If we keep God's commandments we know that we have come to know and continue to know God. See the Notes on 2:3. The section focuses on the consequences of this new nearness to God.

The expression "to know God" is also common in texts of the day, in Plato, in the mystery religions, in Philo, in the Qumran texts and later Jewish texts, and in the New Testament. But the meaning of v. 3 is primarily determined by the Johannine manner of speaking and by texts on the renewal of the covenant. According to John 17:3 eternal life is defined as "knowing the only true God and the one he has sent, Jesus Christ." In the farewell discourse, "to know" becomes a relational word in the description of the relationships between the Son, the Father, and the disciples, parallel to "love" and "abide in" (14:7, 17; 15:21; 17:25). To know God expresses thus a close relationship between God and human beings, like the relationship between man and woman in marriage. It is replaced immediately in vv. 5–6 with "be in God" and "abide in God." See Appendix 15, God in Them and They in God. Knowing God becomes knowing the Father in 2:14, a formulation that leads to thoughts of the Son and of being children. To know the Father stands in parallel to what is said just before, in 2:12, regarding the letter's recipients, that they have forgiveness of their sins through Jesus' name. See the Interpretation on these verses. To know God is parallel to being born of God (4:7–8). The one who knows God loves, because God is love. Whoever knows God is of God and listens to the Elder and the tradition he imparts (4:7). It is the Son who has given the recipients understanding so that they know the true God (5:20). The phrase "know Him" gets its primary content from these Johannine parallels.

Thus, from an intra-Jewish perspective, I have interpreted the words "to know God" on the basis of ideas of a renewed covenant and other related statements in the letter. Other perspectives draw attention to the opponents in the letter, and thus many interpreters read the words "I have come to know Him" in v. 4a as what the secessionists say. In a general Christian perspective, these opponents are described as Gnostics who according to Irenaeus have "a universal knowledge of all that exists," and who think that "they have searched out the deep things of God." "They have a sublime knowledge on account of which they are superior to others" (*Haer.* 2.28.9; 2:10.3). Or so they claimed, insisting that they were enlightened with a supernatural knowledge received through mystical experiences or through participation in the light itself. Therefore they claimed to have a special knowledge (*gnosis*) that radically distinguished itself from the understanding that the Elder represented.

In an ultra-Johannine perspective the differences in the knowledge of God are not so great between the Elder and the secessionists. Both of them belonged to the Johannine fellowship, but the latter gradually came to interpret in a new way the Johannine tradition that we have in the Gospel of John (progression hypothesis). Both groups were largely agreed that they knew God, but the secessionists did not want to draw from this confession any conclusions for their way of life. The two sides were united on the issue of knowing God, but not on the issue of keeping God's commandments. The secessionists attributed no particular significance to Jesus' earthly life or his death—the fact of incarnation was enough for them—and thus they could not accept the rule to live as Jesus lived, i.e., to love one another as Jesus loved.

The Elder speaks often, both directly and indirectly, about keeping God's commandments (in the plural: 2:3–4; 3:22, 24; 5:2–3; and 2 John 6; singular: 2:7–8; 3:23–24; 2 John 4–5). See further the Analysis above, point 2. Does this mean that the Jesus-believing Jews in the letters of John kept the commandments found in the Old Testament and in contemporary Judaism? The texts leave the question open. But in what follows, the Elder successively zooms in on the meaning of the general phrase "keep God's commandments," focusing on the more specific phrases "obey God's word" in 2:4–5, "live as Jesus lived" in 2:6–8, and "love those who believe in Jesus" in 2:9–11.

2. Obeying God's Word (2:4–5)

Sometimes the Elder argues in a generally logical way, to which there can be no objection. This happens in vv. 3–4, as several times previously in 1:5—2:2. If we keep God's commandments, we know that we know God. Therefore: If anyone says that he knows God, yet does not keep God's commandments, he is a liar, etc. In a Johannine context a new nuance possibly enters in with the words "the truth is not in him" (2:4d). See Appendix 3, The Truth, and the Interpretation on the corresponding words in 1:6d and 1:8c. But in the first place these words reinforce only the words "he is a liar." Anyone who accepts such a logical conclusion can be expected to accept what follows as well. But here there is something that often happens. The rationale is put off and new concepts are introduced, as in v. 5, e.g., somewhat unexpectedly: "God's word" (singular) and "God's love." The phrase "to keep God's commandments" (*entolē*, in the plural) is replaced with "to keep God's word" (*logos*, in the singular). Are they the same thing?

The majority of exegetes are convinced that this is the case and refer to the use of the word "commandments" and "word" (plural and singular) in the Gospel of John: "if anyone keeps my word" (singular in 8:51–52; also 14:23; 15:20), "if anyone keeps my words" (plural, 14:24), "if anyone keeps my commandments" (plural, 14:15, 21; 15:10), and "this is my commandment that you love one another" (singular, 15:10; also 13:34). At the same time, Jesus' word is God's word: "I have not spoken on my own, but the Father who sent me has himself given me a commandment about what to say and what to speak. And I know that his commandment is eternal life. What I speak, therefore, I speak just as the Father has told me" (John 12:49–50).

The Gospel of John almost always speaks of *Jesus'* words, whereas the letter speaks only of *God's* words. In any case, there is no clear example of "Jesus' word" in the letters of John, but there certainly are examples of "God's word/commandment" (singular:

2:14; 2 John 4). See further the Analysis above, point 2. A good deal speaks for God's word in 1 John having in view the revelation of God that was mediated through Jesus Christ and that is thereby a part of what the recipients of the letter heard from the very beginning (1:1, 10; 2:5, 14). God's word, God's message, and God's testimony in 1 John come very near to one another in terms of their content. For this reason, I see the formulation "God's word" (v. 4) as one of the first instances of the author's making more precise what he means by "God's commandments" (v. 3). The understanding of "God's commandments" thus is related to Jesus Christ. This difference between "God's commandments" and "God's word" can justify other translations of "keep his word," e.g., "obey his word," or "observe his word."

This meaning for "his word" is reinforced by the reference to God's love in the next line. For the letter's recipients, God's love always includes Jesus Christ. Through his having given his life for them, they came to know love. Thus they too must give their lives for the brothers (3:16–17). God's love became visible for them through God's having sent his son into the world to make them partakers of divine life (4:9–10, 14). This love revealed through Jesus attains its fullness in them when it produces ethical consequences in their lives, something that later in the letter is exemplified by their loving one another (4:7–21). This is also the result of the argument for keeping God's commandments in 2:3–11, i.e., for loving one's brother (v. 10).

This first step in the elucidation of the theme in v. 3 is rounded off with a conclusion that then becomes the point of departure for the next step, namely, the words "By this we know that we are in him." The formulation is clearly connected with the beginning of v. 3, while at the same time it replaces "knowing God" with "being in God." Both expressions describe the close fellowship between God and human beings in the renewed covenant, a nearness between God, Jesus, and those who believe in Jesus. More than thirty times in the Johannine writings this new divine fellowship in the renewed covenant is described with the words "to be in" or "abide in." See Appendix 15, God in Them and They in God.

3. Living As Jesus Lived (2:6–8)

The next step proceeds directly to a positive exposition of what has just been said, but without the usual formula "not A but B." B is expressed immediately. Based on what we have said about the first step, it is not so unexpected that "to keep God's commandments" is interpreted as "to live as Jesus lived." The content is already indirectly present in the formulation "to obey God's word." The ethical model "as Jesus" occurs several times in the letter and refers to what Jesus did during his earthly ministry (as he lived, as he loved, as he died) and to what Jesus was and now is (as he is pure, as he is righteous, as he is; 2:6, 29; 3:3, 16–17; 4:17). The commandment in the new covenant, according to John 13:34, runs as follows: "Just as I have loved you, you also should love one another." In most of these cases, a special word for "he" (*ekeinos*), is used of Jesus. See the note "he" on 2:6.

The meaning of this life-rule is explained only in part in the letter. It implies first of all loving one's fellow believers (3:11–24; 4:7–21), i.e., not disrupting the fellowship of truth and love that has come as a consequence of God's renewal of the covenant with his people. To live as Jesus lived also implies sharing of one's own assets with the brothers and sisters who are in need, even to the point of giving one's life for them (3:16–17), as well as praying for those who have committed a sin and thereby giving them life (5:14–17). Even the exhortation not to love anything that is in the world—e.g., what the body craves, what the eyes lust for, and what pride in a person's status and possessions encourages (2:15–17)—can be read as a general commentary on living as Jesus lived.

The subject of vv. 7–8, the expansion of the second paragraph in 2:3–11, is the commandment that the readers should live as Jesus lived, not just that they should love one another. See the Analysis above, point 2. The new commandment is lived out in Jesus' life and in theirs, v. 8b. Its general motivation is the fact that the darkness is in the process of passing away; therefore the reference is to the current situation. The former age is disappearing and the coming age has already arrived, with divine life and the divine manner of life in its train. Compare Rom 13:11–14. There are ethical consequences in the readers' life. And if they keep God's commandments they can be certain that they know God (v. 3).

Here too the Elder plays with words. The interpretation of "God's commandments" in terms of Jesus and his life is old, yet also new. It is old because it was part of the message that the letter's recipients heard from the beginning; it is new because it is closely connected to the renewal of the covenant and the new participation in God. Even Jesus describes the commandment to love one another as new (John 13:34). They now know God through Jesus Christ, and they know what God's will is and can bring it into reality. The true light is already in the world. "God is light" (1:5). Or with the words of the evangelist: "The true light, which enlightens everyone, was coming into the world" (John 1:9). But "people loved darkness rather than light because their deeds were evil" (John 3:19–21). To walk in the darkness or in the light is a matter of ethics.

With the expansion of the second step in 2:3–11, the argument for this Jesus-rule acquires a special weight: (1) it is part of what the letter's recipients heard in the beginning; (2) it is new as an element in the new covenant with its two-part commandment (3:23); (3) it corresponds to the new life that was realized in Jesus and now is being realized in the recipients; (4) it corresponds to a new situation in which the new age is breaking in more and more; and (5) it has its foundation in Jesus' love and in God's. The last-named item later becomes the main theme in the second part of the letter (3:11–24).

First John

4. Loving the One Who Believes in Jesus (2:9–11)

The repeated antithetical pattern "not A but B" in 1:6—2:11 is extended in the third step to "not A but B and not A" (vv. 9–11). The emphasis is thus laid on the negative statement regarding being in the darkness and hating one's sister or brother. As with previous steps the first line of this one is connected to what has just been said, and the paragraph as a whole becomes both a new and more concrete delineation of what it means to "keep God's commandments," while at the same time providing an ending to the first part of the letter (1:5—2:11).

Being in the light corresponds to the earlier claims of knowing God and abiding in God. God is in the light (1:7). With this image of light and darkness, the Elder binds the final paragraph together with the first one (1:6–7), which itself explains the message from and about Jesus (1:5). The words "to walk in the light" in 1:7 presumably have, as we have seen, a broad meaning of being enlightened through Jesus Christ in thought and deed, enlightened this way by the God who is light. But in 2:10, after a number of intervening steps, the idea of "walking in the light" is finally distilled into loving one's fellow believers. In the then-current situation this was clearly very important.

This is the first time the author speaks about "loving/hating one's brother." In the first part of the letter he has taken his time leading up to this theme, one that later on becomes dominant. But then he immediately drops it in order first to encourage and admonish his audience (2:12–17), and then to remind them about those who had thrown over their faith in Jesus as Messiah, God's son (2:18–27), in order finally to spell out what it means to practice righteousness as Jesus is righteous and to purify themselves as Jesus is pure (2:28—3:10). Is this a form of rhetoric? Why this cautious and gradual, indirect argumentation, one that requires so much attention for perceiving what the author actually means by what he is saying? Is it that delicate, this question about the faith these Jews have in Jesus as Messiah, God's son, with its entailment of a renewed covenant and eternal life? Or is it simply difficult to say with good effect something the listeners actually already know?

Walking in the darkness is the image that dominates the ending. In contrast to the light, the truth, and love, the author opposes the darkness, lying, and hatred. The dualistic phraseology is highly concentrated in these verses. In Johannine tradition expressions with light and darkness are used to describe people's relationship with Jesus. When the light came, humanity was forced to choose: a life in the light or a life in the darkness (John 3:16–21). Those who chose the darkness gradually become blind and do not see that they are on the road to destruction (v. 11). The image goes back to Isa 6:10, which is used in John 12:35–36 of Jews who did not believe in Jesus in spite of all the signs he did. The explanation given there for the Jews' unbelief is twofold: on the one hand, a scriptural explanation—God made them blind, and on the other hand a sociological one—they preferred honor from other people over honor from God (John 12:37–43). In the text of the letter, the issue has to do with Jews who at one time had come to faith in Jesus as Messiah, God's son, but who for various reasons had chosen to give up this Messiah-faith. Thus they themselves have chosen to be made blind. They are further described in 2:18-27.

The word-pair "love/hate" forms part of the dualistic pattern in John. The question is whether it ultimately goes back to covenant texts in which there are only two alternatives: to hate God or to love God and keep his commandments (Exod 20:5-6). "To love" here means primarily "to be bound to, be in solidarity with, to serve, to obey"; "to hate" stands for the opposite. In 1 John the concern is not the relationship one has with God, but the relationship one has with Jesus-believing Jews. In Hebrew these paired words clearly function as words of relationship and not as words of sentiment. It can be used of hating one wife and loving the other, in a case of a man who has two wives; there the words most likely mean prefer/despise (Deut 21:15-17). The NRSV translates the word "hate" in Deut 21:15-16 as "dislike" (cf. Exod 20:5, "reject"). With regard to attitudes toward Jesus, expressions like "love more than" and "love rather than" are used in place of merely "love" (John 3:19; 12:43). "Whoever comes to me and does not hate father and mother . . ." in Luke 14:26 becomes in Matthew's version "Whoever loves father or mother more than me . . ." (Matt 10:37). In the Gospel of John too, "love" is clearly a word of relationship with parallels like "know" and "abide in" (John 14:15, 21-24; 15:9-12). And in the letter the idea of love is determined by the love of God and Jesus for human beings. To be in the light gives an ability to love one's fellow believers, because love comes from God. "To love" stands for the close union and solidarity between God and God's children, and thus also among God's children (5:2). "To hate" stands for the opposite.

The dualistic way of thinking does not imply a static relationship between two positions, but rather a dynamic struggle between two powers. The darkness is not fully gone; it is only in the process of disappearing. Yet already now the real light is here in the dawn (v. 8). There is therefore still a risk of falling away from God. As for the one who loves, however, there is no "stumbling stone" within him that can cause a fall. See the note on 2:10. Jesus says, "Those who walk during the day do not stumble, because they see the light of this world. But those who walk at night stumble, because the light is not in them" (John 11:9-10). Jesus says, "I am the light of the world. Whoever follows me will never walk in darkness but will have the light of life" (John 8:12). Even in the renewed covenant individuals must each day choose the light over the darkness, confess their sins, and live as Jesus lived, thereby making the light visible in the world. They must "walk in the light," day by day.

5. Summing Up 1 John 1:1—2:11

Through the covenant at Sinai, God selected a group of people to be his own, a people separate from all other peoples, a royal priesthood, a people marked by the love of God. Through the tabernacle and the law, God came especially close to these people;

First John

God cleansed them from sin though various forms of sacrifice and required that they keep God's commandments in all things. Thus they would become the nation through whom God would also redeem all other nations of the earth. But repeatedly, God's covenant people Israel fell away from their God, even from the very start at Sinai. At last God promised to intervene again and in his mercy to forgive God's people their sins and to renew their hearts so that they might keep God's commandments. In the promises of a renewed covenant this covenantal relationship is strengthened and deepened. Now here in the beginning of his letter (1:1—2:11), the author of 1 John has focused on a renewal of the revelation, the cleansing from sin, the presence of God, and obedience to God's commandments. The renewal has come about through Jesus, the Messiah, the Son of God. Everything depends on a faith in God that includes him, particularly the possession of eternal life here and now (John 17:3).

4

1 John 2:12–17: Comfort and Admonition

Translation Display

12a	I write to you
12b	little children:
12c	your sins have been forgiven on account of his name.
13a	I write to you
13b	fathers:
13c	you know him who was there from the beginning.
13d	I write to you
13e	young people:
13f	you have conquered the evil one.
14a	I write to you now
14b	children:
14c	you know the Father.
14d	I write to you now
14e	fathers:
14f	you know him who was there from the beginning.
14g	I write to you now
14h	young people:
14i	you are strong
14j	and the word of God abides in you
14k	and you have overcome the evil one.
15a	Do not love the world
15b	or the things in the world.
15c	If anyone loves the world
15d	then the love of the Father is not in him

First John

16a	for all that is in the world
16b	—the desire of the flesh,
16c	the desire of the eyes,
16d	the pride in riches—
16e	it comes not from the Father
16f	but from the world.
17a	And the world is passing away, and its desire,
17b	but the one who does the will of God remains forever.

Notes

2:12. I write. Here Gkt has the present tense, *graphō,* which occurs again in vv. 13a and 13d. In v. 14 the aorist, *egrapsa,* is used three times in a corresponding manner. The difference between the two temporal forms is presumably mainly stylistic, rhetorical. See the Analysis, point 2.

little children. Gkt has the vocative *teknia* ("you children"). See the note, "My little children" on 1 John 2:1.

your sins have been forgiven. Gkt introduces this line with the word *hoti,* which can mean "that" or "because" or both. See the Analysis, point 2. We have this word six times in this section, v. 12, v. 13 (twice), and v. 14 (three times). Here I take it as equivalent to a colon. Gkt continues with a construction in the perfect passive: "your sins have been forgiven you." In fact the corresponding clauses in the remaining five segments in vv. 12–14—all of which are introduced with *hoti,* see the Analysis, point 2—have the perfect (vv. 13c, 13f, 14c, 14f, 14k). The tense implies an event in the past with ongoing effect in the present. Some translations render these verbs with the present, thus the NRSV here and in vv. 13c, 14c, and 14f. The children are merely passive recipients of forgiveness—which is appropriate for children. At this point, the author is not interested in explaining the forgiveness except to indicate that God is the agent (passive construction) and that Jesus is the means ("his name"). Why does he use this indirect way of expressing things? Is it the traditional formulation in a Jewish milieu?

on account of his name, i.e. according to usual New Testament usage, "on account of Jesus' name." A more complete expression of the name is found in 1 John 3:23 and 5:13. In an Old Testament perspective a person's name stands for his or her identity and power. God forgives God's people for the sake of God's own name (Ezek 20:8-9). For God's name's sake, he intervenes and gathers God's people from all nations, cleanses them and gives them a new heart, a new spirit, a share of God's own spirit in fact, so that they can keep God's commandments and follow them (Ezek 36:22–27). Knowing a person's name also gives access to that person's power. The formulation in v. 12 presumably has its background in the baptism that took place in Jesus' name and that among other things had the forgiveness of sins as a consequence (Acts 2:38).

13. fathers. In Gkt the vocative form of *patēr* is in the plural: "you fathers." The same word occurs in v. 14e. It is never used to refer to an entire congregation in the early church. The rabbis could be called "fathers." First Corinthians 4:15 distinguishes between "tutors" and "fathers." The continuation in v. 13 and v. 14f suggests that those being referred to have been Christians for some time. Probably it is older, more mature Christians, both men and women, who are being addressed in this way. See the Analysis, point 2. The use of "fathers" and "young men" in v. 13 and v. 14 with reference to both men and women reflects traditional models. The ancient divisions of the "ages of man" were interested only in men.

know. Gkt has the perfect tense, i.e., a fact in the past that is still valid. See the notes "know" on 1 John 2:3 and "your sins have been forgiven" on 12c above.

him who was there from the beginning. Gkt has here, as in v. 14f, a substantive use of a prepositional phrase—"the one from the beginning"—which can be completed with several meanings of the verb "to be": "is," "was," or "has been." It can mean him who is from the beginning, i.e., before the creation of all things (cf. John 1:1), or him who was there from the beginning, i.e., the Life that was revealed and made known to human beings (1 John 1:1). The expression points in both cases to Jesus. The emphasis lies here not so much on Jesus' existence before the creation, but—as so often in the letter—on the earthly Jesus. I translate it, "him who was there from the beginning." See also the note on 1 John 1:1 and Appendix 10, What you Heard From the Beginning.

young people. In Gkt the masculine vocative form *neaniskoi* ("you young men"). The word *neaniskos* is used most often of younger men from teenage years until the time for marriage. In view here, presumably, are the younger people in the congregation, both men and women, who have come to faith after "the fathers." In terms of society at the time there were only two categories of age, young and older, and the boundary fell at approximately forty years. See further the Analysis, point 2.

have conquered. The young people/addressees are part of the final battle between God and all who are opposing him. Compare 1QM and Rev 2:7, 11, 17; 12:11, and so on. God has the supreme power. They have a place in God's plan and purpose. Such an apocalyptic vision could give them hope and meaning in situations of oppression.

the evil one. The expression in Gkt, *ho ponēros,* is the most common name for the devil used in the letter (1 John 2:13, 14; 3:12; 5:18, 19). This usage is not clearly represented in pre-Christian texts, but it is used in Matt 6:13; 13:19; John 17:15; and Eph 6:16. The use of the phrase "the devil" (*diabolos*), is restricted to 1 John 3:8, 10 (four times). In dualistic speech, conquering the evil one belongs to the realm where the darkness strives to overcome the light. Cf. Luke 11:22 and Rom 12:21.

First John

14. I write. See the note "I write," on v. 12, above.

children. Gkt *paidia*. The word is a diminutive in neuter plural vocative from a common word for "child" (*pais*). It is probably a stylistic variant on "little children" (*teknia*) in v. 12. See the note "My little children" on 1 John 2:1. With regard to children it may be more appropriate to say "know the Father" than "know Him" or "know God."

know. See the note on v. 13, above.

and the word of God abides in you. Although this clause like the next one is introduced with "and," both clauses function as justification and explanation of the words "you are strong" in v. 14i. On "the word of God," see the Analysis on 1 John 2:3–11, point 2. Later on the author uses "the message [of God]" (3:11), "the command of God" (3:23) and "the testimony of God" (5:9–11), but not "the word of God."

15. Do not love. Gkt has the present imperative, which gives a special weight to the first direct injunction in the letter. "To love" as used here approaches the Old Testament meaning: to prefer something over something else for the sake of one's own satisfaction and advantage, to love A more than B. It thus does not correspond to the Johannine conception of loving as an outflow of God's love. See further the Interpretation.

the world. More than half of all New Testament passages containing the word "world" (*kosmos*) are found in the Johannine writings. From a dualistic perspective, "the world" takes on a powerfully negative connotation, especially in John 13–17 and 1 John; this deviates from the positive perception in the Old Testament as well as in Greek texts. The world in the Johannine writings is at enmity with God and his people; it is evil and doomed to destruction. "The whole world lies under the power of the evil one" (1 John 5:19). The devil is called "the ruler of this world" (John 12:31; 14:30). However, in some places the word "world" stands for the entire human race, which God wants to save (John 3:16; 4:42; 6:33, 51; 8:12; 1 John 2:2; 4:14).

Some commentators want to explain this double use of *kosmos* in John 13–17 in terms of the experiences of the Johannine Christians: first an enthusiastic testimony in their Jewish environment to Jesus as the world's savior, then a more and more negative attitude as the hoped-for result did not materialize, resistance against them increased, and none of their compatriots wanted to believe in Jesus as the Messiah, the son of God. When the light came into the world, people loved darkness more than the light (John 3:16–21; 12:27–43).

Here in v. 15, "the world" can have yet a third meaning, the material world and everything that belongs to it, the values, related to the concept "mammon" in Matt 6:24, that can lure humanity away from God. The following qualification, "the things in the world," can point in this direction. The expression in Gkt, *ta en tōi kosmōi*, is another substantive prepositional phrase, like "him who was there from the beginning" in v. 13c and 14f. According to early Christian parenesis, the believers are to keep themselves "unstained by the world" (Jas 1:27). "Friendship with the world is enmity with God" (Jas 4:4). See further the Interpretation.

the love of the Father. The context provides a good reason for reading the phrase "love for the Father" (objective genitive). Translations vary. See the note "the love of God" on 1 John 2:5.

16. all that is in the world. What now follows is a somewhat parenthetical listing of three examples.

the desire of the flesh. Gkt genitive construction is followed by two further, similar constructions: "the desire of the eyes" and "the pride of life" (NRSV: "pride in riches"). How are we to interpret these three genitives? Do they have the same function in all three phrases? Is there a subordination or super-ordination within this little catalog of vices? The answer depends on what meanings are operative in the various words. Translators and commentators give many suggestions.

The word for "desire" in Gkt (*epithymia*) is a neutral term that can be used both of something good (Phil 1:23; Luke 22:15) and of something evil (John 8:44). In the LXX it is mostly the latter (Exod 20:17). In Philo, desire is the root of evil in human beings.

In the first phrase, "desire of the flesh"—often wrongly restricted to a question of sex—the genitive is very certainly subjective, "what the flesh desires," or alternatively a genitive of origin, "desire that comes from the flesh." This reading can be supported from general usage in the NT (Rom 1:24; Rev 18:14) and from the function of the genitive in the following expressions.

The question, however, is what is meant by "flesh" (*sarx*) in this context. In the Greek Hellenistic tradition *sarx* refers as a rule to the most physical aspect of human existence: eating, drinking, having sex, etc. In an Old Testament connection "flesh" stands for humanity in its weakness, humanity as something other than God. Paul seems mostly to be following the Greek tradition when he speaks of "the desire of the flesh" (Rom 13:14; Gal 5:16–17, 24). See also 1 Pet 4:2–3 and 2 Pet 2:10. If we take account of the view of humanity that comes forward in 1 John—and we avoid both the restriction to sex and the traditional Pauline exegesis—the meaning becomes everything that satisfies human need as such; Raymond Brown translates it more positively as "human nature full of desire." Cf. a neutral connotation for *sarx* in, e.g., John 1:14 and 1 John 4:3.

the desire of the eyes. The phrase occurs nowhere else in the OT, NT, or in the Qumran texts. The genitive here must be subjective, "what the eyes desire," or possibly a genitive of origin, "the desires that come from the eyes." The question is what is meant. The OT gives examples of haughtiness (Prov 6:17); greed (Eccl 4:8); sexual desire (Gen 39:7). The question, however, is whether the phrase in a Johannine context—like "the

First John

desire of the flesh"—does not have a somewhat wider sense: something seen that can awaken desire or that can lead to sin (cf. Gen 3:6; Num 15:39). "None will continue in a willful heart and thus be seduced, not by his heart, neither by his eyes, nor yet by his lower nature" (1QS 5:4–5).

the pride in riches. The expression in Gkt, "pride of life," is difficult to interpret because the meanings of both "pride" (*alazoneia*) and "life" (*bios*) are hard to make sense of in this context. The phrase is usually interpreted as pride in one's life and resources, mostly wealth and possessions (objective genitive), in a wider sense, boasting over what one is, has, and owns. The word *alazoneia* means pride, arrogance, boasting/boastfulness. The word *bios* means livelihood, what one has to live on, sustenance, or life. See 1 John 3:17 and Titus 2:2. If we wish to see a subjective genitive here as well, which is unnecessary, the expression refers to a dangerous confidence in external security. People have life and what life provides, and they are content with it.

It comes not from the Father but from the world. There are two clauses in Gkt: "it is not from (*ek*) the Father, but it is from (*ek*) the world." The words "be from" (*einai ek*), imply both origin and belonging. The phrase is used often in the dualistic language of 1 John—55 of some 80 times in the NT. It is most often used positively: of/from God/the Father, of/from heaven, from above, of the truth, or in reference to being Jesus' disciples. There are three negative phrases with this construction: of/from the devil, of/from the world, and from below.

17. is passing away. The present tense in Greek normally indicates ongoing activity. The same verb and verb form are used of the darkness in 1 John 2:8.

its desire. This phrase ends a long list of related expressions: "the world," "the things in the world," "all that is in the world," "the desire of the flesh," "the desire of the eyes," "the pride in riches," "the desire of the world" and "the word." Is this only a rhetorical accumulation of words in order to emphasize the exhortation "Do not love the world"—the section has a strong rhetorical flavor—or does it also intend to give some teaching on how dangerous the world is? I have chosen the latter alternative above.

the one who does the will of God. Literally, "but the one doing God's will." The participle construction is typical in 1 John. See, e.g., 1 John 2:3–11 and 3:4–10. The phrase "do God's will"—with the change from the Father in the foregoing to God—is nonetheless a typical biblical formulation.

remains forever. The phrase is used in the OT (LXX) mostly of God and what belongs to God (Pss 9:8; 102:13; Isa 40:8). The same words are used of David's seed in Ps 89:37 and of Messiah in John 12:34. The one who keeps Jesus' words shall "never see death" (John 8:51).

Analysis

1. Delimitations and Structure of the Text

The short paragraphs 1 John 2:12–14 and 2:15–17 are difficult to fit into the letter's thematic structure. I believe that they have mostly a rhetorical function, which is reflected in the title I have given to this chapter: "Comfort and Admonition." In this they resemble traditional characterizations of the purpose of preaching: to comfort, teach, admonish, and warn.

I read vv. 12–14 as a powerful assurance and encouragement for the listeners. See point 2, below. The author closes the section 1 John 2:3–11 in rather dark colors: the negative alternative, hating one's brother, is mentioned before love for the brothers in the last paragraph, vv. 9–11, and is intensified through expanded repetition in v. 11. The darkness afflicts the one who hates his fellow believers, but the letter's recipients are strong, they have overcome the evil one, they have forgiveness of sins, they have learned to know the one who was there from the beginning, etc. Before the antichrists are brought into the scene in 1 John 2:18, the addressees need a firm reminder of their own identity and their own situation.

The comforting words in vv. 12–14 also prepare the listeners for the first direct admonition in the letter, v. 15a; it is partly thematic in introducing the contrast between God/the Father and the evil one, and partly emotional in the many positive words. As in 2 and 3 John, the author displays considerable circumspection in his attempt to reach his readers. The entire section issues in the negative implications of law-observance: do not love the world, which continues the negative theme in 1 John 2:9–11. The words about the Father's love in v. 15d are also reminiscent of the beginning of the earlier section (1 John 2:3–5), as well as are the closing words on doing God's will (v. 17b). For this reason, some commentators want to combine 1 John 2:3–17 into a unity. It begins with knowing God and keeping his commandments, specified more closely as the requirement to love one's fellow believers, and it ends in the admonition against loving the world and doing the will of God.

The section 1 John 2:12–17 is defined mostly by its form and its surroundings, the two clearly marked units 1 John 2:3–11 and 2:18–27. The structure of the first paragraph, vv. 12–14, is more closely described under the next point.

2. Rhetorical Analysis of vv. 12–14

Expositors have had a difficult time coming to agreement on these three verses, not least because the verses deviate in form from the rest of the letter, and in terms of content they do not seem to fit the context. See above, point 1. The author has a predilection for saying things three times in varying ways (e.g., in 1 John 1:6—2:2, in 2:4–11, and in 2:16bcd). Here now, with a well-structured repetition, he presents the readers with a double set of triples, vv. 12–13 and 14. This is clear in the Translation Display for the section and does not need to be described further here. On the other hand, there are reasons to take up certain generally acknowledged difficulties in these verses before determining their function as a whole.

The first problem is to discern how many groups are being addressed. Is it one, two, or three? All three alternatives are well represented in the history of interpretation. The division may have to do with three different levels of age or with grades of maturity, e.g., the newly baptized, those who have made some progress in their spiritual life, and those who are mature Christians. That we are dealing here—as someone has suggested—with three different offices within the Johannine community, corresponding to deacons, elders, and bishops, is extremely unlikely.

The theory that there is only one group—so, e.g., Augustine, Dodd, de la Potterie, and Marshall—is contradicted by the order in which the three descriptors occur: children, fathers, young people. Similarly, the usual use of "little children" (*teknia* or *paidia*) for all those who are receiving the letter is an argument against three groups— as, e.g., Origen, Bruce, and Stott suggest. The same can be said regarding the descriptions given to each.

The best of reasons speak for a two-fold division—thus Westcott, Wrede, B. Weiss, Loisy, Bultmann, Schnackenburg, and some other contemporary exegetes. All the readers are addressed first, and then they are divided up into groups, fathers and young people, i.e., older and younger within the Johannine community. This is a typical stylistic device in ancient rhetoric, called *distributio*. It is also a common model for presenting God's people in the Old Testament (Exod 10:9; Josh 6:21; Isa 20:4; and Ezek 9:6): first the people as a whole, then the old and the young. The Septuagint uses the words *presbyteroi/presbytai* and *neaniskoi*. See also Acts 2:17–21; 1 Tim 5:1–2; Titus 2:1–8, and 1 Pet 5:1–5. In a covenant perspective the nearest parallel is Jer 31:34, where it is said that all shall know God, from the greatest to the least; in the Septuagint it reads, "both small (*mikroi*) and great (*megaloi*)." What is said here of the fathers gives the impression that they have been Christians for a longer time and thus stand out as both older and more mature than the young ones. The difficult crisis in the Johannine fellowship can be partly attributed to a generational problem. See chap. 12, points 2–4.

A second problem concerns why this model is used twice. The audience is addressed in a fourfold way, twice with "little children" and twice with the combination "fathers" and "young people." Such forms of repetition constitute a common rhetorical device, the so-called *conduplicatio*. Repetitions are thought to reinforce, to give life to speech and to increase emotional engagement.

The use of certain variations (*expolitio*) can be even more effective. What is said about the recipients as a whole—"children"—has differing forms in v. 12 and v. 14. The first utterance leads readers' thoughts to 1 John 1:5—2:2, the other to 2:3–11. The words about the young people are expanded in v. 15, compared with v. 13. The words for child differ in v. 12 and v. 14, different grammatical forms of "father" (*patēr*) are used in vv. 13b, 14c, and 14e. All these many variations within a given pattern are chosen in order to affect the audience positively, even if a later reader may possibly think of them more as distracting. The entire letter has an undeniably powerful repetitive character, but here the repetitions are clearest and most frequent.

Included among the varying repetitions is the tense of "write" in the two triads, first the present (vv. 12–13), then the aorist (v. 14). The question is why. Sometimes commentators refer to the so-called epistolary aorist: the letter writer uses a temporal form that corresponds to the time when the letter is to be read. See as examples 1 Cor 9:15; Gal 6:11; Rom 15:15. But why a change at this particular place? Up to this point the author has been using the present (1 John 1:4; 2:1, 7, 8), but after 2:12–14 he uses only the aorist (1 John 2:21; 26; 5:13), with no apparent difference. Some have suggested that the aorist in v. 14 refers to other texts, e.g., to 2 John, the Gospel of John, or certain parts or even earlier drafts of 1 John. But this is rather unlikely. None of the suggested parallels makes sense in v. 14. What remains then is the conclusion that it is a stylistic variation—as is so often the case in Johannine writings. It can be more precisely described as a rhetorical variation. Ancient rhetoricians discuss how differing tenses can be used to make a speech more lively and engaging. I have already pointed out other rhetorical devices in these verses: *distributio, conduplicatio,* and *expolitio.* All of them reinforce and energize the encouraging and comforting words in vv. 12–14.

In light of this paragraph's powerful rhetorical character, it becomes easier to decide whether the word *hoti* introducing the six statements about the recipients is to be taken as a logical conjunction "since/for" (thus the Vulgate, KJV and much of the English translation tradition, as well as commentators such as Westcott, B. Weiss, Plummer, Brooke, Dodd, Bultmann, Spicq, and Marshall), or as a general introductory "that" (so Bengel, Bonsirven, Noack, Malatesta, Schnackenburg, Brown, and others). Both alternatives are possible. In the Translation Display, the *hoti* of the Greek text is indicated by a colon, but if we must make a choice, introductory "that" is clearly preferable, not least because of the paragraph's generally encouraging character. The same thing applies to 1 John 2:21. In statements with "write," there is a consistently positive tone, and in these verses the author commends and praises his audience. He reassures and comforts, an expressed aim of the entire letter (1 John 5:13).

Based on what has been said above, it is easier to understand how vv. 12–14 fit into the context. There are a number of substantive connections both in the foregoing text (forgiveness, sin, knowing the Father/the Son, from the beginning, God's word, abiding in) and in the following text (the name of Jesus Christ, the evil one, overcomer). But the most important factor is the verses' rhetorical function. Following the stern words in 1 John 2:9–11 about those who hate their fellow believers, these verses turn to the audience in a positive way, extolling their status and instilling them with courage, strengthening the affective relationship between sender and recipients in advance of the first serious admonition in the letter, that they must not love the world (vv. 15–17), and preparing for the coming section regarding the devastating

First John

split between Johannine Christians (1 John 2:18–27). The closer the author comes to describing the recipients' delicate situation—the risk of relapse/backsliding—and to making the decisive division between "they" and "we," the more cautious he seems to become and the more concerned that what he says will come across to the recipients in a positive way. Here again we have the same sort of authority as in 2 and 3 John. See, e.g., the interpretation of 3 John 1, 13–15.

3. Early Christian Parenesis and vv. 15–17

The formulations in vv. 15–17 are not as Johannine as the rest of the letter is, but they can be interpreted in a Johannine direction. Un-Johannine elements occur in other places as well. See, e.g., the interpretation of 2 John 8.

The expectation of the world's destruction belongs to the Jewish and Christian parenesis of the two ways, and it is also found in Paul's apocalyptic argument in 1 Cor 7:31: "the present form of this world is passing away." The words "do the will of God" (1 John 2:17b) function as a traditional formulation in Jewish and Christian preaching. To speak of "desire," *(epithymia)* does not characterize Johannine writings, but it does mark general parenetic sections as in Eph 2:3; 1 Pet 2:11, and *Did.* 1:4. The same is true of the catalog of vices that occurs in mini-form at v. 16bcd. Parallels to vv. 15–17 are primarily found in such texts as Eph 5:11–16 and Jas 4. These expressions of early Christian parenesis within a thoroughly Johannine context give a dual character to these verses that influences the interpretation of the text in a number of ways. See further the Notes and Interpretation.

Interpretation

1. Those Who Have Conquered the Evil One (2:12–14)

Those who "hate" their fellow believers walk in the darkness, and the darkness makes them blind. They do not know where they are going. This dismal close to the section 2:3–11 would easily serve as a transition to 2:18–27, the introduction of those who have gone astray and left the Johannine fellowship. They are also described as those who are leading the letter's recipients astray (2:27). But the Elder breaks off his presentation to encourage his readers by reminding them of what they already have (2:12–14). The sons of light are set in opposition to the sons of darkness. The form of this paragraph deviates considerably from the remainder of the letter, even though the Elder continues to permit the domination of triads, in fact more here than anywhere else in the letter. See the Translation Display and the Notes on it. The interpretations of the section are thus unusually numerous, and in the Analysis, point 2, I have attempted to list various alternatives and to take a position on them. Here I argue my own interpretation.

By different rhetorical means (repetitions, varying vocatives, changes in the manner of expression, etc.) the Elder encourages and comforts his readers and reassures them that they are on the right path. See the Analysis, point 2. In a threefold way, repeated in two paragraphs, he describes what their faith stands upon and shows that they really do have fellowship with God through Jesus Christ. First he addresses all of them with the words "little children," then he divides them into "fathers" and "young people," i.e., into the older and the younger. What he says to them varies somewhat: to the children (that is, to all the addressees) he says, "your sins are forgiven on account of his name" and "you know the Father" (v. 12c and v. 14c); to the fathers, "you know him who was there from the beginning" (v. 13c and v. 14f); and to the young people, "you have conquered the evil one" and "you are strong and God's word abides in you and you have overcome the evil one" (v. 13f and v. 14ijk). The last portion of the two paragraphs thus ends in victory over the evil one, an idea that easily leads to the struggle with the world that is carried on both within them and outside of them (vv. 15–17). This second part of the section 2:12–17 is connected to what is said in 2:3–11 about God's commandments and about the darkness that is passing away, and to what is said in the letter's introduction (1:2) about eternal life.

The words to the "little children" in v. 12c and v. 14c clearly take up 1:5—2:2 (the forgiveness of sin) and 2:3–11 (knowing God), respectively, and they bind 1:5—2:17 together into a longer unit. In addition, we note once more a covenant model behind the statements in the letter. Jer 31:31–34 is especially in view when it is said that God will establish a new covenant with his people "after those days." God shall forgive their sins and they shall all know God. Forgiveness of sins and knowing God. The same combination characterizes the renewed people of God at Qumran (1QS 11:14–16). See further Appendix 9, A Renewed Covenant. God's son has come and given understanding to the recipients of the letter so that they know the true God and through the Son have eternal life (5:20; 5:11–13). Eternal life is defined in the Gospel as knowing the only true God and the one whom God has sent, Jesus Christ (John 17:3).

The addition of "on account of his name" can be taken as evidence that the forgiveness of sin and the knowledge of God belong together with the recipients' baptism. Baptism in the name of Jesus Christ and forgiveness of sin are combined in the depiction of the first Christians. "Repent, and be baptized every one of you in the name of Jesus Christ so that your sins may be forgiven" (Acts 2:38). "Everyone who believes in him receives forgiveness of sins through his name" (Act 10:43). Within the Johannine community, baptism entailed a confession that, according to the aims of both the Gospel and the letter, had to do with the name of Jesus (John 20:31; 1 John 5:13). The fundamental message in the renewed covenant contains as its first article the commandment to "believe in the name of his son Jesus Christ" (3:23). Cf. John 3:19. Thus what is said here to the "children," i.e., to the entire Johannine community, very likely belongs to "what they heard from the beginning" when they came to faith.

First John

The words to the fathers in the two paragraphs, v. 13c and 14f, are identical and refer back to the introduction and especially to "what was there from the beginning" (1:1a). In place of the many verbs of perception, here the author uses the basic word "to know." See 2:3–5. At some point they came to know Jesus Messiah, God's son, and they continue to know him. The use of the perfect tense (see the note) and the vocative "fathers" gives the impression that they have known Jesus a long time. This is implied as well in the formulation "from the beginning" (see the note), which very likely, as in 1:1a, refers to Jesus, his person, words and deeds, which were there from the beginning. It was with him that all this new circumstance came into being. The emphasis is not on the Son's pre-existence, but on his having become a human being and on his work as a human being. The Life became visible to human beings. "The fathers" seem to belong to the same generation as the Elder, to judge by the nearness they have to "what was there from the beginning." It is said of Jesus' disciples that they too can bear witness because they have been with Jesus "from the beginning" (John 15:27).

The words to the young people are mostly followed up by what is said in 2:15–16, even if the contrast between God and the evil one corresponds to the contrasts between light and darkness, truth and lie, and love and hate in the earlier discussion. "You have conquered the evil one" (vv. 13–14) is justified in the second round by the statements "you are strong" and "the word of God abides in you." Their strength has its source in the faith (5:4), i.e., in their faith in Jesus as the Jewish messiah, the son of God (3:23), something that obviously belongs to "what was there in the beginning." This can also be said about "the word of God," one of the expressions for "the message that we have heard from him and proclaim to you" (1:5, 10; 2:5). It is "the word that you have heard" (2:7), which among other things contains the admonition that they must love one another (3:11): to believe and to love (3:23). These encouraging and strengthening words in 2:12–14 all seem to have their roots in the earlier tradition that the Elder stands for and that he delivers to them. They are a part of the gospel, the good news, within the Johannine fellowship. The victor's crown of life is theirs when they hold fast to the tradition.

2. Do Not Love the World (2:15–17)

The young among the addressees have conquered the evil one. It is in connection with these words that all the addressees are warned not to love the world, the first explicit admonition in the letter. Later more will be said about conquering the world (5:4–5). In a dualistic framework, the tension between the world and God becomes even stronger. The world with everything in it is dangerous because it can lead a person to fall away from God. This is probably what has happened with the apostates in the letter. In any case, they have abandoned the God who became visible in Jesus the Messiah, God's son (2:18–27). Perhaps they loved honor from other people more than honor from God, like many authorities who were afraid of being excluded from the synagogue (John 12:42–43). They were clinging to their earthly possessions and did not wish to share them with other members of the community in a situation where it could be perilous to be associated with the Jesus-believers (1 John 3:16–17). This is in any case a potential explanation for the appearance of these verses at this point in the letter. Here and there the formulations resemble more the Old Testament than they do Johannine style. See the notes on these verses.

As a first impression, loving the world can be understood as loving the world more than God, as is the case in John 3:19: "The light has come into the world, and people loved darkness rather than light." It was because of their deeds. This choice led to devastating consequences. According to the summarization of the Johannine message, these people have no part in eternal life; they go lost (John 3:16–21). Loving the world leads to falling away from God, the most serious thing that can happen to a believer. The world plays the same role here as idols do in the Old Testament covenant formulas. "You shall have no other gods before me," says the Lord in Exod 20:3–4. In a dualistic conceptual world, the oppositions become even more pronounced. The entire world is in the power of the evil one (5:19), even though the judgment over the world and its prince was delivered when Jesus died and returned to the Father (John 12:31). In v. 16ef the Father and the world are placed in direct opposition to one another. There is no way both to love the world and to love the Father (v. 15cd). Love of the Father engenders in the Jesus-believers love for their fellow believers, not love for the world.

According to the progression hypothesis, the secessionists have fastened on the idea that God loved the world (John 3:16) and have gone out into the world and spoken the language of the world. They "loved the world." They focused on the incarnation, i.e., on the fact that God demonstrated his love by sending his only son, but they gave no thought to what then happened to the Son and the significance that his death had for the salvation of humanity. Against this the Elder could object that the message of love from God and Jesus first of all had to do with love for one's fellow believers and that according to the Johannine tradition the world hated Jesus (John 15:18–25). Jesus did not pray for the world (John 17:9). At bottom, the words in 2:15–17 are about a struggle over the right interpretation of the Gospel of John.

Using three examples to illustrate a point is common in many contexts, and the author of the letter too is fond of threes. See also in this regard v. 16bcd. There are further related triads in contemporary texts: to love God "with all your heart, and with all your soul, and with all your mind" (Matt 22:37), "desire of money, or glory, or pleasure" (Philo, *Decal.* 28 [153]), a formulation reminiscent of what Justin Martyr says, "not from love of money, of glory, or of pleasure" (*Dialog with Trypho*, 82.4). One of the Qumran texts speaks of three traps that Belial uses to catch Israel: fornication, wealth, and defiling the temple (CD 4:15–18).

In our text, "all that is in the world" is illustrated by the desire of the flesh, the desire of the eyes, and the pride in riches—to use the NRSV rendering. The more specific meaning of these phrases is difficult to determine. In the notes above, I have presented various alternatives. These expressions are frequently compared with sexual desire, carnal desire, and desire for money. I have argued for a more neutral meaning, such as "what the body desires."

"Flesh" (*sarx*) in Johannine texts stands for simple humanness in distinction from God or God's Spirit. The word became "flesh" (John 1:14). The Messiah came "in the flesh" (1 John 4:2); people must be born again through the Spirit (John 3:3–4). What is born of the flesh is flesh, what is born of the spirit is spirit. The formulation "desire of the flesh" is open to both a positive and a negative reading. What the body desires can lead a person to falling away from God.

The eyes see what is visible, but not what is invisible. The desires communicated through them can have the same negative effect as the desires that come from the body. There is a duplicity within human beings, something that in Jewish texts was described in the doctrine of the two inclinations and in Qumran texts is defined as two spirits within a person: "He created humankind to rule over the world, appointing for them two spirits in which to walk until the time ordained for His visitation. These are the spirits of truth and falsehood" (1QS 3:17–19). Jesus Sirach prays, "O Lord, Father and God of my life, do not give me haughty eyes, and remove evil desire from me. Let neither gluttony nor lust overcome me, and do not give me over to shameless passion" (Sir 23:4–6).

The last item in v. 16 has to do with a person's life, what a person is (status) and has (possessions). See the note. What a person has of riches and social position can lead to pride and boasting, to arrogance and overconfidence in the material. The sense of it can perhaps be stated as "what pride boasts in." Most often, however, it is translated something like "pride in this life's goods."

These three examples of "all that is in the world" can lead a Jesus-believer to fall away from the new faith in Jesus as the Messiah, God's son. Humanity finds itself in a conflict between the world and God. Everything that is in the world is of the world and not of the Father (v. 16ef). According to Jesus' intercessory prayer in John 17, his disciples do not belong to the world, even though they are still in the world. "I am not asking you to take them out of the world, but I ask you to protect them from the evil one" (or "from evil"; John 17:15).

The young people in the Johannine fellowship, and rhetorically the others as well, are addressed as victors over the evil one (vv. 13f and 14f). The victors are victorious through holding fast to God's word (v. 14j) and through their faith in Jesus as the messiah, the son of God (4:4), but if because of the world and its allurements they fall away from this faith, they will go lost. The world is passing away (v. 17a); eternal life belongs to those who do God's will, to those who love the Father and follow his commandments (v. 17b).

5

1 John 2:18–27: Schism in the New Community

Translation Display

18a	Dear children
18b	it is the last hour
18c	and as you have heard that antichrist is coming
18d	so now many antichrists have appeared
18e	whence we know that it is the last hour.
19a	They went out from us
19b	but they were not of us
19c	for if they had been of us
19d	they would have remained with us.
19e	But this happened so that they might be exposed:
19f	none of them is of us.
20a	*You* have an anointing from the Holy One
20b	and you all have insight.
21a	I am not writing to you
21b	that you do not know the truth
21c	but that you do know it
21d	and that no lie comes of the truth.
22a	Who is the liar
22b	if not the one who denies that Jesus is the Messiah?
22c	He is the antichrist
22d	the one who denies the Father and the Son.
23a	Anyone who denies the Son does not have the Father either.
23b	He who confesses the Son also has the Father.
24a	As for *you*, let what you heard from the beginning remain in you.

First John

24b	If what you heard from the beginning remains in you
24c	then you too will remain in the Son and in the Father.
25a	And this is the promise that he himself promised us:
25b	eternal life.
26	I am writing this to you about those who are deceiving you.
27a	As for *you*, the anointing you received from him remains in you
27b	and you have no need that anyone should teach you.
27c	Indeed, as his anointing teaches you about all things
27d	and it is true
27e	and it is not a lie
27f	and as it has taught you:
27g	remain in it.

Notes

2:18. Dear children. Gkt *paidia*. See the note "children" on 1 John 2:1 and 14. The word here indicates the beginning of a new section.

it is the last hour. Alternatively, "these are the last times." The same assertion occurs at the end of the verse and thereby forms an *inclusio*.

The word for "hour" (*hōra*) lacks the article in Gkt, but it should nonetheless be rendered definite. The absence of the article can be explained in several ways, e.g., that it is not used with abstract nouns and that *hōra* in John's Gospel does not have the article when it is modified by an ordinal number. The expression "the last hour"—which in the NT occurs only in 1 John—is most readily interpreted as that period of time that issues in "the last day," a phrase that in John 12:48 is used of the Judgment Day and in John 6:39, 40, 44, 54; 11:24 of the day of resurrection. The author of 1 John concluded that the end of time was near. In the OT we find the formulation "at the end of days" (LXX "in the last [of the] days"), in Qumran and the NT "in the last days" (1QSa 1:1; Acts 2:17; Heb 1:2; Jas 5:3).

antichrist. The word is a transliteration of Gkt *antichristos*. The prefix *anti-* in this sort of word formation can mean either "in place of" or "against." The Greek word *antistratēgos* can, e.g., mean both one who stands in for a general and a general who mutinies. An *antididaskalos* is a teacher who turns against others. An *antichristos* is either someone who promotes himself as Christ/Messiah or who opposes Christ. The context in 1 John speaks for the latter meaning. Cf. also *antitheos* as one who opposes God. See further the Interpretation.

is coming. Gkt has the present "comes." In John the Messiah/Christ is described several times as "he/the one who comes" (John 1:15, 27; 12:13). Martha acknowledges that

Jesus is the messiah, the son of God, "who is coming into the world" (John 11:27; present participle in Gkt). Christ and antichrist are described in mutually similar ways.

antichrists. According to v. 26, the Elder has in view people who lead the letter's recipients astray and deceive them; according to 4:1 the reference is to false prophets. They do not recognize Jesus as the Christ/Messiah.

whence. Gkt does not have the usual "by this," but instead a relative adverb, *hothen*, which means "by which," or "from which." See the note at 1 John 2:3. Clauses that begin with this word function to draw a conclusion.

19. They went out from us. Gkt emphasizes "from us" (*ex hēmōn*) by placing it first in the clause. These two words, which occur four times in v. 19, also bring the verse to a close. The verb is in the aorist (hybrid aorist: a second aorist verb with a first-aorist ending), which would indicate that the reference is to an act in the past when these people left the Johannine fellowship. In later exegetical literature they are frequently called "the secessionists."

The word "us" here stands for the community surrounding the author, i.e., the Johannine Christians.

were not of us. Gkt has the construction "to be of" (*einai ek*), which implies both origin and belonging. The same construction occurs at the end of the verse. See note at the end of 1 John 2:16.

if. In Gkt, "if" (*ei*) is followed by the imperfect with the pluperfect in the apodosis, implying a merely hypothetical case (contrary-to-fact).

But this happened so that they might be exposed. Gkt uses the elliptical *all' hina* ("but in order that"), a common construction with *hina*—the words "they went out from us" or, more generally, "this happened," are missing before *hina*. The following words are personal, "they might be exposed," rather than an impersonal "it might be revealed." The word in Gkt can be read either as a passive ("they might be exposed") or as a middle ("they might reveal [regarding themselves] . . ."). Whichever is the case, an explanatory "that" (*hoti*) follows, marked by a colon in the Translation Display.

none of them. The formulation in Gkt is more literally, "not all." Similar constructions occur in 1 John 2:21d, 23a; 3:15b; and 5:18a; presumably they are influenced by Semitic speech.

20. You. Gkt has an emphatic "and you" (*kai hymeis*) at the beginning of the clause. It can mean "you too" (and not just these "anti-messiahs" who left the fellowship) or "but you, on the other hand" (in contrast to those just mentioned) or perhaps simply a stressed "you" (without marked comparison). See 1 John 4:14a. See also the notes at the beginning of vv. 24 and 27.

have an anointing from. From the Johannine perspective, the word in Gkt for "anointing" (*chrisma*) very likely has in view the Spirit, i.e., the spirit of truth that mediates the truth. See the Analysis, point 3.

the Holy One. Probably the reference is to Jesus and not to God. See v. 27. Whichever way we read it, however, the point is that there is a close cooperation between Jesus and God. See the Analysis, point 3.

and. The word indicates here the result of the preceding clause: "so that." See further the note "but . . . remain in him" on v. 27 below.

you all have insight. For "you have insight" the Gkt has the usual word for "know" (*oidate*), followed by "all" (*pantes*; masculine nominative plural)—thus, "you all know." According to other mss, instead of "all," the text reads "everything" (*panta*; neuter accusative plural), thus: "you know all things," knowledge that results from the fact that they have the anointing. It is not easy to discern what originally stood in the text.

The majority of manuscripts, especially from a later time, as well as early translators have "all things" (*panta*), which therefore is found in all older versions. This variant is also supported by the fact that the verb used here usually has an object. At the same time, the reading "(you) all" (*pantes*) is very early and is supported by the weighty manuscripts Codex Vaticanus and Codex Sinaiticus and by an early Coptic version. It is also supported by the context—the anointing leads to all of them having insight—and it is easier to explain how *pantes* became *panta* under the influence of v. 27c and of John 14:26 and 16:30 than vice versa. For this reason I elect to go with this reading. Moreover it yields a good parallel to what is said of the new covenant in Jeremiah 31: "They shall all know (*pantes*) me." See further the Analysis, point 3.

21. I am not writing. Gkt: "I do not write to you," i.e., the same formulation as in 1 John 2:14 plus "not." Possibly the word "write" refers to the letter as a whole. See the note on 1 John 2:14.

that . . . .that . . . that. Gkt has three clauses all beginning with *hoti*. The meaning can be "that" or "because" in all three cases, or a combination of the type "that . . . that . . . because." The triple "that" is grammatically the simplest (whereby the that-clauses are objects of "write") and is appropriate to the verse's encouraging and reassuring character. As in 1 John 2:12–14, I thus interpret *hoti* all three times as "that." See the Analysis for 1 John 2:12–17, point 2. Several interpreters, however, read the third that-clause as dependent on "know" in the second clause and add a "know" or something corresponding to it in the third.

you do not know. Gkt has the verb *eidenai* ("recognize, know, have insight"), as in v. 20b and in the next clause, "that you do know it" (v. 21c).

no lie. More literally: "every lie ... not." This is perhaps an intensification: not even a single lie.

comes of. Gkt phrase "is of" indicates both origin and belonging. See note "comes not from ... the world" at 1 John 2:16.

22. Who is ... if not ... ? The rhetorical question places the emphasis on the final words: "the one who denies that Jesus is the Messiah."

liar. Gkt has the word in the definite form, and some therefore interpret it as "the Liar," i.e., as a title parallel with Antichrist and perhaps also with the Deceiver in 2 John 7. See the note there. According to John 8:44, the devil is a liar and the father of lies. To make God "a liar" (1 John 1:10; 5:10) is to make him like the devil.

In Qumran, the community's chief opponent is called "the Man of Lies," who leads astray many people with his deceptions, so that they "preferred worthless things and did not listen to the "interpreter [*mēlīts*] of knowledge" (4QPs37 1:17–19). The Hebrew term *mēlīts*, which can mean translator, interpreter, but also teacher and mediator, defender, advocate, is an excellent background for the use of *paraklētos* to refer to the Spirit in the Johannine writings. The liar stands as a counterpart to the spirit of the truth. See also 1 John 4:1–6.

denies that Jesus is the Messiah. Gkt inserts a negation in the clause that functions to strengthen the word "deny." There is no corresponding form in English. On the confession of Jesus as Christ/Messiah, see Appendix 14, Jesus as Messiah, God's Son.
23. Anyone who denies. Literally, "everyone who denies," a rhetorical strengthening of the related term in v. 22, "the one who denies."

have the Father. The peculiar expression (even in English) "to have" a person occurs in three contexts in the letters of John: to have the Father (1 John 2:23); to have the Son (1 John 5:12); and to have God and to have the Father and the Son (2 John 9). All three contexts concern the true confession of Christ. To "have God" expresses a very close fellowship between God and human beings, with a background in the idea of the covenant. See the Interpretation for 2 John 7–9 and Appendix 9, A Renewed Covenant.

confesses. For the verb in Gkt, *homologein*, see note on 1 John 1:9.

24. let what you heard from the beginning remain in you. Literally in Gkt: "You, what you heard from the beginning, may it remain in you." "You" at the beginning of the sentence, taken up subsequently in the phrase "in you"—thus constituting a so-called *casus pendens*; see the note on 1 John 2:5—focuses on and emphasizes the recipients. What they heard from the beginning has, like the anointing, a divine origin and divine content (1 John 1:1–5). See further Appendix 10, What you Heard From the Beginning.

First John

you too will remain in. Gkt has the verb *menein en,* which occurs five times in vv. 24 and 27; it can carry the connotation of "always" in contexts like this—perhaps especially in the future, as here—and some translations supply that element. See Appendix 15, God in Them and They in God.

25. And this is. The expression is a typical Johannine introductory phrase that moves the argument further along. See the note on 1 John 1:5. It is possible that the word "this" refers to the foregoing. Being in the Son and in the Father is a form of eternal life. "What you heard from the beginning" is interpreted as a promise that was brought to reality through Jesus. The word "this" would then function to point both backward (anaphorically) and forward (cataphorically).

that he himself promised. Gkt has here a so-called cognate accusative for the verb "promise," literally: "the promise that he promised"—the technical term for this is *figura etymologica.* There is both a present and a future eschatology in the letter (1 John 2:28—3:3). If I must choose a reference for "he," I prefer it to be Jesus, who has a prominent role in the context as the focus of denial and confession. But the argument itself can point to God as subject. See Appendix 8, He: God or Jesus or Both.

eternal life. See the note on 1 John 1:2.

26. I am writing this to you. Literally: "these things have I written to you." In Gkt, the verb is in the aorist and "this" refers especially to what has been said already in vv. 18–25 (anaphoric reference). See the notes on "write" at 1 John 1:4; 2:1 and 12. An anaphoric "this" sometimes occurs at the end of a section (1 John 1:4; 2:1).

those who are deceiving you. Gkt has a present participle, which in the context can carry a conative sense (wish to, try to do something). The description of the false prophets in the letter, however, can suggest the translation, "those who deceive you." See further the note "many false prophets have gone out into the world," at 1 John 4:1.

27. As for you. Gkt has "and you," as in v. 20. Thus this verse too begins with an example of *casus pendens.* See the notes above at vv. 20 and 24.

anointing. The author presumably has in mind the Spirit, i.e., the spirit of truth who mediates the truth to Jesus' disciples. See the Analysis, point 3. In v. 27 the emphasis is on the teaching of this Spirit, on what they heard from the beginning, on the "teaching about the Messiah" (2 John 9).

and you have no need that anyone should teach you. "And" at the beginning of the sentence makes a syntactic coordination to the sentence before but a semantic subordination, marking the consequence, "so that." Gkt uses the conjunction *hina* to introduce what is not needed. For this unusual construction with an explanatory *hina,* see also John 2:25; 16:30. The idea of no need of teachers is found nowhere else in the Bible. The closest parallel occurs in Jer 31:31–34. See Appendix 9, A Renewed Covenant.

1 John 2:18–27: Schism in the New Community

Indeed, as his anointing teaches you about all things and it is true and it is not a lie and as it taught you: remain in it. The sentence structure in Gkt, to say the least, is convoluted. It is not clear whether there is one sentence or there are two, nor what relationship exists among the five clauses. A more literal rendering looks like this:

27c But as (*all' hōs*) his anointing teaches you about all things
27d and it is true
27e and it is not a lie
27f and as it taught you
27g remain in it/him

I read vv. 26 and 27 as a rather clumsy summary of what is already said in this section with an emphasis on the receivers of the letter. See Analysis, point 2. The introductory word in v. 27c, *alla*, can mark a contrast, "but," or a continuation of the argument, "indeed," a conclusive strengthening of what is just said. See the use of *alla* in John 5:24, 41–42; 6:39; 7:28; 8:12, 28; 10:18; 12:49 and 13:10. I take it in the latter sense.

The agent in v. 27c and v. 27f is "his anointing" (or in v. 27f simply "he"). "It," in v. 27de, refers most naturally to the teaching of the anointing and not to the anointing as such. Compare 1 John 2:20–21. The same applies to "it" in v. 27g, even if many interpreters want to read "him" as in v. 28b. See the note on this verse. In my reading v. 27 very strongly focuses on the anointing and its teaching, even if the formulations are open to other referents.

Some interpreters read these five clauses as two sentences, two comparisons: "Indeed, just as his anointing teaches you about everything, so it is true and not a lie. And just as it has taught you, so remain in him." Allowing "and" in v. 27d to follow "just as" in v. 27c is unusual, but not entirely impossible.

Others want to read the text as one single sentence with v. 27de as a parenthesis and v. 27f as a resumption of v. 27c. I tend to prefer this way of reading it, but would perhaps describe the sentence as an anacoluthon. The author begins a comparison in v. 27c, but then breaks it off by adding three clauses, v. 27def, the third of which links back to v. 27c. See the Translation Display. The change of construction in v. 27def makes it easier to read the last sentence as an imperative referring to the teaching of the anointing, "remain in it." The use of the present in v. 27c and the aorist in v. 27f can refer to the present moment and to the point when the letter's recipients received the anointing, i.e., to what the letter describes as "the beginning."

teaches . . . taught. In Gkt the same verb, *didaskein*, is used, first in the present and then in the aorist. The words "teach," "teaching," and "teacher" occur twenty-four times in the Johannine literature and thus occupy a central place in both the Gospel and the letters.

remain in it, i.e. in the teaching of his anointing. Or "remain in him", i.e. in Jesus Christ. I have above argued for the first interpretation, even if the context of v. 28 is a

First John

good argument for reading "him." See note on v. 28b. The referents of the pronouns in 1 John oscillate. Here in a transition from one section to another the author uses the same pronoun twice with primarily different referents: "remain in it" and "remain in him." See further Appendix 8, He: God or Jesus or Both.

Analysis

1. Delimitations

First John 2:18–27 has a well-marked beginning point, but lacks a clear ending. There are many opinions about where the section stops: after v. 25, v. 27, v. 28, or v. 29. These difficulties in delimitation are caused by the text itself.

The author begins immediately, without any introductory particle (asyndeton), addressing the readers as "dear children" and immediately mentioning the new theme: the last hour and Antichrist. New in the section is the discussion of antichrists, liars, and deceivers, of the anointing and its teaching of everyone, and of denial or confession of Jesus as Messiah. The connection to the foregoing is found primarily in tension-filled opposition pairs: God vs. the world, the young people vs. the evil one, and the one who loves vs. the one who hates his brother. Ethics now gives way to eschatology and Christology, and the author becomes significantly more concrete than he has been to this point.

If a boundary is to be placed at the end of chapter 2, I choose to place it after v. 27. As in the letter's first and second sections there is here a summarizing "this" (v. 26), pointing back to vv. 18–25, and it is followed by a closing repetition and defining comment regarding the anointing and its teaching. The sentence structure in v. 27—see the note on this verse—is not at all clear; the verse functions poorly as a preamble to a new section, but better as a rhetorical *accumulation* at the end of the section, even if it is rather clumsy in our ears. And as so often in the letter, a section or a paragraph closes with a phrase that clearly makes a link to what follows, in this case with the words "remain in it/him" (v. 27g and v. 28b). The reasons for regarding v. 28 as the beginning of a new section are put forth in the analysis for 1 John 2:28—3:3, point 2.

2. Structure

The section's structure has been described in various ways. In vv. 18–19, the serious problem troubling the new community is introduced. What is said in vv. 20–21 about the anointing and in vv. 24–25 about the message that was there from the beginning—i.e., what is said about the Spirit and the tradition—surrounds and gives weight to the central statements about Jesus in vv. 22–23. Finally some conclusions are drawn in vv. 26–27. It is possible to see a chiastic structure here—if v. 28 is included.

1 John 2:18–27: Schism in the New Community

As I see it, the composition in this section—with its repeated contrast between "they," i.e., the antichrists, and "you," i.e., the letter's recipients—is not organized as complicatedly as a chiasm would require. See the Translation Display. In the original text, a heavily marked "you" occurs three times, at the beginning of vv. 20, 24, and 27. In addition, v. 18 is clearly formed into a unit by the repetition of the words "it is the last hour" (*inclusio*). Thus, as in earlier sections, I would prefer to see a three-part organization, three internally "antithetical" paragraphs (vv. 19–21, 22–25, 26–27) with v. 18 as the introductory theme verse, comparable to 1 John 1:5 and 2:3. See the Translation Display once more. The first and third paragraphs issue in a word about the anointing that gives insight, while the second paragraph deals with the message that was there from the beginning. This implies that these two themes are to be held together—the verb "remain in" is used of both (vv. 24 and 27)—and that the interest is primarily on the anointing and its effects.

With this three-part structure the tension and opposition are focused between two groups well known to the parties involved, between "they" and "you." They once belonged to the same fellowship. Much is left unsaid, so that the transitions between the six they-paragraphs and you-paragraphs are not always so obvious. An inclusive "we" draws the conclusion in v. 18c, the word "us" in v. 19 I take as referring to the Johannine community (see chap. 12, point 3), and "us" in v. 25 lends itself to a more general reference.

One might ask why what v. 25 has to say is included at all. Would not the argument proceed just as well without it? The author frames the entire letter with words of "eternal life" (1 John 1:2 and 5:20), and includes them when he describes the letter's purpose (1 John 5:13). Eternal life is thus one of the overarching, central concepts in the letter, which generally indicate its eschatological character: the new day, eternal life, is already here. In all three instances eternal life is connected with Jesus Christ. Confessing Jesus is coupled together with eternal life in vv. 24–25 as well. To remain in the Son and the Father (v. 24c), i.e., to have fellowship with God through Jesus, is eternal life. "What they heard from the beginning" is further explained as "the promise" that became reality through Jesus. Cf. 1 John 1:1–3.

The antichrists are allotted more space at the beginning of the section; the letter's recipients receive more space at the end. The text culminates in two admonitions: let what you heard from the beginning remain in you, and remain in the teaching of his anointing, in "the teaching about the Messiah" (2 John 9).

3. An Anointing (chrisma) from the Holy One

The discussion in 1 John 2:18–27 of an anointing from the Holy one (*chrisma apo tou hagiou*) has no linguistic parallels in the world of that day. The word *chrisma* occurs only here in the New Testament three times, the corresponding verb, *chriein*, four times with regard to Jesus (Luke 4:18; Acts 4:27; 10:38; Heb 1:9) and once with regard to Christians (2 Cor 1:21). The following statements occur in the text:

- You all have *chrisma* from the Holy One (v. 20a)
- You received *chrisma* from him (v. 27a)
- His *chrisma* remains in you (v. 27a)
- His *chrisma* teaches you about all things (v. 27c)
- His *chrisma* taught you: remain in it/him (v. 27fg).

To this we can perhaps add what is said in v. 27de, that his *chrisma* is true and that his *chrisma* is not a lie.

It is not altogether clear why the author takes up this concept here. Is *chrisma* an event, an anointing, or is it a thing, an oil of anointing? For some readers, the traditional rendering, "anointing," includes both. Does the word refer to the Spirit or to something else? Who has given them this anointing? When did they receive this *chrisma*?

In fact, the questions here are many, as are the answers to them. With the majority of exegetes from Augustine and on I take *chrisma* primarily as a reference to the Spirit and its teaching. This *chrisma* is described in a way reminiscent of the spirit of truth, the Paraclete, the Helper, in John 14–16. Jesus' disciples received the Spirit/*chrisma*, the Spirit/*chrisma* remains in them, the Spirit/*chrisma* teaches them about all things, and the Spirit/*chrisma* mediates the truth to them. Through *chrisma* they all have insight and know the truth. They need no one to teach them. Compare 1 John 2:27 and 2:20 with John 14:27, 26.

The idea that no teacher is needed leads one's thoughts to the new covenant in Jer 31:31–34 and related texts. God's re-creative gift is described there as heart, spirit, a new heart, a new spirit, God's spirit, or in the words of the text, "my laws in their minds" (Jer 31:33 NIV; LXX: *dianoia*). According to 1 John 5:20, they have received understanding (*dianoia*) so that they may know God. The Spirit in 1 John is closely connected with the new union between God and humanity (1 John 3:24; 4:13). See further Appendix 9, A Renewed Covenant.

With support, e.g., from what has just been said about Jeremiah 31 (God's law in human hearts), some readers want to interpret *chrisma* as a reference to God's word. We would in that case still have the same theme in all three paragraphs in 1 John 2:19–27. But the letter's central problem corresponds better with a variation in these three paragraphs between the Spirit, the tradition, and the Spirit again. It is precisely the combination of the Spirit's teaching and the teaching of Christ that is inalienable according to 1 John. And if the closest parallel is the spirit of truth, then the Spirit and the Truth are closely united with one another. See also Appendix 15, God in Them and They in God.

Greek words ending in –*ma* as a rule refer to the result of the action that lies in the verb, in this case "anoint" (*chriein*); thus the result of having been anointed, or however we might express that in English. Anointedness? Anointed with oil? But words of this kind can also, as exceptions to the rule, stand for the act itself, in this case an act of anointing. The use of corresponding words in the Old Testament and Jewish texts provide support for both meanings.

The formulations in the letter—to have/possess *chrisma*, to receive *chrisma*, that *chrisma* remains in them and teaches them—undeniably indicate that the reference is not to an act. But perhaps what is said in v. 20a speaks of an act, an anointing with oil that mediates the spirit of truth to those who are anointed, and perhaps these formulations have been constructed from the result of the act of anointing, i.e., with reference to the Spirit. The ambiguity on this point suggests that it is not a matter of anointing in a physical sense. The use of oil in baptism is attested later on by Tertullian about the year 200. Baptism could be described as an anointing even without the use of oil (Acts 10:38). Compare Luke 4:18. If this reasoning will not hold, then I am inclined to prefer anointing oil over the act of anointing.

When and how this anointing took place remains uncertain, but other texts in the New Testament, e.g., 2 Cor 1:21–22, suggest that it is baptism that is in view here and that, as he did earlier, the author once again connects it to what took place in the beginning when they became Christians. Even the initiation in Qumran was connected with the Spirit. The novice is to "be cleansed from all his sins through the holy spirit that unites him with God's truth" (1QS 3:6). See also 1QS 4:21–22 and Appendix 10, What you Heard From the Beginning.

The expression "the Holy One" refers either to God (Hab 3:3; Sir 23:9) or to Jesus (Acts 3:14; Rev 3:7). Jesus is called "God's holy one" in a context of "regression" highly reminiscent of 1 John (John 6:69). The question of who is meant remains an open one in v. 20, but the context in v. 27 probably requires that it be answered with Christ. One point in the letter is that *chrisma* and *Christos* belong together. See also Appendix 8, He: God or Jesus or Both.

In John 20:19–23 it is Jesus who mediates "a holy spirit" to the disciples. But with regard to the Paraclete, the spirit of truth, in the Gospel of John, there is a close cooperation between God and Jesus. Jesus is to ask that the Father would send them another Paraclete, the spirit of truth (John 14:16). In John 14:26, it is said that the Father will send the spirit in Jesus' name, and in John 15:26 both are mentioned: Jesus will send the Spirit from the Father, and the Spirit proceeds from the Father. In John 16:6 Jesus alone is the sender. However one interprets "the Holy One" in 1 John 2:20, there is certainly an implied cooperation between the Father and the Son. The anointing is of divine origin and of divine character. When it comes to the Spirit, to judge by the context, God is identified as the sender (1 John 3:24; 4:13).

Interpretation

1. The Last Hour: Antichrist Has Come (2:18)

After the long exposition in 1:5—2:11 of "what was there from the beginning" (1:1–3), of "the message that we have heard from him and declare to you" (1:5), and of the old, but new commandment "that you had from the beginning" (2:7–8), together with a comforting and admonishing addition in 2:12–17, we now come to a description of the central event that lies behind the Elder's writing: a schism within the Johannine community. Some Jesus-believing Jews have turned away from what they had heard from the beginning. "God's light" through Jesus Christ, which had been brought to them by the Elder and his fellow workers (1:5), has been put completely in doubt.

In this situation, everything is concentrated on the confession of Jesus as the Messiah, God's son, the foundation stone for the new fellowship, the renewed covenant with God's people Israel. The Jesus-believing Jews have separated into two camps, something the Elder interprets in terms of a dualistic model: light or darkness, truth or lie, love or hate. Following an introductory vocative and a statement of the theme (v. 18ab), paragraphs regarding those who have left the fellowship (vv. 18c–19, 22–23, and 26) are woven in among paragraphs regarding those who have remained in the fellowship (vv. 21–22, 24–25, and 27). There is a striking alternation between those who are in the darkness and those who are in the light (2:9–11), or to use the group designations from Qumran writings, between children of darkness and children of light. The former group dominates at the beginning (vv. 18–19), the latter at the end (vv. 24–27). This determines the arrangement of the discussion.

As in 1:5, the announcement of the theme is very short: "This is the last hour" (v. 18b). It is repeated at the end of v. 18 and thereby binds v. 18 into a unit. The author is convinced that what is happening belongs to the events of the end time. "The last days" have begun with the life, death, and resurrection of Jesus (Acts 2:17), and they will come to an end with his return, the judgment, and the culmination of what has already begun, described in the letter in terms of those who have been united with Jesus becoming like God (2:28—3:3; 4:17). The author shares with the New Testament generally this conviction that the end is near, but he uses an expression all his own when he speaks of it as "the last hour," or "the last times." See the note. In the Gospel, the same words are used of Jesus' hour, i.e., the point in time when everything is fulfilled in Jesus' departure and return to the Father, and the spirit of truth comes to the disciples (John 2:4; 7:30; 12:23; 13:1; 17:1). In this way the author indicates a connection between what has already happened and what will yet happen. Jesus the Messiah, God's son, occupies a central place in the events of the end times as a whole.

Old Testament and contemporary Jewish ideas of the end-time events are many and kaleidoscopic. One repeated concept is the conflict between good and evil, between God and Satan, a decisive battle in which God at last emerges victorious. It is described through a number of different narratives. The Elder adopts the apocalyptic concept of the antichrist, the terminal manifestation of evil in the last days. See, e.g., Mark 13:21–23; 1 Thess 2:3–12; Revelation 13; and Daniel 7. But these texts make no use of the word "antichrist"; in all of the Bible it is only 1 and 2 John that use the word. It is not attested in Jewish writings from the time of the New Testament, nor is it common in early Christian writings. Its use by Polycarp and Irenaeus in the second century may mean that it was a Johannine tradition in the early church. Summarizing four contemporary motifs, Raymond Brown sketches a background for this Antichrist.

1. *The sea monster.* Remnants of the creation myths about the battle between the god Marduk and the sea monster Tiamat (or Baal or Yamm/Sea) survive in the description of YHWH's victory over the dragon Rahab and the sea monster Leviathan (Isa 51:9; Ps 74:13–14; 89:10; Job 26:12; 41:1–34). Sometimes these mythic figures could be historicized and made to stand for political powers or powerful personages (Isa 30:7; Ezek 29:3).

2. *Satan.* The word means "adversary," "enemy." Satan is sometimes described as one of God's sons or God's angels in the heavenly court and can step forth as the accuser of humanity (Job 1:6; Zech 3:1). He leads the powers of evil against Israel and in the book of *Jubilees* and the Qumran writings he receives like Belial power over human beings and political empires. As the angel of darkness, he leads people astray, away from God's ways (1QS 3:20–21). He is an adversary of Christ (2 Cor 6:15) and hinders Paul's work (1 Thess 2:18; Eph 6:12).

3. *Human ruler embodying evil.* The attempt of the Syrian king Antiochus IV Epiphanes to desecrate the temple in Jerusalem at the beginning of the second century BCE functions as a description of the end time in the book of Daniel. Antiochus fought against God himself (Dan 8:25); he made himself into a god (2 Macc 9:12). The heathen altar he set up in the temple of the Jews, which was given the name "the desolating sacrilege," becomes part of the final scenario, according to Matt 24:15. The awaited ruler from David's line, God's anointed, the Messiah, was expected to lead God's army against the assembled powers of evil in the last battle.

4. *The false prophet.* Deut 13:1–5 describes a prophet who through signs and wonders lures Israel away from God's way and attempts to make them serve other gods. He is presented as the opposite of the prophet like Moses mentioned in 18:15–19. Both had a place in future expectations as one or several persons. A Christian writing roughly contemporary with John's letters says, among other things: "For in the last days false prophets and corrupters shall be multiplied, and the sheep shall be turned into wolves, and love shall be turned into hate; for when lawlessness increases, they shall hate and persecute and betray one another, and then shall appear the world-deceiver as Son of God, and shall do signs and wonders, and the earth shall be delivered into his hands, and he shall do iniquitous things which have never yet come to pass since the beginning" (*Did.* 16:3–4).

First John

These ideas were combined in various ways in Christians' expectations of the end-time. They are most represented in the book of Revelation (chaps. 12–13; 19–20), but are also found in 2 Thess 2:3–12. Various mythological figures are historicized as individual persons. At the end of the second century, Irenaeus identified the Lawless One in 2 Thessalonians as the Antichrist, although without mentioning the letters of John. Since then, the identifications have continued in a long line throughout Christian history. Antichrist becomes the name of the powerful representative of evil at the world's end.

Quite obviously the central feature of what the recipients of 1 John had heard from the beginning was Jesus as the Messiah, God's son. "We know that God's son has come" (5:20). But there were also ideas of an opposing figure: an "antichrist is coming," an anti-messiah (v. 18c). The conflict between light and darkness had not ended (1:5—2:11), even though the ruler of this world had been driven out by the death and resurrection of Jesus (John 12:31; 16:10–11). The struggle against the world was still there (1 John 2:15–17), even though Jesus had overcome the world (John 16:33). The young people's fight against the evil one cannot but have a good ending (2:13–14; 5:4–5).

2. They Split the New Community (2:19).

The Elder's identification of Antichrist with several members of the Johannine community who had abandoned their faith in Jesus as Messiah takes up a very limited range of the ideas that could be associated with the concept of antichrist. It is tempting for later readers to think that the author is merely indulging in word-play. Antichrist is reduced to Messiah-denier. As such, these people can lead the faithful to fall away, and thus they function primarily as liars, deceivers, and false prophets. See the note at 4:1 on false prophets. The fourth motif sketched above thus becomes the most relevant one in this context. A description of these antichrists comes in vv. 22–23.

What happened when the antichrists appeared resulted in a sharp division between "them" and "us" (v. 19), between children of darkness and children of light (2:9–11), between children of the Devil and children of God (3:10), and between those who are driven by the spirit of error and those led by the spirit of truth (4:6). Even the Gospel gives an account of Jews who have come to faith in Jesus, but who then left him (John 6:60–71), sometimes with bitter disputes that led to sharp division into two groups (John 8:31–59). How could this happen? Indeed, the author draws the conclusion that these people had never actually belonged to the new fellowship. Even Judas was included within the Twelve, although in fact he did not really belong there. "Have not I myself chosen the twelve of you?" Jesus asks in John 6:70, "Yet one of you is a devil." Likewise after having washed the feet of the twelve disciples, Jesus says to them, with reference to Judas, "You are clean, though not all of you" (John 13:10–11). This has nothing to do with the idea that certain people are predestined to salvation and others to damnation. It is rather the result of the fact that the light, Jesus the

Messiah, God's son, has come into the world (John 3:19–21). Salvation or judgment: there is no third alternative.

The letter as a whole gives the impression that this schism within the Johannine community lies at some remove from those to whom the letter is directed and that there are no longer any antichrists in their midst. But the circumstances that led these Jesus-believing Jews to renounce their Messiah-faith are presumably still in force, and thus there is also a risk that yet more members may begin to deny their faith. Therefore the author wants to show them just what they have through their faith, namely eternal life (5:13); he wants to clarify the nature of that faith in various ways, to confirm it, and to ensure that it will endure. In the conflict of the last days, it is their faith that overcomes (4:4; 2:13–14; 5:4–5).

3. You All Have Insight (2:20–21)

The words that are addressed especially to the readers through a highlighted "you" at the beginning of v. 20 (see the note) and that deal with them directly recall the form of 2:12–14. There the author encourages and comforts those who walk in the light and confirms what they already have. The same applies to this paragraph. They have an anointing, *chrisma* in Greek, from the Holy One. See the note "have an anointing from" at 2:20. The word functions almost like a conjunction between the two paragraphs, between anti*christoi* (antichrists) in vv. 18–19 and *chrisma* (anointing) in vv. 20–21, a word-play followed up with *Christos* in v.22. There are a number of questions connected with the subject of *chrisma*, anointing, which describes the status enjoyed by the letter's recipients. I have discussed them in the Analysis, point 3, above.

The readers have received a share in God's spirit. With all likelihood that is the meaning of the words "they have an anointing." The formulation certainly has to do with Johannine ideas of one's having (within one) divine life, divine light, divine love, divine words, divine seed, etc. Thus I reject the alternative interpretation that the anointing is to be interpreted as God's word. As we shall see below, under point 4, the spirit and the word do indeed cooperate (vv. 24–27), but the recipients' status of having been anointed has to do with the spirit. In Johannine tradition, the spirit is primarily described as the spirit of truth, i.e., as the spirit that mediates the truth. The spirit is also called the Paraclete, the Comforter, the Helper. The spirit is present in the place of Jesus, ever since Jesus went away (John 14:16–17, 25–26; 15:26–27; 16:7–15; 1 John 4:6). The comfort and help the believers have in the current situation thus comes from the spirit, which they received from God through Jesus Christ.

The reception of this spirit is described here as an act of anointing, whether in a physical sense or an extended, metaphorical sense. In contemporary mystery religions, anointing played a role in the initiation rite; through it one came into possession of special insight (mysteries). In the Old Testament, anointing with oil is coupled together with God's spirit. This was the case with kings (1 Sam 16:13); it was also the case with prophets. Jesus cites Isa 61:1: "The spirit of the Lord is upon me, for he has anointed me" (Luke 4:18). It is connected to Jesus' baptism (Acts 10:37–38; Mark 1:8 parr) and certainly to Christian baptism as well (2 Cor 1:21–22). In the fourth century, anointing became a standard feature of the Christian initiation rite: anointing, water baptism, eucharist. It is likely that the letter's recipients had received a share in God's spirit at baptism (or in their conversion, or when they entered into the new fellowship). It belonged to what was there from the beginning.

The anointing, i.e., the spirit, has just one function in this paragraph: to confirm the truth, i.e., the knowledge of God and his son Jesus Christ. They all have knowledge (v. 20; see the note at 2:20, "you all have insight"). The anointing has taught them and continues to teach them about all things; they need no other teachers (v. 27). The anointing mediates only the truth, no lie (vv. 21cd, 27de). Thus they can be entirely secure in what they have.

That they all have insight the Elder then confirms by saying, "I write that" (see the note "that . . . that . . . that" at v. 21), and does so in the usual threefold way, first negatively (v. 21b), then positively (v. 21c), and finally with the additional comment that "no lie comes from the truth" or "no lie belongs to the truth" (v. 21d). This last point, of course, is self-evident by definition, yet the author intentionally includes such statements in his argument, something that spreads a self-evident quality to the surrounding context as well. It is not so simple to write about what the audience already knows. Varied forms of reinforcing repetitions also dominate the description of the anointing in v. 27. See the notes on this verse. There can be no doubt about it: they all have insight. The antimessiahs need not be seen as a threat.

The fact that the Jesus-believing Jews who remained within the Johannine fellowship possess a special knowledge has a biblical background. The same is claimed for the people of God in the Old Testament (Prov 28:5), for Jesus' disciples (Mark 4:11; Matt 11:25; 13:16), and of the Christians (1 Cor 1:18–31; Col 1:28). At the very beginning of the second century, Ignatius writes to the Christians in Ephesus (14:1): "Nothing remains hidden for you if you have a mature faith in Jesus and love." But the background to the statements about the anointing in 2:18–27 are above all found in the promise of a new covenant in Jer 31:31–34 (they shall no longer need to teach one another, not the one brother the other; they shall all know me, for God has put the law in their heart). The words "you have an anointing" can also be understood in terms of the various statements regarding the renewal of the covenant, especially those referring to having a new heart, a new spirit, God's spirit, or God's law in one's inmost being (Ezekiel 36). Those truly belonging to the renewed covenant cannot leave the Johannine fellowship or the knowledge of the True One that comes through Jesus Christ, God's son (5:20).

1 John 2:18-27: Schism in the New Community

4. They Denied That Jesus Was the Messiah (2:22-23)

The antichrists, the enemies of the Messiah, are presented in more detail in vv. 22-23. The link-words *chrisma* and *antichristoi* in the two preceding paragraphs are now followed up with *Christos*, which we can render with "Messiah" or "Christ." The decisive question for the Jews in the Johannine community was this: Is Jesus the Messiah or is he not? Or in the words of John the Baptist: "Are you the one who is to come, or are we to wait for another?" (Matt 11:3). All Johannine Christians answered "yes" to the question and confessed that Jesus was the Messiah, the son of God (John 20:31). But many of them had changed their minds and denied that Jesus was the Messiah. As we have already seen, the author describes them as "antichrists," as "antimessiahs," as enemies of the Messiah.

The antichrists are given several names in the letter: liars, deceivers, false prophets. According to 2:22-23, they can also be called deniers, and when they reappear in 4:1-6, they are referred to first as "spirits," and then as "spirit of antichrist" and "spirit of error." In v. 26 they are described as people who want to deceive, or who are deceiving (see the note). Lying, deception, and falsehood belong close together in the description of the last times and the rebellion against God. See further the note "many false prophets have gone out into the world" at 4:1. The ultimate aim of these people, according to the believers, is through word and deed to get other people to fall away from God. In the Johannine letters the concentration is on people's relationship with Jesus as the Messiah, son of God. Who God is, is confirmed through him. For this reason the first descriptor applied to the opponents in this section is "antichrists," "antimessiahs."

When the antichrists are more closely described in vv. 22-23, the first word used of them is "liar," in fact "*the* Liar" in definite form (see the note), presumably because the concept of lying is mentioned immediate before this verse. They deny that Jesus is the Messiah. From an intra-Jewish perspective, I take these words in their simplest conceivable meaning. Other alternatives are presented in point 6, below. At one time they had come to faith in Jesus as the Messiah, the one who was to come—the more complete confession was Jesus as the Messiah, the son of God—but for some reason had cast over their faith and had not remained in the "teaching about the Messiah" (2 John 9).

What is implied in this denial is explained in what follows, with help of statements about whether or not one "has the Father." The confession of Jesus as Messiah in the Johannine tradition has a close connection with the relationship between Jesus and God, between the Son and the Father. God has sent his only son into the world to give life to human beings (4:9-10). The Elder has seen and bears witness: "The Father has sent the Son as the savior of the world" (4:14). Faith in the Son and faith in the Father are linked together in the Gospel (John 5:23; 10:30; 14:6-7; 15:23). The Messiah in the Johannine writings is tied to this mutual relationship. For this reason, denying

First John

that Jesus is the Messiah becomes more narrowly defined as denying the Father and the Son (v. 22b and v. 22d).

In typical Johannine style, the denial is first described negatively (v. 23a), and then positively (v. 23b). It is a matter of participating in the renewed covenant or not participating in it. "To have God" is a covenant formula, probably coined in a Greek-speaking milieu. It occurs also in 5:12 and 2 John 9. The expression is attested only here in the New Testament, but we meet it many times in the so-called Apostolic Fathers (to have God/Jesus within oneself/one's heart). See the Interpretation for 2 John, the end of point 3. The basic rule for YHWH's covenant with Israel is this: "You shall have no other gods before me" (Exod 20:3). In the letter, having God is related to having fellowship with God, to know God, and to remain in God. Thus the Elder regards the antichrists as Jews who have fallen away from the (renewed) covenant with God and at the letter's end warns his readers away from idols (5:21). Those who have chosen to leave the Johannine community have lost that close contact with God in the renewed covenant and consequently their part in the divine life. For further discussion on the antichrists, see the commentary on 4:1–6; Appendix 14, Jesus as Messiah, God's Son, and chap. 12, point 4.

5. You Have the Word and the Spirit That Guarantee Eternal Life (2:24–27)

The paragraph about the secessionists, at the end of this section, is very short, only one sentence long (v. 26). That is probably an indication that the author has his thoughts much more on those who have remained in the fellowship than on those who have left it. The two last paragraphs, which directly address the letter's recipients with a stressed "you" in vv. 24, 27 (see the notes on these verses), are thus brought together here.

What was said earlier about the anointing, the truth, and the renewed covenant can with good reason be applied to what was there when the recipients came to faith in Jesus as the Messiah, God's son. But in v. 24, the focus is directed to the tradition, "what you heard from the beginning," for which the Elder and his fellow workers have a special responsibility (1:1–5). Like the anointing, it is something that can be found "within them." See Appendix 10, What you Heard From the Beginning, where I have tried to sum up what constitutes this Johannine tradition. With it the recipients of the letter have two criteria for evaluating what has happened: the anointing, i.e., the spirit within them, and the tradition, which the Elder mediates and interprets; in terms of later formulation, they have the Spirit and the word. All believers have the Spirit; all are likewise entrusted with the tradition, but there are also those who are especially charged with responsibility for the tradition. The question of how this responsibility is to be conceived has been answered variously by various churches at various times. The section in 4:1–6 will show later on that it is not enough simply to insist that it is the spirit that speaks.

The covenant formula "to have the Father" is replaced in v. 24 with "to remain in the Son and in the Father." As I see it, even the expression "remain in" has a relationship to ideas of the covenant. See Appendix 15, God in Them and They in God. Here object and person are blended in the Johannine immanence formula: if something (or Someone) abides in them, then they abide in that Someone. What they heard from the beginning was no longer with the secessionists and they are therefore no longer with God, defined here as being "in the Son and the Father." Thus neither do they have eternal life. A reasoning of this sort may lie behind the unexpected continuation in v. 25. The perspective broadens out to include a "we," and the timeframe expands to embrace both promises and fulfillment. To have the Father or to remain in the Son and the Father is a form of eternal life. See Appendix 6, Life, Eternal Life. Thus this section on the antichrists becomes an important part of what the letter aims to accomplish: to make sure the audience knows that they have eternal life through Jesus the Messiah, the son of God (5:13).

The last verse, v. 27, emphasizes what has already been said: You have an anointing that teaches you about all things. Remain in this teaching. In a rhetorical way this message is strengthened by several additions: You have received this anointing from Him, it is in you, it mediates the truth, it has nothing to do with falsehood, it has already taught you, so now you need no other teachers. Such an accumulative way of expressing himself is not foreign to the Johannine author and creates the sense that the section is ending. The focus is on the anointing within them and the relation to its teaching. They are to "remain in it."

6. Perspective-Dependent Interpretations (2:18–27)

In this section of the letter it is perhaps more obvious than elsewhere which perspective serves as the foundation for the interpretation. As I have previously indicated, I adopt an intra-Jewish perspective in which some Jesus-believing Jews within the Johannine community have given up their faith in Jesus as the Messiah (2 John 9), which is the absolutely decisive ground of the new fellowship with God, of a renewed covenant between God and Israel. They are therefore regarded as apostates (2:19), as enemies of the Messiah (2:18, 22; 2 John 7), as liars (2:22), as deceivers (2:26; 4:6; 2 John 7), as false prophets (4:1–3), and also, indirectly, as idol worshipers (5:21). One's relationship to Jesus determines in a decisive way one's relationship to God the Father (2:23; 5:20). As in the Qumran community, the renewal of the covenant causes a sharp division within Judaism, something reinforced by an overarching dualistic mindset.

In a general Christian, Gnostic perspective there is as a rule no limiting of the situation to a special Johannine form of Christianity. The conceptions of an antichrist, which the author refers to in v. 18, are seen as a part of the early Christian tradition, and the antichrists are understood to have been influenced by contemporary Gnostic ideas. The deviation from Christian faith that the author combats "is gnostically oriented." This is shown by both the terminology and the thought-world. This view requires "no further proof" (Rudolf Schnackenburg). Presumably the author adopts the concept of "anointing," e.g., from Gnostic language in order to make the claim against his Gnostic opponents that the Christians have an inner divine, spiritual capacity that leads to a true gnosis. The expression "you all have insight" is undoubtedly aimed directly at the false Gnostics. Various opinions prevail about which form of Gnosticism has influenced the Christians in the letter. Many refer to the teachings of Cerinthus, while others argue for the docetic ideas described in the writings of Ignatius. See further Appendix 14, Jesus as Messiah, God's Son. What these alternative forms hold in common would be their devaluation of Jesus' historical person as the only real savior and their denial of salvation through his flesh and blood. Their heresy belonged to "the dangerous pseudo-Christian spirituality that revealed itself openly in Gnosticism" (Schnackenburg).

In an intra-Johannine, progression perspective, the antichrists are equated with Johannine Christians who had further developed their belief-system and had arrived at a conception of Christ that the Elder could not accept. Raymond Brown, e.g., lays the emphasis on Jesus in the confession formula "*Jesus* is Christ" and equates Christ with God's son. The antichrists also confessed that "Jesus is Christ"—they were Johannine Christians after all—but they interpreted those words in a new way that weakened the human side of the formula, not the divine side. The problem then did not have to do with the predicate "Christ" in the statement "Jesus is Christ," but rather with the subject "Jesus." Could the human Jesus be the same person as the divine Christ? The secessionists admitted that the divine Word was Christ, but to emphasize Jesus as the Christ would mean that Jesus' life and death took on a decisive meaning for the life and salvation of humanity. Their understanding was based on a lopsided reading of the Gospel.

Thus the secessionists would have readily acknowledged the pre-existent Word as Christ, God's son, without laying any great weight on the incarnation. The Elder, on the other hand, professed the incarnated Word in Jesus' life and death. If Jesus' life was unimportant, as the secessionists believed, then one could not affirm the rule "to live as Jesus lived." Ethics would be placed in a subordinate position. And if Jesus' death were unimportant, then neither would sin be important. The secessionists sought support for these ideas in certain verses of the Gospel.

The secessionists also claimed, according to Brown, that they were anointed with the spirit and that they followed the tradition. But they gave a significantly larger role to the spirit in reinterpreting the tradition, such that the Elder could no longer see that "what they heard from the beginning" was still with them. The secessionists could then point to the fact that Jesus had said that he had not revealed everything to the disciples, but that the Paraclete would proclaim what would come to pass (John 16:12–13). In this way there arose a serious disagreement over the interpretation of the tradition (the Gospel), and the Johannine community split into two groups who could never acknowledge one another.

6

1 John 2:28—3:10: Children of God and Children of the Devil

Translation Display

28a	And now, dear children,
28b	remain in him
28c	so that when he appears we may have boldness
28d	and not turn from him in shame at his appearing.
29a	If you know that he is righteous
29b	then you know
29c	that also everyone who does righteousness is born of him.
1a	See what love the Father has given us
1b	that we are called God's children
1c	and so we are.
1d	For this reason the world does not know us
1e	because it has not known him.
2a	Beloved,
2b	now we are God's children
2c	and it has not yet been revealed what we shall be.
2d	We know that when it is revealed, we will be like him
2e	for we will see him as he is.
3a	And everyone who has this hope in him purifies himself
3b	just as he is pure.
4a	Everyone who commits sin also commits lawlessness,
4b	and sin is lawlessness.
5a	You know
5b	that he was revealed in order to take away sins

First John

5c	and that sin is not found in him.
6a	Everyone who remains in him does not sin.
6b	Everyone who sins has not seen him
6c	or come to know him.
7a	Dear children
7b	let no one deceive you.
7c	The one who does righteousness is righteous
7d	just as he is righteous.
8a	The one who commits sin is of the devil
8b	for the devil has sinned from the beginning.
8c	For this the son of God was revealed,
8d	in order that he might destroy the devil's works.
9a	Everyone who is born of God does not commit sin
9b	because his seed remains in him.
9c	And he cannot sin
9d	because he is born of God.
10a	By this, the children of God and the children of the devil are obvious:
10b	anyone who does not do righteousness is not of God
10c	and anyone who does not love his brother.

Notes

2:28. And now. Gkt *kai nyn*. The phrase is the usual introductory one for marking a transition and new beginning with focus on what follows, in this case coming after the long introduction in 1 John 1:5—2:27. There is probably still a temporal nuance as well in this "now," referring to "the last hour" in 1 John 2:18, which is followed up there immediately with "so now" in v. 18d. The same temporal marker is found in John 17:5, with reference to Jesus' "hour": "So now, Father, glorify me." A vocative, "dear children," and an imperative, "remain in him," reinforce the new beginning and introduce a deepening of what has been said.

dear children. Gkt *teknia*. See the notes on 1 John 2:1 and 12.

him, in this context probably a reference to Jesus, the Messiah, God's son. See the note "remain in it" at 1 John 2:27.

when. Gkt *ean* ("if") approaches the meaning of *hotan* ("when") in the Greek of the day.

he appears. Gkt has the passive verb: "he is revealed," which can also have a reflexive meaning, "he reveals himself." The verb, *phaneroun*, is used five times in this section (1 John 3:2, 5, 8). In v. 10, moreover, we have the adjective "revealed, obvious" (*phaneros*). In other Johannine passages it is often used of Jesus, but never of God.

1 John 2:28—3:10: Children of God and Children of the Devil

we may have boldness. Literally, "we have boldness." With the final judgment in view, the sender and the receivers are united as "we." The Greek word for "boldness" here, *parrēsia*, occurs nine times in John and four times in 1 John (1 John 2:28; 3:21–22; 4:17; 5:14). It indicates a posture of audacity, openness, and confidence, sometimes combined with a trusting nearness, in 1 John always in relation to God or Jesus.

turn from him in shame. Gkt has the passive, "be shamed away from," or the middle, "turn oneself in shame from." Words having to do with shame are not unusual in writings related to the coming judgment (Isa 1:29; Mark 8:38). According to Daniel 12—the only passage in the OT that speaks of eternal life—some will rise again to "eternal life" and others to "eternal shame" (Dan 12:2).

at his appearing. The word *parousia* is used 24 times in the NT as a technical term for Jesus' return, but it occurs only here in the Johannine literature. The readers are presumed nonetheless to be familiar with the concept. The expression in this context cannot refer to anything other than Christ's return, which consequently determines the meaning of "he" and "him" in the context. As a whole, v. 28 forms a chiasm:

a	when he appears
b	we may have boldness
b'	and not turn from him in shame
a'	at his appearing

These formulas are more generally apocalyptic than Johannine. Likewise in 2 John 8.

29. If you know. Gkt does not have "if" (*ei*) followed by the indicative with the sense "now that you know," but instead *ean* with the subjunctive, yielding a nuance of self-testing: "If you know—and you do know, don't you? You have realized this, have you not?"

he is righteous. Probably a statement about Jesus. See the Analysis, point 1, and Appendix 8, He: God or Jesus or Both.

then you know. The Greek verb form used here can be read either as an indicative, "thus you know," or as an imperative, "know then." The former fits better with the letter's way of speaking about the information that the recipients already have.

everyone who does righteousness. Literally, "everyone doing the righteousness." This construction with "everyone" + article + participle (with a qualifier) is very common in this section. See the Analysis, point 2. With regard to "do" in this type of construction, see the note "do the truth" at 1 John 1:6. To "do righteousness" in this connection is the opposite of "doing sin." See Appendix 12, They Cannot Sin.

is born of him. A typical phrase in 1 John, clearly common enough that the author can use "him" of God without specially indicating it. The same applies to "have fellowship with him" (1 John 1:6) and "know him" (1 John 2:3). Possibly the connection is to a Jewish milieu where "he" is used instead of the divine name. See Appendix 11, Begotten/Born of God.

3:1. See what. Both the word "see" and the indirect question fasten the recipients' attention on the fact that what follows is very important. The imperative "see" introduces revelatory formulas at John 1:29, 36, 47; 19:14, 26, 27. "What" (*potapos*), marks both quantity (how large) and quality (how remarkable).

has given. Gkt has the perfect of the standard word for "give." God's gifts to Jesus (John 3:27, 35; 5:22, 26, 27, etc.), to those who believe in Jesus (John 1:12; 3:34; 4:14–15, etc.), and to all people (John 3:16; 6:32, etc.) form a dominating theme in John. The use of the perfect lends weight to the statement.

that. Gkt *hina* is explicative, introducing an expansion on the word "love" earlier in the sentence.

God's children. Gkt has the usual word for "child" (*teknon*), in the plural. In the OT and Jewish literature, the designator "God's children" expresses that God and the people are closely associated in the covenant ratified at Sinai and that the people of the covenant are to live as God's children. In 1 John the meaning of this term is enhanced through the notion of being born of God. See Appendix 11, Begotten/Born of God.

and so we are. A repetition reinforcing what was just said. It is said yet a third time in v. 2.

For this reason the world does not know us, because it has not known him. Gkt indicates the connection between the two clauses in double fashion: "for this reason . . . because (*hoti*)." The word *hoti* can thus function either explanatorily, making "this" a forward reference (cataphoric), or causally, making "this" a backward reference (anaphoric). The former construction occurs six times in John, but an anaphoric "this" (nine times in John) is never followed up with *hoti*. See also the note at the beginning of 1 John 1:5.

On the use of "world" in the letter, see the note "the world" at 1 John 2:15.

him. The word can refer to Jesus, as in 1 John 3:6 and John 1:10, or to God, as in 1 John 4:8 and John 17:25. The context here speaks in favor of the latter. See Appendix 8, He: God or Jesus or Both.

2. Beloved. See the note at 1 John 2:7. The beginning of v. 2 connects to words in the foregoing text: "love" and "God's children" in v. 1 and "now" in v. 28.

now . . . and . . . not yet. Moreover, the formulations not only refer to the prevailing situation (1 John 2:18, 28) but also indicate a present and future eschatology in the letter.

1 John 2:28—3:10: Children of God and Children of the Devil

and. Some translations render Gkt *kai* here as "but." See the note "and" at 1 John 1:6. Here the term functions also to mark an important additional clause. Later manuscripts of the Byzantine tradition insert the word *de* ("but" or "however") in the next clause, easily explained from the context. Some translations complete the sense by adding a corresponding equivalent.

when it is revealed. See the note on v. 28 above. Some interpreters render the clause, "when he is revealed." I however prefer the generalized subject, since the immediate context does not mention Jesus. Moreover the direct parallel in the same verse has "it" as subject and 1 John 3:1–3 is dominated by God as agent and object.

2–3. him . . . him . . . he. The words refer to God, assuming God is taken as the agent in vv. 1–3, up to the change to Jesus with the pronoun "he" (*ekeinos*), in the phrase "just as he is pure" (v. 3b). See Appendix 8, He: God or Jesus or Both. The recipients are now God's children; in the end they will be like God. In this world they are already like Christ (1 John 4:17). Moses was not permitted to see God when the covenant was renewed at Sinai (Exod 33:20, 23). Neither have they been allowed to see God in the renewed covenant (1 John 4:12, 20). But they have seen his son, Jesus Christ (1 John 1:1–3; 4:14).

3. And everyone who . . . The construction dominates this section. See the Analysis, point 2. On the "and" (*kai*) advancing the argument, see the note "and the life was revealed" at 1 John 1:2.

hope, Gkt *elpis*, is an important theological word in the NT concerning Christian hope for the future. It occurs only here in the Johannine literature. The strong sense of a realized eschatology in the Johannine writings may be an explanation for this.

in him, i.e., in God, who has already bestowed love on the letter's recipients and made them his children (1 John 3:1).

purifies himself . . . pure. The words in Gkt, *hagnizein* ("sanctify oneself/purify oneself") and *hagnos* ("holy/pure") are not common in the NT. Only here is Jesus described as *hagnos*. The word-group often has a cultic use. Behind the word-choice there may be allusions to God's establishing a covenant with his people at Sinai. In preparation for meeting with God, the people were to purify themselves (Exod 19:10–11). The verb *hagnizein* is used in both texts. Later the Levites were to purify themselves whenever they came into God's presence (Num 8:21). In view of the imminent confrontation with God, the letter's recipients must also be made pure. See the Interpretation and Appendix 9, A Renewed Covenant.

just as he is pure, i.e., just as Christ is pure. For "he," Gkt has "that one" (*ekeinos*), which refers to Jesus in 1 John. See the note "he" at 1 John 2:6.

The words "just as he is pure" now lead the Elder back to the statement "he is righteous" in v. 29 and thus to the theme of righteousness and sin.

First John

4. Everyone who commits sin. See the note "everyone who does righteousness" at v. 29, above. The construction binds v. 4 to v. 29 and to what follows. According to some interpreters, the reference is to a very specific sin: the secessionists' apostasy from faith in Jesus as the Messiah, God's son, with the consequent schism within the new fellowship.

commits lawlessness. Gkt *poiei tēn anomian* ("does the righteousness"). See the previous note. The word *anomia* is a common word for sin in the OT (LXX). The word construction itself suggests the idea of law-breaking, transgressing the Law, which in a Jewish milieu is a typical description of sin. The word *anomia* is thus frequently a synonym of "sin" (*hamartia*; Ps 32:1 as quoted in Rom 4:7; Ps 51:3 [LXX]; and in connection with discussion of a new covenant, Heb 10:17). Elsewhere the letter does not support viewing the reference as an offense against the Law of Moses. It may have in mind a violation of "the law" in the renewed covenant (1 John 3:23). In apocalyptic texts the word *anomia* most readily carries the sense of lawlessness, godlessness, rebellion against God. The evidence for such an apocalyptic content is manifold. Besides passages in the Qumran writings and in the LXX, see *T. Dan* 6:1–6; Matt 7:22–23; 13:41–42; 24:11–12; 2 Thess 2:3–8; *Did.* 16:3–4; and *Barn.* 4:1–4. *Anomia* in the sense of transgression against the Law of Moses is not attested in the NT. See further the Interpretation.

sin is lawlessness. Literally, "and the sin is the lawlessness," where from the context "and" acquires a sense of motivation and clarification. When both nouns in clauses of the type *x is y* are definite in form, the first is regarded as subject. On the basis of what has been said in the preceding note, this clause can be interpreted either as a reinforcing definition (sin is a violation of the law) or as a way of placing sin within an apocalyptic situation. Sin is part of the great lawlessness and godlessness that characterize the final battle between God and Satan.

5. You know. Literally, "and you know," with yet another argument-advancing "and." See the note "and the life was revealed" at 1 John 1:2. The formulation is a reaffirmation that the recipients already have the needed understanding (1 John 2:20–21, 27).

he, Gkt *ekeinos,* therefore Jesus the Messiah, God's son. See the note "he" at 1 John 2:6. "He" is parallel to "God's son" in v. 8, below.

was revealed. Gkt has the aorist passive, which can also carry a reflexive or middle sense, as at 1 John 2:28; 3:2, 8. See the note "he appears" at 1 John 2:28. The reflexive sense—"reveal himself"—leads most readily to thoughts of the Word that came into the world, but the verb "be revealed" was not usually employed as a reference to the Incarnation itself. Most likely the idea here is of the real existence, including the death, of Jesus as the one who came both with water and with blood (1 John 5:6), and in that case the passive "was revealed" fits better. See also 1 John 1:7 and 2:2. John the Baptist, immediately following his testimony about "the lamb of God who takes away the sin of the world," says that Jesus would "be revealed to Israel" (John 1:29–31).

take away sins. Literally, "take away the sins." Gkt has the same verb as John 1:29. The sense of the letter's perspective is probably best described by 1 John 1:7 and 2:2. Exod 34:9–10 can provide a possible background: when Moses at Sinai prays that God would "take away" the people's sins (*hamartia*) and transgressions (*anomia*) and make the people his own possession, God replies by establishing a covenant with them. Jesus' death renews the covenant. See Appendix 9, A Renewed Covenant.

sin is not found in him. The same is said about Jesus in John 7:18, but with the word "unrighteousness" (*adikia*) instead of "sin" (*hamartia*). As advocate and reconciler, Jesus is "righteous" (1 John 2:1–2). See also John 8:46 and 14:30. If Jesus' "purity" is now the life-model for those who look forward soon to becoming like God (1 John 3:3), it is not surprising that in what follows the author claims that they do not sin.

6. Everyone who remains in. The same construction as in vv. 29c, 3a, and 4a. See the notes on these passages. The formulations connect to the important shift at the boundary between v. 27 and v. 28, with the imperative "remain in him." See further the note "that he abides in him" at 1 John 2:6, which is yet another principal text regarding the recipients' way of life. See Appendix 15, God in Them and They in God.

does not sin. Gkt has the present tense, indicating a process, but without saying anything about how often the concerned parties do sin. No good linguistic support exists for solving the problem with sin in 1 John by distinguishing between occasional sins and habitual sinning. See Appendix 12, They Cannot Sin.

has not seen him or come to know him. Gkt has both verbs in the perfect: "has not seen" and "has not known." The two verbs reinforce each other and express a close relationship to Jesus Christ: the first perhaps a more general experience of him, the second a more intimate knowledge of him, an acquaintance that extends in to the present. To "see Jesus" scarcely means here to have been in his company during his earthly days. Cf. verbs of perception in 1 John 1:1–3.

7. Dear children. See notes at 1 John 2:1, 12, 14 and 28. Since what follows is a repetition and sharpening of what has already been said, this direct address and the following clause function as an appeal for the readers' attention, not as an introduction to a new section. The increasingly serious subject matter dealing with the opposition between God and the devil requires breathing room. Cf., e.g., the vocative "Beloved" at 1 John 4:11.

the one who does righteousness. This is the same formulation as in 1 John 2:29c. See the note there.

he. Gkt has "that one" (*ekeinos*), referring to Christ, as in v. 3. See note "he" at 1 John 2:6.

8. The one who commits sin. Again, the same formulation as in the beginning of v. 4. See the note above.

is of the devil. The expression indicates both origin and belonging. See the note "comes not from the Father but from the world" at 1 John 2:16. The phrase "to be of the devil/the evil one" occurs three times in the Johannine literature; "to be of God/the Father" eleven times.

The word "devil" occurs four times in 1 John 3:8 and 10. The rest of the letter uses "the evil one." See the note on 1 John 2:10. The Gospel of John uses additionally the terms "Satan" and "the ruler of this world" (John 13:27; 12:31, 14:30; 16:11). The devil is portrayed as the great counterpart to God. Both have children; both are described as father. Cain—who "was of the evil one" (1 John 3:12)—is represented in Jewish sources as born of the devil. See Appendix 13, Cain as the Devil's Son.

has sinned from the beginning. Gkt reads "from the beginning the devil sins," emphasizing "from the beginning" by placing it at the front of the clause. The present tense expresses a process that has been operative "from the beginning," i.e., from the ancient event in Eden's pleasure garden, or from the time before the world's creation, or from the point of the world's creation, or from the first act of murder, or more generally from the time covered in Genesis 1–4, a section that opens with the words "in the beginning" (Gen 1:1). The temporal reference is not precisely indicated. Cf. the use of "from the beginning" in 1 John 1:1 and 2:13–14. The devil is defined as one who sins.

For this the son of God has been revealed, in order to. That the revelation of God's son has a purpose is expressed both by "For this" (*eis touto*) and by "in order that" (*hina*). See a parallel syntax in 1 John 3:3 (see the note). Here a cataphoric (forward-referencing) "this" is taken up by a "that"-clause (explicative *hina*). On "was revealed/revealed himself," see the note on the same expression at v. 5, above.

destroy the devil's works. Both God and the devil carry out their works. Cf. good and evil works in John 3:18–19 and 1 John 3:12; 2 John 11; 3 John 10. Here "the devil's works" are probably equivalent to "the sins" in v. 5. Confrontation between Jesus and the devil does not, however, form part of the Johannine narrative, although it does in other NT texts (Matt 4:1–11 par; 12:38; Mark 1:24; 3:11; Luke 10:18; Heb 2:14). In a strongly realized eschatology, the struggle between Jesus and the devil becomes part of the final resolution (John 12:31; 14:30; 16:11). The letters of John provide evidence for a body of older apocalyptic material (1 John 2:18; 28; 2 John 7–8).

9. Everyone who is born, the same type of construction as in 1 John 2:29c; 3:3a, 6a, 6b, 7c, and 8a (although the last two passages lack "everyone"). See the notes on these texts.

born of God. See Appendix 11, Born of God.

his seed remains in him. The reference here in v. 9b is to God's seed, as is shown by the parallel in v. 9d, "he has been born of God." See Appendix 11, Born of God.

1 John 2:28—3:10: Children of God and Children of the Devil

And. The word introduces the result of the previous clause. See the notes on 1 John 2:20b and 27b.

cannot sin. See Appendix 12, They Cannot Sin.

10. By this . . . are obvious. At the end of a section in 1 John, we often have an anaphoric (backward-referencing) "this" (1 John 1:4, 2:1; 4:6). Such is also the case here, even though "this" may also refer (cataphorically) to what follows, namely, the two substantive participles that come last of all in this closing verse: "anyone who does not do righteousness" and "anyone who does not love his brother." Cf. 1 John 4:21. The words "does not do righteousness" in v. 10 and "do righteousness" in 1 John 2:29 form an *inclusio* in this section.

does not do righteousness. See the previous note.

is not of God. See the note "is of the devil" at v. 8 above, and the references there.

and likewise. Gkt "and," *kai*, introduces an addition to what the preceding line (v. 10b) says. Some interpreters take this "and" as explanatory and translate it, "that is to say."

who does not love. Literally, "the one not loving." The expression is the last of the many substantive participles in this section. It provides a definitive characterization of "everyone not doing righteousness" and leads into the second part of the letter, which begins with 1 John 3:11. Augustine says that the love of God is the "most true, full, and the perfect righteousness" (*De natura et gratia* 49 [42]).

Analysis

1. Closing and Introduction

With the section 1 John 2:28—3:10 the letter changes character. The words "we/I write," which had earlier identified the communication situation, disappear and do not reappear until the final formula at 1 John 5:13. The cautious and often indirect manner of writing is replaced by a more open posture. The content is concentrated (if for the moment we ignore 1 John 2:28—3:10) on the two themes clearly indicated in 1 John 3:23, i.e., on faith in Jesus as the Messiah, God's son, and on the mutual love between fellow believers, with a strong emphasis on the latter. The author quite openly wishes to stem further schism within the community of the renewed covenant. God's children of the last times are united as one.

By making a sharp division between children of God and the children of the devil, the section brings to a close what has been said earlier. The earlier sections—similar to the structure of 1 Peter—can be seen as a long introduction in which the author in careful and rather ordinary terms lays a foundation for himself and for his actual subject and purpose. First it is a matter of the sin among the believers, followed by the schism within the community of faith, and finally the fundamental division between those who sin and those who do righteousness. In several ways, what is said in this section has been foreshadowed earlier, but it is now set out more straightforwardly in a fundamental argument. By means of this altered form the section introduces what follows, i.e., the letter's second part, which is concerned with mutual love among the believers. Thus the section 1 John 2:28—3:10 both closes and introduces, thereby becoming a central pivot point in the letter as a whole.

This double character of closing and introducing may perhaps explain the difficulties interpreters have had with fitting these verses into an overarching arrangement. Suggestions here are unusually many, both in commentaries and in translations. Here, more than in any other section, the author speaks directly to his audience. Among others, the following phrases show this:

- And now, dear children
- If you know that . . . then you also know . . .
- See what love the Father has given us . . .
- Beloved!
- And you know that . . .
- Dear children

In addition there is also a theme very central for the recipients: being children of God. In this way 1 John 2:28—3:10 displays a greater emotional intimacy than any earlier section in the letter.

The section begins with a direct exhortation and then follows it up with several indirect exhortations of various kinds: if you know, then know (v. 29); he purifies himself (v. 3); the many formulations with "everyone who" (vv. 3, 4, 6, 7, 8, 9, 10). The audience may apply these things to themselves as they see fit. They must also fill in the reference for the many third-person pronouns found in the section. "He," *ekeinos*, is used of Jesus three times (vv. 3, 5, 7). Not until the end does the intended referent, Jesus or God, become explicit.

According to my reading, Jesus is at the center in this section, with the exception of vv. 1–3 and the fundamental statements about the children of God and the devil in v. 10. God is brought in with the phrase "born of him" (v. 29c) and Jesus returns in the pronoun "he" at v. 3b. But the change at v. 29 is troublesome. The phrase "his coming" in v. 28d certainly refers to Jesus' coming, and thus it is natural to read "he," "him," and "his" in this verse as referring to Jesus. Similarly at the beginning of v. 29, "that he [i.e., Jesus] is righteous." But because the idea of a person's being born of Jesus does not occur in the New Testament, the phrase "born of him" (v. 29c) should, as always in Johannine writings, be understood to refer to God. This otherwise ambiguous phrase leads then to the discussion of the children of God and God himself (vv. 1–3). See further the notes on these verses.

1 John 2:28—3:10: Children of God and Children of the Devil

The ambiguity in the personal references, which requires an extra effort on the part of the listeners, gives a special coherence to the entire section similar to the audience-oriented formulations and the implicit exhortations. In spite of difficulties with discerning a thematic structure, 1 John 2:28—3:10 is an engaging section, thematically and emotionally charged. Its unity and coherence are above all rhetorically motivated.

2. Delimitations and Structure

The delimiting of the text at v. 10 is, in Johannine fashion, very clearly marked by a summarizing verse introduced with the typical "by this," a framework around the entire section (inclusio) with the words "do righteousness (1 John 3:10b and 2:29c), and an overly explicit link in v. 10c to what follows.

Even the beginning is linked together in the Johannine manner with the words "remain in him," closing the previous section at 1 John 2:27 and opening this one at 2:28. The phrase "and now, dear children" functions very well as a new beginning point. And v. 28, like numerous section openers in 1 John, picks up the theme of the entire preceding section, the eschatological situation, but directing it now solely to the audience. The secessionists are included only at the end (1 John 3:7–10), and then in more general terms. This, together with what I have said about the delimitation of the previous section, leads me to insert a whole-note rest between v. 27 and v. 28.

The thematic structure, as already noted, is fairly unclear. See the Translation Display. By coupling together the present and the future, v. 28 envisions an introductory scene at the last judgment, i.e., the encounter with Jesus when he returns. Verse 29 functions almost as a theme verse, in which the concept of righteousness is also related to the recipients' situation at the final judgment. In one sense, it is people's deeds that determine the outcome. Through its content and with the phrase "everyone who does righteousness," v. 29 pre-announces what dominates vv. 4–10 and the repeated antitheses that are found there. At the same time, the final words of v. 29 lead to an emotionally intimate representation of the recipients as God's children both now and in the future. On the other hand, v. 3 returns listeners' attention to "everyone who does righteousness" in v. 29c. This phrase, finally, links together the beginning and the end (v. 10). The content of the two final verses also rounds things off by generally taking up the earlier themes: being born of God, living righteously, being God's children and being revealed as such (1 John 2:28—3:3), and committing sin (3:4–9).

The many participial constructions introduced with "everyone/the one who" are especially observable in this section. This has led some interpreters to attempt reconstructing a special source behind the text. The antitheses occur throughout the section. See the Translation Display.

- Everyone who does righteousness is born of him
- Everyone who has this hope in him purifies himself

- Everyone who commits sin . . .
- Everyone who remains in him does not sin
- Everyone who sins . . .

- The one who does righteousness . . .
- The one who commits sin . . .
- Everyone who is born of God does not sin

- Everyone who does not do righteousness . . .
- The one who does not love his brother

In the more embellished beginning the positive perspective is mentioned twice, whereas the negative formulations are given somewhat more space at the end. This very clause structure, like parallelism, is common in the Johannine writings, and thus it is hardly necessary to presume a literary *Vorlage* behind the section. More likely it is a case of a Johannine speech pattern of a more or less consistent shape, even to the point of fixed phrases and sentences.

Taken as a whole, this section is dominated by a very general, collective, and foundational perspective: it has to do with the present and the future, with "we" and every individual, with practicing righteousness or sin, with being the children of God or the children of the devil. The basic conditions for being a child of God are concretized later in the two-fold covenant commandment in 1 John 3:23, to believe and to love, brought together in 1 John 3:11–24 and 5:1–12, but taken separately in 1 John 4:1–6 and 4:7–11. In this section, vv. 28–29 form an introductory paragraph on the final judgment, 3:1–3 have the children of God as a cohesive theme, and the remainder, vv. 4–9, broken into two parts by an admonition at v. 7, is concentrated around the principle that "the children of God do not sin." The second part, vv. 7c–9, repeats, varies, sharpens and deepens the first part, vv. 4–6. In v. 10 the result of the entire argument is summarized with a clear division between the children of God and the children of the devil, with an indication, finally, of what comes now in the letter's second main part. See the Translation Display.

Interpretation

1. On Judgment Day (2:28–29)

This new section begins in the usual way with a reference to the end of the previous section, in this case with a verbatim repetition: "Remain in it," or "Remain in him";

1 John 2:28—3:10: Children of God and Children of the Devil

the Greek text can be translated either way. The earlier section focused on those who opposed the Messiah (antichrists) and would not confess Jesus as being the Messiah. Neither would they hold fast to what was there from the beginning, which likewise had Jesus as the Messiah at its center. The context in v. 27 is an argument for translating "remain in it," i.e., in the teaching of the anointing; that in v. 28 argues for "remain in him," i.e., in Jesus the Messiah, God's son. To end one section with "Remain in him" (v. 27) and then to continue in the next with "Remain in him" carries special weight in the context. It is most natural then to interpret "remain in him" as "remain in Jesus the Messiah, God's son."

But it is not just these words that make the connection with the foregoing. The entire section does so by maintaining the perspective that "it is now the last hour" (2:18). The eschatological orientation is pushed one step further and we arrive in v. 28 at the Day of Judgment. The very first words in v. 28 indeed mark a new beginning (see the note), but in terms of content they continue the theme from the section before, though in a varied and deepened form. It is necessary to remain in Jesus the Messiah, God's son, especially in view of what happens on the Judgment Day. There will then be only two alternatives: confidence (see the note) that makes it possible to stand steady before the judge, or shame that drives people away from him and thus from eternal life with him.

According to Daniel's apocalyptic vision of the future, there will at last come "a time of persecution such as never before," but after that the people will be rescued, "everyone who is found written in the book. Many of those who sleep in the dust of the earth shall awake, some to everlasting life, and some to shame and everlasting contempt. Those who are wise shall shine like the brightness of the sky, and those who lead many to righteousness, like the stars forever and ever" (Dan 12:1–3). God's people are here divided into two camps. The Septuagint speaks of "everlasting life" and of "dispersion and everlasting shame." Those recorded in the book, those who are wise, "those who hold fast to my words" (LXX), will be delivered.

Jesus too speaks of a division on the resurrection day: "those who have done good will be raised to life, those who have done evil will be raised to judgment" (John 5:29). He also says, "Those who hear my word and believe in him who sent me, shall have eternal life. They will not come under judgment, but have passed from death to life" (John 5:24).

According to John 5, it is Jesus who judges. "The Father judges no one, but has given all judgment to the Son" (John 5:22). It is true nonetheless that he does only what the Father does. "I can do nothing on my own," he says. "As I hear, so I judge, and my judgment is just, because I do not follow my own will, but the will of him who sent me" (John 5:30). It is thus not so very strange in Johannine perspective when it is said in v. 28 that the judgment occurs "when he appears," at his return (v. 28d). Only here in all Johannine literature do we find the word "return," in Greek *parousia*, which in the first century was used of a god incognito who manifests himself through wonder-working, or of the visit of a Caesar or a king to a particular vicinity (in Latin, *adventus*). Here Jesus clearly functions as judge, but in 2:1 he is defender and advocate before the Father. The Day of Judgment is also expressly mentioned in 4:17. The only thing said there is that the confidence that the letter's recipients can have depends on the fact that just as Christ is, so are they too in this world.

The comparison with Christ is also found in v. 29, if we interpret the words "he is righteous" to refer to Jesus (see note). In 2:1 he is described as righteous, likewise in 3:7d, which should be read as equivalent in meaning to "sin is not found in him" (3:5c). Verse 29 is indirectly an admonition: "Live righteously, just as he is righteous." Righteousness is indicated at the end of this section as the criterion for who is a child of God and who is a child of the devil, and thus it has to do with the double result of the judgment. The idea of righteousness belongs closely with the theme of the Judgment Day, something that can also be explained by what is said about this day in 4:17 (just as Christ is). But the train of thought is broken by the unexpected closing words in v. 29: "is born of him," i.e., of God (see the note). It recurs later in v. 9 and in the letter's second part. See Appendix 11, Begotten/Born of God.

2. Already God's children—not yet like God (3:1–3)

The words "born of Him" at the end of v. 29 inspire thoughts of the Messiah-believers as God's children. This theme is explored with considerable energy in vv. 1–3. The point of view changes from "you" to "we"; God and we occupy the stage; Jesus is not mentioned until the last line of the paragraph; exclamations, admonitions, repetitions, direct addresses, and assurances draw the listeners into what is said; and the words take on a warmth lacking in the immediate context. Thus these verses contribute in their way to the section's peculiar character. See Analysis, point 1.

"We are called God's children," "and that we are," "now we are children of God" (vv. 1–2): three times this is stated in this short paragraph. And the children of God are identified even more precisely through being contrasted with "the world" (v. 1de). God's children know God (see Interpretation for 2:3–4); the world does not. By this means God's children are distinguished from the people in their environment. A dualistic model dominates the entire section: confidence—shame on the Judgment Day; God's children—the world; do righteousness—do not do righteousness; not sin—sin; God's son—the devil; God's children—the devil's children. Verses 1–3 can seem like a glaring sidetrack, but they actually contribute to the overall argument in 2:28—3:10 by assuring the letter's recipients that they belong to the category of God's children.

The concept of God's children recurs often in later Christian parlance, but it is not very common in the Bible. See Appendix 11, Begotten/Born of God. It presumably has a double background in the Old Testament and in contemporary Jewish writings, and is anchored in a special way in Johannine ideas. According to Jesus' words in Matt 5:9, peacemakers will one day be "called sons of God." In the Old Testament, we sometimes hear of "sons of God," figures of divine nature around God's throne in heaven (Ps 29:1;

89:6; Job 1:6; 2:1; 38:7; Dan 3:25). Later writings portray righteous persons who have died as being "numbered among God's sons" and having their place "among the saints" (Wis 5:5). The sons of God are equated with angels in God's presence (Luke 20:36). According to Paul, God's sons will appear together with Jesus at his return, when the new creation becomes a reality (Rom 8:19–23). Jesus therefore promises his disciples, the peacemakers, that one day they will be in God's immediate presence and be numbered among the sons of God. All this can contribute to our grasp of what being children of God means in the Johannine writings. They have been born as God's children, begotten of God, and they bear God's seed within them, i.e., they are in one sense divine, and already now, in contrast to God's sons in other New Testament writings (John 1:12–13; 1 John 3:9–10). The phrase "God's son," however, is reserved for Jesus in the Johannine literature, and the Jesus-believers are called God's children.

A potentially more immediate background occurs in the description of the covenant between God and the people and of the renewal of this covenant. "You are children of the Lord, your God," says Moses in Deut 14:1, with reference to the covenant at Sinai and with conclusions about what that implies for their way of life. When God renews God's covenant and re-establishes his people, according to a Jewish text from the second century BCE, God will give them "a holy spirit" and cleanse them so that they return to the Lord and keep God's commandments. "I will be a father unto them, and they will be sons unto me. They shall all be called sons of the living God." All angels will see and confess "that they are my sons and I am their father in truth and righteousness. And I shall love them," (*Jub.* 1:22–25). See further Appendix 9, A Renewed Covenant, and Appendix 11, Begotten/Born of God. The concept of God's children/God's sons/God's sons and daughters in these texts thus designates a covenant relationship to God and a commitment to God's commandments. It also characterizes God's children in 2:28—3:10.

They have become God's children through a divine begetting, through having "been born not of blood, or of the will of the flesh, nor of the will of man, but of God" (John 1:13). See Appendix 11, Begotten/Born of God. This is what is most unique about the Johannine concept of God's children. In every passage, the begetting is coupled together with being God's children (John 1:12–13; 1 John 2:29—3:2; 3:9–10; and 5:1–2). It is God himself that has made them to be children of God through a second birth, which is spoken of in John 3 as a birth from above or a birth by the Spirit. It is all a gift of God to them, an expression of God's love for them (v. 1). God has given them a part of himself, of his spirit (3:24; 4:13). They have God's *sperma* within them (3:9). Saying that they are now already God's children can be seen as way of saying that the last hour has arrived. As they see it, the relationship with God has been radically altered by the renewal of the covenant. Eternal life, divine life, is already a reality for those who know God through Jesus the Messiah, God's son. Thus the idea of God's children is also an important expression for the new fellowship with God. Now they are God's children; in the future they will be sons of God. Their present existence is determined by the relationship to God, and the description of the imminent consummation in heaven is also framed in terms of the relationship with God, i.e., seeing God as God is, becoming like God.

The last hour is a time of "revelation," i.e., what is godly and what is demonic will be obvious on earth. Everything has its beginning in the life and work of Jesus, his words and deeds, from birth to death, whether as a revelation of life, divine life (1:1–3; 3:5, 8), or a revelation of God's love (4:9). Antichrist, or rather the antichrists, have already appeared (2:18); Christ will appear very soon (2:28); God's children and the children of the devil will become manifest (3:10). But not everything has been revealed. There is already now much of God in the believers on the earth, including the confrontation with evil and what that implies. But at least one thing remains as yet unrealized: that God's children become like God. *Now* they are God's children, with all that is implied by that in the Johannine context, but it has *not yet* been revealed what they shall be, i.e., like God (v. 2).

I have taken God rather than Jesus to be the primary reference in vv. 1–3, and therefore the hope mentioned in v. 3—the only time hope is mentioned in the Johannine literature—is a hope in God, the Father, the origin and source of love. The hope of seeing God, of being with him, and of becoming like him, leads to the question of how they should live in anticipation of the Judgment Day, when they will be able to meet their judge with confidence. They know that they must live in righteousness, just as Christ is righteous (2:29). This is now formulated with words reminiscent of how the people cleansed themselves in preparation for meeting God at Sinai. Here they are to purify themselves as Christ is pure (v. 3). In view of the Judgment Day, they can remind each other that "just as Christ is, so are we in this world" (4:17).

3. Sin As Lawlessness at the End of Time (3:4–9)

The words "everyone who purifies himself . . . as he is pure," at the end of v. 3, lead the argument to the theme that was formulated in v. 29. It is developed here in two stages, vv. 4–6 and vv. 7c–9. The words "children" in v. 7a and "let no one deceive you" in v. 7b, a reminder of the great risk of deception (1:8b, 10b; 2:22, 26; 4:1–6), underscore the gravity in the repetition that follows, with its reference to the devil and his works. Verses 7c–9 further develop the discussion in vv. 4–6. See the Analysis above, point 2.

The continued argument for a life of righteousness in view of Judgment Day implies a definition of what sin is: "Sin is lawlessness" (3:4b), i.e., lawlessness in a particular form. The word in the Greek text, *anomia*, represents a long list of words in the Hebrew Bible, and in the Greek translation of the Old Testament it can sometimes be associated with Satan and even render the Hebrew "Belial," another word for Satan (2 Sam 22:5; Ps 17:3). In later Jewish texts Israel's end-time sin is coupled together with Satan and his works. *T. Dan* 6:1–6 warns readers to be on guard against Satan and his spirits and to cling to God and to the angel who speaks for them. God will fight

1 John 2:28—3:10: Children of God and Children of the Devil

against the enemy's kingdom and will one day obliterate it. In this "time of lawlessness for Israel, the Lord will not desert his people and therefore they will seek to do his will. According to some manuscripts, the angels at Jesus' grave at the end of Mark's Gospel also speak of "this age of lawlessness and unbelief under Satan" (Mark 16:14 *v.l.*)

One of Qumran's most important texts concerning the righteous (1QS 3:17—4:18) claims that human beings are driven by "the spirit of truth or of deception," with the consequence that they are divided into "the sons of righteousness," those who walk in the light, and the "sons of deception," who walk in the darkness. See also 1QS 5:2, 20; 10:20. Deception is thus set in opposition to both truth and righteousness, and the list of many sins belonging to deception is long (1QS 4, 9–11). The word translated here as "deception" also means fraud, falsehood, injustice, and unrighteousness, and it is translated numerous times in the Psalms as "lawlessness" (Ps 37:1; 58:2; 64:6; 89:22). In 2 Cor 6:14—7:1, which has many similarities in phrasing with the Qumran writings, it is also said, "What has righteousness to do with lawlessness, and what does light have in common with darkness?"

When the weeds are separated from the wheat at the world's end, according to the parable in Matthew 13, the Son of man will send out his angels and they will remove from his kingdom "all causes of sin and all evildoers" (13:41). In Matthew's Gospel, Jesus speaks several times about the lawlessness of the end-time (Matt 7:22–23; 24:11–12) and his words lie behind the description of the situation at the end of time in *Did.* 16:3–4, a Christian text contemporary with the Johannine writings: "For in the last days false prophets and corrupters shall be multiplied, and the sheep shall be turned into wolves, and love shall be turned into hate; for when lawlessness increases, they shall hate and persecute and betray one another, and then shall appear the world-deceiver as Son of God, and shall do signs and wonders, and the earth shall be delivered into his hands, and he shall do iniquitous things which have never yet come to pass since the beginning." Besides the fact that these lines are in many ways reminiscent of 1 John, they are also, together with certain passages in Jesus' apocryphal speech in Matt 24–25, evidence that the word "lawlessness" at this time could have a special meaning in connection to the events of the end of all time. Thus whoever sins does the deeds of lawlessness (1 John 3:4).

The idea that sin will one day vanish also belongs to Jewish conceptions of the end-time. In a renewed covenant, God shall free his people from everything that makes them impure (Ezek 36:29). "And he made for all his works a new and righteous nature, so that they should not sin in their whole nature forever, but should be all righteous each in his kind for all time" (*Jub.* 5:12). The *Testament of Levi* speaks of the priest of the end-time: "to him all the words of the Lord will be revealed." When he comes, "sin shall vanish, and the lawless shall rest from their evil deeds, and the righteous shall find rest in him" (*T. Levi* 18:2, 9). At the Judgment Day God will put an end to all that is called "deception" and destroy it forever. Through God's holy spirit, God will purify from all unrighteous deeds those who enter into the new fellowship in Qumran. Thus shall the righteous gain insight into the knowledge of the Most High and into the wisdom of the sons of heaven. "For these God has chosen for an everlasting covenant" (1QS 4:19–23).

With this Jewish background, the continuation in 3:5 is not unexpected. Jesus the Messiah, God's son, came to take sins away, which is how his earthly work can be summarized. Sin is a central theme in the letter because it separates humanity from God. This finds expression in many ways in the letter: purify, forgive, reconcile, take away, destroy sin; indeed even intercession is available as a means of taking sin away (2:1; 5:16–17). At the renewal of the covenant in Exod 34:9–10, Moses is already praying for his people: "Take away our sins and our iniquities [*anomia* in the Greek translation] and we shall be yours." To this, the Lord responds by once again making a covenant with them. The words "take away the sins" come close to the description of Jesus' work in John 1:29, where John the Baptist says, "Behold the lamb of God who takes away the sin of the world." In the letter it is natural to understand "take away sins" on the basis of 1:7 and 2:2. Jesus dies as a sacrificial lamb and his blood purifies from sin. Jesus is the atonement for the sin of all humanity.

The one who takes sins away is himself without sin, which is expressed in 2:29 and 3:7d with the words "he is righteous." This is a very common thought in the New Testament (Heb 4:15; 1 Pet 2:22; 2 Cor 5:21) and occurs as well in the Gospel of John (John 8:46; 14:30). It is a consequence of his union with God, of the fact that the Father and the Son are one. Likewise the letter's recipients' union with the sin-free Christ means that they do not sin (3:6a; here as in 2:27–28 expressed with the words "remain in"). It is then reinforced in the Johannine writings with two other common verbs of experience that express extreme closeness, namely "see" and "know." Whoever has seen the Son has also seen the Father (John 14:9); whoever has learned to know the Son also knows the Father (John 8:19). Thus here too, just as in 1 John 2:29 and 3:9, union with God indirectly becomes what leads them not to sin, what leads them to do righteousness.

What has now been said about sin is strengthened in vv. 7c–9 through sin's being made to depend fully on the devil, through the status of the righteous person being described as born of God (divinely begotten), and through the categorical claim that anyone born of God cannot sin. The dualistic model becomes therefore more pronounced: practice righteousness—practice sin; Christ is righteous—the devil is a sinner from the beginning; some are of the devil—some are born of God. Once more Jesus' earthly work is presented in formulations similar to those in 3:5. He will destroy "the devil's works" (3:8).

After what we have said above about the time of lawlessness, it is not unexpected that the devil would show up here. According to Jewish conceptions he will become much more sinful in the end-time, and the battle between him and God or God's anointed one will reach its culmination. According to John's Gospel, Jesus has overcome the ruler of this world through what happened in Jesus' "hour" (John 12:31; 16:11). Consequently sin exists no longer. The Jews who abandoned their faith in Jesus in John 8:38–44 are described by him as those who do the works of the devil. Unbelief is the great sin. They are of the devil; the devil is their father. See Appendix 13, Cain as the Devil's Son. In the letter we read that human beings "are of the devil" or that they "are the devil's children," but not that they "are born of the devil."

In his great love, God has made those who believe in Jesus the Messiah, God's son, to be God's own children (vv. 1–2). In God's love God renewed the covenant with them, and as a result nearness to God became more intensive than ever before. In the Johannine texts, especially in the first letter, this is expressed through the image of divine begetting. In his great love, God has begotten them and made them his children. They have God's *sperma* within them. Some interpreters read God's *sperma* as God's offspring, with reference to Jesus Christ, but this is not supported in the context. See Appendix 11, Begotten/Born of God. Being a child of God is a gift of God, a result of God's action. God creates through God's word as well as through God's spirit. If we must choose between these two alternatives for the meaning of the formulation about God's *sperma*, then I choose the latter one. By God's spirit God is the constantly active power that gave them life, a divine life, when they came to faith and were baptized. God is the constantly active power that enables them not to sin, but to act righteously. See further Appendix 11, Begotten/Born of God.

4. God's Children and the Devil's Children Become Manifest (3:10)

The entire rationale in this section, based as it is on the imminence of the Judgment and the intensive presence of the Lawlessness and the devil, issues in a conclusion in v. 10. The children of God and the children of the devil are here set side by side. At the final judgment, they will become definitively visible and will be compelled to go their separate ways. But even in the last days before the Judgment they can be distinguished from one another. The children of the devil do not practice righteousness, they sin, they do the works of the devil, and they do not love their fellow "believers."

It should be possible then to assert the opposite regarding God's children, but the author says nothing about them in the conclusion. He has, however, admonished them earlier to do righteousness as Christ is righteous, and he assumes that they will purify themselves as Christ is pure. At the same time, he also claims that they do not sin, that they cannot sin. They remain in Christ, who has taken away sins, and he is without sin. God has made them God's own through a divine begetting. Here we have a powerful tension between admonition and declaration, something that can be understood in light of the strong eschatological direction taken in this section. The completely decisive thing is to remain in Jesus the Messiah, God's son. By rejecting Jesus as Messiah, God's son, those who have left the Johannine fellowship become children of the devil. Perhaps the author is thinking of the sin "unto death" when he says that God's children cannot sin. See further Appendix 12, They Cannot Sin, and Appendix 19, The Sin unto Death.

7

1 John 3:11–24: Love One Another

Translation Display

11a	For this is the message
11b	that you have heard from the beginning
11c	that we should love one another.
12a	Not like Cain
12b	he was of the evil one
12c	and murdered his brother.
12d	And why did he murder him?
12e	Because his works were evil
12f	but his brother's were righteous.
13a	Do not be amazed
13b	brothers
13c	if the world hates you.
14a	We know that we have passed from death to life
14b	because we love the brothers.
14c	The one who does not love remains in death.
15a	Everyone who hates his brother is a murderer
15b	and you know that no murderer has eternal life abiding in him.
16a	By this we have learned to recognize love:
16b	he laid down his life for us.
16c	We, too, ought to lay down our lives for the brothers.
17a	But if anyone has worldly provisions
17b	and sees his brother in need
17c	and shuts up his heart against him
17d	how can God's love abide in him?

18a	Dear children
18b	let us not love with words or tongue, but with action and truth.
19a	By this we know
19b	that we are of the truth
19c	and we shall assure our heart before him
20a	that if our heart condemns us
20b	that God is greater than our heart
20c	and he knows everything.
21a	Beloved,
21b	if our heart does not condemn us
21c	then we have confidence before God.
22a	And whatever we ask for we receive from him
22b	because we keep his commandments and do what is pleasing before him.
23a	And this is his commandment:
23b	that we should believe in the name of his son, Jesus the Messiah,
23c	and that we should love one another
23d	as he gave us a commandment.
24a	And the one who keeps his commandments remains in him and he in him.
24b	And by this we know that he remains in us
24c	by the spirit that he gave us.

Notes

3:11. For this is the message . . . that. See notes on 1 John 1:5.

that you have heard from the beginning. Literally, "which you heard from the beginning," i.e., the same formulation as in 1 John 2:24. See Appendix 10, What you Heard From the Beginning.

12. Not like Cain. The formulation renders exactly the three words in Gkt. It is probably a shortened form (ellipsis) of "not like Cain loved/acted toward his brother," which is then followed by "he was of the evil one." Some translations expand slightly with "we must not be like Cain" (NRSV) or "Do not be like Cain" (NIV). Cain is used in contemporary texts as an example of people who do not believe. On the Jewish background, see Appendix 13, Cain as the Devil's Son.

of the evil one. See the note "is of the devil" at 1 John 3:8.

murdered. Gkt has the usual word for slaughtering a sacrificial animal. Rev 5:6, 9, 12, and 13:8 speak of "the lamb that was slaughtered." According to Gen 22:10, Abraham took up his knife in order to "slaughter" his son. The expression is also used in other contexts for brutal killing.

First John

And why did he murder him? Questions of this sort heighten the drama of the presentation. See also 1 John 3:17 and John 9:36.

works . . . evil . . . righteous. A continuation of the dualistic formulations in 1 John 2:28—3:10. See the note "destroy the devil's works" at 1 John 3:8, and Appendix 13, Cain as the Devil's Son.

13. Some manuscripts—among others, Codex Sinaiticus and early versions—introduce v. 13 with an "and" indicating that these words are linked to what was said earlier, and therefore imply that it does not begin a new paragraph. The words ought to have the same function as does the beginning of 1 John 3:7.

Do not be amazed . . . if. The same admonition is found in John 3:7 and 5:28, where, however, it is followed by "that" (*hoti*) and not with "if" (*ei*), as it is here. The sense of "if" with the indicative—something like, "when"—closely approximates the declarative "that." According to John 15:18 and 17:14, the world hates those who belong to Jesus.

brothers. This common NT word of address is used only here in the Johannine texts, presumably motivated by the use of "brother" and "the brothers" in this paragraph. Familial concepts such as fathers, children, and brothers emphasize the close inner relationship within the Johannine community. See the description of the recipients of 2 John as a family of truth and love, in the Interpretation of 2 John 1–3, 12–13.

14. We. Gkt has the pronoun "we" (*hēmeis*) placed first in the clause, which gives the word a contrastive emphasis. Cf. the same use of "you" at the beginning of 1 John 2:20, 24, and 27.

from death to life. Verse 15b uses the related expression "has eternal life abiding in him." See Appendix 6, Life, Eternal Life.

because, Gkt *hoti*, introduces a clause that gives the rationale either for "we know" or for "we have passed from death to life." If human love is seen as an outflow of God's love, the latter works better, and this is reinforced by what is said in v. 14c.

the brothers. In this context it is fellow believers in the Johannine fellowship that are probably in view, or possibly Messiah-believing Jews who were more loosely associated with them. For the latter use of the word, see 3 John 3 and 5.

remains in. The verb in Gkt, *menein,* is nearly always used with a positive extension, but here it is with something negative (death), as in John 12:46 (the darkness). "To be in the darkness" (1 John 2:9) has a similar sense. See Appendix 15, God in Them and They in God.

15. Everyone who hates. Gkt employs the usual construction with "everyone" (*pas* + article + participle).

1 John 3:11–24: Love One Another

murderer. Gkt has an expression very unusual in Greek: *anthrōpoktonos*. It can be applied concretely to Cain, but the expression can also have a weakened sense. Jesus includes, e.g., "to be angry with one's brother" as part of the commandment not to kill (Matt 5:21–22), and Eliezer ben Hyrcanus, a scribe contemporary with 1 John, says, "The one who hates his brother belongs to those who shed blood" (*Derek Erets Rabba* 11.13).

no murderer has eternal life abiding in him. Anyone who kills another person forfeits his own life (Gen 9:6). The one who does not love his brother/hates his brother loses out on all eschatological blessings, now and in the future.

16. By this we have learned to recognize love: he . . . See the note on 1 John 1:5. A cataphoric "this" is taken up in a subsequent that-clause (in Gkt, *hoti*).

he, Gkt *ekeinos,* refers to Jesus. See the note "he" at 1 John 2:6 and 3:3.

laid down his life. Gkt has a typical Johannine expression (eight times in John and two in 1 John): to lay aside one's life as one takes off clothing. It has the nuance of an act of free will.

We, too. In Greek, *kai hēmeis,* which can also be translated "and we." The word *hēmeis* adds emphasis to "we."

ought. The formulation is Johannine and often refers to Jesus as the model for a disciple's lifestyle. See the notes on 1 John 2:6 and 3 John 8.

17. But if anyone has worldly provisions and sees his brother in need and shuts up his heart against him. The three clauses introducing this verse exemplify the so-called *casus pendens,* where the subject is taken up by "him" at the end of the sentence. See the note at the beginning of 1 John 2:24.

A "but" (*de*) beginning v. 17 indicates that what follows is in contrast with the end of v. 16.

worldly provisions. Gkt has just one word, *bios,* which means life, life's necessities, resources, possessions, things needed for living. See the note "the pride in riches" at 1 John 2:16.

in need. Literally, "have need," as a contrast to what immediately precedes.

heart. Gkt does not have the usual word for heart, *kardia,* but *splangchna,* which in the OT often means mercy, compassion. The person in question does not even have sympathy for the suffering brother.

God's love. See the note at 1 John 2:5. The person in question obstructs God's love, which works through human beings.

abide in. See Appendix 15, God in Them and They in God.

First John

18. Dear children, Gkt *teknia*. See the notes on 1 John 2:1, 12, and 14.

not . . . with words or tongue, but with action and truth. In Gkt, "words" and "tongue" are in the instrumental dative; "action and truth" are governed by "in" (*en*). Verse 18 may sound like a general maxim. It is to be interpreted, however, in terms of its Johannine context and its clear connection to the beginning and main theme of this paragraph.

The Gospel of John has a penchant for expressions in which two words are to be interpreted in relation to one another, e.g., "in spirit and truth" (John 4:23). At the same time, the meaning of these double expressions is not so clear. Several interpretations have been put forward for the formulation in 1 John 3:18:

a. not with many words, but with a multiplicity of deeds (the words in both halves are synonyms and reinforce one another).

b. not with fine-sounding words, but with genuine deeds (a form of hendiadys in both halves).

c. not with lip-service, but with deeds of truth (the second word in both halves clarifies the first). The most characteristically Johannine formulation is thus the last word, "(with) (the) truth." See the notes on 2 John 3 and 3 John 1–3. Similarly, the word "truth" provides a link to the next verse. "In deed and truth" can also be understood as "with the deeds that come of the truth." In a corresponding way the first half of this expression would then be "with words that come of the tongue." This last alternative fits the context best.

19/20. By this we will know . . . The convoluted structure of v. 19 is addressed below in the Analysis, point 2. Some translations bring vv. 19 and 20 together into one sentence in order to alleviate the difficult syntax. A more literal rendering is provided in the Translation Display.

One difficulty in v. 20 is the repetition of the word "that" (*hoti*) in v. 20a and v. 20b. In the present context, this word can also be rendered as "since." In v. 20a it is followed by the word "if" (*ean*), which can be taken as equivalent to *an*, and thus the combination *hoti an* takes on the meaning "whatever." It is read then as an indefinite relative pronoun in the accusative (restrictive accusative) combined with the particle *an*, which gives the clause a conditional nuance.

we are of the truth. See the notes "comes not from the Father but from the world" at 1 John 2:16 and "of the devil" at 1 John 3:8.

our heart. The word "heart," which comes close to our word "conscience," has an OT background. It is God who knows the heart of human beings (1 Chr 28:9). The just man avoids doing what is evil, "being condemned not by another, but by his own heart" (*T. Gad* 5:3). "Happy are those whose hearts do not condemn them" (Sir 14:2).

assure. The word in Gkt, *peithein*, normally has the meaning of convince, persuade, i.e., to convince a person to believe in something he or she does not usually believe in, or to persuade someone to do something that he or she otherwise does not want to do. This "something" is most often expressed with a that-clause, as evidently here in v. 20b. Translators choose a meaning appropriate to this sense: calm, still, fill with confidence. This seems to fit the context better and enables what follows to be understood as a motivation. See Analysis, point 2.

21. Beloved. See the note on 1 John 2:7.

have confidence. See the note "we may have boldness" at 1 John 2:28. The ongoing discussion suggests that what is most in view here is a confidence in the present and not merely with regard to the future judgment.

22. ask for. The word in Gkt, *aitein*, means desire, ask to receive. Occasionally the verb *erōtan* can be used as a synonym (1 John 5:14–16; John 16:23). Prayer (in Jesus' name) and God's full attention to prayer constitute a typical Johannine theme (John 14:14–16; 15:7, 16; 16:23–26).

his commandments. See the note "we keep his commandments," at 1 John 2:3.

what is pleasing before him. The implication is that it is certain deeds that are pleasing to him. The redundant expression—to keep God's commandments and to do before him deeds that are pleasing to him—gives weight to the rationale in v. 22 and leads thoughts to God's covenant with the people of Israel, which demands love for and obedience toward God on the part of the people.

23. And this is his commandment: that. Gkt has the same construction as in the beginning of 1 John 1:5 and 3:11. See the notes there. The cataphoric "this" is unpacked by two that-clauses (governed together by a single explanatory *hina*): "that we should believe . . . and that we should love . . ." The word for commandment is in the singular here. For the thematic chiasm in vv. 23–24, see the Analysis for 1 John 2:3–11, point 2.

believe in. The verb "believe" (*pisteuein*) is a central feature of John's Gospel (98 occurrences) and of 1 John (nine occurrences). It can be construed in various ways: 39 times with a preposition that usually means "to, in the direction of" (*eis*), 21 times with the dative, 16 times with a that-clause, and once with an accusative object. In other instances it has no qualifiers, i.e., "believe" stands alone. Here in v. 23, we have believe + the dative. Many grammarians think that the first construction expresses an especially close relationship between subject and object: commit oneself to, bind oneself to, unite oneself with. The use in 1 John 5:10 of the first two constructions side by side can be taken as an argument that there does not need to be any great distinction between them.

First John

in the name of his son, Jesus the Messiah, i.e., in everything implied in the name Jesus the Messiah, the son of God. See the note "on account of his name," at 1 John 2:12.

as he gave us a commandment. Judging from the numerous references to God in vv. 18–24 and the chiastic model mentioned in the note on v. 23, these words presumably parallel the beginning of the verse. See the Analysis for 1 John 2:3–11, point 2.

This commandment in the renewed covenant is one of the many gifts that God conveys through his son Jesus the Messiah. See the note "has given," at 1 John 3:1.

24. The one who keeps his commandments. Literally, "and the one keeping his commandments." Gkt has a continuing "and" followed by a substantive participle. The context implies that the commandments in question are God's commandments.

remains in him and he in him. See Appendix 15, God in Them and They in God.

And by this we know that he. See the opening comments on 1 John 2:3. This is the third time that this sort of phrase occurs in the paragraph: the first time was with the verb in the perfect tense (v. 16); the second with the verb in the future (v. 19); and the third with the verb in the present (v. 24). A cataphoric "this" is taken up first by a that-clause (Gkt *hoti*) and then by a prepositional phrase—"by the spirit that he gave us"—in which the word "spirit" foreshadows the next paragraph. God's commandment (v. 23) and God's spirit (v. 24) are paralleled to one another here as the gifts that define the existence of the letter's recipients. See Appendix 9, A Renewed Covenant.

by the spirit. Apart from 1 John 4:1–6 and 5:6, 8, the spirit is mentioned only here and in 1 John 4:13 in the Johannine epistles. Both cases use the preposition *ek* ("from, by"), which in 4:13 is most naturally understood as partitive: God has given them a portion of his spirit. In 3:24 *ek* seems to indicate the source or the cause for knowing that God remains in us. The spirit in 1 John comes close to the concept of the spirit of truth, the Helper, as it is presented in John 14–16. The concept "truth" is found in this paragraph and in 1 John 4:1–6, as well as in connection with the anointing in 1 John 2:20. See the note there.

that. In Gkt, the relative "that" (*hou*) is in the genitive case by attraction to the antecedent "spirit," which is in the genitive.

he gave us. According to the Gospel of John, it is both the Father (John 14:26) and the Son (John 15:26) who send the spirit of truth to the disciples. The context here supports understanding "he" to refer to God. Cf. 1 John 4:13.

Analysis

1. Delimitations and Structure

The Johannine way of ending and introducing a section in 1 John 3:10 and the thematically cohesive unity in 1 John 4:1–6 make it easy to delimit this portion of the letter. The allusion to the following section through the word "spirit" in 1 John 3:24c and a thematically effective introductory verse in 1 John 3:11 contribute to this as well. Beginning a new section with "for/since" (*hoti*) is of course not typical. It may have to do with the link between the two sections: " . . . anyone who does not love his brother, for . . ." This can also be compared with "and" (*kai*) as the opening word in 1 John 1:5; 2:3, and 2:28, and is perhaps to be explained in terms of a more oral culture and the Johannine way of moving from one section to another. Raymond Brown regards v. 11—which admittedly is very similar to 1 John 1:5—as introducing the letter's second part, and he thereby obtains the same structure as in the Gospel. From a functional and thematic point of view, this does not work well, but the rough bi-partite structure can perhaps be attributed to a revision of the letter. See further chap. 12, point 3.

The section's internal structure is in greater dispute. The author addresses his audience with vocatives in three separate passages: vv. 13, 18, and 21, which some readers take as indicating new sections. In general, the recipients are drawn powerfully into the interactive process found in this section with phrases such as:

- that you have heard from the beginning (v. 11b)
- why did he murder him? (v. 12d)
- Do not be amazed (v. 13a)
- brothers (v. 13b)
- how can God's love abide in him? (v. 17d)
- Dear children (v. 18a)
- let us not love with words or . . . (v. 18b)
- Beloved (v. 21a)

In addition to this, there are several indirect admonitions: we should love one another (v. 11); do not be like Cain (v. 12); we ought to lay down our lives for the brothers (v. 16); a commandment to believe and to love (v. 23); and other more general formulations in vv. 15a, 17, 22bc, and 24ab. With the many vocatives, admonitions, questions, references to the recipients' understanding and insight (vv. 11, 14, 15, 16, 19, and 24) and some strong expressions—slaughter one's brother, man-killer, give one's life for the brothers, not with words and tongue, but in deed and truth—this section takes on a clearly hortatory and argumentative character. Its coherence is perhaps to be found more at a rhetorical level than in its content.

First John

As often elsewhere in the letter, this section opens with a theme verse (v. 11). From that point, it can be divided into two paragraphs (vv. 12–17 and 18–24), each of which in turn is divisible into two parts. See the Translation Display. The first paragraph, in good rhetorical style, gives two examples: first a negative, Cain (v. 12), and then a positive, Jesus (v. 16). Both cases are supplied with an argument, most extensively in the negative case of Cain, and the content is made more profound by a connection to "eternal life" and to "God's love," respectively (vv. 13–15 and 17). The second part of the paragraph, with its context-appropriate direct address, "brothers" (v. 13), heightens the emotional level and expands on the dualism between "they" and "we": Cain, the Evil one, the world, hatred, and death, all stand in opposition to Cain's brother, the righteous one, Jesus, we/the brothers, love, and life.

The second paragraph is introduced with a strong linking verse (v. 18), which follows up the two examples by connecting to and reinforcing what was said in the theme verse (v. 11). The connection to the continuation (vv. 19–20) seems rather superficial, with "in/with truth" and "of the truth" as key terms. By direct address, repetition, and reformulation in v. 21, the argument is concluded, and it happens simultaneously with this verse's use of the words "confidence before God" to introduce the subject of the new intimate fellowship with God, expressed in the promise of God's full attention to prayer (v. 22). The double chiasm in vv. 22–24 has been described in the Analysis of 1 John 2:3–11, point 2. The final portion of the section (vv. 21–24), like the linking verse (v. 18), is also connected to the beginning of the section, especially v. 23a to v. 11a, v. 23c to v. 11c, and v. 23d to v. 11b.

This joining together of the beginning and the end, plus the other peculiarities of the text I have described, lead me to read 1 John 3:11–24 as a section divided into two paragraphs. The first paragraph is dominated, like 1 John 2:28—3:10, by a number of oppositions: Cain–his brother, Cain–Jesus, evil deeds–righteous deeds, the world–we, hate–love, and death–life. The second paragraph concentrates on the letter's recipients and their relationship to God, not least the connection, essential for life, between the covenant fellowship with God on the one hand—the open confidence, the immediate audience with God through prayer, and the mutual existence in one another—and obedience to God's commandments on the other hand.

2. Three Difficult Verses (vv. 19–21)

Verses 19–21 are troublesome for several reasons and therefore deserve special treatment in the analysis. According to some scholars, these verses are the most difficult to interpret in the entire letter. Scribes have attempted to alter the text in several places, and the suggestions for its interpretation are many.

Vocabulary and internal relationships bind vv. 19–21 into a unit: "heart" four times and only here in the letter, "condemn" twice, "before God" twice, and a kind of word play with "understand/know" (*ginōskein*) and "condemn" (*kataginōskein*). But

1 John 3:11–24: Love One Another

the language in these verses is neither Johannine nor early Christian in general; there is possibly an Old Testament ring to it. See the note on 1 John 3:19. Perhaps the unusual language has to do with the letter's Jewish roots.

The literary setting of vv. 19–21, however, has a Johannine color. The words "by this" in v. 19 are most readily understood as a reference to the content of v. 18 and thus to all the preceding discussion. Active love for the brothers testifies to belonging to the truth. Holding love and truth together is fundamental in the Johannine letters. As has already been mentioned, the phrase "in truth" in v. 18 leads to the related phrase "of the truth" in v. 19.

Verse 21, with its Johannine vocative, follows up and drives home what has just been said and proceeds to another main idea in the letter: confidence before God. Confidence in 1 John 2:28–29 directed attention primarily to the final judgment, but here as in vv. 14–15 it has to do with eternal life here and now. The Elder first of all wants to assure his children that they have fellowship with God, that they have eternal life by faith in Jesus as the Messiah, God's son, even if they sometimes sin, or still are not what they shall be, or are condemned by their hearts, or feel fearful. See the Interpretations for 1 John 2:1–2, 12–14, 28–29; 4:17–18; 5:13, 20. It is from this perspective that I read vv. 19–21.

In the Interpretation below I take up the question whether v. 20 deals with God's severity and judgment or with God's mercy and forgiveness. Here I will confine my remarks to the sentence structure in vv. 19–20. Some readers view v. 20a and v. 21b as two independent parallel alternatives: "if our heart condemns us" or "if our heart does not condemn us." But these two verses are completely dissimilar in their reasoning, and in v. 21 the argument is carried forward. The line of thought in v. 21 is as follows: if the heart that earlier condemned us no longer does so, then we have confidence, etc. In v. 19, "and" introduces a conclusion drawn from the foregoing: we are to understand the connection between love and truth and so assure our hearts, etc. "And" in v. 20c, on the other hand, makes this verse parallel to the preceding clause or clarifies it. What remains then is the meaning of the Greek word in v. 19c translated as "assure" (*peithein*) and the use of the word "that" (*hoti*) in the beginning of v. 20a and v. 20b.

The Greek word *peithein* normally means to assure, to convince, but some exegetes claim that the context and subsequent discussion demand the meaning "calm," "still," "fill with insight." The conjunction *hoti*, introducing both v. 20a and 20b, can be rendered with "that," "since," or "whatever." See the notes on vv. 19–20. These various possibilities yield then several alternatives. The two most common are: (1) And so we must calm our hearts before him no matter what our heart may accuse us of, because God is greater etc. (2) And so we must assure our hearts before him that, if our heart accuses us, that God is greater than our heart etc.

In the latter alternative, the second *hoti*—some scribes have omitted it in order to improve the syntax—is read as a repetition of the first one, both with the meaning "that." One can also choose to translate it "because" and thereby indicate what it is that we assure our heart of. I prefer alternative 2 with the more usual meaning of *peithein* and the repeated "that." The author often uses repetitions, even of "that." See, e.g., 1 John 2:21; 3:2, 14. "Whatever" is expressed three times in the Johannine writings with *hoti an*, but never with *hoti ean* as we have it here. Since the assurance results in the heart's no longer condemning (v. 21b), perhaps the differences between the two alternatives are not so very great. But viewed linguistically, the verses remain problematic.

The content then can be freely formulated in this way: Let us love one another. This is the kind of effect that God's love within us must have. Do not love with empty words alone, but show love in deeds that correspond to the truth. We know that we are the children of the truth when we love one another. But what happens if we are at times unable to love as we ought, or when our hearts accuse us? Assure yourselves then that God is greater than your hearts and knows everything. God can forgive. Then when our hearts no longer condemn us, we have open access to God: everything we ask God for we receive. This effect then is followed by God's being in us and our being in God. And by yet another gift from God: the Spirit.

Interpretation

1. We Should Love One Another (3:11)

The last words of 3:10 lead to a new theme: "that we should love one another" (v. 11). Doing righteousness in the final stage of the time of salvation, before the last judgment (2:28—3:10), takes on concrete form in loving the brothers, i.e., one's fellow believers, women and men (3:11-24). Following the opening thematic verse (v. 11), comes first a paragraph that in good rhetorical style provides two examples, a negative one (i.e., Cain, vv. 12-15) and a positive one (i.e., Jesus, vv. 16-17). The second paragraph (vv. 18-24) sharpens the exhortations and pushes the argument and its rationale yet further by showing the blessings that follow in the path of obedience to God's covenant commandments. By frequently addressing his audience, referring to their understanding and insight, subjecting them to rhetorical questions, and varying his admonitions in form and content, the Elder gives this section a powerfully exhortative and argumentative character. See further the Analysis, point 1.

By using the "we"-form, the Elder includes the entire Johannine community in his admonition: "let us love one another." This reciprocal love applies to all of them. Unity, unanimity, concord, and solidarity characterize every aspect of the new community in the renewed covenant. What is new about it has its origin and its source in God, and God is one. It is God's love alone that has created the Johannine community. Love for fellow believers is an outflow of God's love. To disrupt the community is to dissolve the renewed covenant between God and his people. This is why the Elder insists that being in concord with one another is completely decisive for the life of the community. Jesus has revealed God to his disciples "that they may be one as we are one, I in them and you in me, that they become completely one, so that the world may know that you have sent me and have loved them even as you have loved me" (John 17:22–23). See further Appendix 16, God is Love.

The introductory words "For this is the message" put what is said in this verse on the same level as what follows the words "And this is the message" in 1:5. Then the double message receives a more focused content through v. 23: "And this is his commandment." Believing in Jesus as Messiah, God's son, and loving one another is the best summarization of the core of the renewed covenant. Mutual love belongs to the very hub of the Elder's message and thus becomes completely central to his letter. The fact that some people have disrupted this fellowship of love (2:18–19) gives the question an urgent immediacy. The message in 1:5—2:2 is bound up with the tradition from Jesus, which the Elder passes on to them, and the message in 3:11–24 is something they had already heard when they came to faith. The twofold message is thus well anchored in the tradition that formed the Johannine community.

2. Not Like Cain, But Like Jesus (3:12–17)

Let us love one another! The words are immediately explained with two examples. "Like Jesus" has previously stood out as the fundamental principle for the Johannine Christians' way of life (2:6, 29; 3:3, 7). Now the same kind of rule is used, but in a negative way: "Not like Cain" (v. 12). In the description of the relationship to "the brothers" Cain becomes a counter-principle to Jesus. The story of Cain and Abel (Gen 4:1–16) has fascinated readers throughout the ages and raised many questions. In early Jewish tradition Cain is made into a primal type of the wicked and Abel into a primal type of the righteous. Cain was "evil" because his deeds were evil; Abel was "righteous" because his deeds were righteous (v. 12).

Cain's evil is traced back to the devil himself. Cain was begotten of the Evil one and not of Adam, and he did the deeds of the Evil one. Thus we have something like two families in the world, Cainites who have the devil as their father, and Abelites who have God (through Adam) as their father. See further Appendix 13, Cain as the Devil's Son. These depictions of Cain explain the formulations in v. 12 as well as the author's argument regarding God's children and the devil's children in the preceding section. "The one who commits sin is of the devil" (3:8). The one who has God's *sperma* abiding in him cannot sin (3:9). The images developed around Cain (and Abel) corresponded well enough to the dualistic shape of Johannine thought, in which human deeds play an important role (John 3:16–21). Here Cain becomes a counter-example to Jesus. Cain kills; Jesus gives life.

Whenever the Elder wants to take an idea a further step, or to make more precise, comment on, reinforce, or apply what he has just said, he often begins with a vocative (2:1, 7; 3:7; 4:11). He uses the word "brothers," which undeniably fits the context. See the note on 3:13. In this section he also employs the usual words "dear children" (v.

18) and "beloved" (v. 21). He is concerned to reach his readers with his message. "Do not be amazed" has a general introductory and delaying function, like "let no one deceive you" in v. 3:7. At the same time, the perspective shifts from Cain and Abel to "the world" and "we" (which has an emphatic place at the beginning of v. 14) and from death and hatred to their opposites, life and love.

The Elder is not the first to have associated physical death with hatred. "For as love would make alive even the dead, and would call back them which are condemned to die, so hatred would kill the living, and those that had sinned little it would not allow to live" (*T. Gad* 4:6). "Because forever those who are like Cain in envy and hatred of brothers will be punished with the same judgment" (*T. Benj.* 7:5). Clement of Rome (90s CE) cites the Cain story and adds, "You see, brothers, how envy and jealousy led to the murder of a brother" (*1 Clem.* 4:1–7). See also the citations in Appendix 13, Cain as the Devil's Son.

In the author's dualistic vocabulary, hatred is primarily the opposite of love. Anything that does not express love, compassion, nearness, fellowship, and solidarity comes in under the concept of hatred. In the letter, love, like life, has God as its origin and source. Therefore anyone who hates has nothing to do with life, i.e., with the divine life in which the recipients have become partakers though union with God and God's son. In v. 15, the author "proves" this by equating hatred with murder and reiterating the obvious fact that a murderer does not belong to God's kingdom, to use a concept that approximates the letter's use of eternal life (Rev 21:8). Passing from death to life is expressed in John 3:5 with the words to enter into the kingdom of God. Those in view here are clearly indicated by Jesus' words in John 5:24: "Anyone who hears my word and believes in him who sent me has eternal life, and does not come under judgment, but has passed from death to life." See Appendix 6, Life, Eternal Life.

"We" in v. 14 thus stands for the Johannine fellowship; "the world" in v. 13 primarily stands for those who have left the fellowship and thereby have shown that they hate—i.e., do not love—"the brothers." The division between Cainites and Abelites appears to lie behind the argument even in vv. 13–15. It is debatable whether mutual love is a sign of or a cause of passing from death to life (v. 14). The word "because" can of course be construed either with "we know" or with "we have passed from death to life." See the note on "because" in v. 14.

Is love for the brothers an outward sign that divine love and divine life exist within them? Or have they passed from death to life *because* they love "the brothers"? John 13:35 speaks in favor of the first option. But if love for "the brothers," like all love in the letter, is an outflow of God's love, could not one then imagine that love for the brothers would be both a sign and a cause? Hatred is more than a sign of death; it is part of the kingdom of death (v. 14c). Thus love, too, can be more than a sign of life (v. 14ab).

The Elder brings in Jesus as a model, using the typical formulation "By this we have learned to recognize," with "love" as object (v. 16). See the note on the beginning of v. 16. We have similar introductions in v. 19a and v. 24b. See the note on v. 24. The

Elder says merely "love," but the section as a whole focuses on mutual love. It should be so regarded here as well. He has earlier described Jesus as righteous and pure (2:29; 3:3), when he presents him as an example. It happens here with the words, "He [i.e., Jesus] laid down his life for us." The formulation is typically Johannine (see the note "laid down his life" at v. 16), but the idea that Jesus died "for us" is found in several crucial passages in the New Testament (Rom 5:8; Mark 14:24).

Jesus' suffering and death are used rather often as a model of a Christian lifestyle (1 Pet 2:21–24; Heb 13:12–13; 2 Cor 5:15; Phil 2:5–12). The words "for us" can mean both "in our place" and "for our benefit." The application here speaks for the latter. See also Appendix 7, Expiation and Forgiveness. The special Johannine formulation for giving up one's life is used both of Jesus and of the letter's recipients. They are to give their lives for the brothers, i.e., to sacrifice everything for their fellow believers, up to and including their own lives, in accordance with the model. Jesus says, "This is my commandment, that you love one another as I have loved you. No one has greater love than this, to lay down one's life for one's friends" (John 15:12–13). When Clement of Alexandria, around the year 200, writes about the Apostle John in Ephesus, he has him cry out, "I will willingly endure death for you, just as the Lord did for us" (Eusebius, *Hist. Eccl.* 3.24.17).

The example of love that now follows, sharing one's possessions with the poor in the Johannine community (v. 17), can seem rather petty in relation to the weighty words about life and death. The author uses strong words like "kill," "murder," and "hate," but the only example he gives is that some Christians refuse to share their possessions with fellow Christians in need. They are also indirectly said to have left the Johannine fellowship. Is this the same thing as hatred and murder, as in Cain's case? Or is the author driven to gross exaggerations by his dualistic model? The most concrete example of what it means to "live as Jesus lived" (2:6) is given here. It is reminiscent of a fundamental idea in both Judaism and early Christianity: sharing of one's goods with the poor, concerning oneself with those in need (Deut 15:7; CD 14:14–16; Mark 10:21; Luke 10:25–37; Jas 2:15–16). Ignatius writes of those who preach against the teaching of Christ's grace and are opposed to the will of God: "They have no regard for love; no care for the widow, or the orphan, or the oppressed; of the bound, or of the free; of the hungry, or of the thirsty" (Ign. *Smyrn.* 6:2).

In 1 John love is bound up with the new fellowship. The world beyond the horizon of the faithful flock is not in view here. Possibly this has to do with the eschatological situation and its dominating focus on the new thing that came with Jesus the Messiah, God's son. They are participants in divine life and divine love. God's love applies to all humanity, but here everything is limited to its consequences precisely for the Johannine Christians. How can God's love remain within those who do not accept God's love? This is the issue underlying the rhetorical question that closes the first paragraph of this section. How can God's love still be found in one who feels no compassion and does not share in the new fellowship that has come with Jesus the Messiah, God's son?

First John

Even in the Qumran community very heavy demands are laid upon members to show love for the brothers (1QS 3:13; 4:5). See Appendix 9, A Renewed Covenant.

3. Love in Action and Truth (3:18)

The Elder takes a fresh run at it in v. 18, putting a sharper point on the admonition to love one another. He does so by speaking of love expressed "not only with words, but with deeds" and of genuine actions, actions directed by the truth. God's love in the letter is an active power that must express itself in concrete deeds. The Qumran texts also frequently speak of "deeds of God's truth," i.e., actions corresponding with the truth (1QM 13:2; 1QS 1:19; 1QH 1:30). Perhaps the sense is similar in kind to the Jewish admonition: "And now, my children, each one love his brother, and put away hatred from your hearts, love one another in deed and in word" (*T. Gad* 6:1). The author appears to use a well-known contemporary manner of speaking, such that it is not so easy to define precisely the meaning or to apply the words within the context. See the note on v. 18. Using maxims is a common feature of Johannine rhetoric (John 2:10; 4:35–36; 5:19; 13:10; 1 John 5:2). At the same time words with a deep resonance within the Johannine linguistic world are used: love, truth. The latter word is linked to the statement, "we are of the truth" in v. 19. I understand v. 18 as a serious exhortation to love one another in deed and truth.

The paragraph beginning with v. 18 is also divided into two parts: vv. 18–20 and vv. 21–24. Both parts are introduced with a vocative, "dear children" and "beloved," respectively. Judging from what immediately follows, v. 18 appears to emphasize the risk of failing to love one another in the right way. What happens if someone does not have compassion for a sister or a brother, mostly talking instead of acting? What if someone does something that does not correspond to the truth? Some commentators perceive primarily the secessionists as standing behind the argument in this section. These secessionists are assumed to have claimed that the Christians' lifestyle was not particularly important. Deeds had no significance for salvation. The Elder countered by insisting that God's love must come to expression in the believers themselves. Thus he must also address situations in which a brother commits a sin. What happens if my heart judges me because of my actions?

4. God Is Greater and Knows Everything (3:19–20)

The first thing the Elder says then is that the letter's recipients need not doubt that they are the children of the truth. They have their origin and their position in what has been revealed about God through Jesus the Messiah, God's son. See Appendix 3, The Truth. They know this because they love one another. This mutual love, as in v. 14, is a sign that they belong to God. The beginning of v. 19 points back to v. 18 and thus to the theme for the entire section, v. 11. But what if someone does not love another person in deed and in truth? This idea may lie behind what follows. The following text is probably one of the most difficult parts of the letter to interpret. In the Analysis, point 2, I have enumerated the difficulties and offered my opinion. I let the verb in v. 19c retain its usual meaning of "convince." I give the word "heart" a meaning that approaches our idea of conscience, a meaning that can be attested in the Old Testament, but not in the New Testament, least of all in the Johannine writings, which otherwise do not use the word "heart." And I let the author repeat the word "that" twice. See the Translation Display.

The other thing that the Elder would like to say is that when the hearts of the letter's recipients judge them for failing to love in deed and truth in accordance with the exhortation in v. 18, they are to assure their hearts that God is greater than their hearts. This last point can be interpreted to mean that God is greater in his severity and judgment (so early Church fathers, Augustine, medieval commentators, and Calvin). The addressees must convince their hearts of the great significance of their actions. For if their hearts judge them for not putting love into action in their dealings with people, they should be made to understand that God is even greater than their hearts and is aware of everything, and thus judges them even more severely. The idea that God is greater thus becomes a motivation for actually taking the exhortation in v. 18 seriously.

God's being greater can also be understood in terms of his clemency and love (so Luther and the majority of modern interpreters). The letter's recipients are to assure their hearts that God is merciful and great in leniency, as when the covenant was renewed at Sinai (Exod 34:6–7). See Appendix 9, A Renewed Covenant. God is greater than their hearts, which judge them. God is aware of the entire situation. God can forgive. Thus, in the situation mentioned in v. 21, their hearts do not condemn them. The idea that God is greater becomes a reminder of the possibility of forgiveness when a person has committed a sin (2:1–2; 5:16). See Appendix 19, Sin that Leads to Death. The Elder usually has encouraging words to say when he speaks of judgment (2:1–2, 28; 4:17–18). And the entire section, in fact the entire second part of the letter, is dominated by the concept that God is love. See Appendix 16, God is Love. I therefore prefer the latter alternative, that God is greater in mercy and leniency than their own hearts are.

5. God's Gifts in the Renewed Covenant (3:21–24)

If then the recipients keep God's commandments and do what pleases him, if they love one another in deed and truth, what is the result? The remainder of the section treats this as a further argument that they should love one another (vv. 21–24). The Elder explores this partly by listing the blessings it entails—confidence before God, assurance of answered prayers, a fellowship where God is in them and they are in God, and the gift of the spirit—and partly by setting forth the core of God's commandments: to believe and to love (v. 23).

Confidence before God means here primarily an open pathway to God, an access to God that makes possible a new form of prayer, assuring believers that God listens to the one who prays. In the Gospel, as a rule, this is referred to as prayer in Jesus' name (John 14:14–16; 15:7, 16; 16:23–26). It has its foundation in the new unity between Father, Son, and those who believe in Jesus as the Messiah, God's son. When he calls Lazarus back to life, Jesus says, "Father, I thank you that you have heard me. I knew that you always hear me, but I say this for the sake of all who are standing here, that they may believe that you have sent me" (John 11:41–42). The Elder returns to this kind of prayer in 5:14–17, where it is applied to those in the Johannine fellowship who have committed a sin. The one who prays can lead the sinner back to life, eternal life. See Appendix 19, Sin that Leads to Death.

Similar statements about prayer are found as well in other parts of the New Testament (Matt 7:7; Mark 11:24, and Jas 1:5–6), but only the Johannine texts place prayers within a clear concord between God and humanity. God keeps his covenant promises, because they express his very nature as a loving and righteous God. If the people respond by loving him and obeying his commandments, they come close to God. Eliphaz tells Job that if he humbly returns to God, if he removes evil from his house, then he will be able turn with confidence to God. "You will pray to him, and he will hear you, and you will pay your vows" (Job 22:23–27). According to Philo, God listens to a nation's prayers if the people are inspired by true piety, and God draws near them when they call upon God with a pure conscience (*Praem.* 14.84).

What is said next, in vv. 22b–24a, is framed by the assumption that the letter's recipients keep God's word and do what pleases him. See the closing of point 2 in the Analysis for 2:3–11. Jesus, who is their great example, also says, "I always do what is pleasing to him" (John 8:29). The double formulation of obedience toward God surely implies that the author places great weight on this stipulation. In v. 22a, it leads to God's listening to their prayers, and in v. 24a to their being in God and God in them. I have interpreted the latter expression as a Johannine form of the words "they shall be my people and I shall be their God," in light of the renewal of the covenant. The renewal has "interiorized" the relationship between God and the people, i.e., it has placed that relationship within the inner being of every individual. See Appendix 9, A Renewed Covenant, and Appendix 15, God in Them and They in God.

Even the so-called double love command, which is sometimes identified as the core of the covenant between God and the people (Matt 22:34–44), can be said to have assumed a special form in the letter. The covenant commandment, "You shall love the Lord, your God, with all your heart and with all your soul and with all your mind," has been completed within the Johannine tradition with "You must believe in Jesus as Messiah, God's son." To "believe in the name of his son, Jesus Christ" (v. 23b) has this sense in the context of the letter. See Appendix 14, Jesus as Messiah, God's son. The names reveal who Jesus is. See the note "on account of his name," at 2:12. See also John 20:31. Faith in God has been tied to Jesus Messiah, God's son, and the revelation of God that came with him (John 1:18). The command, "You shall love your neighbor [fellow Jew] as yourself" has in the Johannine situation become "you must love one another." It is this that is the core in the Elder's message in 3:11–24, which is further amplified and discussed later on in 4:7–21. What he thinks of people outside the Johannine community is not clear, apart from his saying that God in God's love sent his son to rescue all humanity (2:2; 4:14).

The closing words in this section (v. 24bc) mostly function as a transition to the next section. The author uses the theme of God in them and they in God in order to introduce the concept of "God's spirit," which he then takes up in 4:1–6. God has given God's people a commandment (v. 23); God has also given them a portion of God's spirit, or, in Johannine terms, the spirit. See the note "by the spirit" at v. 24. According to the texts concerning a renewed covenant, God shall place God's law in the people's hearts and give them of God's spirit. Then they will know God and obey God's commandments. See Appendix 9, A Renewed Covenant.

The spirit in the letter takes its meaning mostly from what is said about the Spirit of Truth, the Helper, the Paraclete, in John 14–16. Obedience to God's commandments, particularly to the commandment to love one another, has been put forward earlier as a sign that they belong to God (vv. 14 and 19). Here, as in 4:13, the reference is to the spirit as a sign of the new union with God, but it is remarkable that the author does not further pursue the spirit's function beyond its relevance to confessing Jesus in 4:1–6. The question is why. Was the concept of the spirit problematic in the dispute between Jesus-believing Jews and non-Jesus-believing Jews, which lay behind the letter? Earlier he had firmly bound the anointing together with what they heard from the beginning, i.e., the Spirit and the tradition (2:18–27). The Elder had authority over the tradition, but not over the Spirit. As he does earlier, he now connects to the tradition what comes with the Spirit.

8

1 John 4:1–6: Test Every Preacher

Translation Display

1a	Beloved,
1b	do not believe every spirit
1c	but test the spirits
1d	whether they are of God
1e	because many false prophets have gone out into the world.
2a	By this you know the spirit of God:
2b	every spirit that confesses Jesus as the Messiah come in the flesh is of God
3a	and every spirit that does not confess Jesus is not of God
3b	and this is the spirit of the Antichrist
3c	which you have heard is to come
3d	and which is already in the world.
4a	*You* are of God
4b	dear children
4c	and you have overcome them.
4d	For he who is in you is greater than he who is in the world.
5a	*They* are of the world.
5b	Therefore they speak of the world
5c	and the world listens to them.
6a	*We* are of God.
6b	The one who knows God listens to us
6c	the one who is not of God does not listen to us.
6d	By this we know the spirit of truth and the spirit of deception.

Notes

4:1. Beloved. See the note on 1 John 2:7.

every spirit. Gkt has an alliteration with *p* in the beginning of v. 1: *mē panti pneumati pisteuete* (literally, "do not believe every spirit"). From what follows it becomes clear that there are actually two spirits active within humanity, a spirit that imparts the truth and one that stands for lying and deception. In biblical tradition, God's spirit and the prophets belong closely together (Ezek 2:2; Isa 61:1; Luke 4:18–19). According to John 14–16 and 1 John 2:20, all who are in the Johannine community are prophets. Likewise prophets are the Jesus-believing Jews—men and women—who praised God's great deeds in Acts 2, according to the quotation from the book of Joel used there. The Johannine Christians possess the Spirit; they all have insight. The Spirit speaks through them. The Elder probably has in mind Johannine Christians who have left the Johannine fellowship and perhaps other visitors as well, e.g. itinerant brothers mentioned in 3 John, or others who can be suspected of infiltrating the Johannine community.

test. Prophets were tested even in the OT (Deut 13:2–6; 18:15–22). In the Qumran community every member was examined annually regarding obedience to the Law as interpreted within the Qumran society. There it is referred to as testing "their spirits" (1QS 3:13–14; 5:20–21, 24). Itinerant teachers in the early church were also subjected to testing (Herm. *Mand.* 11:7–17). See Appendix 2, Itinerant Brothers. The Gkt uses the present tense of "test," which gives it the nuance of an ongoing activity. There are many who come and go.

whether, Gkt *ei*, introduces an indirect question.

are of. The phrase "be of" (*einai ek*), is used in every verse in this section. It signifies both origin and belonging. See the note "comes not from the Father but from the world" at 1 John 2:16.

many false prophets have gone out into the world. The formulation is reminiscent of other statements in the Johannine letters: "they went out from us" (1 John 2:19); "many antichrists have appeared" (1 John 2:18); and "many deceivers have gone out into the world" (2 John 7). Here the verb is in the perfect tense, in 1 John 2:19 and 2 John 7 the aorist, a change without any great difference in meaning, and something rather common in the Johannine letters (1 John 1:1–3, etc.). Regarding these four passages, the following can be noted:

   a. These people are described as false prophets (*pseudoprophētes*), deceivers (*planos*), and antichrists. According to Jewish apocalyptic expectations, the coming end time will be characterized by grievous forms of false teaching, delusion and deception, often attributed directly to Satan or the devil. Cf. 1 John 2:26; 3:7, and 4:6). One of the names of the Evil one in Rev 12:9 is "the deceiver (*ho planōn*) of the whole world."

Truth and delusion/deception are set in opposition to one another in a Johannine dualistic perspective. This manner of speaking has its roots in Jewish writings from the Intertestamental period, e.g., in the Qumran writings and the *Testaments of the Twelve Patriarchs*. There the truth is opposed by lying, falsehood, and delusion/deception. Words with the root *pseud-* are very closely related therefore to the many words with the stem *plan-* in Johannine speech. Compare 4QpNahum (4Q169) 2:8: "This refers to the *deceivers* of Ephraim, who through their *false* teaching, *lying* talk, and *false* speech *deceive* many."

b. The false prophets, like the deceivers and antichrists, are described as "many," which underscores the general situation and its seriousness.

c. The words "have gone out into the world" echo "went out from among us" in 1 John 2:19. Among the deceivers there are those who once belonged to the Johannine community but who left it and became part of the world, i.e., part of that portion of humanity that sets itself against God. See the note "the world" at 1 John 2:15. It is also possible here to understand "the world" in a more neutral way, as the place where people live and work, including the letter's recipients, but the strong contrast between the world and God in vv. 4–5 speaks against that reading.

2. By this you know, *en toutōi ginskete*. "This" is cataphoric and looks ahead to the latter part of the verse. See the first note on 1 John 2:3. Most commentators take the verb as indicative, "you know," but it can also be read as an imperative, "know." In the manuscripts there are other variants: *ginōsketai* ("it is known") and *ginōskomen* ("we know"). The Johannine phrase "By this you know/recognize/see" always has the indicative. Even the text-critical variants are in the indicative.

the spirit of God. The genitive "of God" indicates both source and belonging. The Johannine letters never use the expression "the Holy Spirit."

confesses. Gkt has the usual word for "confess" (*homologein*).

Jesus as Messiah come in the flesh. For Messiah, Gkt has the word *Christos*. This Jesus-confession is the most emphatic in the letter and closely approximates the one in 2 John 7. The only difference is that 1 John uses the perfect participle, "come," while 2 John uses the present participle, "coming." Codex Vaticanus has improved the latter by making it a perfect infinitive. Similarly Polycarp, who cites this passage at the beginning of the second century in his letter to the Christians in Philippi (7:1), has the perfect infinitive. The words "in the flesh" (*en sarki*) very likely mean "as a human being," "in human form."

From the point of view of syntax, the words "Jesus Christ come/coming in the flesh" can be read in at least three ways, depending on how they are related to one another in the clause as a whole:

a. As a single, cohesive concept, i.e., the entire phrase is the direct object of the verb: "confess Jesus Christ come in the flesh."

b. With "Jesus Christ" as the direct object of the verb and "come in the flesh" as an expansion on this object, i.e., "confess Jesus Christ as having come in the flesh." Here, as in the first alternative, it is most natural to render *Christos* as "Christ."

c. With "Jesus" as the object and "Christ come in the flesh" as an expansion on this object, i.e., "confess Jesus as Messiah come in the flesh." I chose here to translate *Christos* as Messiah. According to John 1:40, Christ (*Christos*) corresponds to Messiah (*ho Messias*).

From an intra-Jewish regression hypothesis, alternative (c) is to be preferred; according to other perspectives alternative (b) or possibly (a). For a more detailed discussion, see Appendix 14, Jesus as Messiah, God's son.

The present tense in 2 John—"coming"—can indicate a future reference: "shall come in the flesh." The author would in that case have in mind Jesus' return. But that is hardly likely. The conception of Jesus as Messiah that is combated in 2 John is with all probability the same as the one combated in 1 John. The present tense can be explained as an emphasis on the incarnation's timeless character, with its effects in the present, or more likely as a consequence of the formal phrase referring to Jesus as "the coming one" (*ho erchomenos*; John 1:15, 27; 12:13). See also "the prophet who is to come into the world" (John 6:14).

3. and. See the notes "and the life was revealed" at 1 John 1:2 and "and" at 1 John 1:6. The beginning of v. 3 is formulated to follow on v. 2, and there is a clear antithesis spanning the two verses. For text-critical variants to v. 3, see the Analysis, point 2.

is not of. See the note "are from," at v. 1 above.

and this is the spirit of the Antichrist . . . in the world. The spirit of delusion is further described—the clause begins with "and," moving the argument forward another step—in a manner reminiscent of 1 John 2:18. See the notes there.

4. You. Gkt places the pronoun "you" (*hymeis*) first in the sentence. There is no introductory particle; the structure marks an emphasis and contrast.

dear children. Gkt *teknia*. See notes at 1 John 2:1, 13, and 14.

you have overcome them. This likely means that the letter's recipients have exposed the false prophets as possessing a spirit that does not come from God and that they have therefore repudiated them. According to 1 John 2:13–14, the young people have overcome the Evil one.

he who is in you . . . he who is in the world. More literally: "he in you . . . he in the world." The definite article in this construction is in the masculine, which leads to the translation "he who." Many commentators see here a contrast between God and the devil. In v. 4, the author has progressed from speaking of spirits to speaking of persons. Others, however, point to the fact that "he who is in the world" corresponds to "the ruler of this world" in John 12:31; 14:30; 16:11, and equate him with the "spirit of Antichrist." In that case, we are dealing with a comparison between God's spirit and the spirit of Antichrist. But then the question is why does the author not use the neuter—"spirit" is neuter in Greek.

5. They. Gkt has here indicated the subject with a pronoun, "they" (*autoi*), with the same effect as the corresponding stylistic feature in v. 4.

are of. See the note on v. 1, above.

the world. The word occurs three times in this verse and stands in opposition to God. See the note on 1 John 2:15.

6. We. See the note "You" on v. 4, above. Probably only the bearers of the tradition within the Johannine community are in view; they thereby become a counterpart to the false prophets in v. 5.

are of. See the note "are of" on v. 1, above. The same expression recurs once more here in v. 6.

us. The word presumably refers to the bearers of the Johannine tradition. See Appendix 5, We in the Johannine Letters.

By this we know. Literally, "of this [*ek toutou*] we know." The phrase resembles "through this [*en toutōi*] we know." See the second note on 1 John 2:3. "This" is anaphoric, referring back to the entire section.

Analysis

1. Delimitations and Structure

Thematically and rhetorically, this section is well defined. Certain expressions recur especially often: "spirit" seven times, "to be of God/the world" seven times, "the world" six times. Oppositional pairs of various sorts dominate the entire section: believe and put to the test, God's spirit and Antichrist's spirit, confess and not confess, be of God and not be of God, God and the world, he who is in you and he who is in the world, you and they, listen to them and listen to us, the spirit of truth and the spirit of deception. See the Translation Display. By means of these expressions two separate spheres are depicted, and the crucial question is to which of them a person belongs. The Johannine dualism is at its most intense precisely here. See chap. 12, point 8.

There is a clear thematic connection with what comes earlier: the close association between love and truth/faith continues here with a concentration on the latter.

1 John 4:1–6: Test Every Preacher

See the Analysis on 1 John 3:11–24, point 2. The word "spirit" in 1 John 3:24c operates as a transition to a new section.

This "dogmatic" highpoint in the letter also has a clear rhetorical structure. See the Translation Display. In v. 1, the theme is formulated. Then comes an initial investigation in vv. 2–3, where the end is clearly reminiscent of the end of v. 1. Verses 4–6c are dominated by three emphatic pronouns, one at the beginning of each verse: *you—they—we*. These three verses are likewise introduced with a new term of address: "dear children." The subject of spirits shifts to the subject of persons. With the phrase "by this," as a reference to all the foregoing, and by its very content, v. 6d is marked as an obvious conclusion to the section. First John 4:7–21, then, takes up the second main theme: love.

Anyone so inclined may find numerous chiastic parallels in this section, perhaps most clearly in vv. 2–3c: God's spirit—confess Jesus—not confess Jesus—Antichrist's spirit. If we extend the context to include vv. 2–6, the pattern takes on a seven-part structure:

God's spirit (v. 2a)
    spirits from God (v. 2b)
        spirits not from God (v. 3)
            you are of God (v. 4)
        they are of the world (v. 5)
    we are of God (v.6a)
the spirit of truth (v. 6d)

If v. 1d and the end of v. 6d are included, then the false prophets and the spirit of deception enter the picture and provide a situation and framework for the entire section. These parallels, even if they are vague and not entirely consistent, contribute to the sense of coherence in the section.

The thematically introductory verse, v. 1, acquires by various means a substantive and emotional gravity: the vocative "beloved," the antithetical form "not A but B," the alternation between "every spirit" and the plural "the spirits" and back again to the singular, together with the observation that the false prophets are "many."

The first paragraph following the theme verse, vv. 2–3, provides a content-based criterion for testing every individual spirit, formulated in Johannine fashion as a parallelism, first positively and then negatively. In terms of their content, the paralleled assertions have a conditional character: if a spirit (does not) confess . . . then it is (not) . . . See the Translation Display. Expanding v. 3b to include 3cd yields a concluding effect. The verb "know" in v. 2a can also be read as an imperative—see the note—and vv. 1–3 thereby take on a more admonitory character.

The second paragraph following the theme verse, vv. 4–6c, contains only assertions and begins by reassuring the recipients in two-fold way that they are on the right side.

First John

Here there is no doubt; here no test is needed. God/God's spirit is in them and is greater than the devil/Antichrist's spirit. These lines have the same function as 1 John 2:12–14 does. Exhortation and reassurance often tightly follow one another in 1 John.

This reassurance is further strengthened and justified in what follows regarding the false prophets (v. 5) and regarding the true prophets, i.e., regarding the we-group the author represents. Where one belongs depends on to whom one listens. First, negatively: the world listens to the false prophets; then positively: the one who is of God listens to the true prophets. Fellowship with God is possible only through fellowship with "us." See also 1 John 1:3. Indirectly, then, there is stern exhortation in this paragraph: Continue listening to us!

2. Preachers Who "destroy" Jesus (v. 3)

As a rule, the beginning of v. 3 is translated, "every spirit that does not confess Jesus." From the context it is natural, then, to understand as implied what is said in the preceding line: "Jesus as Messiah, come in the flesh." This yields a typical Johannine parallelism of the same sort as occurs in 1 John 5:12: "the one who has the Son . . . the one who does not have the son of God." But the shorter formulation raised questions early on. From a grammatical point of view, the Greek should have the negative *ou* here, rather than *mē*, which is what it actually does have. Can this be dependent on 2 John 7, where the use of *mē* belongs with the participle? See the note there.

In the Greek manuscripts there are several alternative readings:

1. who do not confess Jesus.
2. who do not confess Jesus the Lord come in the flesh.
3. who do not confess Jesus Christ come in the flesh.
4. who do not confess Christ.

Most manuscripts have alternative 3, which agrees completely with the first portion of v. 2. It is found in the Byzantine tradition, in the Textus Receptus, and thus in the King James Version of 1611. Codex Sinaiticus has alternative 2, in connection with the confession "Jesus is Lord," e.g., in 1 Cor 12:3. The translation should then be "who do not confess that Jesus is Lord, come in the flesh." Codex Vaticanus and Codex Alexandrinus, together with a handful of other Greek manuscripts have alternative 1. Alternative 4 occurs only in one late minuscule. Of these alternatives, it is easy to defend alternative 1 as the original.

Polycarp, bishop in Smyrna, uses this verse in his letter to the Christians in Philippi around the year 140. According to tradition, he knew the Lord's disciple John in Ephesus. He quotes v. 2b almost verbatim—"For whoever does not confess that Jesus Christ has come in the flesh"—and then interprets it with the words "and whoever does not confess the testimony of the cross is of the devil" (Pol. *Phil.* 7:1). Compare "the one who came through . . . blood" in 1 John 5:6. Even Polycarp did not seem to be satisfied with the formulation "who does not confess Jesus."

There is also an old text-critical variant, certainly from the second century, that is not attested in any Greek manuscripts. The Greek historian Socrates (fifth century) says that in older manuscripts this passage read, "every spirit that destroys (*lyei*) Jesus," and the variant is found as well in the margin of a Greek minuscule from Athos, written in the tenth century from an exemplar of the sixth century. It is also noted there that this verb is used in named writings of Irenaeus, Origin, and Clement of Alexandria. This does not necessarily mean, however, that Socrates has seen any Greek manuscripts with this reading.

The writings mentioned unfortunately exist only in Latin translation and there the word used is *solvit*, or occasionally *dividat* ("divide"), a verb that clearly reflects the Greek *lyei*. The manuscripts of the old Latin translations, with one exception, have *solvit* like the Vulgate and the Latin fathers (the latter sometimes also use *destruit* ["destroy"] or *negat* ["deny"]), e.g., Tertullian, Augustine, Priscillianus. The question is when this variant made its way into the biblical text. Can it be the original reading?

The Greek verb *lyein*—like the Latin *solvere*—means dissolve, destroy, annihilate, obliterate, annul, cancel, invalidate, withdraw. It is used in 1 John 3:8 regarding God's son, who "destroys" the devil's work. The verb is quite common in the Gospel of John with a variety of direct objects: the temple (as a sacrificial institution; John 2:19); the Sabbath (5:18); the law of Moses (7:23); and the Scripture (10:35). To "destroy" Jesus in 1 John 4:3 would then mean to render worthless Jesus' life and work, to annul what Jesus had done, to make Jesus inconsequential. The verb scarcely means "divide," such that it would accommodate the idea of dividing Jesus into a human being and a divine being.

In the early church, this text came to be used of Jesus' two natures, e.g., by Leo the Great in the fifth century. With reference to 1 John 4:3 and 2 John 7, Irenaeus says at the end of the second century, "all who make a distinction between Jesus and Christ as the Gnostics do stand outside the order of salvation" and their teaching "divides God's son into many parts" (*Adv. Haer.* 3.16.8). According to the German scholar Hans-Josef Klauck, the reading fits the docetic, Gnostic conflicts, and thus probably came into the text in some such connection.

The fact that the variant is attested in early Latin translations perhaps speaks against Klauck's explanation. There is no proof that this verb was used in the debate with the Gnostics. The application to Jesus' two natures—taking the verb in the sense of "divide"—must be seen as a later usage.

It is probably necessary to point out that it is impossible to know with full certainty which word first stood in the text. B. F. Westcott suggested in 1880—with reference to the formulations in Polycarp—that both expressions come from the debate in question and that "destroy" (*lyei*), with its clearer and severer meaning, later on entered into the early Latin translations. Perhaps he was right. But usual text-critical rules and the context give preference to "who do not confess Jesus." It also corresponds

First John

best with an intra-Jewish perspective for the letter as a whole. The formulation "dissolve," *lyei,* became current during the later part of the second century, when there began to be disputes within the church over various types of Christologies, i.e., over various Christian conceptions of Jesus Christ.

Interpretation

1. Test the Spirits (4:1)

"You must believe in the son of God, in the name of Jesus Christ" and "You must love one another." These two exhortations constitute the Johannine version of the double love commandment, the very center of the renewed covenant (3:23). The first is examined in more detail in 4:1–6, the second in 4:7–21. The theme of 4:1–6—"Test the spirits!"—was pre-announced at the very end of the foregoing section with the introduction of the concept of spirit. After a thematic verse introduced with "Beloved" (v. 1) come two paragraphs, the first regarding various spirits (vv. 2–3), the second regarding various prophets and teachers, introduced with a second vocative, "dear children" (vv. 4–6a). In v. 6d, the section culminates in a closing statement: "By this we know the spirit of truth and the spirit of deception." See the Analysis, point 1, and the Translation Display.

The repetition of a vocative and the constantly recurring array of oppositional pairs form the entire section into a tightly coherent unity and give the impression of a more general line of reasoning. The letter's recipients are the center of attention in the argumentation and the goal is to guide them and to strengthen them in their faith in Jesus as the Messiah, God's son.

In the Roman world of the day, many Jews and Christians traveled freely. They visited their co-religionists in various localities and, like Paul and Apollos and many others, had opportunity to speak in various gatherings. See Appendix 2, Itinerant Brothers, and Appendix 1, Hospitality. All three of the Johannine letters bear witness to the fact that the attitude toward visitors gradually changed, especially after a number of Jesus-believing Jews left the Johannine fellowship, according to 1 John 2:18–19. It had become necessary to test everyone who spoke in the Jewish or the Christian communities.

Testing of prophets and teachers is commanded already in the Old Testament and is found in later Jewish writings; it is mentioned even in other Christian writings. See the note on "test" in 4:1. According to the *Did.* 11–12, all itinerant prophets are to be tested by their message and especially by their way of life. The latter is even more important in the rules set forth in Hermas, *Mand.*11:7–17, for deciding who "is a prophet and who is a false prophet." "Test by deeds and life the man who claims to have the Divine Spirit."

The Elder regards the situation here in the same way as he does in 2:18–27. "It is the last hour." The false prophets belong to the end time (Matt 24:11) and are described in a similar way to the antichrists in 2:18–27. The spirit of Antichrist is mentioned in connection with them (4:3bcd). See the final note on v. 1. It is completely obvious that the Elder is thinking about these secessionists and Messiah-deniers, but his description of the eschatological situation is generalized. Among the visitors he has in mind may be some of the brothers mentioned in 3 John or other Jewish visitors. Three times he emphasizes the concern for "every spirit" (vv. 1b, 2b, 3a). There are many false prophets in the recipients' vicinity, which highlights the seriousness of the situation. Test the spirits!

The formulations in the three first verses concentrate on the spirits. The Elder is careful to observe where the message comes from, whether from God or not from God. Ultimately the spirits can be reduced to two: God's spirit and Antichrist's spirit (vv. 2–3), the spirit of truth and the spirit of deception (v. 6d). A close connection between spirit and prophesying is attested in Old Testament, Jewish, and Christian texts. See the note on "every spirit" in v. 1. "The Spirit made an announcement to me," insists Ignatius regarding his own instruction. The spirit "spoke with a loud voice—the word is not mine, but God's" (Ign. *Phld.* 7:1–2).

The term "prophet" in this context does not need to mean more than teacher or preacher. "Prophet" and "teacher" approximate one another in New Testament usage (Acts 13:1; 1 Cor 12:28) and at times cannot be distinguished (2 Pet 2:1; *Did.* 11:3–12). "Spirit" can mean several things in biblical texts. The reference here is to unearthly powers that are able to rule human beings. In John 16:1 the Spirit of Truth is set in opposition to the ruler of this world. The Spirit of Truth can be described as being within Jesus' disciples (John 14:17), and Satan entered into Judas (13:27). Thus spirits are understood as operating together with human beings and determining their actions. See also the references under point 4, below.

2. The Confession of Jesus As Messiah (4:2–3)

In vv. 2–3, then, the criteria are provided for testing the spirits. The sense of these verses is much disputed, and every interpretation is tied to the overarching perspective a person chooses for understanding the Johannine letters. In a note on v. 2, I have presented various possible translations of "Jesus Christ come in the flesh"; under point 2 of the Analysis, I have reviewed the variant manuscript readings for v. 3; and in a special treatment in Appendix 14, Jesus as Messiah, God's son, I have presented solutions arising from the three perspectives considered in this commentary. Now, in the Interpretation, I have chosen not to focus especially on which group the author is opposing, but to read the text as the Elder's way of leading and strengthening the faith of those who share his views; and I have taken an intra-Jewish perspective as the foundation for interpreting the letter. From this perspective, the two criteria-oriented verses ought to be translated in the following way: "Every spirit that confesses Jesus as Messiah come in the flesh is of God" (v. 2b). "And every spirit that does not confess Jesus [as Messiah come in the flesh] is not of God" (v. 3a).

As so often in Johannine texts, we have a so-called parallelism: an important message is expressed twice, first positively and then negatively. The decisive confessional question is whether the Messiah, he who was to come, sent by God to the world, has in fact come or not, and whether the Messiah has appeared in the life and work of Jesus, from his birth to his death. On this point stands or falls the entire message that the Elder imparts to the letter's recipients. On this point stands or falls the renewal of the covenant. Indeed, the Elder wants by all available means to convince his readers that they have eternal life when they believe in the name of the son of God (5:13). It is this Messiah in the person of Jesus that he is thinking of in the opening words about what he has seen and heard and equates with eternal life. And he finishes by saying in plain speech that Jesus Christ, the son of God, is eternal life (5:20). That the son of God has come is the prerequisite for eternal life through Jesus Christ, God's son (5:20).

The Elder is especially keen to include the death of Jesus, because it cleanses people from sin and gives them sure guidance in how they should live. Jesus' death is also the prerequisite for the renewal of the covenant. There is in 5:6 a particular emphasis on Jesus' death, but his death is implied even in the phrase "in the flesh" (v. 2), as is indeed his entire life. As I see it, the text contains no emphasis on a special form of the incarnation or on Jesus' humanity, other than that Jesus' life as a human being and his earthly work constitute the life of the savior that God promised to send his people. Even less is this a statement about Jesus' human nature in contrast to his earthly nature. It is only later, when the intra-Jewish problem had faded away, that the criteria in 4:2–3 took on new meanings dependent on various Christological disputes within the early church. This change in meaning is noticeable in, e.g., Irenaeus and his general Christian perspective. For interpretations from other perspectives, see Appendix 14, Jesus as Messiah, God's son.

3. False and True Preachers (4:4–6c)

Beginning at v. 4, the author turns the focus from spirits to people. The pronouns "you [plural]" (v. 4), "they" (v. 5), and "we" (v. 6) are emphasized by being placed first in their respective clauses. The Elder reassures the letter's recipients that they have their origin in God and belong to him, just as God's spirit does in v. 2. They are on God's side, they all have insight, they know the truth (2:20–21, 27). For this reason, they have overcome these false prophets, who do not belong to God. Earlier in the letter it has been said that the young people have overcome the Evil one because they have God's word abiding in them (2:13–14). According to 5:5, people overcome the world when they believe that Jesus is the son of God. Faith, as it is defined in this section, is what gives victory (5:4). In 4:4, overcoming is explained with reference to the fact that God (or Christ or God's spirit) is within them and that he is greater than Antichrist (or the spirit of Antichrist), who is in the false teachers. The formulation in the original text is open to a number of interpretations (see the note). The context speaks in favor of a comparison between God and God's fearsome opponent in the end time, namely Satan, the devil, the Evil one, Antichrist.

In vv. 5–6, similar formulations are used to refer to "they," i.e., the false preachers, and to "we." Thus it is easiest to interpret "we" as the true preachers, i.e., as the bearers and interpreters of the Johannine tradition represented by the Elder. See Appendix 5, We in the Johannine Letters. The false teachers belong to the world and speak in the world's terms. In the Gospel, "world" became a term for all who repudiated Jesus, all who chose darkness over light (John 3:19; 7:7; 16:33). The world is in the power of the Evil one (5:19). The true teachers belong to God and therefore speak words from God. Both categories have their listeners and followers. The boundary runs between those who know God and those who do not know God. The formulations can be viewed as a type of predestination doctrine, but they should be interpreted in the specific historical context of the Johannine letters and be understood in terms of the dualistic pattern found in the letter.

4. The Spirit of Truth and the Spirit of Error (4:6d)

The two spirits in 4:2–3, God's spirit and Antichrist's spirit, are further described here with the words "the spirit of truth" and "the spirit of error." The spirit of truth, according to John 14–16, is the spirit that is stamped by the truth and that conveys the truth. The truth is Jesus' spirit, and Jesus is the truth; it defines Jesus' entire life (5:6–8). See Appendix 3, The Truth. The term "the spirit of error" or "the spirit of deception" is found only here in the New Testament, but deception, fraud, and lying, according to many texts, belong to the last days. See the citations in the last note on 4:1. In 2 John 7 the Deceiver is equated with Antichrist.

Similar appellations are attested in the Qumran texts, e.g., in the summation of the sect's dualistic theology: "He created humankind to rule over the world, appointing for them two spirits in which to walk until the time ordained for His visitation. These are the spirits of truth and falsehood" (1QS 3:17–19). Later they are referred to as "the spirits of light and darkness" (3:25). *The Testament of Judah* says to readers, "Therefore know, my children, that two spirits are devoted to humanity: the spirit of truth and the spirit of deceit" (20:1). *The Shepherd of Hermas,* a Christian apocalypse from the second century, speaks in a similar way: "There are two angels with a man, one of righteousness, and the other of iniquity." Then it is explained how one can recognize these two angels, since both are said to be active within the Christian (Herm. *Mand.* 6: 2).

The Elder's presentation in this section thus is anchored in certain Jewish, dualistic ways of thinking, but these are used here for describing the situation in the renewed covenant from the end time's perspective. God and Satan operate within and among people in many different ways. For this reason it is important to test every preacher.

9

1 John 4:7–21: God is Love

Translation Display

7a	Beloved,
7b	let us love one another
7c	because love is of God.
7d	And everyone who loves has been born of God and knows God.
8a	The one who does not love has not come to know God
8b	because God is love.
9a	In this the love of God has been revealed in us:
9b	God has sent his unique son into the world
9c	that we might live through him.
10a	In this is love:
10b	not that we have loved God
10c	but that he loved us
10d	and sent his son as an offering for our sins.
11a	Beloved,
11b	if in this way God loved us
11c	then we too ought to love one another.
12a	No one has ever seen God.
12b	If we love one another
12c	then God remains in us,
12d	and his love has been made complete in us.
13a	By this we know that we remain in him and he in us:
13b	he has given us of his spirit.
14a	*We* have seen and testify
14b	that the Father has sent the Son as the savior of the world.

15a	If anyone confesses that Jesus is the son of God
15b	then God remains in him and he in God.
16a	And we have known and believed in the love
16b	that God has in us.
16c	God is love
16d	and the one who remains in love remains in God
16e	and God remains in him.
17a	In this love has been made complete among us:
17b	that we have confidence on the day of judgment,
17c	because just as he is
17d	so also are we in this world.
18a	Fear does not exist in love
18b	but complete love casts out fear
18c	for fear has to do with punishment
18d	and the one who fears has not been competed in love.
19a	*We* love
19b	because he first loved us.
20a	If anyone says, "I love God,"
20b	and hates his brother
20c	then he is a liar.
20d	For the one who does not love his brother
20e	whom he has seen
20f	he cannot love God
20g	whom he has not seen.
21a	And this commandment we have from him:
21b	the one who loves God must love his brother also.

Notes

4:7. Beloved. See the note on 1 John 2:7. This verse begins with three words alliterated in *a*: *agapētoi, agapōmen allēlous*.

let us love. Gkt has the same verb as in 1 John 3:23, there governed by *hina*, here as a hortatory subjunctive.

is of. See the note "It comes not from the Father but from the world" at 1 John 2:16. The continuation of the argument makes it clear that the reference is to the origin.

everyone who loves. The word "love" is used here without any explicit object, which has led some to claim that the word has a meaning more general (love for one's neighbor) than the basic theme of 1 John 4:7–11, namely, love for one's fellow believers.

First John

Codex Alexandrinus reads "love God." Yet the entire section is dominated by an argument for loving one another/loving one's brother.

has been born of God. Gkt has the perfect *gegennētai*. See Appendix 11, Begotten/Born of God.

knows God. The two final clauses in v. 7 are mutually strengthened and deepened by means of two words beginning in *g*—*gegennētai* ("have been born") and *ginōskei* ("knows")—and by the change in time from perfect to present. To know God is a central theme in the letter. See Interpretation to 2:3–11, point 1.

8. At the beginning of this verse, what has already been said is stated a third time in negative form (antithetically). Scribes wished to change the aorist form to the perfect or the present as in v. 7d, but the combination of perfect, present, and aorist is certainly the original reading. No great distinction of meaning is to be attributed to the difference among these tense forms.

God is love. The words primarily state what God does. See the note "God is light" at 1 John 1:5 and Appendix 16, God is Love.

9. In this. Gkt *en toutōi*. The phrase occurs in 1 John 4:9, 10, 13, 17, and 5:2. "This" is cataphoric, and is taken up by the following that-clause (*hoti*, represented with a colon in the Translation Display). See the note "by this we know" at 1 John 2:3.

has been revealed. See the notes "and the life was revealed" at 1 John 1:2 and "was revealed" at 3:5.

the love of God. See the note on 1 John 2:5.

in us. Gkt *en hēmin*, as in 1 John 4:12d and 16b, but in 4:17a "with us" (*meth' hēmōn*). Based on the word order, the words "in us" can be attached to "the love of God" and translated "God's love for us," which works well with vv. 10c and 11a. Or more likely they belong with the verb, either "revealed for us"—the phrase taken as replacing the dative—or "revealed in/among us," with a local connotation. In favor of the last alternative, note the corresponding phrase in John 9:3 and the formulations in 1 John 4:12. If "us" refers to human beings in general, we should render it "among us"; if it points to the Johannine Christians, then "in us." See Appendix 5, We in the Johannine Letters.

unique. Gkt emphasizes the word "unique" (*monogenēs*) by placing it after the word it modifies. The Greek term has often been translated "only born," but the Greek etymology and the Hebrew background—the word is used *inter alia* of Isaac when Abraham intends to offer him as a sacrifice—speak for the meaning "unique, the only one of its kind." See also Luke 7:12; 8:42; 9:38. The Hebrew word, *jāchīd*, is translated in the LXX both with *monogenēs* ("unique") and with *agapētos* ("beloved"). According to Gen

22:2, 16, Isaac is "beloved," and according to Heb 11:17, he is "unique." See also Mark 1:11 and 9:7.

"Beloved" (*agapētos*) is often used of the believers in the Johannine letters (see the note on 1 John 2:7), while "unique" (*monogenēs*) is used of Jesus exclusively.

the world. The word is used here in a positive sense as in v. 14. See the note on 1 John 2:15.

that we might live, or "so that (*hina* of result) we have life." Gkt uses the verb "live" rather than the usual "have (eternal) life." See Appendix 6, Life, Eternal Life.

10. In this. A cataphoric "this" pointing forward to a that-clause introduced with *hoti*, which is represented in the Translation Display with a colon. See the note "In this" at v. 9 above.

not that we . . . but that he. Gkt emphasizes both "we" and "he" by employing the pronouns, which strengthens the contrast.

as an offering for our sins. Gkt has "offering" (*hilasmon*) as a predicate appositive for "his son," followed by the preposition "for" (*peri*). This preposition is used in the LXX to describe the effect of a sacrifice. In a context lacking reference to sacrifice the preposition *hyper* is preferred (1 John 3:16). See Appendix 7, Expiation and Forgiveness.

11. Beloved. This address is used here for the last time in the letter. See the note at 1 John 2:7.

if. Gkt has *ei* plus the indicative, which usually indicates that the condition corresponds to reality; roughly, "now, since . . ."

in this way God loved us. Based on the context, the reference is to Jesus' earthly life, including his death. The phrase "in this way" (*houtōs*) summarizes what has been said in vv. 7–10. The same expression occurs in John 3:16.

then we too ought. More literally, "we too are obliged to." The words "we too," with the pronoun *hēmeis* expressed, gives emphasis both to "we" and to the conclusion drawn. Regarding the Johannine use of the verb "ought," see the note "ought to" at 1 John 2:6.

12. No one has ever seen God. There is a possible sound-based word play: *theon . . . theasthai*. See the alliteration in v. 7 and the notes "Beloved" and "knows God." The same expression is found as well in John 1:18; 5:37; 6:46; 1 John 4:20.

If. The new sentence begins with "if" (*ean*), which normally indicates that what follows is something assumed.

remains in. See Appendix 15, God in Them and They in God.

his love. The genitive can be subjective, objective, or both. See the note "the love of God" at 1 John 2:5.

First John

has been made complete in us. In some manuscripts "in us" is associated with "his love." See the note "in us" at v. 9, above.

13. By this we know that we remain in him and he in us: he has given us of his spirit. Gkt: "In this . . . [that (*hoti*)]: he has given us of (*ek*) his spirit." The cataphoric "this" anticipates the explanatory that-clause, which is introduced by a colon in this translation. Some readers take the *hoti* as causal, "because."

of his spirit. Gkt here has an explicit partitive sense: "of his spirit." See the note "by the spirit" at 1 John 3:24.

14. We. Gkt "and we" (*kai hēmeis*). See the note "*You*," at 1 John 2:20. The formulations at the beginning of v. 14 are reminiscent of 1 John 1:1–2 and some commentators have therefore interpreted "we" as a reference to the Johannine tradition bearers. See Appendix 5, We in the Johannine Letters.

have seen and testify. A combination of perfect and present is common in 1 John.

as the savior of the world. The expression is a predicate appositive for "the Son." The word "savior" (*sōtēr*) is used of the Lord in the OT (LXX) and of Jesus in later NT writings (the Pastoral Letters, Lukan writings, John 4:42). Zech 9:9 (LXX) speaks of the coming king as "saving" (*sōzōn*). Greek gods are also called *sōtēr*, e.g., Zeus and Asclepius, and thus in time the Roman Caesars as well. Hadrian (117–38 CE) had among his other titles "the savior of the world."

15. The first clause, in Gkt a relative clause, is taken up in the next clause by "him," forming a so-called *casus pendens*. See the note at the beginning of 1 John 2:24.

confesses. See the note "confesses" at 1 John 4:2.

Jesus is the son of God. "God's son" is taken as a rule to be a predicate appositive, but it can also function as subject. The confession answers to the question: Is God's son Jesus? And the answer is: "God's son is Jesus." On the same basis, the formula in 1 John 2:22 can be translated "Jesus is Messiah." See also Acts 18:5, 28.

16. And we. As in v. 14, Gkt has an emphatic we. See the note "*You*" at 1 John 2:20.

we have known and believed in. Gkt has two verbs in the perfect that are frequently combined in John in different orders and tense forms (John 6:69; 8:31–32; 10:38; 14:7–10; 17:8). Everything favors taking "know" and "believe" as two ways of describing the same relation, put together here in order to strengthen the expression. Besides the passages just mentioned, see also 1 John 4:1–2.

the love that God has. The verb "have" is often used in this way in the letter (have + object), but only here with God as the subject. The formulation "to have love" occurs also in John 5:42; 13:35; and 15:13.

in us. See the note "in us" at v. 9, above.

and the one who remains in love. The introductory "and" has here a consecutive nuance: "so that." The words "remain in love" most likely mean to continue loving.

17. In this . . . : that . . . for. Gkt has "in this . . . that (*hina*) . . . for (*hoti*)." This ordinary construction—see the introductory note at 1 John 2:3—offers here an inordinate number of alternative interpretations:

a. A cataphoric "this," which is taken up by the *hina*-clause, an explanatory *hina*. This is how the text seems to have been taken in the NRSV, which translates it with both a colon and a "that" (see the Translation Display). The content of v. 17, namely, that love has reached its full maturity in something that has as yet not happened, speaks against this alternative.

b. A cataphoric "this," taken up by the *hoti*-clause. This yields a better sense, but the *hina*-clause becomes oddly parenthetical in that case.

c. An anaphoric "this" referring to v. 16de—they in God and God in them—with a consecutive *hina* ("so that") and a causal *hoti* ("because"). This produces the translation, "In this, love has reached its completion among us, so that we can be confident on the day of judgment, because just as Jesus Christ God's son is, so are we in this world." This alternative gives the text an excellent sense. The beginning of v. 17 summarizes the earlier discussion in order to turn now to speaking of confidence and fear.

among us. Gkt has the preposition *meta* ("with/among/in"). See the note "in us" at v. 9 above. Probably it refers to the mutual love among fellow believers in the Johannine community.

have confidence. See the note "we may have boldness" at 1 John 2:28.

just as . . . so also. Gkt has "just as He is, *we* too are," with the emphatic pronoun *hēmeis*, which strengthens the comparison.

he. Gkt has "that one" (*ekeinos*). See the note "he" at 1 John 2:6. The reference is to Jesus Christ, God's son.

18. fear has to do with punishment. Literally, "fear has punishment," i.e., fear has to do with punishment (as rendered here) or fear has/is its own punishment. The word in Gkt for "punishment" (*kolasis*) means pruning, cleansing, correcting, punishing for one's own good, but later it took on the more common sense of punishment. It is used of eternal punishment in Matt 25:46.

been completed in love. The word for "completed" in Gkt is the usual verb *teleioun* in the perfect middle (1 John 2:5; 4:12, 17, and 18).

19. We. Gkt has the emphatic pronoun, giving special weight to "we." It introduces a closing portion of the section 1 John 4:7–21. Cf. the similar use of "you" (*hymeis*) at the beginning of 1 John 2:20, 24, 27, and "we" again at 4:14, 16.

20. If anyone says . . . and . . . then. See notes at 1 John 1:6. The latter portion of v. 20 contains in Gkt a simple chiastic shape:

> He who does not love
>
> his brother, whom he has seen
>
> God, whom he has not seen
>
> he cannot love.

then he is a liar. The same conclusion is drawn in 1 John 1:6 and 2:4. This phrase, like the direct quotation in v. 20, is according to some readers a sign that the Elder has in mind the secessionists.

21. And this is the commandment we have from him: . . . Gkt includes "that" (*hina*) in place of the colon. The clause includes a cataphoric "this," taken up by the *hina*-clause. The reference of "him" is God.

Analysis

1. Delimitation

The thematic change between 1 John 4:1–6 and 4:7–21 is an unusually sharp one. It corresponds to the two main themes of the letter, faith/truth and love, which clearly figure in 1 John 3:11–24, especially in the new covenant's dual commandment in 1 John 3:23. The sections 4:1–6 and 4:7–21 thus become two high points in the letter, which powerfully put forward Faith/Truth and Love as characteristics of the renewed covenant and its intimate family-like fellowship.

Verse 7 very obviously introduces a new section by means of its theme, a new vocative, and a direct exhortation in first person plural. With a continued tight argument, vv. 7–10 form a foundational introductory paragraph.

It is much more difficult to determine a suitable end to this section. Where does 1 John 5:1–4 most naturally belong? With some hesitation I have taken these verses together with the following section. Like 1 John 3:11–24, 5:1–12 deals with both love and faith. It is not unusual that a new section first takes up what was treated in a preceding section. First John 5:1–4 becomes a door to a new room.

The end of 1 John 4:7–21 explicitly takes up the theme of the section's beginning, especially with a reference in v. 19 to the content in vv. 7 and 11. Following a repetition of the basic thought of the section—"We love because he first loved us"—the very same thing is said three times, first twice in negative form in v. 20abc and v. 20defg, then once in positive form in v. 21. The three-fold reinforcement of the main message of the section—to love fellow believers—makes a strong final impression, as does "this" in v. 21, which points both backward and forward. The formulation "the commandment we have from him" (v. 21a)—where "him" in this context can only refer to God—leads the readers' thoughts to the double covenant commandment in 1 John 3:23 and thereby prepares for the introduction to the next section: "Everyone who believes that Jesus is the Messiah" (1 John 5:1).

This attempt to analyze the boundaries of the text thus renders a more foundational introduction in vv. 7–10 and a less obvious closing in vv. 19–21.

2. Structure

Most interpreters look for a thematic structure in 1 John 4:7–21 and consequently encounter difficulties with the text. To be sure, a list of familiar thematic terms appears, especially from the lexical field of "love": the noun "love" 12 times; the verb "love" 15 times, and the vocative "beloved" twice. In addition, there are such Johannine words as remain in, send, the Spirit, see, know, confess, witness, believe, confidence, and hate/love one's brother. But it is not easy to discern a logical structure. The coherence seems—as in 1 John 2:3–17—to be more rhetorical than logical.

The vocative "beloved" in vv. 7 and 11—the last time the recipients are addressed in this way—divides the section into two paragraphs. Following a foundational exhortation in v. 7ab, the text is clearly shaped by repetitions, by a chiasm in vv. 7c–8b, and in vv. 9–10 by matching lines both introduced with "in this," where the word "this" points forward. See the Translation Display. As already indicated, vv. 7–10 function as the foundation for the entire section.

What follows, vv. 11–21, is mostly a reasoned exposition of vv. 7–10. The content of these introductory verses is repeated, expanded, strengthened, and rationalized. Verse 11 functions as a preamble: new address, reference to the first paragraph, mostly to vv. 9a and 10abc, and a reinforced repetition of the exhortation in v. 7 employing the formulation "we too ought to love one another." The closing, vv. 19–21 has already been treated under point 1, above.

What remains, vv. 12–18, has a more evidential character and consists of three loosely assembled parts, with two arguments for what each part asserts:

- Verses 12–13, like vv. 14–16, are dominated by the idea of close union with God: God in them and they in God. The proof of this intimate fellowship is two-fold, as in 1 John 3:11–24: mutual love and God's spirit within them.
- Verses 14–16, which begin by repeating vv. 9bc and 10de, likewise give a two-fold proof of the new covenant relationship: their confession of Jesus Christ/Messiah, God's son, and God's love within them.
- Verses 17–18 draw a conclusion similar to 1 John 3:21. By means of a backward-pointing "this" in v. 17a, what has just been said is summarized before a new

theme is introduced. God's love as active within them—God in them and they in God—leads to confidence on the day of judgment, as does their belonging intimately with Christ. In all these three parts there is a double proof for the new divine fellowship. In v. 18 a more general discussion about fear is added to what was said in v. 17 and the content of that verse is thereby reinforced.

In this way, the section 1 John 4:7–21 takes on a character wholly different from that of 1 John 4:1–6, even though both have the function of strengthening the recipients' faith and unity. The secessionists are conspicuous mostly by their absence; the negative formulations are few. Talk of love dominates the entire section and related themes are piled on one another without much logic. Everything points toward encouraging the Jesus-believers to continue in loving one another. The origin and source of this mutual love is God's love for them. It is no wonder that the section has sometimes been given the title "Song of Songs of Love." See Appendix 16, God is Love.

Interpretation

1. Love is of God (4:7–10)

In response to the question regarding which is the greatest commandment in the law, Jesus points to the so-called double love command. "'You shall love the Lord your God with all your heart, and with all your soul, and with all your mind.' This is the greatest and first commandment. And a second is like it: 'You shall love your neighbor as yourself.' On these two commandments hang all the law and the prophets" (Matt 22:34–40). According to 1 John 3:23, these two Old Testament commandments have been expanded, or we might say, made more precise in a particular way within the Johannine tradition. In the first commandment, love has been bound together with a faith in him whom God has sent into the world to save it, Jesus Messiah, God's son. In the second commandment, "your neighbor" has been interpreted as "your brother," in the sense of a member of the Johannine fellowship. This explains the repeatedly occurring commandment that "we should love one another" (3:23; 2 John 5), or "let us love one another" (4:7, 12), or "we ought to love one another" (4:21). This second element of the core Johannine commandment is the subject of this section, 4:7–21.

The Elder first assembles some basic theses in a more foundational introduction in 4:7–10 with "beloved" as an appropriate word of direct address. As is his custom, he repeats himself several times, though with variation in the formulations. The repetitions are probably provided to give weight and depth to the presentation. There comes then in 4:11–21 a more loosely arranged segment of evidential character containing material that had appeared earlier but that is now knit together with the theme of love, both God's love and the mutual love of the believers. This paragraph, too, is introduced with the vocative "beloved." The special rhetorical form and repetition of the main theme in vv. 19–21 makes them an appropriate ending for the section. See the Analysis, points 1 and 2.

The very first words, "Let us love one another, for love is of God" (v. 7), express the central principle that characterizes the entire section. There are only two primary axes in the love described in the letter: a vertical axis, God's love for human beings, and a horizontal axis, human beings' love for each other, the latter limited to the Johannine community. This reduction of potential subjects and objects is worth noting, since in the Gospel of John, there is frequent mention of love between Jesus and his disciples and between Jesus and God, as well as of the disciples' love for God, even though in a lesser sense. See Appendix 16, God is Love.

The letter's inverted T-model for love—God's loves people and people love one another—presumably has its background in the covenant love defined in Old Testament and Jewish writings (Exod 34:6; Joel 2:13; Jonah 4:2; Psa 69:13; 103:8; 145:8–9; Neh 9:17). See Appendix 9, A Renewed Covenant. Even in an Old Testament context "loving one's neighbor" has a natural limitation to the people of the covenant. The people's response to God's love, to wholeheartedly love God in return, is replaced in the letter's argument with faith in God's son, Jesus, Messiah. What remain, then, are God's love for the letter's recipients and their love for one another. Thus the section in the Bible that has the most to say about love places a definite limit on its range.

The repetition of the first main motivation, "for love is of God" (v. 7) in a renewed form, "because God is love" (v. 8), gives it a more complete, well-rounded content. God is love, and as such God is both origin and source of the mutual love among the believers. Everything began with God's love, a love directed toward human beings and one that must manifest itself among and within human beings. God is a God who wants fellowship with human beings and who therefore takes the initiative and acts. We have the same sort of meaning in the expressions "God is light" and "God is spirit." See the Interpretation for 1 John 1:5—2:2, point 1, and Appendix 16, God is Love.

Even in the exposition of "God is love," the three dimensions of "God is light" are present: revelation, salvation, and lifestyle. But before the Elder goes on, he connects "God is love" together with divine begetting (being born of God) and with being in close union with God (knowing God), the latter first in a positive statement (v. 7d) and then in a negative statement (v. 8a). This rhetorical form of parallelism does not need to imply that the Elder focuses the negative clause particularly on the opponents, whether Gnostic teachers or ultra-Johannine secessionists. He simply wants to establish the fact that those who love know God and those who know God love. To know God implies, in the letter, a very intimate union with God (see the Interpretation for 1 John 2:3–11, point 1, on 2:3) and thus also with love, because God is love. Mutual love is merely a natural consequence of knowing God, and vice versa.

Fellowship with God is expressed even more intensely in the concept of divine begetting: the one who loves "is born of God." This connection is emphasized later in a special way in 5:1. See also the Interpretation for 2:28—3:10, point 4, and Appendix

First John

11, Begotten/Born of God. Here too we can turn to the clause: The one who is born of God loves. Thus it becomes completely clear that God's love and the mutual love among God's children are inextricably bound together with one another. In 2:3–11 "knowing God" is joined together with keeping God's commandments, which is then successively reduced to keeping oneself faithful to God's word, i.e., to the revelation of God through Jesus Christ, to living as Jesus lived, and to loving one's brother. See the Interpretation there. The world and Jews who do not believe in Jesus do not know God (1 John 3:1; John 16:3). The world hates Jesus' followers (John 15:18; 17:14; 1 John 3:13). From this it follows that in his argument the Elder restricts himself to God's children, which in the letter means the Jesus-believing Jews within the Johannine community.

The meaning of "God is love" is further defined in vv. 9–10 in two formulations, both dominated by the idea of God's sending the Son into the world. The first formulation is marked with "has sent" (perfect); the second with "sent" (aorist). Jesus as "the one whom God has sent" is a very common formula in the Gospel (John 3:34; 4:34; 5:23, 24, 30, 36, 37, 38, etc.). The core of the disciples' faith can be summed up in the words, "they believe that God has sent him" (John 17:8, 25). The sending of the Son is mentioned only here in the letter. The emphasis lies on the fact that God *sent* his son into the world. The sequence of thought is unfolded in three stages: Love is of God, God is love, and God's love is revealed in us (see the note "in us" at 4:9).

The revelation of God's love is therefore tied to Jesus Christ. God's steadfast love (grace) was already there in the covenant at Sinai, but it took on a new form in Jesus Christ (John 1:16–17). God gave the world "his unique son"; that was what was new. And the purpose is indicated in two ways: through the Son life is mediated to humanity (v. 9c), and through the Son humanity is cleansed from sin (v. 10d). Something is added; something is taken away. By saying, "that we might have life," and "for our sins," the Elder shows that he is thinking of the Johannine community. Only God lives by virtue of Godself; God's son has received life from the Father and he has mediated this divine life to those who believe in him (John 5:26; 6:57; 1 John 5:11). See Appendix 6, Life, Eternal Life. We have the same message in John 3:16–21. The "sending" entails not only Jesus' having become a human being (the incarnation), but also Jesus' atoning death. It is Jesus' entire life and work that is in view, as in 1:1–3; 3:5, 8, 4:2; 5:6. "By this we have learned to recognize love: he laid down his life for us" (3:16). Thus, Jesus' love is also present in this exposition of love, even though it is not expressly said here, as it is in the Gospel, that Jesus loves the Father and his own.

In this way, in this first paragraph, the Elder develops, explains and strengthens the encouragement to the letter's recipients to love one another by seeing mutual love as an outflow of God's love and by joining it together with being born of God, knowing God, having eternal life and being cleansed from sin. God's love includes within itself not only revelation (God sends God's son to the world), but also salvation (people are cleansed from sin and become participants in eternal life) and a way of living (people

1 John 4:7–21: God is Love

love one another). I have earlier tried to show that all these concepts have to do with a renewed covenant. That covenant has been implemented by God's sending God's son into the world in the form of Jesus as Messiah, the one who was to come. Love in this section is a form of covenant love.

2. God in Them and They in God (4:11–16)

With a summarizing of the introductory verses and perhaps not least a reference to Jesus' sacrificial death, "if in this way God loved us," and a repetition of the admonition in v. 7, "then we too ought to love one another," the Elder continues in v. 11 with his teaching about love. To modern readers, his argument may seem poorly structured. The two first parts, vv. 12–13 and vv. 14–16, are held together by the concept of God's being in them and their being in God. In both parts, the Elder gives criteria for this intimate union with God. Verses 17–18 then take up confidence and fear on the day of judgment in relation to how love has attained fullness among the believers. As in vv. 14–16, one reason for confidence is the union with God, and the other is being bound to Jesus Christ, God's son. Faith in Jesus and Jesus as an example have an important role in vv. 11–18, but are conspicuously absent from the section's opening and closing.

The words "No one has ever seen God" in v. 12a are the most disruptive in the context. It would seem simpler if the line were removed. It then recurs at the end, in v. 20. Is it merely a preview of what is coming? The claim that no one has seen God occurs three times in the Gospel (see the note) and then always in connection with the question of Jesus' mission and his relationship to the Father.

It is easy to believe that this clause had an important place in the intra-Jewish discussion about who Jesus was. Moses had not been permitted to see God, but Jesus had (John 1:18). Here in v. 12a then, the words could be reminiscent of Jesus' role with regard to God's love. Jesus reappears as an argument in this paragraph. But the immediately following text and v. 20 connect the words to God's love and to love among the brothers. Is it the point, then, that although no one has seen God, God's love has been visible in Jesus' life and ministry (vv. 9–10) and in the mutual love of the believers (vv. 7–8)? The latter corresponds to what is said in 1 John 2:8, that what is "new" has been actualized "in him and in you." Then this line would make sense with what follows regarding God in us and God's love in us. In this way, v. 12a and 12bcd can be seen as expressing a relationship of counter-expectation: "although 12a, nevertheless 12bcd."

"We remain in God and God remains in us" or "God remains in us and we remain in God" is the cohesive theme in what now follows (vv. 12b–16). The formulation occurs three times in this very short paragraph (vv. 13, 15, and 16). In addition we have "God abides in us" (v. 12) and the mention of God's love within us (vv. 12 and 16). The discussion issues in a final formulation of the condition for this close union between God and humanity: "if we remain in love" (v. 16), i.e., in the love that has just been described, i.e., in God's love, i.e., in God's love within us, i.e., in the love that has been perfected within us. The final stipulation thus includes the first: "If we love one another" (v. 12).

This idea of God in them and they in God intensifies what was expressed in the introduction with the words "to know God" and "to be born of God" (vv. 7–8). The Elder takes care to work love into it, both God's love and the mutual love among fellow believers, in the divine fellowship that has become a reality in the renewed covenant. See Appendix 9, A Renewed Covenant; Appendix 11, Begotten/Born of God; and Appendix 15, God in Them and They in God. Gathered up here are the typical concepts in the letter's patterns of expression. God is love; love is of God; God's love is within them; God's love is fulfilled in them; they love one another; Messiah, God's son, has come in the form of Jesus and his life here on earth, from birth to death, and with him eternal, divine life here and now (5:20). These formulations are unique to the letter. It is extremely difficult to find any parallel material in extra-biblical texts that corresponds to 4:7–21. Here, according to the Elder, we have the core of the Johannine message, forming together with 4:1–6 an exposition of God's "law" in the new covenant (3:23).

There are four conditions and criteria for this fellowship of divine love within the world, or perhaps three, since the first one and the last one are so closely related to each other. "If we love one another" (v. 12b) is a clear repetition of the central theme of the section (v. 7 and v. 11 and vv. 19–21). The connection this condition has with God's love, already laid out in vv. 7–10 and mentioned in v. 12, is recognized in the words "*we* have known and believed in the love that God has in us" (v. 16ab) and is summed up in the letter's typical construction "the one who remains in love," i.e., "if we remain in love," formulated with each and every member of the Johannine community in mind.

The two other criteria or conditions—that God has given them of his spirit and that they confess that Jesus is God's son (v. 13 and v. 15)—have been regarded by many readers as somehow foreign to this particular context. But they have been mentioned previously, and if we read the section as an exposition of the Johannine love command in 3:23, we can see that they fit in naturally here. See the Interpretation on 3:24 and on 4:2. The Elder formulates the conditions for the new covenant, for mutually abiding in one another (referred to in the literature as the Johannine immanence), in several ways: to keep God's commandments (3:24), to remain in God's love, to let God's love reach its fullness in them, to love one another and to confess Jesus as God's son (4:11–16). The Jesus-confession is introduced with the words "we have seen and testify that . . . ," a phrase that leads to thoughts of 1:1–3 and also of 4:6. The Elder clearly has in mind himself, the readers, and tradition-bearers close to him. Thus Jesus once more becomes a necessary part of this Song of Songs of Love.

3. Confidence on the Day of Judgment (4:17–18)

The Elder first briefly summarizes what has just been said and what was said at the beginning of the paragraph. If the letter's recipients remain in love, God is in them and they are in God (4:13, 15, 16), and "in this," i.e., in the fact that God is in them and they are in God, love attains its fullness in them (v. 17). This is how the somewhat complicated beginning of v. 17 is to be understood (see the note). From this it follows that they have confidence on the day of judgment. Likewise in 3:22–24, this mutual immanence and the readers' confidence before God are placed in parallel with one another, there primarily with regard to prayers being heard, and now here with regard to the final judgment. See the Interpretation on these verses. Confidence before God implies complete openness and complete access into God's presence. See the note on 2:28.

Then comes yet another reason for this confidence: Just as Jesus Christ God's son is, so are they in this world. Both Jesus and those who believe in Jesus are very closely united with God. Just as Jesus loves them, so they love one another (3:16; John 13:1; 15:12). As in vv. 14–16, a theological motivation is combined with a Christological motivation for what is put forth. The Elder then reinforces the motivation even further by claiming twice that complete love drives out fear. Indirectly this functions as one more exhortation to love, in order that love attains its full maturity in them. There is no fear in love, evidently a maxim the Elder applies to his readers. Fear goes with punishment. Because the letter's recipients have confidence on judgment day and are not compelled to turn away in shame under the eye of the judge (2:28; 4:17), there can be no risk of punishment. It is out of his love that God indwells them. For this reason as well, all fear vanishes.

4. "We Love Because He First Loved Us" (4:19–21)

With a proverb-like formulation, the Elder introduces the final paragraph of this section: "*We* love because he first loved us." The word "he" is emphatic in the original text. The words can be understood to contain everything that has been said in the foregoing regarding God's love and the mutual love among fellow believers. They repeat particularly what stands at the beginning of the two previous paragraphs, v. 7 and v. 11, namely the obligation to love one another. Not to love one's brother is to hate one's brother (v. 20). This becomes the sole theme in this last paragraph. What is new in the argument is, as later in 5:1–3, the reference to the love people have for God. It is used, however, in a rather formally logical way. No explanation is given of what it means to love God beyond the fact that it belongs indissolubly with loving one another. The formulations are built to a considerable degree upon the double love command, to love God and to love one's neighbor. We have established earlier that the first half of this command, to love God, primarily means to believe in Jesus as Messiah, God son.

First John

The first stage of the "final plea" is given a rhetorical form that the Elder used earlier in the beginning of his letter (1:5—2:2 and 2:3–11). Many scholars would like to see this as a direct reference to the opponents in the letter, whether Gnostic teachers or advanced Johannine Christians. "If anyone says, etc." The use of direct quotation in a statement labeling it as false, together with supportive rationale—similar to the parallel between the brother, whom one has seen, and God, whom one has not seen—can probably be interpreted as an intensification the rhetoric at the end of the letter. Loving God and loving one's fellow believer belong inextricably together. Love is of God. The claim that no one has seen God (v. 12) thus returns here. The letter's recipients have God's love within them; they have experienced its effects in the new fellowship of God's people. They "have seen" the one God has sent into the world (v. 14), but they have not seen God. Only Jesus the Messiah, God's son, has been able to mediate God to them (John 1:18). Thus God's love for them is not primarily to be reflected back as love for God—apart from the need to believe in the name of God's son—but is to be reflected as love for fellow believers, whom they have undeniably seen (3:17).

The second stage of the "final plea" is shaped in the form of a word of commandment, a commandment from God himself: The one who loves God loves his brother also. The command from God has been characterized earlier as "new," i.e., as belonging to the renewal of the covenant (2:7–8) and formulated in the words "let us love one another" (2 John 5–6). See the Interpretation on these verses. It then receives its fullest form in 3:23, to believe in Jesus as Messiah, God's son, and to love one another. The Elder often speaks of what cannot be seen, of God, of knowing God, of being born of God, of being in God, etc. What can be seen is the fruit of what cannot be seen; the visible is the criterion of the invisible. Throughout the letter, what is visible is concentrated in Jesus, that which was there from the beginning, etc. (1:1–3), and in mutual love among the brothers and sisters. We have the same two points in 1 John 2:8, "in him and in you." In this section all the emphasis lies on the latter.

10

1 John 5:1–12: Faith, Love, Begetting, Victory, and Eternal Life

Translation Display

1a	Everyone who believes that Jesus is the Messiah
1b	he has been born of God
1c	and everyone who loves the One who gave birth
1d	he loves the one born of him.
2a	By this we know that we love the children of God
2b	when we love God and do his commandments.
3a	For this is love for God
3b	that we keep his commandments.
3c	And his commandments are not heavy
4a	for whatever is born of God overcomes the world.
4b	And this is the victory that has overcome the world:
4c	our faith.
5a	Who is the one who overcomes the world
5b	if not the one who believes that Jesus is the son of God?
6a	This is the one who came through water and blood
6b	Jesus Messiah
6c	not by the water only, but by the water and by the blood.
6d	And the Spirit is the one who testifies,
6e	for the Spirit is the truth.
7a	For there are three who testify:
8a	the Spirit, the water, and the blood
8b	and these three are in harmony.
9a	If we accept the testimony of human beings

First John

> 9b   then God's testimony is greater.
> 9c   For this is God's testimony
> 9d   that he has testified concerning his son.
> 10a   The one who believes in the son of God has the testimony in himself.
> 10b   The one who does not believe God has made him a liar
> 10c   because he has not believed in the testimony
> 10d   that God has testified concerning his son.
> 11a   And this is the testimony:
> 11b   that God gave us eternal life
> 11c   and this life is in his son.
> 12a   The one who has the Son has this life.
> 12b   The one who does not have the Son of God does not have this life.

Notes

5:1. Everyone who believes . . . everyone who loves. Gkt in both phrases have the familiar formula "everyone" + article + participle. The longer variant with "everyone who" and not simply the definite article alone gives a certain weight to the paragraph's opening line. Cf. 1 John 3:4–10.

Jesus is the Messiah or "Jesus is the Christ" or "the Messiah is Jesus." See the note "Jesus is God's son" at 1 John 4:15. This confession is denied in 1 John 2:22. In 1 John 5:5 it is followed up with "Jesus is God's son." See Appendix 14, Jesus as Messiah, God's son.

he has been born of God. See Appendix 11, Begotten/Born of God.

everyone who loves the one who gave birth loves the one born of him. Gkt has "who gave birth" in the aorist active and "born of him" in the perfect passive. The wordplay gives the saying the character of a proverb. As with all proverbs, the words can be filled with various meanings. It can be a general proverb regarding any parents whatsoever, or one regarding one's own parents: "whoever loves his father also loves his siblings," or applied to God and the children of God: "whoever loves the Father (i.e., God) also loves her fellow Christians." In fact, some readers, with reference to 1 John 5:18, interpret the first phrase as "whoever loves Jesus," but that gives an unacceptable sense to the entire argument in this context. John the Evangelist sometimes uses proverb-like statements that in their own right are logically self-evident, and he applies them to what is said in the context, e.g., in John 13:10. Here the context calls for a general way of speaking that applies to God and fellow Christians.

2. By this we know that. Gkt: "by this we know that (*hoti*) . . . when (*hotan*)." The construction is common in the letter. See the note at the beginning of 1 John 2:3. Here, however, there are two subordinate clauses, the second of them introduced with the word *hotan* ("when/whenever"), unusual for 1 John.

1 John 5:1–12: Faith, Love, Begetting, Victory, and Eternal Life

The question is whether the word "this" points backward or forward. Many commentators take it as anaphoric with reference back to v. 1cd: "From what has just been said, we see that we love God's children when we love God." We have the same effect if we reverse the clauses: "Therefore, when we love God and do his commandments, then we know that we love God's children." This is a repetition of 1 John 4:20–21. Love for God becomes a test of love for fellow believers. A few commentators take it as both anaphoric and cataphoric.

But many others insist on holding to the usual pattern in 1 John, whereby the word "this" points forward, and thus to the clause that begins with "when" (*hotan*), and is thereby completed and strengthened with "and do his commandments." To love God becomes then a proof that we love God's children and not the reverse, as in 1 John 4:20. A variation of this kind is not impossible in the Johannine writings. The effect of what is said in vv. 1c–2 thus issues in a single statement: loving God's children and loving God are completely inseparable. It is expressed in double fashion—the content of v. 2ab interprets the meaning of v. 1cd—and loving God is further developed by the idea of doing God's commandments.

do his commandments. Gkt does not use the typical word for "keep" (*tērein*), which occurs nine times in the Johannine letters, but instead uses "do" (*poiein*). But *tērein* is used again in the next verse. Both verbs are used as well in 1 John 3:22. Presumably this is just a stylistic variation. Regarding "his commandments," see the Analysis for 1 John 2:3–11, point 2.

3. For this is . . . that. A Johannine statement of definition, where "this" points forward and is taken up in the following clause, which is introduced with "that," *hina*.

love for God. Gkt has a genitive construction: "love of God." The context here justifies taking "love of God" as love for God (objective genitive). But see the note "the love of God" at 1 John 2:5 and Appendix 16, God is Love.

his commandments. Literally, "and his commandments." The word "and" introduces a comment on "his commandments" in the preceding clause. The word "commandments" in the plural refers thus to "the commandments from God." See the Analysis on 1 John 2:3–11, point 2.

4. whatever is born of God. Gkt: "everything begotten of God." The word "everything" is neuter singular and can sometimes be used of persons when the community or category as a whole is in view, and not the separate individuals. See John 6:37 and 17:2.

overcomes . . . has overcome . . . overcomes. The word in Gkt, *nikan*, is used three times in vv. 4–5, first in the present indicative, then as an aorist participle modifying the word "victory," and finally as a present participle. The aorist can be rendered with the present "overcomes" and corresponds thus to the present in vv. 4a and 5a. It can also be translated as a perfect, "has overcome," as in 1 John 4:4, or with the imperfect "overcame." In the latter case, it can especially be taken to refer to Jesus' victory (John 16:33) or to the baptism of the letter's recipients (see the "baptismal confession" in v. 5) or to the expelling of the secessionists (see 1 John 4:4, and possibly 1 John 2:14).

and this is. The clause is a typical Johannine definition statement. See the note "And this is" at 1 John 1:5.

victory. The word in Gkt, *nikē*, stands for that which gives victory.

world. See the note on 1 John 2:15.

faith, Gkt *pistis*. Faith occurs very frequently as a verb ("believe") in the Johannine writings, but only here as a noun. Cf. 1 John 2:13–14, where it is with the help of God's word that the young people have overcome the Evil one.

5. Who is the one who overcomes. Gkt expresses this with a present participle.

Jesus is the son of God or "God's son is Jesus." See the note "Jesus is the son of God" at 1 John 4:15 and Appendix 14, Jesus as Messiah, God's son.

6. This. Gkt uses the more precise demonstrative pronoun, "this one" (*houtos*), which in the context takes up the nearest noun, "God's son" (v. 5), and then is identified as "Jesus Messiah." See Appendix 14, Jesus as Messiah, God's son. Introductory formulas such as "this is" or "this one is" are typical for both the letter and the Gospel (John 1:34; 4:42; 7:40–41; as well as examples in the note "And this is" at 1 John 1:5). See also Matt 3:17 and 26:26. In John 6:50, 52, 58, the formulation "this one is" comes quite close to the self-designator "I am."

the one who came. Gkt uses the substantive participle, "the coming one" (*ho elthōn*). Because the participle is in the aorist, the formulation should be taken to refer to a historical event of some kind, e.g., that God's son was born into the world and died on a cross.

through water and blood, Gkt *di' hydatos kai haimatos*. The preposition *dia* plus genitive normally indicates means (instrumental sense), i.e., it signifies by what means one event makes possible another event—here, the coming of God's son. The difficulties with determining what "water and blood" refers to are obvious in the manuscripts. Some readings have "spirit and blood," others "water and spirit and blood," which clearly depends on John 3:5. See further Appendix 17, By Water and Blood.

not by the water only, but by the water and by the blood. Both "water" and "blood" have definite articles, which point out the water and blood as the water and blood just mentioned (demonstrative function). Gkt does not use the usual preposition for "through" (*dia*), but rather *en* ("in, by, with"), preceding both the water and the blood. It clearly emerges that we are dealing with two phenomena: "the water" and "the blood." Most interpreters take *en* here in roughly the same sense as *dia,* but some claim that *dia* focuses on the means itself that made the coming of God's son possible, while *en* indicates the circumstances under which his coming actually occurred. See further Appendix 17, By Water and Blood.

And. The word indicates here a thematic proximity to the foregoing. See the note "and the life was revealed" at 1 John 1:2.

the one who testifies. Gkt has the definite article and participle in the present. See Appendix 18, Testify.

for the Spirit is the truth. The assertion is reminiscent of "the Spirit of truth" in the Gospel of John. The spirit bears witness to Jesus, to what he said and did, and guides those who trust in Jesus into all truth (John 15:26; 16:11–15). See Appendix 3, The Truth.

7. **For there are three who testify.** Literally, "for three are they who testify." The word "for" (*hoti*) repeats "for" in the preceding clause (v. 6d) and is sometimes omitted by translators or rendered with an epexegetical "indeed." The three that testify—the Spirit, the water, and the blood (v. 8a)—are all neuter nouns in Greek, but the author uses the masculine for the participle "who testify," presumably because these three are personified in the text. In Gkt, the emphasis lies upon "three." Older translations had here a longer addition: "in heaven: the Father, the Word, and the Holy Spirit. And these three are one. And there are three who testify on earth." See the Analysis, point 2.

8. **are in harmony.** Literally, "are into one," where the preposition "into" (*eis*) can introduce a predicate adjective (typical in the LXX) or indicate direction, goal. In the former case, the translation becomes "are one," in the latter case "are in agreement," or "in harmony." John 11:52 and 17:23 have a similar construction regarding the fellowship surrounding Jesus.

9. **If we accept . . . then.** Gkt uses a much abbreviated "if . . . then" construction: "if/when we accept the testimony of human beings, then [we ought also to accept God's testimony, because] God's testimony is greater."

the testimony of human beings. It is not clear just what is in view here. It may refer to human testimony quite generally, or to the three witnesses just mentioned, or to the testimony of John the Baptist (John 1:6–8, 32; 3:31–33; 5:34). The Elder's penchant for using common "logical" formulations that can then be applied to what he wants to say speaks in favor of the first option. The wordy reasoning regarding God's testimony in vv. 9–10 has a general, syllogistic character.

God's testimony. The question is whether God's testimony is something in addition to what the three witnesses say—that God's son is Jesus—or whether it coincides with them. Rhetorically, the first alternative works better. God's testimony is likewise focused on God's son, but it carries a different connotation because of the divine life that this son imparts. Regardless of alternatives, it is a new way of saying what in the main has already been said.

For this is. The word "this" in this kind of phrase normally points forward, pointing here to the following that-clause, introduced with *hoti*. Some read *hoti* as a relative pronoun *ho ti* and get thus the translation "(for this is God's testimony), something that...". Cf. the use of the relative pronoun in v. 10d "that God has testified concerning his son." The same construction occurs in v. 11, where *hoti* naturally means "that." See the note "And this is" at 1 John 1:5.

10. believes in the son of God. Gkt has the verb "believe" (*pisteuein*) plus the preposition "in" (*eis*). The same construction is found at the end of the clause: "not believed in the testimony...". See the note "believe in" at 1 John 3:23.

has the testimony in himself. The formulation in Gkt—"to have the testimony in oneself (*en heautōi*)"—is presumably intended to strengthen the simple formulation "to accept the testimony." The believers have embodied the testimony with their entire life. See Rev 6:9; 12:17; 19:10. The opposite idea is formulated in the second half of the parallelism. The manuscripts have *heautōi* or *hautōi* or *autōi*, without any great difference in meaning.

does not believe God. Gkt has the verb "believe" (*pisteuein*) plus the dative. See the note "believe in" at 1 John 3:23.

has made . . . has not believed . . . has testified. Gkt has the perfect in all these verbs. The last verb is part of a so-called *figura etymologica*, "the testimony . . . has testified," which strengthens the concept of "testimony." See the note "the message we . . . proclaim" at 1 John 1:5 and "that he himself promised" at 1 John 2:25.

11. And this is. The clause is a typical Johannine definition statement, where "this" points forward to a clause introduced with *hoti*. See the note "And this is" at 1 John 1:5.

gave. Gkt has the aorist. God gave human beings eternal life when Jesus came into the world and human beings put faith in him as the Messiah, the son of God (John 3:16).

eternal life. See Appendix 6, Life, Eternal Life.

12. has. Regarding to "have the Son" and to "have God," see the note "have the Father" at 1 John 2:23.

the Son . . . the Son of God. When the author chooses to say "the Son of God" in the second clause, instead of "the Son," the second clause takes on a greater weight. It can indicate that this is the end of the section. The formulation "God's son" forms an arc with the closing words of the first paragraph, v. 5b, and its description in vv. 6–8.

this life . . . this life. Gkt has the usual word for "life," plus the definite article, which here clearly indicates that the reference is to the eternal life mentioned in v. 11b.

Analysis

1. Delimitations and Structure

In 1 John, the content of one section can be repeated and even deepened in the beginning of the next section. This is the case with 1 John 5:1–12. As a whole, these first lines are diverse, rich with various themes, and open to multiple interpretations, not least with regard to the relationship among the various clauses. The reader gets the impression that a good deal is forced together in these opening lines before the second half of the section begins. The one is linked to the other: to believe in Jesus as the Messiah → to be born of God → to love God who gives birth → to love those who are born of God → to love God's children → to love God → to keep God's commandments → to love God → to keep God's commandments → to be born of God → to overcome the world → to believe in Jesus as God's son (vv. 1–5). This condensing of the central concepts in the letter indicates to the reader that the end of the letter is approaching.

First the theme that dominates vv. 1–12 is announced, i.e., faith in Jesus as the Messiah, the Son of God, if vv. 1 and 5 are read together. Then comes the theme of mutual love, coupled with old and new arguments: they are born of God; they obey God's commandments. This comes to a close in v. 4 with a comment on the victory over the world, a theme carried further by the definition statement in v. 4bc and broadened out by a question with the answer supplied in v. 5. See the Translation Display. The end of v. 4, "our faith," and v. 5, "the one who believes," link back to the faith in v. 1 and, by means of the confession of God's son, prepares for what follows.

This son of God is presented in more detail in vv. 6–8 as he who came by the water and the blood. To this then the Spirit is added as witness, and thus there are three witnesses: the Spirit, the water, and the blood. And these three are in harmony. The content of this concise, compact paragraph requires filling out from the letter generally and from the Johannine world of thought.

The word "testify" leads into a rather redundant paragraph concerning God's testimony regarding God's son (vv. 9–12). God as witness weighs heavily in the argument in v. 9. God's testimony has as its goal that humanity should believe in God's son (v. 10). And this has for its content something God guarantees: whoever believes in the Son—or has the Son—possesses eternal life (vv. 11–12). The testimony has the power to impart divine life to everyone who believes in it. Parallel formulations, with small variations of expression, abound in this short paragraph: this is God's testimony (vv. 9c and 11a); that God has testified concerning God's son (v. 12a and 12b); the one who believes and the one who does not believe (v. 10a and 10b), together with the one who has the Son and the one who does not have the Son of God (v. 12a and 12b). The participles "the believing one" and "the having one," four times in vv. 10 and 12, repeat the participle "the believing one" from the beginning and end of the first paragraph (vv. 1 and 5), and give a certain rounding off to the entire section. The mediation of divine life at the end (vv. 11–12) replaces in a way the concept of divine begetting in the beginning (vv. 1, 2, and 4a).

From this we have a rather varied flood of ideas consisting of three paragraphs: vv. 1–5, 6–8, and 9–12. See the Translation Display. Some readers bring v. 13 into this section as well, because it deals with eternal life through faith in God's son. The words "these things have I written" in v. 13, the switch to first person singular, and the structure of the entire letter, however, make it more natural to see this verse as the introduction to the letter's closing section, which—like the closing of the Gospel of John—is then continued with additional closing formulations. For this reason, I take this verse with the letter's final remarks.

2. The Three Witnesses (Comma Johanneum)

In the King James Bible of 1611 (and in the New King James Version of 1982), vv. 7–8 read as follows: "For there are three that bear record *in heaven, the Father, the Word, and the Holy Ghost: and these three are one. And there are three that bear witness in earth,* the Spirit, and the water, and the blood: and these three agree in one." I have italicized the words that are not usually found in modern translations. Verse 7 was a very important passage in the Bible and in some versions (e.g., official Swedish editions of previous centuries) was even printed in bold font. The verse was used as a clear testimony to the Trinity. There is in fact no better such testimony in the New Testament. The words were removed in translations coming out toward the end of the nineteenth century and early twentieth, e.g., the American Standard Version of 1901, often following heated debates among those involved in the work of translating. The issue arose because it became clear that none of the oldest sources or manuscripts contains the words that I have italicized above.

These omitted words—usually called *Comma Johanneum* (the Johannine insertion)—are with all likelihood a marginal note that gradually found a place within the text itself. Nothing in the context, however, can be said to deal with the Trinity. The words are found in five very late Greek manuscripts, where they appear to be a translation from the Latin Vulgate. The earliest evidence for them is found in a writing from the end of the fourth century, *Liber Apologeticus*, which is usually attributed to the Spanish bishop Priscillian. Teaching about the Trinity come from an earlier period of course, but it is limited to Latin texts. None of the older translations have this addition, other than the Latin ones, among them eventually the Vulgate itself. Thus it was included in medieval translations and even in later versions. The *Textus Receptus*, which lies behind translations right up to the end of the nineteenth century, contains the addition. What began as a Trinitarian interpretation of 1 John 5:7–8, presumably in North Africa in the third century, gradually found its way into nearly every subsequent translation of the Bible, until the last hundred years. Those few who today argue for the *Textus Receptus* as the basic text still retain the *Comma Johanneum* in their translations (e.g., the New King James).

Interpretation

1. Faith, Love, and Victory Over the World (5:1–5)

The words "everyone who believes" in v. 1 indicate the theme that holds together the final section of the letter before the ending in 5:13–21. They are repeated in 5:5 and in the parallel formulations at the end: the one who believes and the one who does not believe in v. 10 and the one who has and the one who does not have in v. 12. Both believing in God's son and having God's son express a very close union with him. See the note "believe in" at 3:23 and the note on "have the Father" in 2:23. The formulation "the one who believes that . . ." shows that faith also has a definite content.

To begin with, faith is in many ways coupled together with other themes in the letter. This condensing of the letter's content gives the impression that the Elder is now bringing his writing to a close. Faith and love, the core of the new covenant's commandment (3:23), are once more brought together with divine begetting, obedience to the law, and victory over the world, and this forms the first five verses of the section into a separate paragraph. Then follows a deepening of faith in Jesus as Messiah, God's son (vv. 6–8), and the entire section takes on a special weight with a final paragraph on God's testimony about his son (vv. 9–12). Determining the boundaries of the section and its paragraphs is not as simple here at the end of the letter, but I have, as often before, chosen a three-part division. One thing is clear: the Elder is partial to the number three in his rhetorical structuring of the text. See further the analysis above, point 1, and the Translation Display.

The Elder binds his theme together in a familiar manner: partly in an interlocking way, where the form *A and B* is followed by *B and C*, which in turn is followed by *C and D*, etc., and partly by paralleled lines and verses. Compare John 1:1–5. Faith and divine begetting, the first combination in this section (like love and divine begetting in the beginning of the previous section), transition to the combination of begetting and love for God and for God's children. Love for God then moves on to keeping God's commandments, the possibility of keeping the commandments leads to victory over the world, victory over the world leads to faith, and so the circle is complete. Love for God and love for God's children are paralleled in v. 1cd and v. 2ab; loving God and keeping his commandments also occurs twice (vv. 2b and 3ab); likewise victory over the world and faith (vv. 4bc and 5). Even the full Johannine confession of Jesus as Messiah, God's son (1 John 1:3; 3:23; 5:20; John 20:31) is divided here into two lines, the first and the last of the paragraph. There is nothing actually new in this paragraph apart from the heavy concentration of the letter's central themes. The Elder has his own way of expressing himself.

First John

The Johannine rhetoric also includes the use of a "Johannine maxim" in v. 1cd: "everyone who loves the one who gave birth loves also the one born of him." The form is a maxim in the sense that it resembles a byword or a general saying. It is Johannine in the sense that it contains characteristically Johannine words, love and beget. It is not easy to determine whether this is a known proverb, perhaps in Johannine dress, or whether it is a formulation that the Elder created for his argument in this particular context.

There are other similar formulations in the Johannine literature (John 2:10; 5:19; 11:50; 13:10). As a rule, such general formulations are interpreted in context, often by an immediate application to what is said in the text. Thus it is here as well. Verse 2ab speaks of loving God and loving God's children. It has been debated whether this maxim is a general formulation about every father ("the one who loves a father") or whether it is limited to the relationships within a family ("the one who loves his or her father") or whether it has to do with God ("the one who loves the Father"). I prefer the first alternative in view of similar rhetorical features in other passages in the Johannine literature. See the note on v. 1. A maxim is readily understood as self-evident in its logic and it influences the argumentation in which it is found.

The word order and the logical relations among the various thematic elements in this paragraph pose a number of questions for a modern reader. This is evident not least with the interpretation of the well-known phrase "by this we know that..." in v. 2, which here meets the reader for the last time in the letter. See the first note on 5:2. In 4:20–21 the readers are invited to test love for God in terms of love for the brothers. Here it appears to be that one can test mutual love in terms of love for God. The variations are by no means impossible in the Johannine argumentation. Love for God (= A) and love for those born of God (= B) belong indissolubly together. Saying "yes" to A and "no" to B is a lie (4:20abc); "no" to B is a "no" to A (4:20defg). God's commandment in 4:21 is clear: A (i.e., in Jewish thought the basic condition of the covenant with God) and B constitute a unity. If A, then B. If B, then A. The latter is expressly said in the explanation of the general rule in 5:1cd. By A we know B (5:2). Certainly no one after reading these verses can avoid the realization that A and B belong inextricably together.

The connection between love for God and obedience to God's commandments (v. 2b and v. 3) is made on the basis of the Old Testament concepts of the covenant. See Appendix 9, A Renewed Covenant. And for those born of God it is easy to keep the commandments, because everything born of God has overcome, is overcoming and will overcome everything that opposes God. The Elder has an interest in using various tenses for the verb "overcome" both here and in other places in the letter. See the note on "overcome" at v. 4. Those born of God find themselves in a state of constant victory. How is this possible? Through their union with Jesus Messiah, God's son, who by his earthly work and especially its culmination in his "hour," i.e., when he dies and returns to the Father, they have overcome the world and the ruler of this world (John 16:33; 16:11; 1 John 5:18–19).

Or is the Elder thinking of when the letter's recipients were converted and baptized? In v. 5 we have a confession that could very well have belonged to baptism. Or is it their victory over the secessionists that is in view? See 4:4 and 2:14. An additional presentation of this son of God in the next paragraph is not as unnatural as some have insisted. In an ultra-Johannine perspective this and the following paragraph are read to a considerable degree as a polemic against the secessionists—compare 4:4—whereas I have interpreted it mostly as the Elder's energetic argument that his adherents should continue to love one another, because it is an overflowing of divine love or a result of divine begetting and thus an implied aspect of the renewed covenant.

2. Faith in the One Who Came by Water and Blood (5:6–8)

These are perhaps the most debated verses in the entire letter. Suggested interpretations are very much dependent on where the interpreter begins, consciously or not, when he or she comes to this paragraph. Should it be read as a final polemical lunge of the sword against the opponents in the letter, or as yet a further defining of the Elder's way of showing what faith in Jesus as Messiah, God's son, entails? Or both?

If the verses are essentially interpreted on the basis of the secessionists' ideas, who then are these secessionists? Are they Gnostics in general, or are they ultra-Johannine? Or are they Johannine Christians who have abandoned their faith in the Messiah? In a separate treatment (chap. 12, sect. 4), I have described the most important alternative interpretations of the letters that have emerged within the full range of research. For my own part, I have chosen to see the argument in this letter as based on an intra-Jewish problem, i.e., as based on a question of whether Jesus is the Messiah, God's son, or not. Or put the other way around: Whether or not God's son, the Messiah, he who was to come, was Jesus.

The Elder writes to Johannine Christians—i.e., to Jews who believe that Jesus is the Messiah, God's son—in order to strengthen them in their faith and to encourage them in a situation in which Jesus-believing Jews within the Johannine community have abandoned this "teaching about the Messiah" and returned to their previous faith. It turned the question whether Jesus was Messiah, a question so decisive for their existence, into a delicate issue, even after all contact with these secessionists had come to an end.

In vv. 6–8, as I see it, the Elder picks up a central theme, one that has operated in the letter from the very start, and defines it and deepens it even more. According to ancient handbooks on rhetoric, this is what a skilled writer of the time would do as he neared the end of his message. The theme is included in the final lines in the words "God's son has come," without further comment, and thereby vv. 6–8 and what follows regarding faith in God's son become a wrapping up of what the Elder began with in the letter's opening words: "What was there from the beginning, what we have heard, what we have seen with our eyes, what we have looked at and touched with our hands."

This divine life was revealed on earth and became the content of the Elder's proclamation and the message that he and others had delivered to the letter's addressees (1:1–5). It is also taken up in the expression "what you heard from the beginning." See Appendix 10, What you Heard From the Beginning. It is already clear in the letter's prologue that "Jesus the Messiah, God's son," is the center of this message, he who was there from the beginning (2:13–14). Jesus, his life and work, then reappears in various forms and gradually takes on a significance that, according to the Elder, is absolutely decisive for his life and for that of all Johannine Christians in the prevailing situation (1:7; 2:2, 6, 22; 3:3, 5, 7, 8, 16, 23; 4:2–3, 9–10, 17; 5:1, 5–8, 11–13, 18, 20). Jesus' death is especially highlighted as an atoning sacrifice that cleanses them from sin and as a model for their way of living. The Messiah, he who was to come according to God's promises to the people of Israel, God's son, he whom God would send to God's people, had appeared in this Jesus, in his words and deeds.

God's son is "the one who came by water and blood," i.e., Jesus, the Messiah (v. 6). In the context of the letter as a whole, the word "blood" refers to Jesus' death. There can be scarcely any doubt about this. The word "water" occurs only here, in this paragraph, which makes it more difficult to determine what "water" stands for. Like "blood," it is a symbol of something central to Jesus' life. In Appendix 17, By Water and Blood, I have suggested that "water" is a symbolic expression of Jesus' birth, of God's son's becoming a human being. In ancient texts, birth and begetting are associated with water. The words "by water and blood" would then be a way of speaking of Jesus' entire earthly act. It becomes synonymous with the phrase "in the flesh" in the confessional formula in 4:2. See the Interpretation of this passage.

What is said in a single word at 4:2, "in the *flesh*," is here divided up into two words, "by *water* and *blood*," in order to make it possible for the Elder to put special emphasis on Jesus' death. The continued formulation in v. 6 can be understood in this way. We know that it was especially difficult for Jews to accept a crucified Messiah, clearly illustrated in the Gospel by Peter's vehement reaction against Jesus' intention to wash Peter's feet (John 13:1–11). See also Mark 8:31–38 par; 1 Cor 1:23. The death of God's son naturally presupposes his humanity, but the letter particularly emphasizes Jesus' death and its significance for everyone and especially for the Jesus-believing Jews who remained in the Johannine fellowship.

Most often, however, the formula in v. 6c is connected strictly with the false teaching that would be current among the secessionists, and thus other interpretations of "water and blood" are required. See Appendix 17, By Water and Blood. Both "water" and "blood" are often used as symbols of various kinds, and when the words in v. 6 took wing and left behind the situation belonging to the letter, they came to be filled with other content, whether connected with Jesus' baptism and death, connected exclusively to Jesus' baptism, exclusively to Jesus' becoming a human being (which, according to some, was coincident with his baptism), or quite naturally in a limited Christian reading connected to the baptism and eucharist. This last interpretation, however, stands out as something foreign to the letter as we have it.

The transition from focusing on Jesus' earthly work to speaking of the Spirit as the one who bears witness is natural, based on what is said about the Helper, Comforter, Spirit of truth in John 14–16. The revelation of God through Jesus' words and deeds could not get through in its fullness to Jews who knew Jesus in his earthly life (John 16:12, 25). Jesus' disciples could testify of Jesus, but in order to understand everything, they needed the witness of the Spirit regarding what Jesus said and did (John 15:26). This is illustrated also in several passages in the Gospel (John 2:13–22; 12:12–16). The Spirit of truth led them into and with the whole truth (John 16:12–15). In v. 6, therefore, the Elder reminds them that "the Spirit is truth."

Thus there are three that bear witness, but the witness remains visible in two phenomena. The Spirit is active in all who keep Jesus' commandments and is thus visible within the Johannine community. The tradition of Jesus, which includes Jesus' life from birth to the grave, is passed down through the Elder and his closest associates. For this reason, the fellowship between "we" and "you" in 1:1–5 is absolutely decisive for fellowship with God. Because the Spirit and the Jesus-tradition ("the water and the blood") are, according to the Gospel, inextricably bound together with one another (John 16:12–15), the testimonies of the three witnesses are one and the same. The Spirit and the tradition affirm that God's son, the Messiah, was Jesus, something that the Elder has already asserted in the section 2:18–27, when he dealt with the Johannine Christians who broke away from the Johannine fellowship.

3. God's Own Testimony: Eternal Life Through Faith in the Son (5:9–12)

Finally, the Elder refers to God's own testimony and the confidence people have in it (vv. 9–12). Two or three witnesses are sufficient, according to a Jewish way of thinking, but the question about whether Jesus is the Messiah, God's son, clearly requires a word from God himself as well. Both Jesus the Messiah, God's son, and the Spirit of truth have a divine origin, but nonetheless, they cannot be equated with God in a Johannine world view.

A general formulation in v. 9 indicates that God's testimony carries more weight than a human testimony. The Gospel too speaks sometimes of a graduated scale of witnesses (John 5:31–40; 4:42; 10:38). The testimony of God and the testimony of human beings are thus distinct, and this makes it less likely that God's testimony is just another way of speaking of the Spirit, the water, and the blood as witnesses. But in that case, where can one find God's testimony and what is its content? Some have laid hold especially on the idea in v. 10 that the testimony is to be found within the believer; others have based their views on the two definitions of God's testimony given in the text: "God has testified concerning his son" (v. 9) and "God gave eternal life to the one who believes" (v. 11).

Often enough in these verses, God's testimony is described as an inner testimony that makes it possible to recognize the outward testimony when it is given. The sixteenth-century reformers spoke of "the Spirit's inner testimony." The Spirit's witness, however, has already been mentioned and then tied to an interpretation of Jesus' earthly activity. Nor is there anything in the Johannine thought world that would give rise to the reformers' view. Still others refer to the Holy Scriptures as God's testimony, since they have an important role in the interpretation of Jesus (John 2:22; 12:16). Eternal life is also described in 2:25 as the result of God's promises.

Taking as our point of departure the two definitions of God's testimony in v. 9 and v. 11, we could perhaps reason things out in the following way. God's testimony in vv. 9–11 is separate from and additional to what is said in vv. 6–8. It has a historical character, in that it is said twice that God "has testified" (perfect tense, which implies that something has happened that has ongoing validity in the present). It is clearly directed to the fact that Jesus is God's son, but at first it is not clear when or how God bore such witness about his son. There appears to be just one testimony. Verse 10 shows that the question has to do with believing and not believing. Having the testimony within one is an expression for having completely embodied it with one's life. The antithesis is to reject what God says. The second definition (v. 11) goes one step further when it describes the content of the testimony as a gift of God: God gives eternal life to the one who believes, and God does so through God's son. See Appendix 6, Life, Eternal Life. Possession of eternal life here and now through faith becomes God's testimony about God's Son. The relation between the Son and Life thus becomes the final word in this paragraph.

11

1 John 5:13–21: Jesus, the True God and Eternal Life

Translation Display

13a	These things I have written to you
13b	in order that you may know that you have eternal life
13c	to you who believe in the name of the son of God.
14a	And this is the confidence that we have toward him
14b	that if we ask for anything according to his will
14c	then he hears us.
15a	And if we know that he hears us in whatever we ask for
15b	then we know
15c	that we have the requests we have asked him for.
16a	If anyone sees his brother committing a sin not worthy of death
16b	then he shall ask
16c	and he shall give him life
16d	to those who commit a sin not worthy of death.
16e	There is a sin worthy of death.
16f	It is not regarding such a sin that I say one should ask.
17a	Every unrighteous act is sin
17b	and there is sin that is not worthy of death.
18a	We know that everyone who has been born of God does not sin.
18b	He who was born of God keeps him
18c	and the Evil one cannot touch him.
19a	We know that we are of God
19b	and the entire world lies in the power of the Evil one.
20a	And we know that the son of God has come
20b	and he has given us understanding

First John

> 20c   so that we may know the True One.
> 20d   And we are in the True One, through his son Jesus Messiah.
> 20e   He is the true God and eternal life.
>
> 21a   Children
> 21b   keep yourselves away from idols.

Notes

5:13 These things. The words here refer backward (anaphoric use), presumably to everything written before v. 13.

have written. Gkt has the aorist, most simply interpreted as a so-called epistolary aorist. See the Analysis for 1 John 2:12–17, point 2.

in order that. Gkt has the word *hina*, which can indicate both purpose, "in order that," and result, "so that."

you have eternal life. In Gkt "eternal" and "life" are separated; thus literally "life you have eternal," a kind of rhetorical expansion. This gives special emphasis to the word "eternal." See further Appendix 6, Life, Eternal Life.

who believe in the name of the son of God. This description of the recipients comes oddly at the end of the text; some translations reposition it. The phrase is reminiscent of "believe in the name of his son Jesus Christ" in 1 John 3:23.

14. And this is the confidence that we have toward him. This formulation, with *pros* ("toward"), is typically Johannine. See the note "And this is" at 1 John 1:5. The preposition *pros* is rendered in 1 John 1:2 and 2:1 as "with" and in 1 John 3:21 as "before." Cf. "and the Word was with God" in John 1:1. Participation in eternal life fosters openness and confidence before the face of God.

if. Verses 14–16 contain several clauses beginning with "if" (*ean*), sometimes followed by the subjunctive, sometimes by the indicative. This is presumably a stylistic variation. As a rule, the use of the subjunctive gives a greater hypothetical character to the clause.

ask for. See the note at 1 John 3:22.

15. have. Use of the present instead of the future can express a greater assurance of prayers having been heard.

the requests we have asked him for. Gkt has a construction of the type "the requests that we have requested from him," a so-called *figura etymologica*. See further 1 John 1:5; 2:25; 5:10, 16.

1 John 5:13–21: Jesus, the True God and Eternal Life

16. committing a sin. Literally "sinning a sin," which is a variation on "doing a sin" (1 John 3:4, 8, 9). See the previous note.

not worthy of death. Gkt has "not unto death," where "unto death" means resulting in death. Yet is it not fully clear whether this sin will lead to death or whether it has already led to death. The phrase occurs four times in vv. 16–17: "a sin not worthy of death," "[commit] a sin not worthy of death," "a sin worthy of death," and "a sin that is not worthy of death." The focus of this paragraph is on such sins as are not worthy of death. See Appendix 19, Sin unto death.

he . . . he. The word probably refers in both instances to the one who prays.

It is not regarding such a sin that I say. Literally, "not regarding this [sin] do I say."

one should ask. Gkt uses here the verb *erōtan* and not as previously the more usual *aitein*. It means both to ask and to request. Presumably this represents a typical Johannine stylistic variation without any significant difference in meaning.

17. Every unrighteous act. The same expression, *pasa adikia*, is rendered in 1 John 1:9 as "every wrongdoing," and more traditionally as "all unrighteousness." It is used there in parallel with "sins," i.e., the individual sins that one has publically confessed before the congregation.

and. Gkt *kai*, which can also introduce a clarifying repetition of foregoing ideas, here perhaps in the sense of "but." See the note "and the life was revealed" at 1 John 1:2.

18. We know. The expression is a successor to all the previous instances of "we know" in the letter, although they vary from *oidamen* (as here and in 1 John 3:2, 14; 5:15, 16–18), to *ginōskomen* (1 John 2:3, 5, 18; 3:24; 4:6, 13; 5:2), to *gnōsometha* (1 John 3:19), and *egnōkamen* (1 John 2:3; 3:16; 4:16). The words also have a nuance of confession (John 3:2; 4:42; 9:29; 16:30; 21:24).

everyone who has been born. See the note "everyone who" at 1 John 3:3 and Appendix 11, Begotten/Born of God.

He. In Gkt, the clause is introduced with "but" (*alla*), which normally marks a clear opposition or contrast. Here the clause functions more as a clarification or an explanation for the foregoing. See the note "Indeed . . . remain in it" at 1 John 2:27.

who was born of God. The context and the use of the aorist in this Johannine phrase suggest that the reference is to Jesus. This has implications for how the following verb is interpreted. See the Analysis, point 2, and Appendix 11, Begotten/Born of God.

the Evil one. See note at 1 John 2:13.

19. are of God. See the note "It comes not from the Father but from the world," at 1 John 2:16.

lies in the power of the Evil one. Literally, "lies in the Evil one," an expression that also can be interpreted as a very close relationship between the world and the Evil one. Cf. the phrase "to be in someone" (1 John 2:15). The choice of "lies in" instead of "is in" would make it possible to indicate that it is a very firm relationship indeed.

20. And we know. Gkt: *oidamen de*. Some manuscripts have *kai oidamen*. But the word *de* here surely does not have an adversative sense—"but"—but rather marks the end of a series. Some translations read "We know also."

has come. The text does not read "was revealed," as in 1 John 3:5, 8, or the perfect of the verb "come" (*erchesthai*), as in 1 John 4:2. Rather, it uses a form of *hēkein*, which expresses the idea that something has come in the past and at the same time is currently present. In everyday Greek the verb can be used of a god's appearing. It occurs with Jesus as subject also in John 4:47; 8:42; Heb 10:7, 9, 37; cf. John 6:37.

understanding so that we may know. The formulation is a clear reference to Jer 31:31–34. The words "within them," which stand in parallel with the words "on their hearts," are translated in the LXX with "in their understanding" (*dianoia*). The heart, in OT usage, is the seat of thinking and willing. See Appendix 9, A Renewed Covenant.

For "so that" Gkt has *hina*, followed here by the indicative, which is very unusual. Possibly it reinforces the now-character in "know the True One." The present underscores the constancy of the action.

the True One. The context and Jer 31:31–34 make it likely that "the True One" is here synonymous with God, the God who has been revealed through Jesus Christ. Cf. John 17:3.

And we are in. "And" moves the thought along to the next stage. See the note "and the life was revealed" at 1 John 1:2 and Appendix 15, God in Them and They in God.

through his son Jesus Christ. This phrase describes the fellowship with the True One, either as an expression of the means of fellowship, introduced with "through," or as an apposition to the foregoing, introduced with "in," as in some translations. The preposition *en* in Greek can mean both "in" and "through." With "in" here, a change of person from God to Jesus is indicated. The full formula "his son Jesus the Messiah" creates an arc that extends from 1 John 1:3 over 3:23 to 5:20.

He. Gkt has "this one" (*houtos*), which most naturally refers to Jesus Christ. He is thereby described as "the true God" and "eternal life." The words "eternal life" applied to Jesus as Messiah, God's son, clearly connect the letter's beginning with its ending (1 John 1:1–2 and 5:20).

eternal life. Gkt has the indefinite form, something that binds these words more closely together with "the true God," the one who (for the believer) is eternal life. See Appendix 6, Life, Eternal Life.

21. Children. See note at 1 John 2:1.

Keep yourselves away from. The expression in Gkt, *phylaxate heauta apo,* can mean protect yourselves from, be on guard against, be careful of, keep yourselves away from—depending to a great extent on how one understands the object in this verse. The use of the neuter plural, *heauta,* is not unusual in Hellenistic Greek. Numerous manuscripts alter it to the masculine plural.

idols. Gkt uses a common word for idols, *eidōlon.* It normally means depictions of idols, but in Jewish and Christian texts depictions of idols are equated with the gods themselves. In the history of interpretation, it has been difficult to determine just what may be intended with this very unexpected and forceful warning at the end of the letter. See the Analysis, point 3.

Analysis

1. Delimitations and Structure

The content and certain formulations in 1 John 5:13–21 indicate that these verses form a concluding section of the letter. From a rhetorical point of view, the section consists of four paragraphs: v. 13, vv. 14–17, vv. 18–20, and v. 21. Each paragraph has its own particular character: a concluding reassurance that the recipients have eternal life, possibly with an indirect condition (that they believe in the name of God's son; v. 13); a wordier argument regarding prayer and the answering of prayer on behalf of a fellow believer who sins (vv. 14–17); a three-part, almost hymnic confession of what they already know and have (vv. 18–20); and finally a warning delivered in a sharp and pleading tone (v. 21). Verse 13 perhaps belongs more with vv. 14–17 and v. 21 more with vv. 18–20, which then would yield two paragraphs for the section. If we wish to retain a three-part division for vv. 18–21, then the last part clearly becomes expanded and powerfully set off in its own right. Possibly vv. 20e and 21—the antithesis to v. 20abcd?—can be taken as a strong concluding trumpet blast that for now brings to an abrupt close this written communication. See the Translation Display.

Verse 13 is internally very reminiscent of the end of John's Gospel (John 20:31). The backward referring "these things" and the indication of the communication situation with sender and receivers and of the purpose in writing (v. 13b) also give the verse a concluding character. The added description of the recipients in v. 13c reminds us of the entire letter and its message: hold fast to faith in Jesus as Messiah, God's son. Without this faith, there is no eternal life.

Verses 14–17 are held together thematically by words having to do with prayer (six times), sin (six times), and death and life (five times). See the Translation Display. This content connects with the beginning of the letter (1 John 1:5—2:2), and with the beginning of its central part (1 John 2:28—3:10). The emphasis lies on sin that does not end in death. If any members of the community commit such a sin, others in the community are to pray for them and thereby give them life. The first part of this paragraph (vv. 14–15) deals with the immediate hearing of their prayers that has become possible in the renewed covenant (1 John 3:21–24). The second part admonishes them to pray for those who commit a sin that does not end in death (vv. 16–17).

If vv. 14–17 carry further the thought of eternal life mentioned in v. 13, then vv. 18–20 support the word "know" in v. 13. The paragraph is clearly structured by the three cries of assured faith: "We know that." In v. 20d, the third member is expanded by an "and." See the note "and the life was revealed" at 1 John 1:2. To know God, said differently, is to be in God, and this fellowship with God is knit together with Jesus as Messiah, God's son. Then, as has been said, it is possible to bring together v. 20e and v. 21 and achieve an antithetical, final statement regarding the true God and false gods, or to let v. 21 with its direct address and its admonition be a summarizing final word in a different tone.

The change in the form of presentation in this ending of the letter is worth noting. According to the rhetoric of the day, a speaker—or a writer—concluded by repeating what had already been said, at least the most important portion in what had been said, especially with varying formulations and with words that the listener would remember. Handbooks called such a paragraph a *peroratio*. Many commentators have noticed changes in style and word-choice in this ending, and on this basis they have wanted to draw the conclusion that it must be an addition by a person other than the author of the letter. I definitely prefer an explanation based on rhetoric. The main themes are repeated: know, believe, eternal life, sin, divine begetting, the power of the Evil one, union with God, God's son has come, knowing God and being in God and in his son Jesus Christ. Words from the letter's beginning recur here: eternal life, Jesus Messiah, God's son. Formulations are varied, rhetorical figures are used, e.g., "to sin a sin." See the Notes. The style changes in the five parts and some unexpected formulations likely stuck with the listener: "sin unto death," Jesus as "he who was born of God" and Jesus as "the true God and eternal life," and the final words regarding "idols." The ending thus assumes an important role in the interpretation of the letter as a whole.

2. He Who Was Born of God

The first two lines in 1 John 5:18 employ two forms of the verb for "beget/give birth," *gennan*, first the perfect passive and then the aorist passive:

"Everyone who has been born (*gegennēmenos*) of God" (v. 18a).

"He who was born (*gennētheis*) of God" (v. 18b).

In accordance with long tradition, Bible translations have frequently interpreted the two forms as a stylistic variation, taking them to refer to the same thing, i.e., to persons who are born of God. This has presupposed their having read "himself," *heauton*, in this clause, a variant reading attested already in Codex Sinaiticus from the fourth century. The oldest manuscripts assuredly had just the letters *AUTON*, which normally means "him," although it could also be read as *hauton*, i.e., "himself." The usual word for "himself," *heauton*, eventually came to dominate the manuscript tradition and found its way into the *Textus Receptus*, the Greek text lying behind all translations up until the end of the nineteenth century. However, the verb is not normally construed with *heauton*, unless it is accompanied by a complement of the type "keep oneself pure."

Today, most commentators are agreed that the second line refers to Jesus. According to John 17:12, it is Jesus' mission to safeguard his disciples. On the other hand, this is the only place in the New Testament where Jesus is described as the one who was born of God. But the author sometimes plays with words; see e.g. 1 John 5:1, and perhaps the formulation is also a reminder of the great likeness that exists between the Jesus-believer and Jesus himself. "Just as he is, so also are we in this world" (1 John 4:17). If the formulation in v. 18b expresses the same thing as that in v. 18a, then probably the beginning of v. 18b will have to be interpreted as a so-called *casus pendens*: "The one who was born of God, [God] keeps him." See notes at 1 John 1:5; 2:24; and 3:17. But if "he who was born of God" is allowed to refer to Jesus, then both the use of the verb and the immediate context become completely clear: "He who was born of God keeps him, and the Evil one cannot touch him." Verse 18c then becomes most obviously a consequence of the content of v. 18b. Those who are born of God cannot be afflicted by sin unto death (1 John 3:9), i.e., those who left the Johannine fellowship actually, according to the author, never belonged to it (1 John 2:19).

3. A Strange Warning At the end

Viewed from the perspective I have used for interpreting the Johannine letters, with an emphasis on an intra-Jewish problem, on concepts of a renewed covenant, and on a pastoral purpose for the letter as a whole, this final verse is not at all strange. It is a warning against falling away from the God of the covenant as he has now become visible through Jesus Messiah, God's son, and thereby also abandoning the renewed covenant with Israel's God. In Jewish terms, this can be expressed the way it now happens to be in v. 21. It was a matter of "having God" or not having him, of "having eternal life here and now" or not having it. Some within the Johannine fellowship had clearly given up their faith in Jesus as Messiah, God's son already (1 John 2:19), and there was always a risk that more would do the same. The Jesus-believing Jews in the Johannine letters presumably also lived under pressure from both Jewish leaders and Roman officials. See further the Interpretation. But there are several other suggestive interpretations of this verse that are worth listing here, perhaps primarily to provide examples of reading the letter on the basis of other presuppositions.

Raymond Brown, with accustomed thoroughness, has worked through the literature up to c. 1980 and catalogued ten suggested interpretations of the content in the term "idols": (1) phantoms, figments of the imagination, images of the Platonic world of ideas; (2) heathen images; (3) worship of idols (food offerings); (4) compromising with paganism; (5) mystery religions and their practices; (6) Gnostic concepts; (7) Jewish worship at the temple in Jerusalem; (8) sin; (9) visual expression of anything taking the place of God; and (10) a term for apostasy or secession. Brown himself choses the last alternative and says, "the secessionists have themselves become 'idols.'"

Terry Griffith, who has written a dissertation on 1 John 5:21 and its significance for interpreting 1 John, summarizes earlier interpretations in four categories.

1. *Conceptual interpretations.* Here he has in mind interpretations of "idols" as mental constructs of various kinds, false concepts, false teaching, etc. This is the most common type of interpretation. Reference here is primarily to some types of Christological heresies. The antonymous pair, then, becomes the true god–false gods. In Old Testament and Jewish texts, however, the opposition is God–idols or God–other gods. See Tob 14:6; Acts 14:15; 1 Thess 1:9. In the Septuagint, the Greek word *eidōlon* almost always refers to images of idols. In v. 21 the concern has to do with "idols," not with "idol worship."

2. *Socio-historical interpretations.* Here *eidōlon* is understood more concretely. It can have to do with confessional situations during a time of persecution, where a believer would be expected to renounce his or her faith by making an offering to the image of an idol (cf. the confessional formulations in 1 John 2:22–24; 4:2–3, 15), or by eating meat offered to idols (Acts 15:20, 29; 1 Corinthians 8; Rev 2:14, 20), or by participation in mystery religions or other pagan rites. Such activities, however, are not attested in the letter.

3. *Metaphorical interpretations,* i.e., primarily an interpretation of "idols" as sin or apostasy. Here texts from Qumran are important, especially 1QS 2:11–18, which some readers take as evidence that "idols" stand for sin, and 1QS 2:25—3:1 and 7:25–26 as examples of apostasy and expulsion from the community. See also *T. Reu.* 4:6 as evidence for the interpretation as sin: "For the sin of fornication is the destruction of the soul, separating it from God and bringing it near to idols."

4. *A literary interpretation,* or better, a rhetorical interpretation that binds together the beginning and the ending of the letter (*inclusio*) and joins the content in the beginning to a biblical polemic against idols, seen especially clearly in Isaiah 40–48. The phrase "that which was from the beginning" is found only in one place in the Septuagint, Wis 14:13, in a context that perhaps more than any other in the Septuagint criticizes idols.

> Griffith finds something positive in each interpretive model: an interpretation on the basis of the letter as a whole according to (1); *eidōlon* in a literal sense according to (2); anti-idol rhetoric in Qumran texts according to (3); and the opposition God–idols in biblical tradition according to (4). In Griffith's view,

the author of 1 John uses a well-established, almost formalized Jewish polemic, which is well attested in the contemporary literature. It is used for promoting a Jewish identity and for perpetuating an inner social fellowship. Griffith refers especially to *Joseph and Aseneth* 7–13, and cites among other texts the following: "Be on your guard, my children, against the strange woman" (7:6). "It is not fitting . . . to kiss a foreign woman, who with her mouth blesses dead and mute idols" (8:5). Through conversion "she may live in your eternal life forever and ever" (8:11). Israel's God "hates all those who worship idols . . . But I have heard many saying that the God of the Hebrews is a true God, and a living God, and a merciful God" (11:7–11). Using a typical Jewish polemic against other Jews can seem surprising, but it is attested in various ways in Qumran texts, *Apoc. Ab.* 27:7, *Sibylline Oracles,* Gal 4:8–10, Acts 7:48 (?), Rev 2:9 and 3:9, *Epistle of Barnabas,* and in Justin Martyr.

Griffith and I in large measure have the same starting points for our interpretation of the letter and it is therefore easy to opt for his interpretation, though with some adjustments of his rhetorical analysis. See the Interpretation, below. I have yet another strong argument in favor of this reading, namely concepts of a renewed covenant, clearly present within the immediate context (1 John 5:20). Many of the texts adduced above, not least the Qumran texts, have a clear covenant context for their discussion of idols.

Interpretation

1. Eternal Life Here and Now (5:13)

The Elder has come to the end of his letter. One last time he indicates his communication situation, his method of communication (I, you, write), and the purpose of the writing: "that you may know that you have eternal life," with emphasis on the adjective "eternal." See the note. It is clear that the author has a pastoral aim. He wants the Jesus-believing Jews he is addressing to have full insight and to know assuredly that they possess eternal life here and now. Full joy was the goal, according to 1:4, full insight and conviction is the goal according to the letter's end. The word "know" occurs again in a threefold confession in vv. 18–20. According to the last verses of the preceding section, there are just two alternatives: to have eternal life or not to have life (v. 12). Those who hear the writing being read aloud have Life.

The Elder does as Moses did when he took leave of the people in Deuteronomy, the preeminent book of the covenant in the Old Testament. First, Moses sets forth the choice between life and death (30:15–20), then he assures the people that they are on the path of life, because God is with them. "He will not fail you or forsake you" (31:6). It closes with a song of praise regarding the covenant people and their future destiny, in which apostasy and faithfulness to the covenant alternate with one another. Just as Moses in Deuteronomy wants the people to look back to their beginning in the desert, the Elder points back to "what was there from the beginning." The content of what he says in these final verses shows that this is indeed the case. Even the formulation "the name of God's son" can remind them of their conversion, baptism and confession of Jesus and Messiah as names for the son of God (2:12; 3:23).

There is no song of praise at the end of 1 John, but the style of the last verses differs from the preceding text. The Elder knows how to follow rhetorical handbooks and repeats in abbreviated form the most important themes from the earlier presentation, makes a connection to the letter's beginning, uses rhetorical figures, varies his expressions, makes them more precise or concrete, alternates forms of style more than usual, and seeks expressions that will stick with those who are listening. All this in order this one last time to grip the audience and bring them where he wants them to be. Although the different parts belong rhetorically together, I have divided up this conclusion into four parts: v. 13, vv. 14–17, vv. 18–20, and v. 21. See the Analysis, point 1, above.

The conclusion shows that Life, eternal life, is the main concept in the letter; indeed, it is the concept that can be said to hold the entire presentation together (1:2; 2:25; 3:15–16; 4:9; 5:1–13, 16, 20). It would also entail within itself the resurrection of the dead, which is not mentioned in the letter. The Jews expected a new world order, a renewed creation and a renewed covenant, i.e., new relations between God and humanity, between human beings, and between human beings and the entire creation. There are few texts that speak of this world as fated for destruction, but many texts describe how God will fulfill God's promises to the people and alter their situation and consequently the whole world. What God had imagined for the creation and for humankind would become reality. This could be described in many ways: purification from sin, liberation from violence and evil, return to Jerusalem, purified worship in Jerusalem's temple, resurrection of the dead, peace and joy, a paradise on earth. In the presence of all nations, God would once again justify God's people, the people of the covenant, and show that God is Lord over God's creation. The new condition was sometimes summed up in the concept of "the new age." Faith in the one and only God and confidence in God's election of Israel led inevitably to eschatological expectations.

I have claimed that the concept of "eternal life" in the Johannine writings is a way of speaking of this new age. See Appendix 6, Life, Eternal Life. Because the divine Word/Life became a human being and thereby visible to other human beings (John 1:14; 1 John 1:1–3), human beings were able to participate in the divine. They could have eternal life. Jews who confessed Jesus as Messiah, God's son, were convinced that the new age had been realized in Jesus and in them. The darkness was fading away; the true light was already shining (2:8).

The incarnation carries within itself a dual effect: divinity becomes human and humanity becomes divine. The Elder has just one message for the Jesus-believing Jews he is writing to: By believing in the name of God's son (Jesus, Messiah) and loving one another (3:23), they are partaking of eternal life. Because God's son came (v. 20), as

1 John 5:13-21: Jesus, the True God and Eternal Life

Messiah in the form of Jesus, in his words and deeds, the covenant, i.e., the relationship with God, was renewed. The letter's purpose is to strengthen this faith and to steady and encourage those who remained in the Johannine fellowship. "You must know that you have eternal life" (v. 13).

2. Prayer That Imparts Life (5:14–17)

The new eternal life is described in many ways in the letter, among them, for example: to have fellowship with God, to know God, to be in God, to be begotten of God, to be God's child, to have confidence before God, to love one another. God's word is in them; the truth, the anointing, God's *sperma*, God's spirit, as well as other manifestations, are in them. A number of these descriptions of the relationship recur also in the letter's final section. The first mentioned is confidence before the face of God (v. 14). See the note. This is important with regard to the judgment (2:28; 4:17–18); it is important with regard to prayer (3:21; 5:14). Because the Jesus-believers stand very close to God, in Jesus Christ, they are able to pray in accordance with God's will. The Gospel speaks of prayer in the name of Jesus (John 14:14–16; 15:7, 16; 16:23–26). God hears such prayers, and the praying believer knows that God receives what he or she prays for.

Thus this form of direct prayer to God is applicable to prayer on behalf of a fellow believer who has committed a sin. Part of the new life with God is the ability to keep God's commandments, i.e., to live as Jesus lived, to love one's brother, to do righteousness, to avoid sinning, etc. Can one have eternal life and still sin? This is a recurrent problem in the letter, especially in 2:3–11 and 2:28—3:10. In view of eschatology, that the last hour is here, the Elder argues that the one who is part of the renewed covenant cannot sin. In view of everyday life, however, he has to admit that such a person can indeed commit sin. See Appendix 12, They Cannot Sin. He says as much in several passages in the letter and explicitly so also in the conclusion (v. 16 and v. 18). Yet eternal life and sin are mutually exclusive. For this reason a brother is to pray for a brother who has committed a sin and thereby give him life.

The Greek text does not clearly indicate who gives life to whom, but it is likely the praying brother who gives life to his fellow. See the note "he . . . he" at v. 16. According to Old Testament texts, holy persons can pray on behalf of sinners (Gen 18:23–32; Exod 32:11–14; Amos 7:1–6; 2 Macc 7:37–38). The same is said of Christians in the New Testament (1 Thess 5:25; Heb 13:18; Jas 5:15). "Let us then also pray for those who have fallen into any transgression" (*1 Clem.* 56:1). Even in the Gospel, disciples "rule" over sin. Jesus transfers his commission to them and gives them the spirit of God. "If you forgive the sins of any, they are forgiven them; if you retain the sins of any, they are retained" (John 20:23). This is a defining characteristic of the fellowship in the renewed covenant. Jesus and the Jesus-believers are in a very close relationship

First John

to one another. In v. 18, the author describes them respectively as "the one who was born of God" and "the one who is born of God."

The admonition to pray for a fellow Christian who has committed a sin requires a distinction that recurs several times in vv. 16–17: sin unto death and sin not unto death. There are those who sin "unto death" and they are not to be prayed for. But "sin unto death" is viewed, with all probability, as breaking the commandment in the renewed covenant to believe on the name of God's son, Jesus Messiah, and to love one another. The author is therefore thinking of those who left the Johannine community (2:18–27; 4:1–6). This apparently hard attitude is also attested in other contemporary texts. See Appendix 19, Sin that Leads to Death.

3. Jesus, God's True Image and Divine Life (5:18–20)

This paragraph is clearly divided into three parts by the words "we know that," which introduce the three last verses before the final verse of the letter. See Translation Display. It thus follows up the theme of knowing from v. 13 and simultaneously culminates in the theme of eternal life found in the two earlier paragraphs. The content of these three verses is hardly anything new, but some of the formulations are arresting. The paragraphs vary in length and structure. Parallels are typical, but they are of different kinds. In v. 18, the assertion in v. 18a is followed by a double rationale or explanation, one referring to Jesus the other referring to the Evil one. Verse 19 sets "we" and God against "the world" and the Evil one. Verse 20 is constructed of the two final lines, which especially focus on God's son, Jesus Messiah (v. 20de). At the same time, they set the stage for the concluding admonition in v. 21.

The formulation "he who was born of God" in v. 18 as a designation of Jesus deviates from Johannine patterns of expression. It can be used of people (John 1:13), but the usual formulation referring to people is "they are born of God." See the Analysis, point 2, above. Interpreting it as a reference to Jesus, however, renders the entire verse less complicated, and the formulation can be explained in terms of the author's occasional desire to play with words (e.g. 5:2) and in terms of the fact that he is thereby enabled to express a profound closeness between Jesus and the Jesus-believers. Otherwise what the verse says is in large measure a repetition of 3:9 and 4:4. See Appendix 12, They Cannot Sin. To touch someone in the sense of doing harm is a common formulation in biblical and Jewish texts (Gen 26:11; Ps 105:15; Job 2:5; T. Jud. 3:10). Satan threatens to destroy the believer, but he can be overcome (1 Pet 5:8–9; 1 John 2:13–14; John 10:28; 17:15). Jesus taught his disciples to pray, "Rescue us from the evil one" (Matt 6:13).

In v. 19, what has been said in 3:8–10 and 4:4–5 is repeated, and the believer's situation is described from a dualistic perspective. Those who have left the Johannine community and travel around with deceptive teachings have gone out into the world (4:1) and belong to the world (4:5). The contrast in v. 19 can therefore be illustrated with the opposition between the secessionists and those who have remained in the Johannine community. The formulation is reminiscent of the dualism in the Qumran texts. "All the children of injustice are ruled by the Angel of Darkness" (1QS 3:20–21).

The final part of the conclusion's three-part assurance of the letter's recipients' full insight is characterized by concepts of a renewed covenant. "The True One" is a description of the God of the covenant. According to Jer 31:31–34 the new covenant is characterized by the fact that everyone "knows God" and this new close relationship to God becomes possible through God's gift within them, rendered in the Greek translation with *dianoia,* i.e., the same word used in v. 20, often translated "understanding." See Appendix 9, A Renewed Covenant. And the reason for this renewal of the covenant is clearly indicated: "God's son has come." Throughout the entire letter it has been claimed that he is there in the figure of Jesus as Messiah, the one who was to come. This is why the full description, "God's son, Jesus Messiah," is used in v. 20d. The relationship of "knowing God" is replaced in v. 20d with the words "to be in God," which then are connected with God's son, either as "in his son Jesus Messiah," or as "through his son Jesus Messiah" (see the note). In the former option, the words come close to what Jesus says at the end of his prayer for the disciples in John 17: "I pray that ... as you, Father, are in me and I in you, may they also be in us" (John 17:21).

The final description of Jesus in the letter is surprising: "He is the true God and eternal life" (v. 20e). Both the letter and the Gospel begin and end with a confession of Jesus as divine, powerfully expressed through the word "God" (John 1:1, 20:28; 1 John 1:2; 5:20). The point is not an identity between Jesus Christ and God, but both the word "true" and the word "God" can be applied to the Father and to the Son. He is the true image of God, the one who is able to mediate who God is (John 1:18). The Father alone is the source of life, but the Son has received life from the Father and can mediate it to human beings. See Appendix 6, Life, Eternal Life.

4. Apostasy and Worship of Other Gods (5:21)

The entire message from and about Jesus was summed up at the beginning in the words "God is light." In Jesus Messiah, God's son, God has once more revealed Godself as the one who saves God's people by forgiving and cleansing from sin and as the one who gives content to the expectations God sets forth in the covenant with God's people. See the Interpretation on 1:5. In this way, Israel's covenant with God has been renewed.

The entire letter closes with a warning against leaving the God of the covenant, who has now become visible through Jesus Messiah, God's son, and against beginning to worship other gods. Jews who apostatized were called idol worshipers. It happened already at Sinai. Slay those "who have forsaken the true God, and made for themselves false gods," writes Philo regarding the event (*Mos.* 2:171). The Elder uses a polemical formulation that Jews used for confirming their own identity and defending the boundaries of their own people, and even used against other Jews. This may be surprising, but there are numerous examples in contemporary texts. See the Analysis, point 3, above. Those who had left the Johannine community no longer belonged to the elect, true Israel. See the descriptions of the Johannine Christians in the Interpretation of 2 John, point 1. In his dualistic and eschatological description of the situation, the Elder has saved the strongest words for last: "sin unto death," "the true God and eternal life," "idols."

12

The Johannine Letters as a Whole

1. Their Place in Canon and Church

First John has always had a large place in church and devotional life. The two smaller letters, on the other hand, have seldom been used, apart from the portions of 2 John that resonate with 1 John. The three letters together constitute only a small percentage of the New Testament's text, but they have had a decisive significance for our understanding of the Johannine writings, their origin and milieu, their language and content, their message and usage both in their first context and in later periods. This can be seen not least in the present commentary, which brings together both the Gospel and the letters into one and the same intra-Jewish conflict over whether or not to believe in Jesus as the Messiah, God's son. Here the contrast between faith and no faith replaces the usual distinction between true faith and false faith, between orthodoxy and heresy. In this way these texts open up even more to questions of encounters between people of differing faiths and, more generally, to questions of believers' attitudes toward outsiders.

More than any other writing, the first letter speaks of God's love toward all humanity. Yet it simultaneously limits love of one's neighbor to the little flock of Johannine Christians. The language and rhetoric employed are strongly polarized, both in regard to ideas (light and darkness, truth and lie, etc.) and in regard to persons (we and they, God's children and the children of the devil, etc.). Is this the heritage of internal Jewish movements such as that at Qumran, or a particular form of Christian theology at the end of the first century, or a consequence of particular relationships within the Johannine community? The answers to these questions to a great degree determine the exposition of these individual texts.

For the most part, the Church has read the Johannine letters in terms of correct faith (dogmatics) and correct living (ethics). Irenaeus used 1 John and 2 John with contemporary Gnostic false teachers in mind. Clement of Alexandria and Tertullian discussed the question of various sorts of sin, based on a text at the end of 1 John (5:16–17). Even for Cyprian, the letters were instructive for ethical questions, while Augustine constructed his theology of love with the help of the first letter. In the course of historical biblical research other questions have taken center stage, not least the issue of the opponents represented within the letters and their theology. Is 1 John a polemical letter to be read with the secessionists in mind, or is it a parenetic letter to be understood as a serious attempt to comfort and encourage the addressees in their faith? All commentaries from recent times find themselves somewhere along the spectrum between polemical and parenetic readings. It must be said moreover that the history of these letters within the areas of theology, church, piety, art, literature, philosophy, and law has not yet been written, nor can it be written here.

Little is known about the early history of the Johannine letters within the Christian Church or of their place in the canon. At the beginning of the fourth century, Eusebius of Caesarea placed them among the seven catholic letters. Four of these have named senders, but the three letters of John are anonymous. In the East, the word "catholic" was mostly interpreted as referring to the letters' receivers, that the letters were addressed to Christians in general, rather than to a particular group or person. But in the West the term was understood to imply that the letters themselves were generally accepted for use in the Church. From the first, the Johannine letters were unnamed. The titles we now have appeared in the middle of the second century or later.

We know most about the first letter. Researchers have pointed to many words and statements in the apostolic and early church fathers as potentially reminiscent of 1 John, but few of those texts are really convincing. The earliest of the more certain indicators of the letter's use is found in the letter of Polycarp of Smyrna to the believers in Philippi (*Phil* 7:1), from around the year 140. There he writes, "For anyone who does not confess that Jesus Christ has come in the flesh is an antichrist." This very closely approximates the wording in 1 John 4:2–3 and 2 John 7. Polycarp's acquaintance with the letter is further confirmed by phrases he goes on to use, such as, among others, "[to be] of the devil," and "let us return to the word that was handed down to us from the beginning" (*Phil.* 7:2; cf. 2 John 7), and possibly also by a note in Eusebius that according to Irenaeus, Polycarp knew the Apostle John in Ephesus. All this speaks in support of Polycarp's having had access to 1 John. According to Eusebius, Polycarp's contemporary Papias also used 1 John.

The first known citations appear in the works of Irenaeus, bishop in Lyons; according to Eusebius, Irenaeus in his youth had listened to Polycarp. In his *Against Heresies,* from around the year 180, he cites 1 John 2:1–2, 21–22 (3.6.5); 1 John 4:1–2, 5:1, and 2 John 7–8 (3.6.18); and 2 John 11 (1.6.3). Irenaeus clearly knew two of the Johannine letters, but his way of citing them leaves the reader unsure whether he thought of them as one or as two documents. His use of the letters is tied exclusively to his anti-Gnostic polemic. For Irenaeus, the Apostle John was the author of the Gospel, the letters, and the Revelation of John.

During the third century, 1 John is quoted quite frequently: by Tertullian (d. c. 220) over forty times, and by Cyprian (d. 258), Clement of Alexandria (d. before 215), and Origen (d. 253/254). Tertullian disputes the doctrine of sin in 1 John; Cyprian makes use of 1 John 2:1–2, Clement of 1 John 2:2–6, and Origen of 1 John 3:2.

Although Irenaeus used the first two Johannine letters, he clearly did not regard the catholic letters as completely useful witnesses in the fight against the heretics. Only gradually did 1 John attain a secure place in the canon. According to Eusebius, Origen knew of the three Johannine letters but also noted that not everyone recognized the two lesser ones as genuine. Origen's student Dionysius (d. 265) claimed that the Apostle John wrote both the Gospel and the "catholic letter," and further acknowledged a disputed second and third letter of John. Even in North Africa, all three letters were known at this time (according to a council in Carthage in the year 256). Eusebius himself, who wrote at the beginning of the fourth century, placed the first letter among the commonly accepted books, but the smaller letters among the disputed books, even though they were "well known and recognized by most people." Jerome likewise noted at the end of the century that many people attributed the two small letters to the elder, and not to the apostle. John Chrysostom (d. 407) and Theodore of Mopsuestia (d. 428), in the eastern part of the Church, seem never to have used the smaller letters. Otherwise, there is in the later fourth century a manifold witness to the three letters as a unity with a clear place in the canon: Athanasius (367) and the Councils of Hippo (393) and Carthage (397). The first commentary on the three letters as a unit was also written at this time by Didymos the Blind. In the year 407, or perhaps 415, Augustine delivered his famous sermons on 1 John.

The situation was different, however, in the Syrian church. The first letter is included in the Peshitta, the more commonly used translation from around 400, but not so the two other letters. Nor are there any citations from the latter among the early Syrian church fathers. The smaller letters made their way into a later Syriac version at the beginning of the sixth century, but the Nestorians continued to reject them as a part of the Christian canon.

The first and second letters seem thus to have attained a more common use at the end of the second century (Irenaeus, *Canon Muratori*, Clement of Alexandria). During the third century all three letters are mentioned together, but in most cases with the comment that the two smaller letters are not recognized by everyone. See above. The discussion continued during the entire fourth century. The third letter is known to Origen, but the surviving literature after him shows no use of either of the two smaller letters. The earliest known uses of the third letter are those by Ambrosiaster (comparing Gaius in Rom 16:23 with Gaius in 3 John 1) and Jerome (interpreting the names Diotrephes and Demetrius; 3 John 9, 12). Thereafter it appears in the discussions of the canon in the fourth century. See above.

From all that has been said so far, it is obvious that the three letters were variously regarded. They were not preserved together; instead, for a long time, they existed independently and each acquired its own history. The first letter came into use as early as the second century, regarded as presumably written by the author who penned the Fourth Gospel, namely the Apostle John. The letter was of course anonymous and was easily associated with the Gospel. The other two letters, written by the Elder, were unable to attain a reputation of apostolic authorship as easily. Presumably the second letter was very soon attached to the first simply on the ground of similar content, especially since both could be employed in the struggle against the Gnostics. The third letter was accepted later because of its many similarities to the second letter. On its own merits, it would probably never have been canonized. It is a very short letter, only 219 words, addressed to a specific individual, who moreover is unknown. In addition, as I see it, this third letter was originally anchored in an internal Jewish problem. Thus the three letters eventually became a Johannine unity within the Christian canon. Because they were regarded as written by the Apostle John, they acquired a widely recognized status there.

This summarizes the current thinking on the place of the Johannine letters in the early church. Some scholars have recently wished to claim that Irenaeus knew of a collection of five Johannine writings, a *Corpus Johanneum*, all of them written by the disciple John. The fact that the two smaller letters are rarely cited is due to their brevity. When the Fourth Gospel later on became a fixed part of the Gospel collection, the *Corpus Johanneum* was broken up, and each of the remaining four documents went its own way.

2. Letters to Johannine Christians

By the time the letters of John had become part of the Christian canon, their addressees were also regarded as Christians in a general sense, all the more so because the first recipients are not more precisely described in these writings. The letters thus came to be read and applied to Christians generally (something clearly seen already with Irenaeus) and not restricted to a particular segment of the early Church. But that was hardly the case from the beginning. There is much to be said both in favor of the Gospel and letters having arisen among a group of Greek-speaking Jews who believed in Jesus, and in favor of their being directed to that group, at least at the first stage. It is possible that the final stage in the development of the text's written form was carried out with the idea that more Christians should be allowed to enjoy this special tradition within the early Church. See further point 3, below.

Many writers call this body of believers "Johannine Christians." This designation, however, is not one that turns up in the early Church itself, but rather is one used by later researchers for describing a group of Jews who confessed Jesus as Messiah, God's son, Israel's king. Such is the full confession we find in the opening week of John's Gospel (John 1:19—2:11). There we also find other descriptors: rabbi, lamb of God, the one of whom Moses and the prophets wrote. But they all culminate in Nathanael's confession (John 1:49): "Rabbi, you are the Son of God! You are the King of Israel!"

Nathanael—whose name means "God's gift," a description applied to the disciples in Jesus' farewell address (John 17:2, 6, 9, 11, 24)—is, according to Jesus' own words in this introductory week, the true Israelite. In him there is no guile. Everyone who is like Nathanael can be called "Nathanaelite" (God's gift). Perhaps we could visualize some early followers of Jesus calling themselves by such a name, but certainly not by the name "Johannine Christians."

The identity of Johannine Christians can be further determined through the so-called Johannine writings, namely, the Gospel of John, the letters of John, and possibly also the Revelation of John. Together these documents make up a fifth of the New Testament. The two shorter letters have the same author; the second letter has a good deal in common with the first letter, which in its turn must be read together with the Gospel, especially with the beginning of its second main part (John 13–17). It is no new insight that the Johannine writings form a distinct grouping within the New Testament collection. Augustine writes about this already in his *In Evangelium Johannis tractatus* 124[1]:

> There are two states of life . . . that are known to the Church,
> whereof the one is in faith, the other in sight;
> one in the temporal sojourn in a foreign land, the other in the eternity of the
>   heavenly abode;
> one in labor, the other in repose;
> one on the way, the other in the fatherland;
> one in active work, the other in the wages of contemplation;
> one declines from evil and makes for good, the other has no evil from which
>   to decline . . .
> the one fights with a foe, the other reigns without a foe.
> . . .
> Therefore the one is good, but miserable as yet; the other, better and blessed.
> This one was signified by the Apostle Peter, that other by John.

The Johannine texts are unique in the Christian canon. Here we must acknowledge that Augustine is right, even if we do not always understand or subscribe to the ways in which he characterizes the difference. Johannine Christians could thus, according to one definition, be Christ-confessors in the early Church who belonged to "John," that is, to the Johannine texts.

The Johannine Christians can be described on the basis of conclusions we are able to draw from the insights provided within the Johannine writings and from what we know about the first century. The five documents are connected with various situations, but they nonetheless yield a rather consistent picture. The most important points can be summed up thus:

---

1. Translation from *Nicene and Post-Nicene Fathers*, ed. Philip Schaff (Hendrickson, 1994 [1888]), 7.450.

First John

1. *They are Jewish believers who confess Jesus as the Messiah, the son of God* (John 20:30–31; 1 John 5:13). See Appendix 14, Jesus as Messiah, God's son. There were possibly also some members of non-Jewish birth who were closely associated with Judaism: proselytes, God-fearers, or other sympathizers (John 12:20–26; 7:35). Diotrephes may perhaps belong to this group of "Greeks" who took a leading role in the local Jewish community. See the note on 3 John 9. In 3 John, the pronoun "we," referring to the Johannine Christians, is set in contrast to the pagans (3 John 7–8). Passages in Revelation can be interpreted to mean that the prophet and brother John views his fellow believers—that is, those who keep God's word and have the witness of Jesus—as true Jews (Rev 2:9; 3:9; 11:19—12:17; and 21:9–14).

2. *They are deeply anchored in the Old Testament and contemporary Judaism.* This is clear from all Johannine writings, though in varying ways. In the Gospel, the Scriptures are necessary for understanding what Jesus said and did (John 2:22; 12:16). Both the Scriptures and Jesus' words are fulfilled in what happens in connection with Jesus (John 12:38; 18:9, 32; 19:24, 28, 36). Many of the statements and patterns in the Gospel presuppose a great familiarity with Jewish expositions of the Old Testament. This applies as well to the use of Cain as a negative example in 1 John (3:11–15). See Appendix 13, Cain as the Devil's Son. Other evidence of such familiarity with Jewish tradition can be seen in the descriptions of a renewed covenant in 1 John (see below, point 6 in this description of the Johannine Christians), in the last verse of that letter (see the Analysis on 1 John 5:13–21, point 3), and in several apocalyptic formulations in all three letters. Material parallel to the letters is found above all in the book of *Jubilees*, in the *Testaments of the Twelve Patriarchs*, and in texts from Qumran. The Johannine writings have been described as the most Jewish in the entire Christian corpus. The fact that the Old Testament is not cited in the letters is matched in texts from Qumran. Nor is there any discussion with Jews carried out in these letters, but only a background in the regression by some Jewish believers to their former faith.

3. *They are Greek-speaking, at least most of them are.* Such was clearly the case during the latter part of the first century. All the Johannine documents are written in Greek and addressed to readers unable to handle Hebrew or Aramaic. They represent a Hellenized form of Judaism. See Appendix 3, The Truth, and Appendix 6, Life, Eternal Life. The letters also exhibit a blend of Greek, Jewish, and Johannine elements. See, e.g., the Analysis of 2 John, point 2. Certain formulations in the Gospel are difficult to render into Hebrew or Aramaic, for instance, "being born again/from above" (John 3:3; *anōthen*). Whoever edited the letters appears to have had a certain level of training in Greek rhetoric. See below, points 3 and 5.

4. *They hand down and interpret their own tradition about Jesus.* Large portions of the Johannine writings have the character of oral, interpretive material. The

letters refer to a "we"-group responsible for passing on the tradition. See below, point 3, and Appendix 5, We in the Johannine Letters. The Gospel preserves an important depiction of the Spirit of Truth, the Paraclete, who together with Jesus' disciples conveys the Jesus tradition and interprets it (John 15:26–27, etc.). See, e.g., the Interpretation of 2 John 9. The result of this process manifests a clear character of its own, both in content and in form. There is considerable discussion whether the Johannine Christians had access to any of the other Gospels. The final redactor of the letters may have had such access. Regarding various "producers" of the Johannine literature, see below, point 3.

5. *They are described with terms such as "born of God," "God's children," "dear children," "beloved," "brothers and sisters," "friends," "the elect lady and her children," "the elect sister and her children."* These terms—with the possible exception of "friends"—have a clear background in the Old Testament and in contemporary Jewish exposition. In my view, the word "church" (*ekklēsia*), so common in Paul, is used in 3 John 6, 9 with reference to Jewish congregations. See the note there.

6. *They see themselves as participating in a new covenant.* A series of terms in the Gospel has this background, for instance, "grace and truth" (John 1:16–17), and in this commentary I have repeatedly referred to Jewish depictions of God's renewing his covenant with Israel. See Appendix 9, A Renewed Covenant, and the references listed there. These images provide the best framework for holding together a large number of important phrases and concepts in the letters, even though—unlike the case in the letter to the Hebrews—there is not a single quotation regarding how God will renew his covenant. The Johannine Christians view themselves in the light of a new covenant without needing to argue for it.

7. *They live, according to their own view of things, in the last times.* The fulfillment of the promises of a new covenant and of eternal life with God, that is, of the new age in earthly form, corroborates this. They are already "of God," closely united with God, and expect soon to be completely like God. This strongly eschatological theme in the letters reinforces the dualistic perspective.

8. *They can be described as a family of truth and love.* The rich usage of terms of relationship—child, father, lady, brother, sister, the Elder, little ones—and the dominating role played by the concepts of "truth" and "love" motivate such a description. See the Interpretation of 2 John 1–3, 12–13.

9. *They are found in several localities in the world of that day, evidently at some distance from one another, since the Elder must communicate with them by letter.* On the evidence of 3 John, Johannine Christians live in various locations—some of them at least where Gaius is, and "the friends" where the Elder is (3 John 1–3). Second John mentions two Johannine Christian communities: "the elect lady and her children" (2 John 1) and the "elect sister and her children" (2 John 13).

The Revelation of John was sent as a letter to seven congregations in and around Ephesus (Rev 2–3). Many scholars are of the opinion that the Johannine tradition has its roots in Jerusalem and environs, perhaps also in Samaria, probably in a priestly context. We do not know what happened when the Jesus-believing Jews were forced to leave Jerusalem during the war of 66–70 CE. Some seem to have fled eastward; others—Johannine Christians likely among them—turn up in Asia Minor, where there had already been a good number of Jews for a long time. Some scholars wish to reduce the Johannine community to one great, poetic author or to a "Johannine school," that is, to a few witnesses and interpreters of the tradition who "produced" the Johannine literature. See below, point 3. The Johannine letters can be used as an argument against such a perspective.

10. *They do some traveling, visiting one another. They thus have something in common with the itinerant brothers in 3 John, that is, with those Messiah-believing Jews who travel around proclaiming the reign of God in the expectation that Jesus is to return.* See Appendix 2, Itinerant Brothers, and Appendix 1, Hospitality. The description of this situation is reinforced by apocalyptic images of the final time in God's salvation history.

11. *They had experienced a difficult split within the Jewish community: some of them began denying their faith in the Messiah—that is, their faith that Jesus was the Messiah, God's son—probably owing to external pressure from Jewish leaders and Roman authorities, as well as to inner doubts as to whether Jesus really were the Messiah.* Consequently they had returned to their earlier Jewish faith. This schism is reflected also in several texts from the Gospel of John, for example, in the discussion following Jesus' discourse about his being the Bread of Life (John 6:60–71) and in the fierce dialog between Jesus and Jews who had put their faith in him but had then changed their minds (John 8:31–59; cf. 12:37–43). Even the Gospel's depiction of Judas, one of the Twelve, the one who would betray Jesus, can be read in terms of this intra-Johannine schism (John 12:4; 13:2; etc.). Thus there emerges a small minority of Jesus-believing Jews in sharp opposition to a Jewish majority in their vicinity, particularly to former Johannine Christians who now denied that Jesus was the Messiah, son of God. The Johannine writings witness to a strong opposition between "us" and "them," "them" being the Jewish environment.

This description of the Johannine Christians can have varying relevance for various periods in the history of the Johannine community. It is difficult to trace the development from the decade of the 30s to the end of the 90s. The Gospel preserves an ongoing discussion with various types of Jews. In the letters this discussion has died down, with the possible exception of 3 John. The situations behind the letters vary somewhat from letter to letter. See below, point 4.

3. Transmitters of the Tradition, Authors, and Editors

The Johannine writings of the New Testament are anonymous, apart from the book of Revelation, which names its sender as John. This John of the Revelation is presented as God's servant, as a brother among brothers, a prophet among prophets (Rev 1:1, 9; 19:10; 22:9). As a prophet he speaks on Christ's behalf. What he writes, or edits, bears witness that he is a Jesus-believing Jew who migrated westward, presumably from Judea or its environs, as a result of the Jewish uprising against Rome and traveled around among Jews and Jewish Christians in the Roman province of Asia. However that may be, he sends his missive, a kind of apocalyptic letter, to congregations in this district. He is in many ways reminiscent of the itinerant brothers in 3 John. See Appendix 2, Itinerant Brothers. Otherwise we know nothing about this John in the early church. Attempts to identify him with the apostle John or with the elder John are not convincing.

Thus the Johannine writings, with this one exception, are and remain anonymous. This is true also of the recipients, apart from the otherwise unknown Gaius in 3 John. See the note to 3 John 1. In addition there is a troubling lack of early witness to these writings. See above, point 1. Any attempt to determine the identity of the sender and receivers will therefore be little more than an educated guess.

The Gospel and the letters have much in common: central concepts, phrases, clauses, and even sentences, particular features of style, rhetorical figures, linguistic peculiarities such as methods of connecting sentences and larger structures, for example. The most relevant material for this commentary's interpretation of the three letters has thus been the Gospel of John and—although to a considerably lesser degree—the Revelation of John. Yet there are also several noticeable differences: distinct focuses in the two prologues, more God-oriented statements in the letters, more interest in future eschatology and less in the Spirit as a person in the letters, differing use of particles and several similarities to the texts from Qumran in the letters. This combination of proximity and distance can be explained in several ways, not least by differing theories of the origins of the letters and the Gospel.

It is especially clear with regard to the Gospel that it evolved over a longer time, even though a few people today believe that a skilled poet gave it its shape all in one context. The text as we have it bears clear signs of having been redacted, presumably several times. In view of the circumstances prevalent then, it is most likely that the origins of the Johannine material were to a great extent oral. What Jesus said and did was narrated over and over again in a Christian community, while simultaneously being interpreted from the perspective of the Scriptures and prevailing situations.

In some ways this resembles the process followed in the synagogue when an interpreter translated and explained the text of the day in Aramaic, or in more private gatherings where a Jewish teacher instructed his listeners in a way reminiscent of what we have in the book of Sirach. In the Gospel this type of interpreted material clearly appears, for example, in explanatory notes (e.g., John 1:38, 41, 42) and in the depiction of the Spirit of truth, the Paraclete, as the interpreter of Jesus' words and deeds (e.g., John 14:16–31). There is much to be said in favor of a central figure, a Johannine theologian, active in this process of interpretive retellings within a group of Jews who already believed in Jesus. He very likely had his roots in Judea or its environs and possibly had been an eyewitness to some of what he told. The material thus was formed for people who had already heard much of it before and over a considerable period of time.

The primarily oral form of the Johannine tradition presumably has its roots in Jerusalem and vicinity, but its final written form belongs most likely in and around Ephesus. According to several testimonies, Jesus' disciple John was active there to the end of his life. Around the year 190, Polycrates, bishop of Ephesus, referred to John's grave in Ephesus. It was in Ephesus and its surrounding districts where also John who put together the book of Revelation and who was banished to Patmos worked as a traveling brother and prophet.

No other writings in the New Testament stress so emphatically the actual process of their composition (John 20:30–31; 21:24–25; 1 John 1:4; 2:1, 7–8, 13–14, 21, 26; 5:13; 2 John 5, 12; 3 John 13; Rev 1:3, 11, 19; 2:1, 8, 12, etc.). In the first letter the word "write" occurs thirteen times. The question is why. Was there perhaps a need to give a stable written form to the Johannine material in order to preserve it for posterity? This would imply that there previously existed a rather complete Johannine tradition of both oral and written character, and that from it came the final written form of the Gospel and likewise of the three letters, perhaps even of the apocalypse (the book of Revelation). Such a situation can have arisen with the death of the person chiefly responsible for the Johannine tradition, or when those Jesus-believing Jews around him were forced to leave the Jewish community. In that case the Johannine material would have been directed to Jesus-believing Jews, but in a final stage it would have been edited to reach other readers as well. The varying genres can explain many differences observable among these writings.

What then do we know from the text itself about the person who wrote the two smaller letters? It is clear that he is an experienced writer with some training in rhetoric; he is a contemporary writer, a *grammateus,* who is sufficiently confident with the genre of letters that he can manipulate it through small variations so as to convey his special message. See the Analysis of these two letters. In both cases, it is likely that he was successful in convincing his readers of his point. He is a skilled rhetorician, even if at times he is perhaps a bit heavy-handed. He also blends Jewish, Greek, and Johannine forms in a way confirming that the Johannine tradition is clearly Jewish in character, even while exhibiting certain Hellenistic features. Not only is it couched in Greek linguistic forms, but it is also influenced by Greek forms of thinking. See, e.g., the Analysis of 2 John, point 2; Appendix 3, The Truth, and Appendix 6, Life, Eternal Life. There is good reason to think that it is not the Elder himself who does the writing, but rather one of his close disciples. This can also explain why the phrase "the

Presbyter" is used to refer to the sender. Thus the shaping of the two smaller letters could be taken as an argument for the theory that we have here a "redactor" who has had previous instruction, or possibly a secretary to the Elder who played a central role in the group responsible for the Johannine tradition. The different situations of the recipients are described below under point 4. They make it likely that 3 John is intended to function in a situation predating the one behind 2 John.

What can be said about the first letter? Here too we find a consciously rhetorical form that seems to have deceived interpreters throughout history. Whoever put pen to paper had a level of schooling typical for his day and shaped his document on the basis of contemporary rhetorical models. See the Index under the word "rhetorical." Unfortunately, we still have no thorough analysis of rhetoric for this letter. Many formulations appear to be standard and well known to the presumed audience. In terms of language, 1 John has more in common with the Gospel than do the two smaller letters. The basic arrangement itself is the same in both the letter and the Gospel: prologue, main body in two parts, and epilogue.

Which text depends on which has long been debated. Obviously the answer to this question also determines the order in which the two documents appeared. There is some reason to think that the letters all arose in a similar way. Whoever gave the smaller letters their final form also gathered up the Elder's instruction regarding the schism and its consequences, putting them into writing in what is known as 1 John. The same cautionary argumentation occurs in all three letters. The recipients are expected to draw their own conclusions. This same writer probably also edited the Gospel into its final form. The similarities in arrangement are thus explained as the result of the same person's editing both the letter and the Gospel. With regard to the Gospel, then, it is likely that more material was already available in written form. Oral traditions could also have maintained a stable shape over a considerable time.

It would thus be the Elder whose voice we hear even in 1 John. One of his close disciples has given a final written form to his teaching, doing so in response to the fact that some in the Johannine community have abandoned their faith in Jesus as Messiah, God's son. Varied material from different periods and changing situations, different genres, and a writer who gave the material its final written form can explain both the similarities and the differences we see among the Johannine documents. If this same writer also edited the book of Revelation, which is not likely, his name would be John, though not the apostle John, and probably not the Presbyter John either. The name John could also be a pseudonym drawn from the gospel tradition.

This, then, at least for now, is how I would describe the origins of the Johannine letters. We cannot simply speak of an author in our sense of the term. Instead, there is a chain of related "producers" in four stages: Jesus' disciple John the son of Zebedee, the Beloved Disciple, the Elder and his circle, and lastly the writer who in the final stage took pen in hand. It is difficult to say what role the disciple John could have had, but by the mid-second century, the Johannine tradition is connected with him. The role of the Beloved Disciple likewise can be disputed. Possibly he stands for the "brotherhood" that arose as a result of Jesus' death (John 19:25–27), that is, the Johannine Christians. In one sense, of course, it is true that the Johannine community contributed to the form that the Johannine tradition took on. In this way the Presbyter, the Elder, became the primary person in the process of handing on the Johannine tradition; he was most likely a Greek-speaking, literate Jew with connections to the priesthood in Jerusalem, who had become convinced that Jesus was the Messiah, the son of God. If it is he who hides behind "another disciple" in the Gospel of John (John 18:15–16), then he would also have been an eyewitness to some of the things Jesus did. Some scholars, including no less than Martin Hengel and Richard Bauckham, want to identify him with the Presbyter John that Papias (according to Eusebius) refers to, but it is difficult to prove this. Based on the three epistological situations described below under point 4, the letters are understood to function in the order of 3 John, 2 John, and 1 John.

This represents one attempt to describe the origins of the Johannine letters. There are many others. Several of them are based on our own contemporary ideas of what authorship means and for that reason have difficulty accepting an explanation such as the one just given. All of them nonetheless agree that the question of who "wrote" the Johannine letters must be coupled together with the question of who produced the Gospel of John.

The perspective that dominated church and academy up until the beginning of the nineteenth century was that all five Johannine documents were written by one of Jesus' disciples, John the son of Zebedee. Irenaeus, bishop of Lyons (d. 202), states that John, "the disciple of the Lord, who also leaned upon his breast," is the author of the Gospel, the book of Revelation, and 1 and 2 John. He does not seem to have been the first to claim this, but he provides more information than any previous church father. John would have written the Gospel in his extreme old age while he lived in Ephesus, and intended with it to refute the false teachers associated with Cerinthus and the so-called Nicolaitans (Irenaeus, *Haer.* 3.1.1–2; 3.11.1–7). According to Eusebius, Irenaeus in his youth had listened to bishop Polycarp in Smyrna, who likely knew 1 and 2 John, and he had close contact with the congregation in Rome.

Also probably from Rome comes the earliest known canon list, *Canon Muratori*, which due to its poor Latin has been notoriously difficult to interpret. It is likely contemporaneous with Irenaeus. In it the Gospel, two letters and the book of Revelation are attributed to "John," without further precision. The opening words of 1 John are quoted with the conclusion that John was not only an eyewitness and one of those in the original audiences, but also the author. Clement of Alexandria (d. 215) also quotes from John's "longer letter," and Tertullian (d. 225) attributes the Gospel and two letters to the apostle John. Thus during the later second century, there seems to have been a rather general assumption that the Johannine documents were written by John the son of Zebedee. On the other hand, 3 John is never mentioned in this early testimony. These ideas have formed the traditional perspective: in the early days, Jesus' disciple

John moved to Ephesus, wrote the book of Revelation while exiled on Patmos, returned to Ephesus, and there wrote the Gospel and letters.

Few biblical scholars are convinced of this hypothesis today, particularly with regard to Revelation. In it John is not presented even indirectly in a way that brings to mind one of the first apostles. In general, an embarrassing silence prevails throughout all the Johannine material regarding the apostle John as author. Why could this apostle not have used his name, or why could not some other person have presented him as the apostle John when the smaller letters were written? If it were obvious from the very first who the author was, and commonly known besides, then why this silence in the Johannine writings? Is Irenaeus' chain of tradition—John, Beloved Disciple, Polycarp, Irenaeus—as used in the conflict with false teachers during the latter part of the second century, a historical description, or is it partly a theological interpretation of statements in the Johannine texts that was possibly handed down from Polycarp? There are features of the Johannine text that are especially difficult for the hypothesis that the disciple John at an advanced age around the year 100 authored the Gospel and the letters with early christological and theological heresies in mind. It would thus be easier to imagine that the anonymous disciple who appears in Jerusalem during the last days of the story of Jesus' life, the one who knew the high priest (John 18:15–16), is the person who becomes the central figure among a group of Jesus-believing Jews, that it is he who gathers and interprets traditions about Jesus and who eventually in Ephesus finds help in putting the Johannine traditional material into written form. Such a person would possibly have been given the name, "the disciple whom Jesus loved." A hypothesis of this sort can also explain these texts' susceptibility to being viewed as authored by John, son of Zebedee. The Gospel is structured in such a way that it is anchored in fellowship with Jesus during his earthly days and in the subsequent instruction through the Spirit of truth.

4. Various Perspectives and Circumstances Behind the Letters

There is much that we do not know about the Johannine letters. It is therefore especially important to account for the perspective that lies behind a given interpretation of these letters and for the historical situations that are used for understanding the statements in them. Both the perspectives and the situations are constructs developed by interpreters and cannot be simply deduced from the text alone. This becomes clearest perhaps with regard to the smaller letters, where the information is particularly meager. See Analysis of 3 John, point 6. In the introduction to the commentary, I listed three main perspectives for reading the Johannine letters and selected one of them, occasionally then in the course of the interpretation comparing it with others. See especially the Interpretation sections for 1 John 1:1–4, point 6; 1 John 1: 5—2:2, point 5; 1 John 2:18–27, point 6; 1 John 5:1–12, point 2; as well as the Analysis of 1 John 4:1–6, point 2. See also Appendix 2, Itinerant Brothers, Appendix, 12, They cannot sin, Appendix 14, Jesus as Messiah,

God's son, and Appendix 17, By Water and Blood. What follows here is mostly a summarizing and illustrating of what has already been said.

In a commentary on the Johannine letters, the commentator's perspective becomes most visible in the description of the opponents in the letter and in identifying the letters' aims. For the latter, see below, point 5. Most often, the opponents have been described as Gnostic or docetic. The doctrinally and ethically false teachers opposed in the letters are, according to Rudolf Schnackenburg, "gnostically oriented." In a New Testament exegesis textbook used in Sweden since 1969, Lars Hartman writes, "First John warns against Gnostic heretics who are making inroads into the church." During the 1970s, opinion shifted toward so-called ultra-Johannine opponents, especially clear in Raymond Brown's massive commentary of 1982. These are Johannine Christians who further developed certain theological elements of the Johannine tradition and consequently left the Johannine community. The Presbyter spurns these false teachers altogether and sends out "counter-missionaries" in the consequent controversy over the Johannine heritage ("the brothers" in 3 John). Toward the end of the twentieth century voices were raised in favor of seeing the opponents in the letters as of the same stripe as certain Jews in the Gospel. The problem was an internal Jewish conflict. To my knowledge, I am the first to write a commentary in which this way of looking at things influences the entire interpretation of the three letters. It is not difficult to see that the predominant conceptions of the 1960s and of the 1980s, as well as the new orientation found in this commentary, are connected to certain larger cultural changes in our own time.

1. *A general Christian perspective: the influence of Gnostic or docetic heretics (apostasy hypothesis).* This perspective is probably still the most common one. Gnostic and docetic teachers threatened to work their way into the Christian church and lead it astray in terms of both Christian faith and Christian lifestyle. This construct has a very long history, evidenced already in the so-called anti-Gnostic fathers at the end of the second century (Irenaeus, Tertullian, Hippolytus). Commentaries frequently refer to the false teachers in the letters of Ignatius and to Cerinthus in Ephesus, Saturninus in Antioch, Basilides in Egypt, and Valentinus in Rome.

   Those who describe the opponents as Docetists always refer to Ignatius of Antioch. In the second decade of the second century he claimed that "some that are without God, that is, the unbelieving" imagine that Christ only "seemed to suffer" (*dokein peponthenai auton,* Ign. *Trall.* 10). They thus denied Christ's material, earthly and bodily existence. He had what only appeared to be a body. His entire earthly life appears as an illusion. Similar reasoning occurs as well in the letter to the Christians in Smyrna. If the Lord only seemed to suffer, then he too, Ignatius himself, will only seem to suffer even as he is now en route to martyrdom in Rome. These false teachers, he writes, "blaspheme my Lord, not confessing that he was truly possessed of a body" (*sarkophoros*). Condemnation

The Johannine Letters as a Whole

will fall on all who "believe not in the blood of Christ." "They have no regard for love; no care for the widow, or the orphan, or the oppressed; of the bond, or of the free; of the hungry, or of the thirsty. They abstain from the Eucharist and from prayer, because they confess not the Eucharist to be the flesh of our Savior Jesus Christ." (Ign. *Smyrn.* 5:2—7:1)

Against this Ignatius insisted that Jesus Christ truly (*alēthōs*) was born, persecuted, crucified, and raised up, that he truly descended from David's line according to the flesh, that for our sake he truly was nailed to the cross by the authority of Pontius Pilate (Ign. *Smyrn.* 1–2). The opponents in the letters of Ignatius—who appear to be Jewish—obviously can have something in common with the secessionists in 1 John. Docetic ideas are also attributed to Saturninus (before 150), who taught that the Savior was "without birth, without body, and without figure, but was, only by supposition, a visible man" (Irenaeus, *Haer.* 1.24.2). Distinctive of a docetic conception is that during his entire life, Christ had only what appeared to be a body. Those who describe the opponents as Gnostics routinely refer to Irenaeus, bishop of Lyon (d. 202), and the book he wrote to combat heresies. Irenaeus writes:

> Cerinthus . . . a certain man in Asia, taught that the world was not made by the primary God, but by a certain Power far separated from him, and at a distance from that Principality who is supreme over the universe, and ignorant of him who is above all. He represented Jesus as having not been born of a virgin (which was apparently impossible for him), but as being the son of Joseph and Mary according to the ordinary course of human generation, while he nevertheless was more righteous, prudent, and wise than other men. Moreover, after his baptism, Christ descended upon him in the form of a dove from the Supreme Ruler, and that then he proclaimed the unknown Father, and performed miracles. But at last Christ departed from Jesus, and that then Jesus suffered and rose again, while Christ remained impassible, inasmuch as he was a spiritual being. (*Haer.* I.26.1).

Hippolytus of Rome (d. 235) confirms this information and adds that Cerinthus was educated in Egypt, "which was regarded as the home of all heresies" (*Haer.* 7:33; 10:21).

Irenaeus also tells the story of Cerinthus' visit to Ephesus: one day as John was on the way to the baths in Ephesus, he caught sight of Cerinthus there; he hastily left the building and fled, fearing that the bathhouse would collapse, since Cerinthus, the enemy of the truth, was within (*Haer.* 3.3.4). Some teachers in the second century claimed that Cerinthus wrote the Gospel and letters of John. Eusebius describes him as a predecessor of a materialistic, chiliastic eschatology, and Epiphanius of Salamis characterizes him as a fervent Judaizer. How much of this is true is hard to say. Some scholars explain Cerinthus' Christology as based

First John

on Jewish conceptions of how the Shekinah or Wisdom takes up residence in certain people. This "separation Christology"—which separates the man Jesus from the divine Christ—can be found in other texts as well.

These conceptualizations have been primarily used for understanding certain statements in 1 John. The claim that Jesus Christ has not come in the flesh (1 John 4:2–3) is interpreted from a docetic perspective: he only seemed to have a body. The denial that the son of God came not only with water, but also with blood (1 John 5:6–8), is taken to refer to Jesus' baptism and Jesus' death and explained as a "separation Christology." It was not Christ who died on the cross and rose again, but only Jesus the human being. See Appendix 14, Jesus as Messiah, God's son, and Appendix 17, By Water and Blood. The formulations in the letter can certainly lend themselves to such readings, but they cannot be said to be implied in the letter's own statements. From this perspective, the concept of Christ becomes problematic, the conceptions of the incarnation unclear, the arguments complicated and the ethical accusations not as comprehensive as would naturally be invited by a Gnostic belief system, with its distinction between spirit and matter.

2. *An intra-Johannine perspective: ultra-Johannine interpretations of the Johannine heritage (progression hypothesis).* A readily available option for understanding the Johannine literature, especially the Gospel, is a developing-history perspective on the Johannine schism. This is the approach taken by Raymond Brown in his epoch-making commentary from 1982. The Gospel is understood to be commonly shared by the recipients of the letters and by the secessionists. Both parties can easily find support in it for their positions. The split between them thus finds its causes within the Johannine community itself, which can explain the difficulties the Presbyter has in controlling the secessionists. The Johannine tradition carries within itself the seed of what happened. Among other things, the issue had to do with pneumatology, eschatology, ethics and Christology.

All members of the Johannine family are bearers of the Spirit, the Paraclete. They all have an anointing from the Holy One that teaches them and guides them in life. Thus there is a built-in renewal program in the Johannine movement. The Johannine Christians are continually growing. Under the Spirit's guidance, they are advancing in their faith. But Christians can go too far with respect to this leading of the Spirit, and they can lose contact with Christ's teaching. According to the Presbyter, this is what has happened within the Johannine group. As he views it, within the renewal continually taking place, there are two firm points: the Paraclete, that is, the Spirit, and "we," that is, those who hand on and validate the tradition from the earthly Jesus. This is why "what they have heard from the beginning" (1 John 2:24, etc.) is so important. The secessionists flout the tradition and its authoritative tradents. Their spirit thus could not be the Spirit of Jesus; their testimony could not be in union with the testimony of Jesus. In an apocalyptic perspective, they were antichrists, that is, Christians in opposition to Christ.

In a Jewish environment a future eschatology was something taken for granted, and such an eschatology characterized the Johannine community from the beginning. But with the appearance of the Messiah something new had come. God's reign was already present in some sense. Gradually a present-oriented eschatology became all the more prevalent. Christ included within himself all the newness that God had promised his people. Without a Jewish frame of reference, as for example was the case when the Johannine Christians came to Asia Minor, the only eschatology available was a realized eschatology. A change of this sort took place within the Johannine community toward the end of the first century, leading to a fateful division. The Presbyter holds firmly to both a present and a future eschatology.

The secessionists claimed to be without sin, and they were able to find support for that in the Gospel. "One who has bathed does not need to wash, but is entirely clean" (John 13:10; shorter reading), and "You have already been cleansed by the word that I have spoken to you" (John 15:3). In addition Father, Son, and Spirit are said to dwell within the Christians (John 14:23). How then can they sin? They are born of God; they no longer stand under condemnation; they have passed from death to life (John 1:12; 3:18; 5:24). Of course, the Presbyter says something similar: "Those who have been born of God do not sin, because God's seed abides in them; they cannot sin, because they have been born of God" (1 John 3:9). Thus the two groups represented in the letter stand very close to one another, but the secessionists have gone a step further. The Presbyter insists on a "both-and" position—even with regard to this point: "They cannot sin" and "if anyone does sin" (1 John 3:9; 2:1).

Even in the question of Christology we might possibly discern a simple disagreement between those who claim that Jesus is both human and God and those who in a developed form of Johannine thinking claim that he is only God. But this would correspond poorly with the formulations in the text. Raymond Brown therefore believes that the secessionists would have insisted that Jesus' humanly existence, which they perceived as real and not merely an illusion (docetism), lacked any significance for humanity's salvation. They did not deny Jesus' humanity, but only that this humanity had significance for a Christian faith. Brown writes, "For the secessionists, the human existence was only a stage in the career of the divine Word and not an intrinsic component in redemption. What Jesus did in Palestine was not truly important for them, nor the fact that he died on the cross." Even on this point, the secessionists could find some support in the Gospel of John, where Jesus is depicted in a way that downplays his humanity and emphasizes that what is decisive for salvation is believing that Jesus is the one whom the Father has sent. The rest of it is not so important. Both groups in the Johannine schism thus think of Jesus in Johannine terms, but the secessionists have gone a few steps beyond and have thereby lost the balance that the Presbyter regards as utterly necessary.

This interpretation from an intra-Johannine progressivist perspective can find support in many individual parts of the texts, but in my view it seems much too complicated, not least with regard to Christology and the interpretation of 3 John. Nonetheless, Brown's emphasis on diverse eschatological perspectives and the playing off of Christology against the consequences of Christology, namely soteriology, has good support in the letters as a whole. There is much to be said for the idea that the Gospel and 1 John were put into their final edited forms at about the same time.

3. *An intra-Jewish perspective: some Johannine Christians have reverted to their Jewish faith (regression hypothesis).* Those who want to view the opponents as Jews who formerly were Johannine Christians envision a situation where for various reasons some in the Johannine community, possibly many, denied their faith in Jesus as the expected Messiah and left the Johannine community. In this intra-Jewish perspective the conflict is not about Jesus' humanity, but about his messianic status. Was Jesus of Nazareth the Messiah, the one whom God has sent? Had the anticipated end of this age finally come? The few scholars who promote this perspective often take as their starting point the second chapter of 1 John (2:18–23). The opponents had once belonged to the Johannine community, but "they went out from us," as the text puts it, and if this community was made up of Jews who had come to faith in Jesus, then these who had "gone out" were also Jews. They now denied that Jesus was the Messiah, son of God (1 John 2:22; 4:3, 15; 5:1, 5), and thus likewise the Messianic faith represented in the Gospel. They had deserted the teaching about the Messiah described in 2 John 7. They had abandoned as well the conviction that a new covenant had been put into effect, along with everything implied in that. They had returned to their previous Jewish faith and resumed their natural place within the fellowship of the Jewish synagogue. For certain reasons, they no longer demonstrated solidarity with the new community; they no longer loved their brothers and sisters.

The formulation later in 1 John 4:2–3 would then express the same thing as in chapter 2 (vv. 18–23). According to the understanding current among the Johannine Christians, Jesus' deeds demanded that he was human. He gave his body so that the world might have life, etc. The Messiah was the one who would come to earth, sent by God, God's own son, the Word that became flesh. The fact that the opponents denied that Jesus was the Messiah come in the flesh need not imply anything more than this. See Appendix 14, Jesus as Messiah, God's son.

The passage about water and blood as testimony to Jesus Christ as God's son (1 John 5:6) can be taken as justification for this reading. See Appendix 17, By Water and Blood. However, the simplest solution, based on what is said in the letter, is that blood here refers to Jesus' death and water to his birth, or possibly to his baptism. Can these two events be seen as belonging to his messiahship? If someone denied these events, would that person also then be denying that the expected Messiah was Jesus?

According to Johannine faith it was entirely clear that both Jesus' becoming a human being and his death were unalienable aspects of Jesus' work, required in order for him to be the savior of the world. A repudiation of his having come with water and especially of his having come with blood implied a repudiation of Jesus' work as savior, a repudiation of the core of Jesus' messiahship. Even if the water is understood to refer to his baptism, that too, from a Johannine point of view, can be seen as a distinguishing characteristic of the Messiah. It is he who shall baptize with the Holy Spirit, and in his own baptism the Spirit came upon him and remained with him. With the coming of the Messiah, the Spirit came to God's covenant people in a new way. On this point, the two parties in the letter were clearly in greater agreement.

Nothing in the letter explicitly says why these Messiah-believing Jews left the Johannine group and broke up the brotherly, sisterly fellowship that existed there. The Gospel alludes to the fear of Jewish leaders, to the wish to preserve one's reputation in the society, to the risk of being excluded from the synagogue and consequently from privileges Jews enjoyed at that time: freedom from military service, exemption from the worship of Caesar, the right to their own special customs and religious services, and others. At the end of the first century, Caesar regarded himself as "Lord and God." This is the circumstance behind the book of Revelation. Thus, in a situation where Johannine Christians had to choose whether they were a part of the Jewish community or not—for example, by paying the new Jewish tax—a few of them had been forced to leave the synagogue fellowship and to form their own "synagogue." Some writers interpret the closing words of 1 John as a warning against images of Caesar. According to Pliny the Younger, at the very beginning of the second century, one could tell whether a person was a Christian or not by ordering him or her to make an offering before the image of Caesar, the so-called offering test.

If we proceed on the basis of the intra-Jewish perspective, the situation for the three Johannine letters can be described somewhat differently. If we let "the brothers" in 3 John stand for itinerant "Jewish Christian" preachers of the sort found, for example, in Matthew's Gospel and the *Didache*—see Appendix 2, Itinerant Brothers—and if we interpret *ekklēsia* in the letter as referring to the Jewish community—see the note and Interpretation for 3 John 6—then the letter reflects a situation in which an intra-Jewish conflict is beginning to take shape. The leading person among the Jews of this locality, Diotrephes, refuses to receive these "brothers" and expels from his "synagogue" any who would accept them. The Elder understands this to mean that he and other Johannine Christians are also unwelcome in that local Jewish community. Johannine Christians no longer have a place in local Jewish fellowships. This incipient conflict supports the view that the situation in 3 John precedes the one in the two other letters.

In 2 John we have two Johannine communities, the one receiving the letter and the one surrounding the letter's author. A separation from the Jewish community seems to have already taken place. Those who are now traveling to the recipients' congregation appear to be former Johannine Christians. There is no mention of letters of recommendation. It is expected that they will be received by the local Johannine Christians. The addressees are apparently not well informed about the serious split that has taken place within the Johannine community. In any case, they need to be warned. The risks are great. According to the Presbyter, if they listen to these Jews who have not remained in the teaching about the Messiah (2 John 8–9), they risk losing their faith as well as the reward that awaits all who have "the Son and the Father." Chronologically, this situation comes later than the one in 3 John—assuming that the difference is not to be explained in terms of different localities.

The split within the Johannine community mentioned in 1 John is now at some remove from the situation that motivates the letter. But the external circumstances related to the schism remained in effect, namely, efforts by both Jewish and Roman authorities to distinguish Jews from non-Jews, and possibly an inner uncertainty about whether eternal life, or the new age, had actually come with Jesus Christ, God's son. For this reason the Elder's instructions are brought together for the purpose of giving comfort and help both in the present and in the future. This situation postdates those that lie behind the two smaller letters. This is why I have commented on the letters in the order 3 John, 2 John and 1 John.

5. Literary Character and Aim

No New Testament writing has enjoyed as many genre-reclassifications as 1 John: among others, a letter of recommendation for the Gospel, a general letter to all of Christendom, a circular communication, a pastoral letter, a commentary on the Gospel, a treatise, a sermon, a manifest to all Christians, a general circular letter, a religious diatribe, a religious tractate, a catholic pastoral letter, a genuine letter to all of Christianity, a sermonic appeal, a written speech, an epistolary essay, an instruction booklet, an *enchiridion* (handbook, compendium), a polemical writing, an epistolary homily. In the Analysis for 1 John 1:1–4, point 4, I have discussed the degree to which 1 John can be called a letter and have suggested such descriptions as handbook, testament, and pastoral letter. In light of what has been said above under point 3, the designation handbook (*enchiridion*) perhaps functions best, a collection of the Elder's instruction on the subject, written down so that it could be read out to Johannine Christian assemblies and perhaps other Christian assemblies as well.

The Johannine Letters as a Whole

The shorter letters have very concrete aims: to get the recipients to close the door to itinerants who have departed from the teaching about the Messiah and to open the door to itinerant brothers, especially to brother Demetrius, and to supply them with what they need for their further travels. In both cases these aims fit into a larger context: to preserve the new life-giving fellowship with God which had come about through faith in Jesus the Messiah, the son of God, a fellowship referred to with words like "belong to God," "see God," "have God," "have both the Father and the Son." These aims have consequences for the way the author uses the ancient letter format.

The aim of 1 John is not as easy to describe, in any case not on the basis of the extensive scholarly discussion of the question. Simplified, it can be said that all interpreters fall along a spectrum between the poles of sharp polemical aims on the one hand and intensely parenetic aims on the other. Either the letter's author wants to refute the false teachers who are in the vicinity of the recipients and safeguard a correct Christian faith and a proper Christian way of living (polemical aim), or he wants to support, encourage and strengthen the recipients in their faith in Jesus as Messiah, son of God, and to ensure that through this faith they are heirs to eternal life (parenetic aim). It may seem as if the purpose statement in the letter's final chapter (1 John 5:13) clearly supports the latter, all the more so if in addition to the words "so that you may know," we add all other statements in the letter about the fact that they know or can know. See the note "we know" for 1 John 5:18. I have chosen to read the letter as a document meant to comfort, encourage, and strengthen the faith of the recipients. The schism within the Johannine community, with its external and internal causes and with the consequent indecision of individual Jesus-believing Jews, clearly forms a background to the letter, although in some sense it lies at a significant distance from the situation current when the letter was written. The rhetoric of the letter, with its way of framing certain concepts in a straightforward manner (e.g., 1 John 1:6, 8, 10) and its radically polarizing diction heightened by the dualism of the letter's imminent eschatological situation, has doubtless led many people to read the letter as much more polemical than it actually is. The letter's aim is primarily parenetic.

The style in 1 John above all is marked by a limited vocabulary, a limited selection of syntactical constructions, and certain stylistic and rhetorical features. The latter include, for instance, a large variety of repetitions (2:12–14, etc.), antithetical parallelisms (1:5–10, etc.), other kinds of antitheses (1:5; 3:7–10; 5:6, 18–19), inclusios on various levels (1:2; 2:18; 3:9; 4:7–8), summaries of what has already been said (1:5; 5:1–3), pre-announcing of coming themes (3:10, 24), and word-plays (5:1, 18). Many of these same features characterize the Gospel of John as well. In the Notes on 1 John, I have devoted a good bit of space to linguistic peculiarities in the text. See among other things the notes to the verses listed below:

- A rich and varied use of the word "and": 1 John 1:2, 6–7; 2:1, 20, 27b, 28a; 3:2, 9–10; 4:3, 16; 5:3, 17.

First John

- The introductory phrase "and this is": 1 John 1:5; 2:25; 5:4, 11.
- Various forms of conditional constructions: 1 John 1:6–10; 2:4, 19, 29; 4:11–12; 5:9, 14.
- The introductory phrase "and by this we know" and similar forms: 1 John 2:3, 5; 3:16, 24; 4:2, 13, 16; 5:2.
- The so-called "pendent nominative": 1 John 2:5, 20, 24, 27; 3:17; 4:15.
- Various forms of exhortation: 1 John 2:6; 4:11 (ought); 3:23 (commandment that . . .); 2:1, 2:28—3:10 (participle).
- Substantive participles: 1 John 2:4, 29; 3:3, 4, 6, 8–9; 5:1.
- Semitic construction of the sort "all/every . . . not" = no one, none: 1 John 2:21d, 23a; 3:15b.
- The phrase "to be from" as meaning origin and belonging to: 1 John 2:16, 19, 21; 4:1, 3, 5–7.
- Expressions of the sort "to die a death" (*figura etymologica*, or "cognate accusative"): 1 John 1:5; 2:25; 5:4b, 15.
- Double expressions of the sort "A and B": 1 John 3:18, 22; 5:2b, 6; 2 John 3; 3 John 1–3.

Frequent use of these expressions, an almost thoroughgoing simplicity of clause and sentence construction with a small number of conjunctions, a clever rhetorical variation on both the lexical and the syntactical levels, and a number of recurrent central concepts such as light, darkness, life, death, truth, lie, love, hate, righteousness, sin, see, witness, recognize, know, remain in, be born of God, child, brother, boldness, and victory give 1 John a unifying style that binds the letter and the Gospel together. Just like the smaller letters, 1 John also has a peculiar literary character that both fascinates and irritates a modern reader by its meditative style and its open vagueness in the way it expresses its message.

6. Composition

The remarkably similar structure of the two smaller letters is relatively easy to describe. In part they have a genre structure that conforms to the ancient letter, and in part a rhetorical structure that follows ancient rhetorical models. The one wielding the pen is an accomplished writer with some training in rhetoric. The result, in many paragraphs, is fascinating. With small alterations in what would be expected in a text of this type the author is able effectively to convey the message he wants to send. I am convinced that he achieved his aims. In the Analyses of these two letters, to which I here refer the reader, I have described in detail the compositional and rhetorical features of these texts.

The design of 1 John is much more complicated. It is difficult to establish a genre-based structure since there is still no good general description of the letter's genre. See above, point 5. Other structural forms have been described in commentaries and specialist literature without any success in reaching a consensus. I have presented and, on the basis of various criteria, evaluated a number of such forms in an article that appeared in *Discourse Analysis and the New Testament*, where references to literature on the subject may be found. During some periods of the Church's history, 1 John was read as a collection of maxims, and later readings produced mostly thematic analyses. A vacillation between dogmatic and ethical sections has marked many proposals, as well as the view that the letter contains a series of tests for how a Christian should believe and live, a model for facilitating the application of the text to modern readers. With good reason, the letter's beginning and ending paragraphs, 1 John 1:1–4 and 5:13–21, are regarded as coherent units and frequently referred to as prolog and epilog. The remainder is divided up into two, three, or five parts. The three-part scheme is the most common, sometimes with reference to the three persons of the godhead (the Trinity). First John 4:1–6 and 2:18–27 are nearly always viewed as self-contained units, although with a comprehensive discussion about where the boundary falls around 2:28. Suggestions are most varied regarding the analysis of the more ethical paragraphs, 1 John 1:5—2:17; 2:28—3:24, and 4:7–21. The differences often depend on what markers those who describe the structure look for in the text as introducing a new section, or on the fact that most of them are trying to find a thematic introduction.

In every case I have discussed in detail the boundaries between sections and the connections between each and the letter as a whole. The divisions within a commentary can also be based upon the need to work with passages of appropriate length. The way I have organized the commentary is often motivated by rhetorical concerns, but the titles for each section are almost always thematic.

I have proposed the following overall analysis for the letter:

1:1–4	Divine Life, Divine Fellowship, Divine Joy.
1:5—2:2	A New Fellowship with God and its Requirements.
2:3–11	A Renewed Covenant with God and its Consequences.
2:12–17	Comfort and Admonition.
2:18–27	Schism in the New Community.
2:28—3:10	The Children of God and the Children of the Devil.
3:11–24	Love One Another.
4:1–6	Test Every Preacher.
4:7–21	God is Love.
5:1–12	Faith, Love, Begetting, Victory and Eternal Life.
5:13–21	Jesus, the True God and Eternal Life.

First John

The writer has used a series of markers to help the one reading the letter aloud to pause at appropriate places. Some of these markers, of course, have several functions. A vocative form—e.g., "my children" (2:18, 28; 4:1, 7)—together with other features can indicate a new section, but it is also used within a section to heighten reader awareness and to introduce something of importance, often of a negative character (2:1, 7; 3:13, 18, 21; 4:11; 5:21). Vocatives in parts of chapter 2 have their own particular character. See the Analysis of 1 John 2:12–17, point 2. A demonstrative "this" can both conclude (1:4; 2:1, 5, 26; 3:10, 24; 4:6, 21) and introduce a section (1:5; 2:3; 3:11; 5:13). Introductory thematic formulations are common (1:5; 2:3, 18, 28; 3:11; 4:1, 7), often announced in advance in the preceding paragraph (2:17; 3:10). The beginning of a section can also summarize what has just been said (1:5; 5:1–3). These linguistic means are employed also for indicating transitions within a section. See the analysis of each section's structure. I have noted rhetorical structures in the process of commenting on various sections, especially for the letter's introduction (1:1–4), for the section on comfort and admonition in chapter 2 (2:12–17), and for the letter's closing (5:13–21). The rhetoric of 1 John is mostly characterized by various forms of repetitions of both the same and related words, as well as of entire sentences. The use of different words for the same thing, often disturbing to a modern reader, can be understood as part of the author's rhetoric and not as expressions of differing content. Threefold structures are common, not only within sections, but also in certain types of parallelisms and in separate phrases (1:5—2:2; 2:3–11; 2:12–14, 16, 21, etc.). An example appears in the argument in chapter 3 (3:12–17). All three letters have an obvious rhetorical character. There is much in favor of the theory that the same person stands behind the final form of all three letters. See above, point 3.

Many scholars, mostly on the basis of thematic criteria, point out how the sections laid out above fit together. If 1 John 2:3–17 is seen as a single section (and there is some reason to see it that way), then a chiastic structure emerges:

A   1:5—2:2
B   2:3–17
C   2:18–27
D   2:28—3:10
D'   3:11–24
C'   4:1–6
B'   4:7–21
A' 5:1–12

There are several links between the contents of A and A', B and B' and so on, but this is not particularly unexpected, since the entire letter is filled with recurring concepts and themes. I have previously argued that formal correspondences between 1 John 1:5

and 3:11 divide up the letter's main body into two parts. The chiastic analysis above likewise gives a central place to the section 1 John 2:28—3:24, perhaps the most fundamental portion of the letter. Following the double-stranded covenant commandment in 1 John 3:23 regarding faith and love, it is also possible to see the first strand as handled in 1 John 4:1–6 and the second in 4:7–21, and then the two are brought together in 1 John 5:1–12. However, I see the various sections mostly as pearls on a string, held together by an overarching argumentation structure or by rhetorical strategies. The same sort of composition is found in 1 Peter and the letter of James. Thematic introductions are insufficient for describing the letter's composition.

7. A Central Message: God Is Light, God Is Love

The Johannine writings, viewed from an intra-Jewish perspective, can be read as a kind of addition to the agreement God made with the Israelites at Mount Sinai (Exod 19–24, 34). This is clearest in 1 John. The most important words in this alteration are Jesus Christ God's son and eternal life here and now. "And this is eternal life, that they may know you, the only true God, and Jesus Christ whom you have sent" (John 17:3). It is this "and" that dominates the Johannine writings. In 1 John it comes out in the author's exposition of the summary words "God is light" (1 John 1:5) and "God is love" (1 John 4:8, 16). It shines through as well in the concepts of "truth" and "love," which are found repeatedly in all three letters. The demands God placed on the people at Sinai came eventually to be summed up in two commandments: "You shall love the Lord, your God, with all your heart, with all your soul, and with all your strength" (according to the Jewish words of confession; Deut 6:4–5), and "You shall love your neighbor [fellow Jew] as yourself" (the so-called holiness law; Lev 19:18). They are brought together by Jesus in the double love-commandment (Matt 22:34–40). These two commandments from God have corresponding forms in 1 John. The first of them has been filled out more specifically by the new one: "we should believe in the name of his son Jesus Christ" (1 John 3:23), and the second has, so to speak, been refocused in a love for fellow believers in the renewed covenant. See further Appendix 9, A Renewed Covenant. When the Jewish community split apart, the perspective appears to have gradually opened up to other Christians and people of non-Jewish stock, which can be seen in the form that the Johannine writings eventually took on. See above, point 3.

God is light. Thus is summed up the message that the Elder and his fellow leaders received from God through Jesus Christ, God's son (1 John 1:1–5). The metaphorical formulation presents God in an Old Testament, Jewish context as the one who reveals himself to humanity, as the one who saves and sets people free, and as the one who instructs people regarding how they should live. These three revelatory, soteriological, and ethical dimensions of the words "God is light" function well in the letter as a whole. They are expounded twice in the introductory portion of the letter, each time in three stages (1 John 1:5—2:2 and 2:3–11). First it is a matter of walking in the light, that is, of letting the new revelation of God in Jesus Christ put its imprint on all of human life. A child of the light lives in the truth and has fellowship with the Elder and his teaching. Life in the light also has the result that through Jesus' blood God cleanses from all sin. This total forgiveness does not however imply that the recipients of the letter cannot fall into sin. But if any one of them does sin, there is a means of healing it (1 John 1:5—2:2). Then, in a second treatment, the ethical results are added to these revelatory and soteriological explanations (1 John 2:3-11). Those who through God's revelation and God's forgiveness have a renewed covenant relation with God must keep his commandments. This is explained in three steps: to keep God's word, that is, what God has said through Jesus Christ; to live as Jesus lived; and to love one's brothers and sisters. With this, the revelatory, soteriological, and ethical content of the words "God is light" has been clearly presented to the letter's recipients.

God is love. These words, which occur twice in chapter 4, are explained according to a similar pattern. God's revelation corresponds to God's sending of his son into the world; God's forgiveness of all sin is expressed through the presentation of his son as reconciler, life-giver and savior of the world (1 John 2:2; 4:10); and God's ethical instruction is concentrated in the phrase, "to love one another" (1 John 3:16). It is this final ethical dimension that dominates when God is presented in the words, "God is love." The death of Jesus functions in the letter both as reconciliation and as a model.

Truth and love. These two words and the word-forms related to them have a predominant place in Johannine speech. See Appendix 3, The Truth, and Appendix 16, God is Love. Their densest occurrence comes at the beginning of 2 John, where the recipients are depicted as a family of truth and love. See the Interpretation on 2 John 1-3, 12-13. It is likewise clear there that these terms have to do with covenantal ideas. The recipients are also addressed as "beloved," a designation applied to Israel in a Jewish interpretation of what happened at Mount Sinai (Exod 19-24). The truth belongs most naturally with the revelation of God manifested in Jesus Christ, God's son, while love is tied more to God's work of salvation and God's expectations of his covenant people. Jesus loved his own to the uttermost, to the end, something that on the one hand made them clean, and on the other hand gave them a model for serving others (John 13:1-17).

Jesus is the Messiah, God's son. From what has been said so far, it follows that what holds together all these central concepts is Jesus the Messiah, son of God. Everything in the Johannine texts stands or falls with Jesus as Messiah, God's son. Jesus is the one who was to come into the world, i.e., the Messiah (John 11:27). Jesus is the one God sent into the world, i.e., God's son (1 John 4:9-10). Life has been made manifest upon the earth, the eternal life that was with God and became visible to the Elder and others. Thus the Elder places emphasis particularly on the fact that the Messiah, the son of God, came in human form (1 John 4:2-3), and he wants to point to the death of Jesus as an utterly decisive aspect of the way divine life is made effective on earth (1 John 5:6). With total consistency, the first letter ends with the confession that Jesus

Christ is the true God and eternal life (1 John 5:20). The effect of Jesus' life and death can be summed up in the words "eternal life" as something already present in human life on the earth (1 John 1:2; 2:25; 3:14; 4:9; 5:11–13, 20). The darkness is passing away; the true light is already shining (1 John 2:8).

8. A Message Bound by Time and Space

The central message in the Johannine letters is clearly tied to both a definite historical-social situation and a definite comprehensive theological framework. Behind the texts lies a grievous internal conflict among a group of Messiah-believing Jews, in which some had abandoned their Messiah-faith and returned to their earlier Jewish faith. And the entire perspective is stamped with eschatological ideas that the final time of God's salvation history had broken in. Together this creates a dualistic way of thinking with powerfully polarizing language contrasting light and darkness, truth and falsehood, children of God and children of the devil, something found already, e.g., in texts about the pious Jews who withdrew to Qumran on the Dead Sea. Thus other Jewish traditions may have contributed to the dualistic language in the Johannine letters, especially characteristic of 1 John.

Many antichrists have gone out. This is a sign that it is "the last hour" (1 John 2:18). The letters are significantly more permeated with eschatological thought than I had first imagined them to be. There is also here and there some apocalyptic language. See, e.g., what is said in Appendix 2, Itinerant Brothers, and in a long series of passages in the letters (2 John 7–8; 1 John 2:8, 13–14, 15–17, 18–19, 22–23, 26; 2:28—3:10; 4:1–6, 17–18; 5:4–5, 18–20). 1 John has a simple, generalizing, almost philosophical speech that conceals this basic apocalyptic posture. Commentators usually speak of a realized eschatology or an actualized eschatology, i.e., that Jewish expectations of God's final intervention to save and vindicate his people have been realized to a great degree through Jesus Christ, God's son. God's promise of eternal life has been fulfilled, at least in part (1 John 2:25). I have interpreted the concept "eternal life" on the basis of Jewish ideas of a future kingdom of heaven on earth, perhaps coupled together with a Greek concept of the immortality of the soul. Neither Jesus' resurrection nor the resurrection of the dead is mentioned in the letters. See Appendix 6, Life, Eternal Life. To eschatology belong as well ideas of a renewed covenant. See Appendix 9, A Renewed Covenant. The letters' recipients are already in a certain sense made divine, born of God, but there remains a final stage when Jesus returns and judgment is held: they shall become like God (1 John 3:1–3). The nearness of the coming judgment makes the division between God's children and the children of the devil very sharp (1 John 3:4–10). This pervasive eschatological framework intensifies the dualistic language.

They went out from us. The antichrists had previously belonged to the Johannine community, but had broken away from it with pronounced antagonism as a result. Group conflicts of this type among Jews are attested in other texts from the middle of the second century and later. In the so-called animal apocalypse in 1 Enoch 89–90 from the mid-first century before our era, the orthodox author describes in visual form how non-orthodox Jews are obliterated: "And I saw at that time how a like abyss was opened in the midst of the earth, full of fire, and they brought those blinded sheep [= the non-orthodox], and they were all judged and found guilty and cast into this fiery abyss, and they burned." The group conflict had taken on apocalyptic dimensions and thus had intensified to the maximum. According to texts from Qumran, pious Jews had broken away from a Jewish community with violent denunciation of the latter as a consequence. The one who enters into the covenant fellowship at Qumran must "separate himself from all of the perverse men, those who walk in the wicked way, for such are not reckoned a part of His Covenant. They have not sought Him nor inquired of His statutes so as to discover the hidden laws in which they err to their shame. Even the revealed laws they knowingly transgress, thus stirring God's judgmental wrath and full vengeance: the curses of the Mosaic covenant. He will bring against them weighty judgments, eternal destruction with none spared" (1QS 5:10–13). The opponents of the Teacher of Righteousness have excluded themselves from the covenant in the last times, according to the commentary on the book of Habakkuk (1QpHab 8:13). The opponents are described as the "congregation of Belial" (1QH 10:22) Similar descriptions of internal group conflicts are found in the book of *Jubilees* (e.g., 15:33–34) and in *4 Ezra* (10:7, 10). Through an "apocalypticizing" of group conflicts, such conflicts acquire a dimension hardly corresponding with actual circumstances. This is how social conflicts and apocalyptic ideas work together. It is very likely also the case in the Johannine letters.

The message of the texts in other times and other places. What happens with Johannine texts, 1 John for instance, when they are read in a situation not characterized by the letters' powerful sense of realized eschatology or by severe intra-Jewish conflicts? We have seen how Irenaeus reads the first letter with reference to his own intra-Christian situation with its struggle over correct Christian faith and a proper Christian lifestyle. It is easy to show that he has had many followers right up to our own time. What has been said above regarding the letters' central message about God and Jesus Christ can certainly be applied to other situations, but at the same time doing so raises questions about the deep anchoring of Christian faith in Judaism. Can the conditions laid down at Sinai coexist with the demands that belong to a renewed covenant? Does a renewed covenant render the earlier covenant invalid?

From the perspective of positions other than the letter's own, it is also possible to point to the negative effects that lie within the strongly dualistic language. Understood as connected to a conflict with Jews, it can foster anti-Jewish sentiments and activity, and understood as related to intra-Christian conflicts, it can make fruitful discussion impossible. The recommended attitude toward others is different, for example, in other New Testament writings, as well as in our own time. Even if the Elder limits his exposition of God's love to a love among fellow believers, there are other possibilities for letting God's love for the whole world—a very significant idea even in 1 John—lead to a love for all human beings. The ethical principle in the letter—summed up in the words "as Jesus Christ"—should also be able to include thinking such as this. The conflict situation and the strongly eschatological perspectives are what have given the Elder's argument its special character.

The Letter of 1 John is a powerful witness to divine presence on the earth, particularly in the incarnation, that is, in Jesus' earthly life, but also in the life of the letter's recipients. The incarnation is there also in those who are united with Jesus Christ. What is new has been manifested "both in him and in you" (1 John 2:8). Still, the true light shines with significantly more power in this letter than, for example, in the Swedish incarnation hymn of Johan Olof Wallin (1818):

> Kindly over all the earth
> Shine forth rays of heavenly hope.
> Mildly each time-bound day
> The sun of Endless Day comes up.
> So mild that with my earthly eyes
> I may her glorious brilliance bear
> And on God's hidden councils stare.

Here the sun, like the winter sun, is so weak that one can stare directly into it. In 1 John both the light and the darkness become much more pronounced, formed among other things by a grievous internal conflict within the Johannine community and by apocalyptic language.

Appendices

Appendix 1

Hospitality

EXHORTATION TO BE HOSPITABLE occurs frequently in the early church. "Contribute to the needs of the saints; extend hospitality to strangers" (Rom 12:13). "Above all, maintain constant love for one another . . . Be hospitable to one another without complaining" (1 Pet 4:8–9). Love for brothers and sisters in the faith and hospitality cannot be divorced from one another. See also Heb 13:2.

In the Pastoral letters it is the leaders of a church in particular who are to open their homes to itinerant Christians (Titus 1:8; 1 Tim 5:10). Later literature shows that for a long time, hospitality characterized, or was meant to characterize, Christians. See the letter of Clement to the Christians in Corinth, *1 Clem.* 1:2; 10:7; 11:1; 12:1; Herm. *Mand.* 8:10; *Sim.* 9:27; and Justin Martyr, *1 Apol.* 14; 67:6. To practice hospitality is to do what is good (*agathopoiēsis;* Herm. *Mand.* 8:10); the formula is reminiscent of 3 John 11. Ignatius, overseer of the church of Antioch who visited a series of congregations when he was en route to Rome and a martyr's death, gives good examples of early Christian hospitality. The verb *epidechesthai* ("welcome") became a technical term for receiving guests and listening to what they had to say, privately or officially; *propempein* ("send on one's way") became the term for equipping these welcomed guests to that they could travel on to the next place. See 3 John 6, 9, and 10. *Hypolambanein* "receive" in 3 John 8 means to receive in a friendly way in order to give support and protection. The conditions in the Roman Empire of the time facilitated travel for many people. Peace prevailed in the realm, robbers on land and sea had been reduced in number, the network of roads had been constructed in an orderly way, and with Greek a person could make himself or herself understood in most parts of the empire. Not least of all, Jews also traveled a great deal. Most of them at that time lived outside of Judea. Regarding the Essenes, Josephus writes the following (*War* 2:124–25):

> If any of their sect come from other places, what they have lies open for them, just as if it were their own; and they go in to such as they never knew before, as if they had been ever so long acquainted with them. For which reason they carry nothing at all with them when they travel . . . Accordingly there is, in every city

where they live, one appointed particularly to take care of strangers, and to provide garments and other necessities for them. Even Philo notes, thinking of the Essenes, that the door was open to visiting strangers who shared their persuasion (*Prob.* 85). For people of Jewish birth, the synagogue or equivalent sometimes functioned as an inn for travelers, e.g., the synagogue of Theodotus in Jerusalem during the time of Jesus. The mutual concord among Christians promoted similar forms of hospitality.

Christians in the book of Acts are frequently out on the road, not least of all Paul and his co-workers. Many of the greetings in his letters—see especially Romans 16—presuppose extensive traveling. Nor was it only missionaries who traveled, but so did artisans and businessmen. In times of persecution, the number of travelers (fleeing trouble) could significantly increase. In such situations, welcoming fellow believers was an utter necessity. Itinerant brothers and sisters were a highly significant aspect of the early unity among Jesus believers and surely also for retelling the stories about Jesus and for early Christian proclamation.

Appendix 2

Itinerant Brothers

THE DESCRIPTION OF THE itinerant brothers in 3 John has considerable importance for understanding the letter as a whole. According to a standard interpretation they belong to the Johannine community and serve the Presbyter. The word "brothers" in extended meaning, as Paul very frequently uses it, is not however a typical designation for these Jesus-believing Jews—but see John 20:17, 21:23, and 1 John 3:13. Instead it stands more for those of one's own faith-family in general, whether fellow Jews or fellow Christians. Essenes could call one another brothers, and the rabbis distinguished between "neighbor" in the sense of fellow Jew and "brother" in the sense of true coreligionist.

The scanty information in the letter itself is important (vv. 5–10). In fact the entire fabric of the letter indicates that Demetrius belongs to these brothers (v. 12). The following sums up what is said in it:

1. They are consistently referred to as *brothers* (vv. 3, 5, and 10), and not as children, not friends or beloved ones, not teachers, prophets or apostles.

2. They are singled out as a *special category*, as "the brothers" in vv. 5 and 10 and as "such people" in v. 8.

3. They *travel around* among congregations—the Greek word *ekklēsia* can be used both of Jewish and of Christian communities—and clearly expect that the people of a given place are to provide them room and board and then to equip them for their continued journey. The three main personages in the letter—the Presbyter, Gaius, and Diotrephes—have been visited by brothers. Formulas in v. 6 (their testimony before the congregation) and in v. 12 (the testimony of all) can be taken to imply a rather wide-spread distribution of these brothers.

4. They have clearly *renounced all interaction with non-Jews*, which indicates that they are of Jewish origin and that they focus their attentions primarily on fellow Jews.

5. They visit the various congregations *for the sake of the Name*, a formula telling us

that their traveling has to do with their faith in Jesus. Perhaps it is because they wanted to continue Jesus' preaching of the kingdom of God, perhaps because they lived as he did, without home and property, perhaps because they had been persecuted and driven out. Whatever their circumstances, they could testify to how things were in various places (vv. 3 and 6).

6. Their activity concerns *the truth* (vv. 8 and 12). To welcome them is to work together with the Truth; the Truth itself bears a favorable witness regarding the brother Demetrius. In a Johannine perspective, the truth is closely related to Jesus' revelation of God. Here we find a clear connection between the brothers and the Presbyter: both function as links to that which was from the beginning, and both desire to safeguard the tradition handed down from Jesus.

7. In one sense they stand closely related to the letter's three main characters, but at the same time they are presented as *strangers*. This is said explicitly in regard to their relationship to Gaius (v. 5). They are introduced to him (vv. 7 and 12), and they need letters of recommendation (vv. 9 and 12). The formulas in vv. 8 and 12 also reveal a distance between the Presbyter and the brothers. Taking into account this distance and the descriptions of them elsewhere in the letter, we can scarcely view them as envoys of the Elder who work in his "anti-secessionist campaign," as Raymond Brown formulates it. They are not "the Presbyter's indispensable weapon against the spread of the secession," "anti-separatist missionaries," "the Presbyter's countermissionaries." Yet the Presbyter gives these brothers his serious and emphatic recommendation and is anxious to stay in contact with them.

Now there were many Jewish followers of Jesus who during the later part of the first century traveled around testifying about him, about his teaching and his life. Generally speaking, there was a great deal of travel on the part of Jews and Christians at this time. See Appendix 1, Hospitality. According to the Jesus-logia common to Luke and Matthew, the so-called Q-material, the depictions of those whom Jesus sent out with all likelihood corresponded to the way things were when these Gospels took form in the 80s. *The Didache*, a Jewish-Christian writing from around 100, tells of itinerant prophets, teachers, and apostles. In the 90s the author of the book of Revelation presents himself as a brother among brothers, and Papias—bishop of Hieropolis in Asia Minor in the 110s—refers to itinerant elders who passed on the tradition from Jesus.

The wandering preachers who appear in the synoptic narratives of Jesus' disciples, especially in the Q-material—see, e.g., Luke 9:2–5; 10:1–16; Matt 10:5–47; and also Mark 6:7–11—have a number characteristics in common. They lived as Jesus lived, without home or family, without money or possessions, without normal work, without exacting retaliation for wrongs done to them. They set off on their travels because of their faith in Jesus, leaving house and farm, parents and children, and they lived as carefree as the birds of heaven, as the lilies of the field. Their purpose apparently was to deliver Jesus' message of God's kingdom to all of Israel before Jesus returned in

Appendix 2: Itinerant Brothers

glory. As harvest workers, they were bringing in the harvest of the eschatological last times. Thus they turned to the Jews and seemed to have no Gentile mission in their program. Primarily they journeyed around the eastern portion of the Roman Empire, in Palestine and Syria, for the most part outside the large cities. The Roman war of the 60s may have driven some of them westward, e.g., to the many Jews in Asia Minor. They wanted to gather all Israel and thereby usher in the final time of salvation. They constituted thus a living link back to Jesus and the stories about him and functioned as a continuation of his work, his life and teaching.

The description of traveling teachers and prophets in *Didache* 11–15 has a lot in common with these wandering preachers. There it is emphasized that every itinerant prophet must be tested on the basis of his proclamation and even more on the basis of his manner of life. Those who visited congregations had to "hold the ways of the Lord," i.e., they had to live as the Lord lived. "Every prophet who teaches the truth but does not live in accordance with his teaching is a false prophet." At the most, they were to stay two days in any one place. "He who remains three days is a false prophet." As evangelists they were to "increase righteousness and the knowledge of the Lord," to announce "the message" and "the truth" and to spread "the Lord's gospel." They clearly had a high status in the various congregations, even though to some degree they could be replaced by local overseers and deacons.

In the book of Revelation it is prophets and persecuted witnesses who are called brothers. The author, John, belongs to this group (Rev 1:9; 6:11; 12:10). In Rev 19:10 he hears the words, "I am a fellow servant with you and your brothers who hold the testimony of Jesus . . . the testimony of Jesus is the spirit of prophecy." Here we see a group of witnesses and servants who in their prophetic activity are bound to the testimony of Jesus, i.e., to the testimony that came from Jesus. John has at least traveled around the western portion of the Roman Empire, since he knows well the congregations in Asia Minor. At the same time, the way his book presents its material testifies to a Palestinian-Syrian origin.

Although the material from Papias comes from a somewhat later time, there is reason to mention it here, since it is connected with Asia Minor. In his history of the church, Eusebius has an excerpt from Papias, with following commentary, describing some itinerant "elders" (3.39.3–4). According to Papias, they were transmitters of what the apostles had said and guarantors of the genuine tradition. They traveled around like the wandering preachers, some as associates of the apostles, others as associates of the presbyters. Thus the apostles and presbyters formed a firm chain of tradition from Jesus to Papias. They passed on "the truth." Papias preferred what these tradents had to say over what he could find in various written documents. Presumably, Papias had also received from them apocalyptic material of the sort found in the book of Revelation. Among the presbyters he mentions especially Aristion and John, who were clearly more or less contemporary with himself. Eusebius notes that Papias had listened to these two persons. "In any case, he mentions them often by name and writes down their traditions in his writings."

There was therefore a motley band of itinerant evangelists and teachers at the close of the first century: brothers, servants, righteous ones, teachers, prophets, apostles or whatever else they might be called. It is scarcely likely that the "brothers" in 3 John would be Jews or Christians in general, judging by what is said in the letters. They are hardly Johannine Christians in general either. What we are left with then are wandering preachers either within or outside of the Johannine fellowship. That there were many of the latter sort can be concluded from what has already been said, and on the basis of my intra-Jewish perspective and interpretation of *ekklēsia* in 3 John as Jewish communities, I find the latter alternative more likely. Thus we have the following more general pictures of these brothers:

1. It is Jesus-believing Jews who travel around to various Jewish communities in order to proclaim Jesus' message of the kingdom of God to all of Israel, and to do so before Jesus returns in glory.

2. They are sent to various kinds of Jewish fellowships—where there could also be Jesus-believing Jews—in order to carry out their work: there they are to be welcomed locally, to receive board and room, and to be equipped for traveling on to the next place.

3. At least in Asia Minor they needed letters of recommendation in order to be received without further testing as trustworthy Jewish brothers.

4. Through their lifestyle and their delivering the message from Jesus they constituted a living link to him, to his life and teaching.

5. As passers-on of traditions of Jesus, they had a close relationship with the Presbyter, though without actually belonging to the Johannine community.

6. They had been accustomed to being welcomed in the Jewish community where Gaius and Diotrephes lived, but gradually Diotrephes—one of the leaders of the place—said no.

7. Saying no to these native Jewish Jesus-proclaimers, whom the Presbyter had recommended, was tantamount to saying no to the Presbyter himself and a threat both against the Jesus tradition and against the Jews who believed in Jesus. Therefore the Presbyter reacted decisively: it was a matter of "belonging to God" or not, of "having seen God" or not (v. 11).

8. The Presbyter asked Gaius to receive the brother Demetrius and later presumably also other brothers. The fellowship in his house grew, and likely little by little it became a Christian house church. In this way, Jesus-believing Jews left the Jewish community and an initial split between those who believed in Jesus and those who did not believe in him emerged in that locality.

APPENDIX 3

The Truth

THE GREEK WORDS FOR "truth" (*alētheia*) and "true" (*alēthēs* or *alēthinos*) occur frequently in the Johannine literature (eighty-five of a total 163 times in the NT). Researchers have long discussed whether the Johannine concept of truth should be understood from a Hebrew or a Greek background. In the Hebrew Bible "truth" stands for something firm and reliable. God is true in the sense that he can be relied upon. He keeps his promises. A person's life is true when it conforms to God's will. There is thus a moral element in the Hebrew idea of truth.

The Greek word *alētheia* means something that is not hidden, something revealed, and stands for a fact or a relationship that is visible or described. It approaches words like "reality" and "knowledge." In Platonic thought it describes the ultimate reality. The Greek concept is more intellectual than moral.

Scholars such as Rudolf Bultmann and C. H. Dodd have argued for a Greek meaning: "divine reality," which has been revealed to human beings and gives them life, or "what is ultimately real," knowledge and reality. At the same time they have maintained that expressions such as "grace and truth" (John 1:14), "do the truth," or "walk in the truth" have their roots in the Hebrew Bible.

Ignace de la Potterie has with good reasons argued for a background in Jewish apocalyptic and Jewish wisdom literature. Truth becomes almost a synonym of wisdom (Prov 23:23; Sir 4:28), while simultaneously being coupled together with God's mystery, God's hidden plan of salvation (Dan 10:21; 1QH 10:4–5; 1QpHab 7:8). The psalmist says in 1QH 7:26–27: "You have given me insight into your truth and made known to me your wondrous mysteries." In the Qumran texts we hear of sons of the truth, men of the truth, generation of the truth, witness of the truth, and the truth's congregation, always with reference to the renewed covenant community at Qumran. Men of the truth are those who do the Law, i.e., the Law as revealed and interpreted by the Teacher of Righteousness within the Qumran community (1QpHab 7:10–11; 1QS 8:1–2). "The way of the Lord," revealed to the Qumran community, can be replaced by "the way of the truth" (4QS MS E, Frg.1, Col. 3, line 4). Thus, according to Raymond

Appendix 3: The Truth

Brown, it is unnecessary to go beyond a Semitic background in order to find the truth used to refer to God's plan of salvation revealed to human beings.

According to the Johannine writings God's hidden plan of salvation has been revealed through Jesus Christ, the Word, Logos, God's wisdom in human form (John 1:1–18). Grace and truth came through him (John 1:14, 17). He is the way, the truth, and the life (John 14:6). Eternal, divine life for humanity is found there through a renewed knowledge of the only true God and the one whom he has sent, Jesus Christ (John 17:3), ideas that are coupled with a renewed covenant in 1 John 5:20. Those who believe in Jesus as Messiah, God's son, have God's Spirit and God's law in their hearts and can thus realize God's will in a new way. See Appendix 9, A Renewed Covenant. The truth is found in human hearts and can be said to have a more personal character in the Johannine writings than in the rest of Judaism.

The many linguistic constructions with the word "truth" in the Johannine letters demonstrate that the word is both creative and central in Johannine thinking.

- *Do the truth* (1 John 1:6; John 3:21). The combination with "do" in the sense of "carry out" has its background in Hebrew and occurs in the OT (Neh 9:33; 2 Chr 31:20), the intertestamental literature (*T. Reu.* 6:9), and the Qumran texts (1QpHab 7:10–11).

- *Walk in (the) truth* (2 John 4; 3 John 3, 4). In the NT only here, but also in Ps 86:11 and 1QS 8:4.

- *Know/have come to know the truth* (1 John 2:21; 2 John 1). To know the truth (John 8:32) is to understand who Jesus is, i.e., to understand "I am" (John 8:28).

- *To be of the truth* (1 John 2:21; 3:19; John 18:37). The words "to be of" imply both origin and belonging.

- *The truth is in (us/him)* (1 John 1:8; 2:4; John 8:44). What is new in the new covenant is also found in human hearts. See Appendix 9, A Renewed Covenant.

- *To love in (the) truth* (John 3:18; 2 John 1; 3 John 1); *to love because of the truth* (2 John 2).

- *In truth and love* (2 John 3); *in deed and truth* (1 John 3:18). Coordination of closely related terms is not unusual in the Johannine writings: grace and truth (John 1:14, 17); in spirit and truth (John 4:23–24).

- *To bear witness of (your/the) truth* (3 John 3; John 5:33); *to be witnessed to by the Truth itself* (3 John 12).

- *To be a co-worker with the Truth* (3 John 8).

- *The Spirit is truth* (1 John 5:6); *the Spirit of truth* (1 John 4:6). The latter expression is used of the Paraclete in John 14:19; 15:26; 16:13, and occurs also in the Qumran texts. The Spirit of truth can most readily be described as the Spirit that teaches about and reveals who Jesus is, and thus who God is (John 16:12–15).

In the Johannine writings, there is therefore a clear tendency to identify the truth with the revelation in and through Jesus Messiah, the Son of God, i.e., the central content of "what they heard from the beginning," the core of the renewed covenant. Thus, the Old Testament phrases acquired a special meaning in the Johannine context. Those who reverted to their former Jewish faith wanted to deny it, and in dualistic terms they thus appear as the truth's opposite, i.e., as the lie (1 John 2:22, 27; see also 1 John 2:4; 5:10).

APPENDIX 4

House Churches

WE HAVE NO REASON to doubt Luke's information that the first Christians in Jerusalem gathered in the temple and in homes (Acts 2:44; 5:42). "Temple" here does not stand for the actual temple itself, but for the large tract that surrounded it (ca. 300 x 500 meters), with various forecourts, long colonnades, and other spaces. At the time, these accommodations could be used, among other things, for such purposes as were associated in smaller towns with the official communal synagogue. Alongside these communal synagogues there were also private, semi-official association synagogues, e.g., the synagogue of Theodotus or the synagogue of the Freedmen in Jerusalem (Acts 6:9).

The Greek words for "in homes" (*kat' oikon* or *kat' oikous*) can mean "at home" or "from house to house." Thus the Christians gathered not only in the temple precincts but even in private houses. Luke particularly mentions one such situation: Peter "went to the house of Mary, the mother of John who was also called Mark" (Acts 12:12). It was a larger house with a gate on the street set at a certain remove from the meeting room. There were servants in the house, and everything points to the fact that Mary belonged to the more well-to-do. She may have been a diaspora Jew who had returned to Jerusalem. Her son Mark was related to the Levite Barnabas of Cyprus (Acts 4:36–37; Col 4:10). In her house the Christ-believing Jews gathered for prayer.

Saul surely knew of these gatherings within the temple precincts and in various homes (Acts 8:3), and he counted on finding Christ-believing Jews in synagogues in Damascus (Acts 9:2). Information in Acts 9:19 indicates that these Damascus Jews also had gatherings in homes. On Paul's missionary travels entire households came to faith and in his letters he often mentions "house churches": in the homes of Aquila and Prisca (1 Cor 16:19; Rom 16:3–5); of Nympha (probably a woman; Col 4:15); and of Philemon (Phlm 1–2). Especially in the letter to the Romans, he mentions a large number of house fellowships (Romans 16). The recipients of 2 John—"the elect lady and her children"—doubtless form a house church, just as does the group that sends greetings at the close of the letter. In larger cities numerous house churches sprang up, but Paul can nonetheless write to all Christians in a single location, e.g., to

Appendix 4: House Churches

"the church of God" in Corinth (1 Cor 1:1–2; cf. 14:23; Rom 16:23). House churches and "the whole church" in a particular locality could function similarly to association synagogues and communal synagogues.

Gathering for prayer and instruction in the homes of more well-to-do persons was a natural procedure in light of prevailing relationships. "The household," i.e., the contemporary extended family, was the most important structural entity in the society. It was made up of parents, children, and slaves (see Col 3:18—4:7) as well as other relations across several generations. The entire house could become a Christian house and thus an important gathering place for individual Christians. In Greco-Roman society there could also be found a religious cult (honoring household gods) within the walls of the home. The cult of Dionysus and mystery cults were common in private homes, and the many special interest clubs and guilds, the so-called associations or *collegia*, gathered in the houses of the wealthy or in their own quarters.

Jewish homes also served as venues for regular teaching on various commandments, for Sabbath celebrations, and for other religious feasts. Alongside the official village or town synagogue (the communal synagogue) there were more private, "association" synagogues that resembled the Greco-Roman *collegia*. Association synagogues, like private homes, were also natural forerunners of Christian house churches. Sometimes private houses could be remodeled into house synagogues. There are examples at Delos in Achaia, in Stobi in Macedonia, and in Dura-Europos on the Euphrates. A room especially designed for worship services actually formed a part of the building, which in Stobi was still used as a dwelling even after the changes were made. The size could vary. The worship room in Dura-Europos measured ca. 13 x 7 meters.

The house church in Dura-Europos, which lay scarcely 100 meters from the house synagogue, had the same size. The Christians gathered at first in the building's largest room. When the congregation grew, they knocked down the wall to adjacent rooms. One of them seems also to have been made into a baptismal room. The remodeling took place sometime between 165 and 265, but likely the house had already been used for Christian assemblies before this. The expanded room held approximately seventy people. In general, we can assume that early house churches were made up of ten to forty persons.

House churches broke down social, ethnic, and religious boundaries operating in the contemporary society and had a decisive significance for early Christian mission, worship, teaching, and organization. They contributed as well to internal coherence, supportive solidarity, and protection from external pressures. But by the same token there was risk of increased isolation, unnatural independence, destructive models of authority, and unhealthy dependence on individual persons.

Appendix 5

We in the Johannine Letters

IN 1 JOHN THE pronoun "we" is used frequently and in several senses. This is observable not least in the beginning of the letter, but other parts of the letter are also dominated by we-forms (e.g., 2:28—3:3; 3:11-24; 4:7—5:4; and 5:13-21). In 2 John "we" seems only to be used in the sense of all who have learned to know the truth, i.e., in the letter's Johannine perspective, synonymous with the Johannine Christians (vv. 2b, 3b, 4c, 5c, 6b, 8a, and 12d). "We" in 2 John 12d can perhaps be taken as referring only to the letter's sender and its recipients. The use of "we" in 3 John, however, is more like that in 1 John.

The personal pronoun "we" belongs to the more open words in the language. Listeners must usually fill in for themselves the potential or intended reference. This is also true of those who listen to the Johannine letters. There are at least the following alternatives to choose from.

1. "We" as a circumlocution for "I." This usage is found in contemporary Greek, especially in letters. In European tradition, it occurs among other places in royal communiqués (*pluralis majestatis*) and in scientific discourse. The change of "we write" in 1 John 1:4 to "I write" in 1 John 2:1 can be taken as grounds for this interpretation. (In 1 John the pronoun "I" occurs only in "I write" [2:2, 7, 8, 12-14, 21, 26; and 5:13] and in "I say" [5:16].) Some readers wish to argue the thesis that "we" in the sense of "I" is an expression for a person who can with credibility and authority bear witness regarding Jesus' words and deeds. If this is the case, it is remarkable that the author does not argue from a position of authority; quite the reverse in fact.

2. "We" as a reference to the sender and recipients of a Johannine letter: we/I + you (singular or plural) and no others. This is clearly the case in 3 John 14b and possibly also in v. 8b. Likewise "our" in "our joy" in 1 John 1:4 can be understood in this way.

3. "We" as a reference to the sender and recipients of a Johannine letter, together

Appendix 5: We in the Johannine Letters

with those who belong to the same group as they do, i.e., the Johannine Christians. I have interpreted "we" in 2 John in this way, even though this usage can be expanded to include all those who confess Christ. A meaning like this also works well in 3 John 8ab and is the most typical referent in 1 John. If the letter is directed to all Johannine Christians, it becomes synonymous with alternative 2.

4. "We" as a reference to a we-group that does not include the letter's recipients. This is clearly obvious in 1 John 1:3. With many others, I interpret "we" in the letter's prologue as a small group of tradents and teachers within the Johannine community. See chapter 12, point 3. This sense also functions well for "we" in 3 John 9c, 10b, 12bc. The Elder or the Presbyter is thus the main figure in this group. This usage of "we" works well in 1 John 4:14, too, as also in 4:6bc. Compare also John 1:14, 16; 3:11; 21:24. "We" could also refer to other we-groups. Some understand "we" in the words "we have fellowship with him," "we are without sin," and "we have not sinned" (1 John 1:6, 8, 10) as referring to the secessionists mentioned in 1 John 2:18–19.

5. "We" as a reference to "we Christians." When the letter spread to other Christians and gradually became part of the Christian canon, it was usual to read "we" as "we Christians." A few commentators claim that 1 John was directed to Christians in general from the very beginning.

6. "We" as a reference to humanity in general. "We" in "if we say" (1 John 1:6, 8, 10) can be taken this way, thus with the meaning "if anyone says." It corresponds to "whoever says" (2:4, 6, 9) or "those who say" (4:20). The letter's context, however, suggests that most likely the meaning is "if anyone of us says" or "if anyone of you says."

In the course of the ongoing interpretation I will make precise my understanding of these many uses of "we" in the Johannine letters.

Appendix 6

Life, Eternal Life

The words "life" and "live" are among the most crucial concepts in the Johannine writings, in 1 John marked especially by their placement in the beginning and the end of the letter. Second John and 3 John lack these words. They are often used in an absolute meaning synonymous with "eternal life": in the Gospel thirty-six times, in 1 John thirteen times, and in Revelation seventeen times, i.e., sixty-six of a total 135 times in the New Testament. Eternal life stands out as the ultimate goal of God's salvation plan, the final purpose of God's love. The result of Christ's work of salvation can be summed up as eternal life, the greatest gift that faith in Jesus as Messiah, God's son, can give. Both the Gospel and the first letter aim at a deepened conscious faith that gives assurance of eternal life to those who believe (John 20:31; 1 John 5:13).

Statements about life and their distribution in 1 John are worth noting:

- 1:1–2. The letter is about the Life, about the message regarding the Life that was there from the beginning. The Life, eternal life, was with God but was revealed to some who now are able to bear witness to it and tell of it to others.

- 2:25. The eternal life that is now here is a fulfillment of something God long ago promised to give his own.

- 3:14–15. The love of the recipients for their brothers and sisters in the faith demonstrates that they have passed from death to life. Those who hate their fellow believers are classed with murderers; such persons do not have eternal life remaining within them.

- 4:9. God's love became visible when he sent his only son into the world so that human beings would live, i.e., have eternal life, through him.

- 5:11–12. God has testified concerning his son and said that eternal life is found in him. Through him God gives eternal life to humanity. Those who have the Son have eternal life; those who do not have the Son do not have eternal life.

5:13. What is said in the letter is intended to reinforce and deepen the letter's recipients' insight that they have eternal life now, when they believe in Jesus as Messiah, God's son.

5:20. Jesus Christ is the true God and eternal life.

Together the Gospel and the letter provide considerable information about this eternal life, but it is nonetheless difficult to truly nail down the meaning of the concept.

1. The purpose in sending God's son to the earth was to make eternal life available (John 12:50; 3:16; 10:10; 6:35; 10:28; 11:25; 14:6; 1 John 5:20; 4:14). See also John 6:27; 4:36; 12:25; 6:68; and 3:15.

2. Eternal life is something that is already present here and now (John 3:36; 6:47; 5:24; 1 John 5:12–13; 3:14). At the same time it is described as existing both before history (1 John 1:1–3) and after history (John 5:29; 14:19; 11:25). It has an eternal quality unrestricted by humanity's time on the earth.

3. Eternal life actually belongs to the divine world, connected to the divine persons. God alone has life in himself (John 5:26); he is the living Father (6:57); the Life existed with him (1 John 1:2). Through the Father the Son also bears life within himself; he is the bread of Life (John 6:51; 5:26; 6:57; 1:4; 1 John 5:20; 5:11). Eternal life can thus be described as a life of divine quality, i.e., as divine life.

4. God's great plan is that human beings are to share in this divine life. The entire act of salvation can be described as a way of providing eternal life (John 12:50; 3:16–17; 10:9–10; 12:47–50). The ultimate motive and reason is God's love and God's love alone (John 3:16; 1 John 4:9). It is God who takes the initiative (John 6:32–33; 12:50).

   This divine work of salvation is accomplished through the sending of the Son and especially through the Son's death (John 1:29, 36; 3:14–15; 10:11; 11:52; 12:24; 1 John 1:7; 2:2; 4:10). It is sin that separates humanity from God, but Jesus, the Lamb of God, takes away the sin of the world (John 1:29; 1 John 2:2).

   Humanity shares in this divine life through faith in Jesus as Messiah, God's son (1 John 5:12–13; John 3:14–16, 36; 11:25; see also John 1:49–50; 4:42; 6:68–69; 8:24; 10:24–30; 11:27, 42; 13:19; 16:27, 30; 17:8, 21). The point is made very clear in the purpose statements in John 20:31 and 1 John 5:13. This faith is also described as "to know" (1 John 4:16; 2 John 1) and is paralleled with "to see" (John 14:9, 17; 1 John 3:6; 4:14). The relationship with the revealed life, Jesus Messiah, God's son, is described with several verbs of perception in 1 John 1:1–3.

   Humanity also partakes of this divine life though a new birth, i.e., through God's giving birth to them anew (John 1:12–13; 3:3, 4, 1 John 4:7; 5:1, 4). Human beings become God's children (John 1:12; 1 John 3:1–2, 10; 5:2). See further Appendix 11, Born/begotten of God. This divine birth has been described as the central point for all of Johannine piety. Participation in divine life was presumably bestowed in baptism (John 3:5; see also 1 John 2:12–14; 5:1). Note that in the discourse on new birth in John 3, the concepts of God's kingdom and eternal life are combined.

5. Eternal life can be described as the sum-total of all God's salvation gifts. Some commentators—e.g., Johannes Lindblom in his 1914 work, *Das ewige Leben*—deny this and prefer to take the content of eternal life as divine immortality, nothing more. This viewpoint can arise from and be justified by setting the concept against a background of Hellenistic mystery religions. There is certainly a Hellenistic component in the development of the Johannine concept of eternal life. Yet at the same time we must likewise note that eternal life is bound up with a number of Jewish concepts such as sin, guilt, grace, reconciliation, and forgiveness, and that it cannot be explained without reference to faith in Jesus as Messiah, God's son, the incarnation, the crucifixion, and the resurrection. The concept of "eternal life" occurs in some later writings in the New Testament (with early Jewish elements, partly connected to the Diaspora situation: 2 Tim 1:10; 6:16; 2 Pet 1:4; Jas 1:18; 1 Pet 1:23; 2:2; 3:7; Titus 3; Heb 7:16).

Therefore, eternal life is primarily a divine life that belongs to God and to God's son. The ultimate goal of God's love is to make humanity sharers in this divine life. Humanity attains a part in this life through faith and knowledge and new birth. Eternal life is the fulfilling of God's promise to his people regarding the renewal of humanity and the world. According to the Johannine writings, this renewal has already begun with Jesus Christ and those who trust in him (1 John 2:8–11). And that brings us to taking up the question of the concept's background.

6. The idea of "eternal life" dominates the Johannine writings, but it is also found in other New Testament passages: a future gift or inheritance (Mark 9:43); "to enter into life" after the resurrection of the body (Mark 10:17, 30 par; Matt 25:46; Acts 13:46, 48; Rom 6:22–23; Titus 2:2; 3:7). In these texts, eternal life has an obviously Jewish background, and there is reason to claim the same thing for the Johannine usage, even though it has been further developed and colored by Greek ideas of immortality. Words like "enter into" and "inherit" are reminiscent of expressions used in connection with the Jewish concept of "God's kingdom." God's kingdom and eternal life approach one another in Luke 18:29–30 and in John 3:3, 5, 15–16. And as already mentioned, the concept of "eternal life" in the Johannine writings is surrounded by a number of terms central to Jewish thought.

The history of religions school at the beginning of the twentieth century insisted that the Johannine concept had its background in a Greek mystery religion (Johannes Lindblom, e.g.), and later researchers like Rudolf Bultmann and C. H. Dodd have argued for a profound Gnostic or platonic, hermetic influence. The situation was altered partly with the discoveries at Qumran. The Hebrew counterpart to eternal life occurs in just one place in the Old Testament, Dan 12:2. Reflection about life after death developed late in the Old Testament, Jewish milieu. 1QS 4:7 and CD 3:20 speak of a life "without end." The pious believers at Qumran clearly imagined that the messianic time would last forever upon the earth. At this period, the ideas of life after death developed in two directions: faith in a resurrection from the dead (Dan 12:2; 2 Macc 12:43–44) and faith in the immortality of the soul (Wis 3:2–4; 5:15). The Johannine texts appear to combine these two lines of thought.

This Johannine development has probably also been influenced by thoughts of the renewed covenant with God, which resulted in a new, close union with God. This new union with God gave humanity divine character and ability to do God's will. See Appendix 9, A renewed covenant. Eternal life in the Johannine texts is therefore combined with such ideas as knowing God, participating in God, and being born of God. God is in humanity and humanity is in God. God's *sperma*, God's spirit, God's anointing within human beings is what determines what they are to be and how they are to live.

Appendix 7

Expiation and Forgiveness

Words like "expiation" and "expiate" occur only a few times in the NRSV, and then only in the Old Testament and Apocrypha (Num 35:33; 1 Sam 3:14; 2 Sam 21:3; Isa 27:9; Hos 8:11; 1 Esd 9:20). The RSV's New Testament uses it in four places where older and more traditional translations (KJV, NASB) use "propitiation" and related terms (Rom 3:25; Heb 2:17; 1 John 2:2; 4:10, rendering occurrences of the Greek words *hilaskesthai, hilasmos* and *hilastērion*). The RSV's abandonment of "propitiation" for "expiation" in these texts sparked considerable debate at the time. Related terms in the general field of associated ideas include "placate," "conciliate," "do penance" and "recompense," etc. "Reconcile," "reconciliation," and "atone for," "atonement," are the traditional renderings of the original words we are dealing with here.

The results of Jesus' death are interpreted in the New Testament with images and concepts from various areas of human experience. Enemies become friends (reconciliation), slaves are set free (redemption), the afflicted and defenseless are rescued (salvation), debts are canceled (forgiveness), sins are taken away (sacrifice, purification, expiation, conversion), evil is vanquished (the struggle-victory motif), etc. Many people are surprised by the fact that the sacrifice and expiation motif occurs so seldom in the New Testament, presumably because they base their expectations on later theories of atonement that have been enshrined in countless hymns, sermons and inspirational books. There are no attempts in the New Testament to logically organize various concepts, even when several different ones occur in the same text, like images in a poem. Over the course of the church's history, systematic theology has devoted much comprehensive thinking to the meaning of Jesus' death. The results of this systemization can make it difficult to pay close attention to what is actually said in the specific biblical texts. I will attempt to restrict myself here to the Johannine letters.

The word "sacrifice" occurs in a number of modern translations of the word *hilasmos* in the two texts in 1 John where it occurs (2:2; 4:10): "atoning sacrifice" (NIV 1978, NRSV), "victime d'expiation" (TOB), "the sacrifice that takes away our sins" (Contemporary English Version 1995), and "the sacrifice that expiates our sins"

Appendix 7: Expiation and Forgiveness

(the Swedish Bibel 2000). Among the so-called Common Language translations, the TEV has the more general "the means by which our sins are forgiven," while *Die gute Nachricht* has a more detailed description: "weil er sich für uns geopfert hat, kann unsere Schuld . . . vergeben werden" (because he offered himself for us, our guilt can be forgiven). The TEV comes close to the rendering in the New English Bible (1961, 1970), especially supported by one of its translators, C. H. Dodd: "the remedy for the defilement of our sins."

This overview demonstrates that exegetes do not agree on how the word *hilasmos* should be interpreted. This is no doubt related to the lack of unity that prevails regarding the interpretation of Jesus' death. Martin Hengel, Helmut Merkel, and others represent a maximalist reading by speaking of a "substitutionary expiatory death" referred to in Jesus' words at the Last Supper (Mark 10:45; Rom 3:25; 1 John 2:2 and 4:10) and in expressions of the sort Jesus "died for us." This approach brings the cultic expiation in e.g. Leviticus 16 together with a non-cultic "expiation" in Isaiah 53. In fact Peter Stuhlmacher goes so far as to interpret statements about "reconciliation" in, e.g., Rom 5:10–11 and 2 Cor 5:18–19 with the help of the concept of "substitutionary expiatory death." Cilliers Breytenbach and others argue for a minimalist interpretation that on philological grounds clearly distinguishes between expiation and reconciliation/conciliation, between expiating and dying for someone, and between cultic expiation and substitutionary suffering. According to these scholars, the ideas of cultic expiation are assigned a very marginal role in the New Testament. Other scholars find themselves somewhere between these two extremes on the spectrum.

The word *hilasmos* belongs to the New Testament word group (*hilaskesthai, hilastērion, hileōs,* sometimes intensified with the preposition *ek*) that most clearly has to do with expiation and sacrifice. Lexica indicate two meanings: (1) to make someone positively disposed, propitiate, expiate, turn away someone's wrath, and (2) to take away, blot out.

In both cases, it is coupled with sacrifices of various kinds. The first meaning directs attention to the one who has been injured, the second to what brings division between the parties. For *hilasmos,* the first case represents a process whereby someone does something for God that makes God kindly disposed toward him or her, and the second case an act that removes the sin, a means through which the sins are forgiven. For the New Testament usage, most interpreters choose the latter alternative, i.e., they more generally prefer the sense of a person's being united with God by the removal of sin. Louw and Nida are very decisive in their lexicon: *Hilasmos*—like *hilastērion* in Rom 3:25—refers to a means of forgiveness and not a means of expiation. This does not imply that God cannot be the object in the few places of the New Testament where these words occur. The question, however, is whether either meaning is found in texts referring to concrete sacrifices. The question is whether the author of 1 John is thinking about concrete acts of sacrifice or whether he only uses the sacrificial terminology in a more general way.

Appendix 7: Expiation and Forgiveness

The use of the word *paraklētos* ("intercessor," "advocate," "defender") in the immediate context (1 John 2:1) suggests that the person who has sinned is in bad standing with God. That person needs help. In contemporary Judaism, the high priest was the great intercessor on the Day of Atonement. Intercession can blot out sin. Likewise, even *hilasmos* in v. 2 can be read against the background of the Day of Atonement (in Greek, *hē hēmera tou hilasmou*). Thus, the concepts in 1 John 2:1–2 resemble those in Rom 3:25 and in Hebrews, and one can claim that there a context of concrete sacrifice does lie in the background. In the rituals of the Day of Atonement there were both propitiation of God and reconciliation between God and people and between people and other people. But the question is which element in this possible background is to be taken into account in the interpretation of 1 John.

Even if there might be a nuance of expiation in the sacrifice term used in 1 John 2:2 and 4:10, it has precious little support from the rest of the letter. The sacrifice in 4:10 is nothing other than an expression for God's love. Any hint of God's wrath against sin is lacking altogether in the context. For the rest, the following texts are of interest:

1:7 The blood of Jesus his Son cleanses us from all sin.

1:9 [God] is faithful and just and will forgive us our sins and cleanse us from all unrighteousness.

2:12 Your sins are forgiven on account of his name.

3:5 He [Jesus Christ, the son of God] was revealed to take away sins.

3:16 He [Jesus Christ, the son of God] laid down his life for us.

4:14 The Father has sent his Son as the Savior of the world.

5:6 This [God's son] is the one who came by water and blood, Jesus Christ, not with the water only but with the water and the blood.

The last and first of these texts demonstrate that Jesus' death, probably depicted as a sacrifice by the word "blood," was fundamental for the author's way of thinking. Jesus' act of salvation could not be expressed without clearly including his death. The action of God and Jesus is described with several verbs: cleanse from sin (twice), forgive sins (twice), take the sins away, give his life for, save. The formulation in 1 John 1:9 clearly goes back to a covenant rationale. The words in 1 John 3:5 are reminiscent of John 1:29: "Behold, the Lamb of God who takes away the sin of the world!" Jesus is described in several ways in the Gospel as the Pascal lamb that is slaughtered. Compare "the Lamb that was slaughtered" in the book of Revelation. But in 1 John there is no hint of how this act of forgiveness takes place. The decisive thing is that this act resulted in a renewed covenant—an effect indicated throughout the letter by a number of expressions for a new fellowship with God and with one another. Jesus' manner of being and of living, including his death, is presented as model for those who believe in him. Fellowship with God and with one another is what dominates the letter and what influences the interpretation of Jesus' death as well.

Appendix 7: Expiation and Forgiveness

In Appendix 9, A renewed covenant, I have argued that texts like Jeremiah 31 and Ezek 36 were important at an early stage of interpreting what Jesus as Messiah, God's son, implied for the recipients of the letter and for all humanity. Ideas of a renewed covenant seem to me better suited than the Jewish festival of atonement to account for the interpretation of Jesus' death in 1 John. The new covenant in Jeremiah 31 becomes a reality through an intervention of God to blot out sin: "for I will forgive their iniquity, and remember their sin no more" (Jer 31:34). In the first portion of this text, the Septuagint has "I shall be gracious toward (*hileōs esomai*) their sins," which can be translated naturally with "forgive." The Hebrew text has the usual word for "forgive." *Hilasmos* also renders the normal Hebrew word for "forgive" in Dan 9:9 (Theodotion); Ps 130:4; and Neh 9:17. The NRSV translates Ps 130:4 as "there is forgiveness with you." "Forgiveness" would also be a possible translation of *hilasmos* in 1 John 2:2. Without any mention of sacrifice, these passages strongly emphasize that God's blotting out of sin leads to a completely new fellowship with God. This corresponds to "the new covenant in my blood" in Luke 22:20 and 1 Cor 11:25. Indeed the covenant at Sinai was already an answer to the prayer, "Pardon our iniquity and our sin, and take us for your inheritance" (Exod 34:9–10). Even Moses was a great intercessor for his people when God renewed the covenant at Sinai (Exod 34).

There are reasons for using "sacrifice" in translations of *hilasmos* in 1 John, but it is difficult to be convinced that it also implies a nuance of expiation, understood as including the placating of God. The word "reconciliation," then—or even (with reference to the passages mentioned above) the word "forgiveness"—is to be preferred, since either one is more obviously compatible with a meaning in which a broken fellowship is healed.

APPENDIX 8

He: God, Jesus, or Both

PRONOUNS FUNCTION TO SUBSTITUTE for other words or to refer to other words, and thus they become an important means of creating coherence in a text. Through the references they make, they establish a firm underlying structure. "She," "hers," and "her," e.g., usually refer to one and the same person in a paragraph or in a longer text, and as a rule it is not particularly difficult to know what a given pronoun is referring to. But this is not the case with 1 John. There it is not always easy to perceive the reference, and for the reader who wants to know whether "he" refers to God or to Jesus or to both, this uncertainty is frequently frustrating.

In 1 John personal pronouns are used very often. This might perhaps be encouraged by the way Jews do not use the name of God, but prefer instead a variety of circumlocutions for God, among them the pronoun "he." In an earlier appendix, I have analyzed potential references of the word "we." See Appendix 5, We in the Johannine letters. Here we need to take up the words "he," "his," and "him." The use of pronouns in 1 John 2:3-6; 2:28—3:3; and 3:21-24 particularly exhausts the patience of interpreters when they attempt to make sense of the author's thoughts.

The immediate context usually gives an indication of whether it is God or Jesus who is in view. "He" in 1 John 1:5-6; 3:21-22; 4:10, 15, 19; and 5:2-3 refers to God. "He" in 2:2; 3:5, 16; and 4:9 refers to Jesus. Word combinations are also helpful in a Johannine context, so that the reader thinks of God with the phrases "his son," "born of him," "his seed," "the boldness that we have in him," and "what we ask of him," while it is natural to substitute Jesus into expressions like "that we have heard from him," "for his name's sake," and "his coming."

Thus language usage in the Johannine texts—or sometimes in other texts in the New Testament—often provides the necessary information. Yet uncertainty prevails in many passages. To abide in Jesus and to abide in God are both Johannine formulations. This creates problems with expressions like "are in him" and "abide in him" in 1 John 2:5-6. The Gospel frequently speaks of Jesus' commandment, but the letters seem more concerned with God's commandment. The commandment from the

Appendix 8: He: God, Jesus, or Both

Father is expressly mentioned in 2 John 4. The immediate context in 1 John 5:2 and 3:22 gives the meaning of God's commandment. The question then is whether it is still God who is in view in what follows in 1 John 5:3 and in 3:23–24. And how should "know him" and "his commandment/word" in 1 John 2:3–5 be understood? Is the author speaking of God's commandment or of Jesus' commandment in 1 John 2:7–8? Here the answer is sometimes a both-and. It is important for the author to see God and Jesus together. Both fit into phrases such as "know God/Jesus," "abide in the Father/the Son," and "have the Father/the Son." A chief point in the letters of John is that one cannot think about God without simultaneously thinking about Jesus Messiah, God's son, and vice versa.

Still, the author sometimes uses a special pronoun for referring to Jesus, namely, the word *ekeinos,* a demonstrative pronoun that usually points to someone or something located at a certain distance: that one, that, he. It is used in a normal way in 1 John 5:16, but otherwise it refers to Jesus Messiah, the son of God (1 John 2:6; 3:3, 5, 7; 4:17). This is clear both from what is said in these clauses and from the context. To judge from the use of verb tenses, both the earthly Jesus and God's son before and after Jesus' earthly ministry are in view. Four times the word occurs in sentences where Jesus is presented as a model: "as Jesus was and is." 1 John 3:5 deals with Jesus becoming a human being—the corresponding clause in 3:8 has "God's son" as subject—and 3:16 deals with Jesus' death. It is reasonable to assume that this was a special way of speaking among the recipients of the letter. The Gospel, however, uses *ekeinos* in a more usual way, often of God, Jesus, or the Spirit, with the possible exception of John 19:35.

We have no good explanation for this usage in 1 John. The Pythagoreans could use *ekeinos* of their deceased master, and Jewish leaders spitefully referred to Jesus as *ekeinos* (according to John 7:11; 9:28; 19:21). In later Jewish writings the phrase "that man" referred to Jesus. Did the Johannine Christians express their reverence for the divine Jesus in this way? Is this usage dependent on the Jews' habit of using circumlocutions for God, including "he"? Or was it a reference to someone whom only the little group knew, a kind of code name? The answer is that we do not know.

When the author of 1 John uses *houtos,* another demonstrative pronoun meaning this/this one, he has in mind as a rule a general "he" (1 John 2:4, 5, 22), but in 1 John 5:6 it quite clearly refers to Jesus, who has just been designated as God's son. The question is whether this applies as well later on in 1 John 5:20. I find good reasons for that in my interpretation. Jesus Christ is the true God and eternal life. This closeness between God and Jesus in the letter has especially influenced the author's use of "he," "his," and "him."

For the troublesome usage in 1 John 2:3–6; 2:28—3:3; and 3:21–24, I refer the reader to the Interpretations, and for the last named passage also to the Analysis of 1 John 2:3–11, point 2. For 1 John 2:3–6, I have given reasons for choosing God as the reference as far as the change at v. 6 with the use of *ekeinos;* thus know God, obey God's commandment, know God, obey God's commandment, keep God's word, be

Appendix 8: He: God, Jesus, or Both

in God, abide in God, as Jesus lived. A corresponding rationale for 1 John 2:18—3:3 leads to a similar result: abide in Christ, Christ reveals himself, Christ's coming, Christ is righteous, born of God the Father, God's children, know God, God's children, become like God, see God as God is, hope in God, as Christ is pure.

These sections, then, become profoundly God-oriented. But the author can hardly imagine God in relation with human beings without including Jesus Christ. This is most noticeable in 1 John 2:28—3:3. The troubling uncertainty that modern interpreters experience with regard to the use of "he," "his," and "him" in 1 John is caused by a speech pattern that uses certain firm formulas, well known to the Johannine Christians, and by the very fact that the Father and the Son are one, expressed in the letter most clearly with the words, "He is the true God and eternal life" (1 John 5:20 NRSV).

Appendix 9

A Renewed Covenant

Within priestly circles in Palestine during the second century BCE there developed an idea that God renewed his covenant annually. This covenant renewal was connected with the Festival of Weeks/Pentecost, in Hebrew *Shavuot*. The word means weeks. The festival was celebrated seven weeks after Passover. If we change a vowel in the word *Shavuot* we get the meaning "oaths." Changing the Festival of Weeks to the Festival of Oaths can perhaps explain the connection to the covenant.

According to the book of *Jubilees*—remains of fourteen mss of this book have been found at Qumran—there is only one covenant between God and his elect, an everlasting covenant. Already at the creation God separated unto himself a people who would keep the Sabbath. "They shall be my people and I will be their God" (*Jub.* 2:19–20). If the covenant is eternal, then there is no need of a new covenant, but there is indeed need of renewals of the covenant. In the heavenly tablets it is written that the people are to celebrate the feast of weeks "to renew the covenant every year" (*Jub.* 6:17). From time to time the Lord needed to create "in them a holy spirit" and to cleanse them by taking their sins away, and the people would respond with oaths and promises, with sacrifices and festivals. In this way it becomes clear, as the writer says, "that these are my children and I am their Father in uprightness and righteousness, and that I love them" (*Jub.* 1:25).

An annual renewal of the covenant during the Festival of Weeks seems also to have been the practice at Qumran. A regulation for a covenant ceremony is found in 1QS 1:16—3:12. After giving introductory praise to the God of salvation and truth, the priests tell of the marvelous works that God has done toward Israel in his righteousness, grace, and mercy, and the Levites count up all of Israel's sins and transgressions. All the people confess their sins and God, who is true and righteous, forgives them in his grace and mercy. Those who belong to God are blessed; those who belong to Belial are cursed. Finally, too, anyone is cursed who enters into the covenant with "the idols of his heart," something described as a sin leading to a fall. Cf. Ezek 14:4, 7. In a comment it is emphasized that God alone is the one who redeems and purifies those who do his will. The renewal of the covenant leads to "a Community of the truth," "a holy congregation," "sons of the everlasting Company," and those who belong to this community are characterized by goodness, humility, love, mercy and uprightness toward one another. In the Damascus Document, "the new covenant" is mentioned four times, and is most readily understood as a renewed covenant (CD 6:17–19; 8:21; 19:33–35; 20:11–12). This covenant theology is constitutive for the Qumran community's self-understanding and distinguishes the group from other Jewish communities. These ideas of the covenant have their point of origin in the covenant at Sinai (Exod 19–24). Already then, at Sinai, the covenant needed to be renewed, when the people of Israel apostatized and began to worship idols (Exod 32–34). As intercessor for his people, Moses sought God's face, and at last God presented himself:

> The LORD, the LORD, a God merciful and gracious, slow to anger, and abounding in steadfast love and faithfulness, keeping steadfast love for the thousandth generation, forgiving iniquity and transgression and sin, yet by no means clearing the guilty, but visiting the iniquity of the parents upon the children and the children's children, to the third and the fourth generation. (Exod 34:6–7)

There is a clear duality in this picture of God: God forgives and God punishes. In an earlier form this "grace formula" contained a retributive rationale with a sharp division between those who love God and keep his commandments and those who hate God (Deut 5:9–10; 7:9–10). In the later development of the formula (Joel 2: 13; Jonah 4:2; Ps 86:15; 103:8; 145:8–9; Neh 9:17), two things happen. For one, the God of retribution, revenge, wrath, and jealousy disappears, leaving only the God of love and forgiveness. And secondly, the grace of God now embraces all people, not just the people of Israel. Eventually we hear only the liturgical refrain, "O give thanks to the Lord, for he is good, for his steadfast love endures forever" (Psalm 136). The Hebrew word for "steadfast love," *ḥesed*, can also be rendered "faithfulness to the covenant," or simply "grace."

The book of *Jubilees* and the Qumran writings build upon these covenant texts, but not on Jer 31—if we ignore the term "a new covenant"—and certainly not on Ezek 36. The prophets Jeremiah and Ezekiel, both of priestly stock, describe in these chapters a renewal of the fellowship with God that has certain correspondences in 1 John.

> The days are surely coming, says the LORD, when I will make a new (*kainos*) covenant with the house of Israel and the house of Judah . . . I will put my law within them (*eis tēn dianoian autōn*), and I will write it on their hearts; and I will be their God, and they shall be my people. No longer shall they teach (*didaskein*) one another, or say to each other (*adelphos*), "Know (*ginōskein*) the LORD," for they shall all (*pantes*) know (*oida*) me, from the least of them to the greatest, says the LORD; for I will forgive (*hileōs einai*) their iniquity (*adikiai*), and remember their sin (*hamartiai*) no more. (Jer 31:31–34)

Appendix 9: A Renewed Covenant

I have inserted a few words into the text from the Greek translation because they have corresponding terms in the text of the letter. This biblical text is conspicuous by its absence in Jewish texts from the New Testament period, perhaps because among Jewish leaders there was a fear of renewal movements. Jer 31 is cited in Heb 8:8–12 (cf. 10:16–17), and the concept of "new covenant" is used in Luke 22:20; 1 Cor 11:25; and Heb 9:15. See also 2 Cor 3:3–18. According to Ezek 36:25–28, God says this:

> I will sprinkle clean water upon you, and you shall be clean from all your uncleannesses, and from all your idols (*eidola*) I will cleanse (*katharizein*) you. A new (*kainos*) heart I will give you, and a new (*kainos*) spirit I will put within you; and I will remove from your body the heart of stone and give you a heart of flesh. I will put my spirit within you (*didonai en hymin*), and make you follow (*poreuesthai*) my statutes and be careful to observe my ordinances. Then you shall live in the land that I gave to your ancestors; and you shall be my people, and I will be your God.

It is emphatically stated that the reason for this action on God's part is God himself, God's holy name (Ezek 36:22–23). In Jer 31:2–3 reference is made to God's grace and God's love. According to Ezek 36:24, God will also at this time gather in his people, an idea found in John 11:51–52 (see also John 4:36), but not in 1 John.

I have primarily appealed here to texts from Jer 31 and Ezek 36 as an important background for a reading of 1 John. But it must be added that these passages should be seen as a part of God's promises regarding an eschatological covenant (Isa 54:9–10; 55:3; 59:20; 61:8; Jer 32:37–41; Ezek 16:59–63; 34:24–29; 37:26–27). In the future, God will establish a "covenant of peace" and an "everlasting covenant" with his people, a covenant that cannot be broken, since both the conditions and the promises are rooted in God's action. God himself has initiated this covenant, because the people could not meet the conditions in the old covenant. In the eschatological covenant God's entire people will be able to follow his will. It will be the final version and the climax of all covenants. The relationship with God develops and changes in a fundamental way, precisely in that God is now to be found in human hearts in the form of his Spirit and his law. This enables his people to bring to reality what God wants for them.

With these concepts as a background, we can read 1 John and think about what it was "that was there from the beginning." Jews confessed Jesus as Messiah, God's son. What were the consequences of their doing so? Some clearly regarded Jesus' coming into the world and his ministry in the world as a renewal of God's covenant with his people. This is obvious from the introduction to 1 Peter, from Hebrews, from the expression "the new covenant in my blood" in Luke 22 and 1 Corinthians 11, from the material discernable behind Acts 2, as well as from John 20 and the structure of John 1:19—4:54. In 1 John it can be seen clearly in the following passages:

> 5:20. God's son has given the Jesus-believers understanding (*dianoia*) so that they may know (*ginōskein*) the True One. To "know him," i.e., God, and keep his

Appendix 9: A Renewed Covenant

commandments is the main theme in 1 John 2:3–11. See also 1 John 2:14 and 4:6–8. In a social context where God's name is not used it is natural to say merely "him" or "he" or "his." To know God becomes structurally parallel to having fellowship with God (1 John 1:6—2:2).

2:20. All have insight (*pantes, oida*), all know (*oida*) the truth. They no longer need anyone to teach (*didaskein*) them (1 John 2:27). And the reason is that they have an anointing that gives them insight, an expression reminiscent of being given "understanding so that you may know the True One" (1 John 5:20).

3:24. God abides in them and they abide in God. This two-part reciprocal description of the fellowship with God occurs in several forms in the letter (1 John 4:13, 15, 16) and has probably been developed from the typical covenant formula: "I will be their God and they will be my people." See Appendix 15, God in them and they in God.

1:9. God is faithful and just to forgive sins (*hamartias*) and to cleanse from all unrighteousness (*adikia*). One might possibly have expected words like "merciful and gracious," but God's faithfulness and righteousness are part of the covenant formulations in Exod 34:6–7 (LXX) and are especially obvious in, e.g., the renewal ritual in 1QS. See also Appendix 7, Expiation and forgiveness.

2:7–8. A new (*kainos*) commandment, where "new" means new in its essence, qualitatively new, and is explained in the text as what was manifested in Jesus, in the Jesus-believers, and through the images of the darkness that is passing away because the light is already shining. The absence of quotations and exact linguistic correspondences implies that the covenant renewal belonged to a living tradition among these Jesus-believing Jews. It was natural for them to connect the coming of the Messiah with a renewal of the covenant. A background of this sort can also throw light on a number of other expressions in 1 John.

Being born of God, being children of God (1 John 2:29; 3:1–2, 9, etc.). In Jewish perspective, the covenant at Sinai was the great day of Israel's birth. It was then that God became their Father and they became his children, a theme that recurs in many covenant texts. The union with God is reinforced in the letter by the concept of being born of God. See Appendix 11, Begotten/born of God. Eventually they will become like God.

Having eternal life, i.e., having a part in divine life, can also be seen as an intensification of the fellowship with God that the covenant renewal leads to (1 John 1:1–2; 3:16, etc.). See Appendix 6, Life, eternal life. Becoming divine in this way is described as a fulfillment of what God has promised (1 John 2:25).

They have God (1 John 2:23 etc.), a peculiar expression that is most readily explained on the basis of a covenant relationship.

God gave them of his spirit (1 John 3:24; 4:13), something that results in a new fellowship with God. Ezek 36 and Jeremiah 31 refer to God's spirit and God's law.

Beloved (1 John 2:7 etc.). The covenant with God is an outflow of God's love for Israel. The children of Israel are God's beloved in a special way. See the notes "the beloved" and "Beloved" on 3 John 1–2.

God's love, God first loved them (1 John 2:5 etc.; 4:7–10 etc.). The concept of "love" in the letter summarizes the characteristics of God according to the seven-fold "grace formula" in the Old Testament. See above. "Grace and truth came through Jesus Christ," according to John 1:17. In 1 John this is expressed with "love and truth." The reason for the covenant is always God's grace (*ḥesed*).

Cleansing, forgiveness, atonement, taking away of sins are important acts of God in covenant renewal texts (1 John 1:7, 9; 2:12; 3:5 etc.). God's forgiveness and salvation can embrace all humanity even here (1 John 2:2; 4:9, 14). Public confession of sins also belongs to this semantic field (1 John 1:9).

Intercessor, intercession that cleanses from sin (1 John 2:1; 5:16) may very well have as a model Moses at the renewal of the covenant (Exod 34) and does not need to be seen as part of the ritual of the Day of Atonement.

They should love one another (1 John 3:11 etc.), an expression for how God's covenant binds God's people together into a solidified unity, something that is reinforced at the renewal of the covenant (1QS 2:24–25). The use of the word "brother/brothers" (1 John 2:9; 3:14; 5:16 etc.) can also been seen from this perspective of belonging. The central theme of the letter, to love one another, is a constitutive element of the new covenant. See also Heb 10:15–25.

To the elect lady (2 John 1). The covenant is sometimes described in terms of marriage. See further the note on and Interpretation of 2 John 1.

To keep God's commandments, a phrase that occurs frequently in 1 John, has the covenant as a natural framework. Even using the word "commandment" (*entolē*; 1 John 3:23) to refer to the central point in this renewed fellowship with God can be explained from a covenant perspective.

No one has seen God, a completely unexpected assertion, which occurs in 1 John 4:12 in order then to be used in the argumentation in 4:20, alludes to Moses as well, in Exod 34.

To love or to hate (one's brother) (1 John 2:9 etc.) has a meaning similar to that of love or hate in the covenant texts in Deuteronomy.

People sorted into children of God and children of the Devil in 1 John 3:10 correspond to those foreordained to God and those foreordained to Belial in 1QS 2:2, 5.

There is in him no cause for stumbling (1 John 2:10), i.e., something that leads a person to fall away from God. The expression is also found in 1QS 2:12, where it is further qualified as "the stumbling block of his sin," most readily interpreted as a sin that leads him to a fall. Cf. the "sin that is mortal" in 1 John 5:14–17.

Keep yourselves from idols (1 John 5:21). This highly unexpected ending to the letter can be most easily explained on the basis of ideas of a renewed covenant. When God renewed the covenant in Exod 34, the background was the fact that the people had begun to worship idols. Idols constitute the greatest danger for those who have entered into covenant with God. They are mentioned also in the comment on the first commandment (Exod 20:4–5; Deut 5:8–9). The stumbling block in 1QS 2:12 is also connected to the worship of "idols." The major risk contemplated in the letter is that of falling away from the God who now has renewed the covenant through Jesus Messiah, God's son. The cause of stumbling and the mortal sin get their content from what is related in 1 John 2:18–27.

A common objection to this reading of the Johannine letters on the basis of a covenant model is the absence of explicitly covenantal language. The word "covenant" does not occur, relevant Old Testament passages are not cited, and typical covenantal formulations are lacking. These observations are largely correct, but they lose their validity, in my view, if we concentrate our attention on renewals of the covenant within Judaism around the beginning of our era, if we assume that the Jesus-believing Jews who bore the Johannine tradition lived with renewal ideas, and if we allow for the fact that to a considerable degree we are dealing with a Greek-speaking milieu. Ideas of covenant are indeed there, though appearing in other, more general forms.

There are many covenants and agreements in the Old Testament. The most important of them are those established with Abraham and through Moses. The first one places the emphasis on the promises in the covenant, the other on the conditions. In New Testament times they were often combined into one covenant. According to Exod 19–24 and the many provisions and laws that follow, God's covenant with his people has four clear consequences:

1. A group of people are specially chosen by God. They are to be a holy people, a kingdom of priests. God's treasured possession above all other peoples, or as it is rendered in the targums: "a beloved people," which can of course mean both that they are beloved and that they love one another.

2. Not only did the people cleanse themselves in preparation for their meeting with God at Sinai, but God also cleansed his people. This is how we can interpret the act of sacrifice in Exod 24, where blood is sprinkled on the people. See the use of Exod 19–24 in 1 Pet 1:1—2:10. God institutes a number of different sacrifices, and not least of all the Day of Atonement, when the high priest atones for the people's sins through his sacrifice.

3. God is especially present among his people through the tabernacle and through the law. YHWH becomes their God and they become YHWH's people.

4. These people are given a number of commandments that they are to learn and obey. Of considerable note is the fact that the covenant of Moses is strongly conditional: "If you obey my voice and keep my covenant, you shall be . . . "

In a renewed eschatological covenant, these effects of the covenant are powerfully intensified: God forgives them. This is the basis for the renewal. And sacrifices are no longer mentioned here. God becomes even more present among his people through his Spirit and his law in their inner being. They know God. They no longer require instruction. They receive a capacity to obey God's commandment. The first point above can perhaps also be seen as a background to the dualistic language found in some Qumran texts and in the Johannine writings. The further on in time we come, the clearer it appears that everything has its beginning and end in God's unconditional love.

Appendix 10

What You Heard from the Beginning

THE ARGUMENTATION IN 1 John to a significant degree is built on references to older traditions and earlier formulations within the Johannine community. "*You know* that Jesus Christ, the son of God, was revealed to take away sins and that there is no sin in him." Therefore: the one who remains in him does not sin (1 John 3:6). "*You know* that Jesus Christ, the son of God, gave his life for us." Therefore: you must also give your life for the brothers (1 John 3:16). "Take away sins" in 1 John 3:6 is reminiscent of John 1:29, and the Johannine formulation "gave his life for us" occurs as well in John 10:11, 15; 15:13. Many individual stylistic features remind us that the entire Johannine production is part of a long interpretational process, and largely oral, it may be presumed.

The traditions that the author refers to are located in time through expressions like "what you heard from the beginning." What the argument builds itself on belongs to the first stage in the history of the letter's recipients. The following statements can be noted:

1 John 2:24 "what you heard from the beginning" (twice).

1 John 3:11 "the message that you heard from the beginning."

1 John 2:7 "the old commandment/message that you had from the beginning."

2 John 5 "The commandment/message that we had from the beginning."

2 John 7 "the commandment/message that you heard from the beginning."

It is interesting to note that "the commandment" (*entolē*) in 1 John 2:7 is identified with "the word (*logos*) that you heard." Is "the word" or "God's word" (1 John 1:1, 10; 2:5, 14) the same as the divine revelation that was there from the beginning, synonymous to a high degree with the concept "truth" in the Johannine letters? See the Analysis for 1 John 2:3–11, point 2, and Appendix 3, The truth. This definition also gives the word *entolē* a broader meaning of message (law = teaching). This makes the use of *entolē* in the letter interesting, too (1 John 2:7–8; 4:21); and especially interesting is 1 John 3:23: "And this is his commandment/message: We must believe in the name of his son, Jesus Christ, and we must love one another, as he gave us commandment."

Appendix 10: What You Heard from the Beginning

To these texts regarding the foundational tradition in the life of the letter's recipients we can also add:

1 John 1:1–3 "what was there from the beginning."

1 John 1:5 "the message that we heard from him."

1 John 2:13–14 "he who was there from the beginning."

1 John 2:18 "as you heard."

1 John 4:3 "as you have heard."

1 John 5:9–11 "God's testimony regarding his son" (five times).

With these texts there is built up within the letter a content-based connection among God's word, God's commandment, the message that you heard from the beginning, and the testimony of God (*logos*, *entolē*, *angelia*, and *martyria*). Raymond Brown has shown, especially with reference to 1 John 1:5—2:2, the thematic similarities that exist with early baptism and baptismal instruction: light and darkness, truth and lie, the two ways, confession of sin, cleansing, forgiveness, reconciliation, and fellowship. He refers to the beginning of the Community Rule, which deals with entrance into the Qumran community—in my view a form of renewed covenant—and to Acts 26:18; Col 1:13; Eph 5:6–11; Heb 10:19–23; 1 Pet 1:1—2:10; *Didache* 7 and the *Epistle of Barnabas* 18.

How central this early tradition is for the entire argument is shown by the letter as a whole and not least by the introduction and 1 John 2:24. The author stands as a link back to this tradition, the content of which is described as "eternal life" and "fellowship with the Father and with his son, Jesus the messiah." According to all three letters, everything depends on him and the tradition he stands for.

What important features, then, constituted this tradition? The formulations in the letter embrace at least the following:

1. Jesus is the messiah, the son of God. God has sent him to the world. He has appeared in the form of a living human being, all the way from birth up to and including death.

2. Jesus' death is particularly emphasized as what takes sins away and creates a new fellowship with God. It is described in the letter in many different ways.

3. They now know God and through Jesus the messiah, the son of God, they are united with him. They no longer need anyone to teach them.

4. They have received a share of God's spirit, been anointed by the Holy One.

5. They participate here and now in divine life.

6. Jesus' life is a model for all who believe in him. With various formulations Jesus is described as righteous, pure, etc.

7. An important part of the new message is that they must love one another.

Appendix 10: What You Heard from the Beginning

8. An antimessiah is to come.
9. God has renewed his covenant through his son/Messiah/Jesus. In every case it is this idea that best binds together the various elements found in "what you heard from the beginning." See further Appendix 9, A renewed covenant.

Appendix 11

Begotten/Born of God

IN NINE PASSAGES IN the section 1 John 2:28—3:10 and later in the letter the author mentions the subject of being born of God. See the overview below. The word used in the original, *gennan*, can mean both "beget" (with a man as the agent) and "bear" (with a woman as the agent). In profane Greek, the first of these meanings is the more common one and it also occurs in the many biblical genealogies in which a father begets/becomes father to his sons. The word occurs 18 times in the Gospel of John and ten times in 1 John. It is used in the passive (be born), often followed by the preposition "from/of" (*ek*), which indicates the origin: of God, of the spirit, of the flesh. In contemporary English, the term "beget" can carry an antiquated or overly formal tone, which has influenced the more recent translations to use the rendering "born of." God is mentioned explicitly eight times in this phrase—"begotten/born of God—but Christ never. Related to this expression is the idea of God's seed (*sperma*) in the believers (1 John 3:9), and the Johannine concept "children." The formulation with God's *sperma* points to the fact that we are dealing with a metaphorical use of the idea of divine begetting. Thus we are not dealing with a feminine image of God, which the expression "born of" could imply.

The words "be born of him," i.e., of God, occur for the first time in the letter at the beginning of 1 John 2:28—3:10, in v. 29. They recur at the end (3:9), and in both instances they are coupled with the concept "God's children." It is a unique formulation, found only in the following passages in Johannine literature:

- Everyone who does righteousness is born of him (1 John 2:29).
- No one who is born of God commits sin (1 John 3:9).
- He cannot sin because he is born of God (1 John 3:9).
- Everyone who loves is born of God and loves God (1 John 4:7).
- Everyone who believes that Jesus is the Messiah is born of God (1 John 5:1).
- All that is born of God overcomes the world (1 John 5:4).

Appendix 11: Begotten/Born of God

- No one who is born of God commits sin (1 John 5:18).
- What is born of the flesh is flesh, and what is born of the spirit it spirit (John 3:6).
- So it is with everyone who is born of the Spirit (John 3:8).

All these texts use the perfect tense: what took place earlier has ongoing effect. The origin determines existence and life-style expectations. There are additional texts with the aorist tense and one that resembles a proverb or a general principle:

- Those who were born not of blood or of the will of the flesh or the will of man, but of God (John 1:13).
- No one who has not been born from above can see the kingdom of God (John 3:3).
- No one who has not been born of water and the spirit can enter the kingdom of God (John 3:5).
- You must be born from above (John 3:7).
- The one who was born of God protects them (1 John 5:18).
- Everyone who loves the one who begat loves also the one begotten of him (1 John 5:1).

The last example could probably be formulated as a proverb: Whoever loves a father also loves the father's children. Johannine maxims often have a logical form that does not always correspond with reality, but they make their point nonetheless. And as a rule they also contain elements suggesting that they were formulated with a view to their application to the Johannine context. The saying in 1 John 5:1, similar to the use of the word "seed," *sperma*, in 1 John 3:9, shows that the image of begetting corresponds to reality.

To these examples of being "born of God" we should also add two other related expressions in the Johannine writings: "to be children of God" (*tekna theou*; 1 John 3:1–2, 10; 5:2; John 1:12; 11:52) and the somewhat more general "to be of God" (*einai ek tou theou*). See the note "comes not from the father but from the world" at 1 John 2:16. The latter expression is often translated as "to be of God," "to belong to God," "to come from God," or "to be children of God." Taken as a whole, these formulations express a very close relationship between God and humanity, which in other texts can be expressed with "to know God" or with an immanence-formula such as "God is in them and they are in God." See Appendix 15, God in them and they in God. The divine begetting is a kind of character determination for the Jesus believers, which indicates both their status and their way of life. The emphasis is not on how the begetting takes place, but on its effect in the here and now. What other biblical texts refer to as a future relationship the Johannine texts present as something already realized. The divine begetting belongs to the last hour and is therefore seen as entailed in the final struggle between God and the devil. The Elder is completely convinced

Appendix 11: Begotten/Born of God

that everything born of God will overcome (1 John 5:4; 4:4). On the basis of John 3, of other New Testament texts regarding new birth, and of the role played in the letter by "what was there from the beginning," it is probable that the divine begetting took place when the letter's recipients came to faith and were baptized, even though it does not say so. In this way, the new birth is also connected to God's spirit, which according to Ezek 36 would be the driving force and guiding principle for the way God's people should live in the renewed covenant.

There is yet more to be said about the expression "children of God." To judge by later Christian parlance, it is remarkably uncommon in the New Testament. It is used only in 1 John 3:1–2, 10; 5:2; John 1:12; 11:52; Rom 8:16–17; 9:7–8; and Phil 2:15. Paul speaks interchangeably of the children of God and the sons of God and mostly with reference to the future, i.e., to the great transformation that happens at Christ's return and the end of the age. Behind his formulations lie the idea of adoption and the associated right of inheritance. The few statements regarding the sons of God in the synoptic Gospels—Matt 5:9, 45; Luke 6:35; 20:36—are likewise oriented toward the future.

With John, the background notion is different, namely the idea of a divine begetting; the children of God are, as mentioned, something that people already are here and now (1 John 3:1). In this way, the meaning of "God's children" is deepened and concretized, and humanity's status comes nearer to Jesus Christ. The author also says, with reference to the Day of Judgment, that as Christ is, so are the readers in this world (1 John 4:17). In 1 John 5:18, Jesus himself is placed side by side with the believers through the description of Jesus as "the one who was born of God." See the note on that passage. On the other hand, the word "son" in the Johannine writings is reserved for Jesus.

The background of these references to God's children is to be found with all likelihood in the Old Testament. The people of Israel as a whole are spoken of there as God's son, or as God's sons and daughters, expressions that could be applied in the post-exilic period to individual Israelites as well (Exod 4:22; Hos 11:1; Jer 31:9, 20: Deut 32:19; *Jub.* 2:20). According to this tradition, which gained strength in the intertestamental period, there are two features that characterize the concept of God's son/child.

1. The idea of Israel as the children of God has to do with the covenant relation between God and the people (Exod 4:22; Hos 11:1). There is evidence for this even in the book of *Jubilees*—see the quotation in Appendix 9, A Renewed Covenant—and in the rabbinic literature. Israel regarded the event at Sinai as the day of their birth, the day when God by "living word" begat Israel as his son.

2. As sons and daughters of God, they must also live as children of God (Hos 11:1–10; Deut 32:18; Jer 31:9). Deut 32:18 is the only text in the Old Testament that speaks of God's having begotten his people; in the LXX the verb is *gennan*. Sir 4:10 says, "Be a father to orphans, and be like a husband to their mother; you will then be like a son of the Most High." According to *Jub.* 1:24–25, God requires the

Appendix 11: Begotten/Born of God

Israelites to hold fast to him and follow his commandments. Then he will be their father and they will be his children. The status as child and the corresponding way of life belong together. In 1 John the divine begetting is connected with the inability to sin (= the ability to do righteousness; 1 John 2:28—3:10), the command to love one another (1 John 3:10; 4:7), and the confession that Jesus is the Messiah (1 John 5:1). Both the relationship to the covenant and its connection with a way of life are reinforced by what is said about the renewed covenant at Qumran, not least in texts about entering the covenant (1QS 1–4). Being a child of God is part of the new covenant.

Elsewhere in the New Testament, there is little said about being born of God. First Peter speaks of those who are born anew, who have been begotten of an incorruptible seed and who will live as newborn children (1 Pet 1:3, 23; 2:2). New birth is mentioned also in connection with baptism in Titus 3:5, and according to Jas 1:18 God "gave us birth by the word of truth." Rudolf Bultmann and others have claimed that the background to this way of speaking lies in the mystery religions and Gnosticism. It is certainly true that it was relatively easy within contemporary Greek religious thinking to give content to statements about divine birth. But with reference to what I have already said above about the background of the concept "children of God," about the ethical context of the divine birth, and about the background in ideas of a renewed covenant found generally throughout the letter, here again I prefer an Old Testament, Jewish background. Raymond Brown wishes to explain the special use of the words "begotten/born of God" in the Johannine writings from, among other things, the perception in these writings of eternal life as a present experience. The Johannine way of speaking about it strongly underscores God's creative and life-giving power through the Spirit when a person comes to faith and is baptized.

The constantly present and creative power within those who are born of God is described in a special way at 1 John 3:9 with its thematically chiastic structure:

a	Everyone who is born of God
b	he does not sin
c	*for God's seed remains in him*
b'	he cannot sin
a'	for he is born of God

It is completely obvious that the words "God's seed remains in him" are a further development of the idea of divine birth. The word in the original, *sperma,* can mean a grain of cereal, offspring, or a man's sperm, i.e., the life-giving element in the begetting process. In this period, it was thought that only the man was the active agent in conception, i.e., the one who created life in sexual intercourse, while the woman was the passive partner, a field where the embryo received nurture and grew. Thus *sperma* stands here for that which gives life in the act of begetting.

Many interpreters have long preferred the meaning "offspring" in 1 John 3:9 and compared it with phrases like "Abraham's seed" (John 8:33, 37) or "David's seed" (John 7:42). This yields for most of them the meaning "for Christ remains in him," a completely plausible reading for Johannine texts. But it does not fit the present context. Jesus can be described as "offspring" or "descendent" (Rom 1:3; 2 Tim 2:8), but never as God's offspring. Other readers see the words as referring to Christians, i.e., "for God's offspring remain in God," but in that case v. 9 becomes utterly tautological. Nor does it say, "for he is God's offspring," but rather "for God's offspring remains in him."

The immediate context and what was said above about the children of God and about being born of God speak primarily in favor of the meaning "sperm." A switch to the topic of vegetation and taking *sperma* to mean a grain of cereal is hardly likely. In that case we would have a new formulation of the idea divine birth. But then what would this metaphorical image represent? Some commentators have equated it with divine life or God's grace or divine nature. But we may presume that the same choice lies before us here as did in the interpretation of "anointing," *chrisma* (1 John 2:20, 27), i.e., God's word or God's spirit—or both in cooperation with one another.

The interpretation of *sperma* as God's word is supported primarily by other New Testament texts (1 Pet 1:23; Jas 1:18) and possibly by the Stoic notion of *logos spermatikos*, namely that the embryonic divine *logos* is found within a person. God's word is an active power in, e.g., John 15:3, 7, but in 1 John 1:10; 2:7, 14, 24, I have interpreted God's word as the divine message mediated through Jesus Christ, "what you heard from the beginning." See the Analysis for 1 John 2:18–27, point 3. The reference above to what happened at Sinai as a background can be taken as supporting this interpretation, one that has been known since the beginning of the third century.

Reading *sperma* as referring to God's spirit is supported not least by John 3 and by the context of baptism found in numerous New Testament texts. The Spirit is connected in 1 John 3:24 and 4:13 to remaining in God, and I interpreted *chrisma* in 1 John 2:20, 27 as primarily referring to the Spirit. *The Testament of Benjamin* 8:2 describes the pious man in this way: "he has no defilement in his heart, because the Spirit of God rests upon him." Understanding *sperma* to refer to the Spirit can also be justified on the basis of the renewed covenant, in which God gives the people his spirit so that they may follow his commandments (Ezek 36:26–27).

It is not so easy to choose between God's word and God's spirit. Perhaps God's *sperma* in 1 John 3:9 contains a reference to both. As I see it, reading it as referring to the Spirit is the more likely choice. The contextually important thing, however, is what is actually said about God's *sperma*. It is the power that at one point gave the letter's recipients new life, a divine life, when they came to faith and were baptized. God's *sperma* is the constantly working power that enables them not to practice sin, but to do righteousness. It is precisely the combination of these two effects of divine birth that makes them into the true people of God, into the people of the new covenant. The argument in 1 John 2:28—3:10 regarding divine birth rests on an overall,

Appendix 11: Begotten/Born of God

fundamental, and cumulative plan. The section functions both as a summing up of the eschatological discussions in 2:18—3:10 and as an introduction to the second part of the letter, which turns to the subject of love and faith as characteristics of those who are born of God.

APPENDIX 12

They Cannot Sin

BELIEVING IN JESUS AS the Messiah, God's son, and loving one's fellow believers constitute the theme that holds together the content of 1 John. It corresponds to "the law interpreted anew" in the renewed covenant (1 John 3:23). According to the Gospel of John, sin is defined as not believing in Jesus (John 16:9), and according to the letter lack of love toward one's fellow believers is described as unrighteousness and sin (1 John 2:28—3:10). Failure to love one's brother, failure to do righteousness, and committing sin are all placed side by side (1 John 3:4–10). It is no wonder then that sin becomes a recurrent theme throughout the letter.

Sin is therefore a central problem in the letter. It shows up already at the beginning and has an important place in the final section as well. In addition we have the numerous foundational statements in 1 John 3:4–10. The statements about the Johannine Christians' sin can be preliminarily divided into three groups.

A1 Everyone who remains in Christ does not sin (1 John 3:6a).

A2 No one who sins has seen Christ or learned to know him (1 John 3:6bc).

A3 The one who commits sin is of the devil (1 John 3:8a).

A4 No one who is born of God commits sin (1 John 3:9b).

A5 [The one who is born of God] cannot sin (1 John 3:9c).

A6 As Christ is, so are they also in this world (1 John 4:17).

A7 They know that no one who is born of God sins (1 John 5:18a).

I include 1 John 4:17 because there it is implicitly said that the Johannine Christians do not sin. Christ is righteous (1 John 2:29a); Christ is pure (3:3b), and in Christ there is no sin (3:5). As Christ is, so are they now, in this world (1 John 4:17). Moreover, this saying occurs in the same context here as the context it has in 1 John 2:28—3:10, i.e., the day of judgment with the two possibilities people will have then: confidence or shame/fear/punishment in confronting the Righteous One. Even sayings about "doing

Appendix 12: They Cannot Sin

righteousness" could be included here, since in this section "doing righteousness" is the opposite of "doing sin."

The statements in the second group have to do particularly with those who left the Johannine fellowship.

B1 Those who say that they do not have sin deceive themselves and the truth is not in them (1 John 1:8).

B2 Those who say that they have not sinned make God a liar and God's word is not in them (1 John 1:10).

Both the words "deceive" and "liar" allude to those who deny the Messiah, mentioned in 1 John 2:18–27. What is said in group B comes into direct conflict with what is said in group A and can in fact lead us to the third group of statements, which claims that the Johannine Christians commit sin and are admonished to confess it and receive forgiveness, or to pray for those who commit sin, that they may be set free from it.

C1 The blood of Jesus, God's son, cleanses them from all sin (1 John 1:7d).

C2 If they confess their sins, God is faithful and righteous to forgive them their sins and to cleanse them from every wrongdoing (1 John 1:9).

C3 The aim of the letter is that they should not sin, but if anyone of them commits a sin, they have an advocate with God, namely Jesus the Messiah, and he is righteous. He is the atoning sacrifice for their sins and not for theirs only, but for those of the entire world (1 John 2:1–2).

C4 The author reassures his readers that their sins are forgiven for the sake of Jesus' name (1 John 2:12).

C5 Christ was revealed in order to take away sins (1 John 3:5b).

C6 God's son was revealed so that he might destroy the works of the devil (1 John 3:8d).

C7 God sent his son as an atoning sacrifice for their sins (1 John 4:10d).

C8 If any of them commits a sin that is not a sin unto death, they are to pray for him and give him life (1 John 5:16).

I have included in this group the statements about forgiveness and purification from sin, even though they could also be included within group A or B. It is interesting to note that purification from sin, from that which separates humanity from God, is connected both with God and with Jesus, and that various metaphors are used for the latter: his blood that cleanses, a vindicator or an advocate with God (the God of judgment), the idea of an atoning sacrifice, and a destruction of the devil's works. See further Appendix 7, Expiation and forgiveness.

The letter uses three words for sin typical in the Septuagint, *anomia*, *adikia*, and *hamartia*, all three attested in, e.g., the mercy formula from the covenant renewal at Sinai (Exod 34:6–7: "iniquity and transgression and sin"). The letter also contains some more exact definitions of what sort of thing sin is. The discussion about God's children and sin in 1 John 3:4–10 begins with the words "Everyone who commits sin [*hamartia*] also commits lawlessness [*anomia*]. Sin is lawlessness." In the Notes and the Interpretation for this paragraph, I have interpreted *anomia* in its definite form as lawlessness, as rebellion against God in the final struggle between God and the devil. Whoever sins thus aligns himself with the devil. The expression "the sins" in 1 John 3:5b is replaced as well with "the devil's works" in 3:8d. The one who sins is of the devil, *diabolos*. The entire argument in 1 John 3:4–10 must be seen in light of the end of time and the judgment, with its clear division of humanity into the children of God and the children of the devil. The words *anomia* and *diabolos* in the description of sin contribute to the eschatological character of this section.

The second definition of sin follows the admonishment to pray for a brother who has sinned (1 John 5:16–17). The author is careful at this point to say that there are such things as "mortal sins." "Every unrighteous deed is sin," he says. "But there is sin that is not mortal." It should be noted regarding formulations elsewhere that the expression "to have sin" is found only in Johannine texts—see the note on 1 John 1:8—and then is used specifically of Jews who do not believe even though they have heard what Jesus said and seen what Jesus did (John 9:41; 15:22, 24). To have sin carries the nuance of bearing sin's guilt. Some interpreters have preferred to read "do sin" as having the habit of sinning, but that is scarcely in keeping with this Semitic expression. Others chose to make a distinction between sin in the singular and sins in the plural (1 John 1:9; 2:12; 3:5; 4:10). The singular would refer to sin as a power, the latter to sin as specific actions. Even a distinction of this sort is difficult to defend in a text characterized by so many stylistic variations.

From a rhetorical point of view, the clearest information comes at the end of the letter. In 1 John 5:14–17 an important distinction is made between a sinful act that threatens the individual sinner's eternal wellbeing (life) and a sin that leads to death. The former can obviously be cleansed and forgiven, but not the latter. The letter shows that the former sin is committed by a person who renounces the confession of Jesus as the Messiah, God's son, and leaves the Johannine community, i.e., hates his brother. See Appendix 19, Sin that leads to death. In the beginning of the letter, furthermore, the author is at pains to say that individual sins can be forgiven (1 John 1:9). Those who commit a sin have an advocate with God, Jesus Christ, one who is without sin, and they can turn to Jesus as an atoning sacrifice (1 John 2:1–2). It is thus completely obvious from the letter's beginning and ending that the Elder is aware that Johannine Christians actually can sin. At the same time the letter's closing repeats what dominates 1 John 3:4–10, that the one born of God does not sin (1 John 5:18). How can we reconcile these claims?

All expositors of the letter have asked themselves this question, and there have been many answers to it. The overview above, with the three groups A, B, and C, demonstrates quite clearly that there is a powerful tension in the letter with regard to the

Appendix 12: They Cannot Sin

question of sin, indeed many readers would call it a clear contradiction. And all of them have tried to explain it or resolve it. I list here some of the more frequent attempts.

1. *The author uses earlier material—written sources or special traditions—or directs his remarks to different groups of readers.* Some are of the opinion that the author or a redactor in 1 John 3:4–10 and 5:18 has inserted material from another source that is in conflict with what the letter otherwise says. According to certain readers, the formulations in 1 John 3:6 and 9 may be slogans from those who left the Johannine fellowship, and which would have been well known to the letter's recipients. These separatists had been influenced by Gnostic claims of being immune to sin ever since they had acquired knowledge (*gnōsis*) of God and themselves. As an argument against them, the Elder demanded that they do righteousness. A theory like this, however, makes the argument in 1 John 3:4–10 very obscure.

   Can it be that the author in discussing confession of sin and forgiveness is speaking to the secessionists, while in 1 John 3:4–10 and 5:18 he is thinking of those who are of the opinion that this business of sin is not all that important? Or is he thinking in the latter case only of special Christians, elite Christians who live up to the condition of remaining in Christ? His words would then have nothing to do with ordinary Christians. Against this is the repeated formulation "everyone who." I have also argued that there is only one separatist group behind the Elder's message. See chap. 12, point 4.

2. *Sin as a habit and sin as individual, isolated sins.* The most common explanation through the ages is probably the one claiming that Christians sometimes can fall into sin, but they do not live in sin. It is the difference between sin as defining one's lifestyle and sin as a single, specific act. Frequently it is pointed out in this context that the original employs differing tenses, the aorist in 1 John 2:1 and the present in 3:6, 9. The latter form can of course express an ongoing action, but it is hardly possible to claim that it means a continuous action, a habit. Even the Semitic expression "to do sin" has sometimes been interpreted as continuous sinning, especially on the basis of John 8:34 and 1 John 3:8ab. But no lexicon, grammar, or context gives any good support to this alternative.

3. *Freedom from sin as an ideal, and sin as part of reality.* The words in 1 John 3:6–9 provide an ideal vision of how things ought to be, while 2:1 describes how they actually are. Theoretically it is impossible to claim that those born of God can sin. God's will is realized by those who walk in the light. But this interpretation functions poorly in an argument that leads to showing how one can distinguish between the children of God and the children of the devil. A similar way of thinking characterizes those who distinguish between two levels in the text, a pastoral level in 1 John 1:8—2:2 and a theological level in 3:4–10 and 5:18. In the prevailing situation it is important for the Elder to admonish his readers not to sin. The pastoral level is often individualized and oriented toward reality,

Appendix 12: They Cannot Sin

whereas the theological level focuses on the community as a whole and on the struggle against evil. Some people also distinguish between a human perspective and God's perspective, as in the standard Lutheran thesis *simul justus et peccator* (simultaneously a righteous person and a sinner).

4. *Teaching about sin in differing literary contexts.* In 1 John 1:8 and 1:10—2:2 the issue has to do with a portion of the early proclamation. The author reminds his readers of the pronouncement of sins' forgiveness which they heard when they came to faith. In 1 John 3:6, 9, and 5:18 the author speaks in an apocalyptic context. The fact that there will no longer be sin among those who were united with God belongs to the end-time expectations. It can also be associated with the renewed covenant (Ezek 36:29). See further the interpretation of 1 John 2:28–29. But the conditions of the last days are usually more clearly laid out than is the case in the argument of this letter. Other readers note the contextual differences by observing that 1 John 3:4–10 is not a description of the Christians but rather functions as an introduction to an admonition. Still others are of the opinion that the categorical statement that "they cannot sin" must not be read as if it said, "You cannot sin" or "You must not sin," but as an observation and a rule indirectly aimed at the Gnostics who had left the community. The section's character, genre, and place in the context are important for the interpretation of sin in the letter, but that interpretation remains heavily dependent on how one interprets the letter as a whole—and there are numerous possibilities.

5. *Two ways of understanding freedom from sin.* Raymond Brown, who has carefully worked through the various alternatives, finally concludes that it is probably not wise to make too much of the opposition within the letter. No other New Testament author contradicts himself so emphatically within a document of limited scope as does the author of 1 John. Freedom from sin, as presented in the letter, can be understood in either an orthodox or a heterodox way. Both alternatives, according to Brown, are built on an interpretation of the Gospel of John. Brown's theory has been modified to make the heretical standpoint to have been developed under the influence of Gnostic ideas. Of the alternatives sketched out above, Brown finds that the third and the fourth are the most reasonable. But no alternative actually removes the difficulty in the text.

6. *Sin in an eschatological perspective: "now–not yet."* I want to return to the apocalyptic solution mentioned under point 4. To the literary rationale offered there, we can add the strongly eschatological content in 1 John 2:18—3:10. Indeed, this holds as well for the entire letter, viewed in terms of the conviction of the Jesus-believing Jews that God had renewed his covenant with his people and mediated divine life to them through Jesus the Messiah, God's son. There is a strongly realized eschatology in the letter, even though the formula "now–not yet" still applies (1 John 3:2). God is in them and they are in God; God's seed remains in

Appendix 12: They Cannot Sin

them; already here on earth, they are closely united with God's son and with God himself. From this perspective, they cannot sin. As long as they are in the world, this dual existence prevails. Even now they possess eternal life, but it belongs to the future just the same. One day they will be like God (1 John 3:2). A similar argument can be made regarding sin. It has no part in the new fellowship with God at the culminating point of salvation history, but nevertheless it is here now. However, according to Raymond Brown, the vagueness and lack of clarity in the author's argument remains a serious objection even to this alternative. In my opinion, it is simpler to argue it from an intra-Jewish perspective.

There is something to be said for several of the suggested interpretations above. Obviously making a choice among them depends on how the letter as a whole is interpreted. Earlier I described the change in the general character that takes place at 1 John 2:28—3:10, the close connection to what comes before (1 John 1:5–9 and especially 2:18–27). See the Analysis, points 1 and 2. Together, 1 John 2:18–27 and 2:28—3:10 form an eschatological section in the letter, in which the perspective of the end-time, the last hour of God's timetable, dominates with particular power. I have pointed out the role that the final judgment in 1 John 2:28–29 has for the entire section, the use of the apocalyptic concept of "lawlessness" in 1 John 3:4, and the introduction of the devil as the opponent of Jesus/God at the end of the section. See the Interpretation. What is said in 1 John 3:4–10 about sin must be read in terms of the end-time, i.e., in the immediate context of the final judgment. For this reason I much prefer the sixth alternative described above, partly combined with the fourth, and clearly enhanced by the dualistic pattern that marks the letter. The tension between "now" and "not yet" occurs throughout the letter, and in 1 John 2:28—3:10 the final destination of this temporal perspective comes very near. It is self-evident then that a child of God cannot sin. But as soon as the situation is viewed from the audience's own moment in time, it becomes clear that a child of God sometimes does sin. It is thus important to hold fast to public confession of sin and to God's forgiveness through Jesus Christ, to hold to public intercession and to God's answering prayer made in Jesus' name that the sinner may be allowed to live the divine life that became a reality through the renewed covenant between God and Israel. The end has not yet come, even though the eschatological hope has been realized to a remarkably significant degree. The tension is there and remains real for the letter's recipients in their own situation.

Appendix 13

Cain as the Devil's Son

THERE ARE NO QUOTATIONS from the Old Testament in the letters of John. In this regard they are like a few texts on doctrine and practice from the Qumran community. The marginal references found in modern editions and translations deal almost exclusively with linguistic parallels. One exception is the allusion to Genesis 4 in 1 John 3:12. Cain is presented there as a cautionary example (1 John 3:12–15), followed in 1 John 3:16–17 by Jesus as the proper model. The overarching theme is love for the brothers, i.e., for fellow believers. The following information is given about Cain, some explicitly and some implicitly.

- *Cain was of the Evil one* (1 John 3:12). The formulation is connected to the preceding verses, especially vv. 8–10 with their fundamental argument regarding the children of God and the children of the devil. Cain was "of the devil," to use the words in v. 8. He belongs to "the children of the devil," he has "the devil's *sperma* in him," he is "born of the devil," he has the devil as his father, if we may use the words regarding God's children (1 John 2:18—3:10) in a negative way. Referring to the devil as "the Evil one" is probably based on the mention of "evil deeds" in v. 12 and on the Jewish background behind the way Cain is interpreted here. See the note on "the Evil one" at 1 John 2:13. In John 8:39 Jews who had previously believed in Jesus are described as having the devil as their father, and in John 13:2, 27 Judas is depicted as a tool of the devil.

- *Cain murdered his brother* (1 John 3:12). This point is mentioned twice, both times with a verb that is mostly used with regard to sacrificial animals. See the note on "murdered" at 1 John 3:12. There may be a connection here with John 16:2, where some people are portrayed as thinking that they are bringing an offering to God when they kill Jesus' followers. Verse 15 mentions "murderers" (*anthrōpoktonos*) with a clear allusion to Cain's deed. This unusual word occurs also in John 8:44 with reference to Satan and indirectly to Jews who want to kill Jesus. The expression broadens Cain's isolated act to a more general one.

Appendix 13: Cain as the Devil's Son

- *Cain's deeds were evil* (1 John 3:12), but Abel's were "righteous," offered as an explanation for why Cain did what he did. This can be filled out with statements from the surrounding text: Cain "does not do righteousness," Cain "does not love his brother" (1 John 3:10). He carries out "the devil's works," he "commits sin" (1 John 3:8). In the immediate context special attention is drawn to the one who does not love the brothers, everyone who hates his brother (v. 14), the one who does not give his life for the brothers (v. 16). They are all described as "like Cain."

- *Cain belongs to the kingdom of death.* This is indirectly stated in 1 John 3:14. He does not have eternal life within him (v. 15). Cain and those who follow in his footsteps belong to a different category from the letter's recipients.

- *Cain's deeds lead to thoughts of the concept of "the world."* "Do not be amazed if the world hates you" (1 John 3:13). According to 1 John 5:19 the entire world lies in the power of the Evil one and thus belongs to the same family as Cain. In John 15:18—16:4a certain Jews are equated with the world. They hate Jesus' disciples just as they have hated Jesus, and they will exclude Jesus-believing Jews from the synagogue and kill them.

- *It is in this connection that Cain is applied to the Jesus-believing Jews who have left the Johannine fellowship* (1 John 2:18–19), who do not love the brothers. The addressees must not be like these people, they must not be like Cain. They are to love one another.

It is obvious that the depiction of Cain characterizes as well the text surrounding 1 John 3:12 and that the information provided about Cain goes considerably beyond what is found in the biblical narrative in Genesis 4. There are many ambiguous formulations and troublesome gaps in the original description. These have been interpreted and filled out in Jewish tradition, with an extensive and varied tradition history as a result. It has been chronicled by several researchers, with regard to 1 John especially by Judith Lieu in an article from 1993.

Cain and Abel appear early on to have been interpreted as ethical examples on the basis of the division of humanity into "the evil" and "the righteous." This categorization is already present in the Old Testament, e.g., in Psalm 1, but it becomes more frequent in later Jewish writings. Josephus (*Ant.* 1.2.1, §53) describes Abel as a lover of "righteousness" (*dikaiosynē*), but Cain as "very wicked" (*ponērotatos*). Philo calls Abel "righteous" (*Quaestiones in Genesin* 1:59) and warns against taking Cain as teacher or guide (*De posteritate Caini* 1:38). Cain is evil, and Abel is good, judged by the works they do. This characterization is found in the New Testament as well (Matt 23:35; Heb 11:4; Jude 11). Cain is constantly evil, Abel constantly good. In later Jewish tradition, Abel belongs in the list of the righteous and Cain in the list of the evil. Those who "are like Cain in envy and hatred of brethren" are threatened with punishment (*T. Benj.* 7:5); hatred is equated with murder (*T. Gad* 4:6; cf. *1 Clem.* 4:1–7).

Appendix 13: Cain as the Devil's Son

This interpretive tradition surrounding Cain's deeds explains the use of the words "righteous" and "evil" in 1 John 3 and yields a more coherent understanding of this portion of the letter. It has to do with a general, foundational, and more comprehensive rationale regarding "Cainites" and "Abelites"—with a vocabulary influenced by the Cain narrative.

Even the question of Cain's origin appears to have been the occasion for scholarly meditation. According to Aramaic translations of Genesis, Cain was physically the devil's son. In *Targum Pseudo-Jonathan,* on Gen 5:3, we read: "And Adam . . . begat Sheth, who had the likeness of his image and similitude: for before had Hava born Kain, who was not like to him." This view of Cain's origin—possibly attested also in 4 Macc 18:8—becomes very clear in a Gnostic writing, *Gospel of Philip* 61:6–10: "First came adultery, then murder. Cain was begotten in adultery, for he was the son of the serpent. Thus he became a murderer, like his father, and he killed his brother."

These depictions may have their origin in the biblical text itself. In Gen 4:25 it says literally that God had given Eve "another seed/descendent," a formulation that could be linked with Gen 3:15 and its mention of the woman's "seed" and the serpent's "seed," also taken as a collective noun: "race." Since it says in Gen 5:3—the text where the targumim note Cain's special origin—that Seth was "a son in his [Adam's] likeness, according to his image," Seth therefore, according to these expositors, has his origin, through Adam, in God. Thus we get two races within humanity: Adam's/Seth's descendents, who are begotten of God, and the serpent's/Cain's descendents, who are begotten of the devil.

The statement about Cain's origin in 1 John 3:12 is therefore nothing new, but rather has its background in Jewish exegesis of the Cain figure. It is possible that the basic distinctions between Cain and Abel are strengthened through Johannine dualism. Even the mention of "seed" (*sperma*) in 1 John 3:9 may have a background in these Jewish interpretations of Cain's origin, as in the altercation in John 8, where Jews who wish to kill Jesus are viewed through a Cain-filter. They are Cainites, and not Sethites. It seems as if Cain and Abel themselves have returned when the world is divided into two fundamentally distinct groups. In John 8, those who believe and those who do not believe are all Jews. The same can apply to 1 John 3. People characterized by faith in Jesus and by the love of God are set in opposition to people characterized by apostasy and hatred, i.e., Jesus-believing Jews who have left their messianic faith and the Johannine community.

Appendix 14

Jesus as Messiah, God's Son

Sin and unrighteous deeds constitute a central theme in 1 John; Jesus Christ, God's son, is another. The former includes failure to live as Jesus lived and failure to love one's fellow believers; the latter entails failure to confess Jesus' death as both a cleansing from sin and an ethical model. Described in this way, these two central themes stand quite close to one another. They are basic as well for various attempts at discerning the conceptions of Jesus—the Christologies—represented by the Elder and his opponents. The particular perspective an interpreter takes in reading the Johannine letters becomes more obvious here perhaps than in any other context in the letter. Thus, in this appendix, after an inventory of the christological material, I will take up in turn each of the three main interpretive perspectives.

In the Johannine letters, there are both formulations about Jesus that are more confessional in nature and descriptions of him and his acts that are more general in nature. The former take center stage for this appendix.

1. *Jesus is Christ/Messiah.* Some people deny that Jesus is Messiah (1 John 2:22); others believe that Jesus is Messiah (1 John 5:1). The first characteristic of the secessionists is precisely their relation to Jesus as Messiah. In an intra-Jewish perspective it is natural to translate *Christos* as "Messiah," in other perspectives as "Christ." See below. The Johannine Christians appear to have been Greek-speaking and thus said *Christos*, but there was always an implication of Messiah. Cf. John 1:41; 4:25. I use both "Christ" and "Messiah" in this commentary. Some commentators want to make "Jesus Christ" into a double name or to equate "Christ" with "God's son." But the independent use of "Messiah" in 1 John 2:22 and 5:1, the more precise explanation of "Messiah" in 2:23, the reference to the name in 2:12 and 3:23, the abbreviation to merely "Jesus" as object in 4:3, and the discussion of "Messiah's teaching/teaching about Messiah" in 2 John 9 can be taken as grounds for interpreting "Christ" as "Messiah," i.e., for taking "Messiah" as an independent designation for Jesus. The word "Christ" was so common, however, that it also came to function as a name. It is also used in more complete

formulas. See below under points 3–5. *Christos* occurs eight times in 1 John and three times in 2 John.

2. *Jesus is God's son.* The positive confession in 1 John 4:15 and the content of faith in 1 John 5:5 are formulated in this way. To believe in God's son (1 John 5:10) is certainly the same thing as to believe that Jesus is God's son (1 John 5:5; expanded in 5:13 to believing in the name of God's son). "God's son" is also used by itself as subject in 1 John 3:8 and 5:20, and as object in 4:9–10 and 4:14 (the Son). God has testified regarding his son (1 John 5:9–10). Additionally, the expression "God's son" occurs in the form of "the Son" (1 John 2:22–24; 5:12) and in combination with other names: "Jesus, God's son" (1 John 1:8) and "Jesus Messiah, God's son" (1 John 1:3; 3:23; 5:20). To have the Son/God's son (1 John 5:12; 2 John 9) implies an intimate relationship with this person. See the note "has the Father" at 1 John 2:23. Related to the designation "God's son" is "the true God" and "the one who was born of God." See points 6 and 7 below. The Son is also described in 1 John 4:9 as "only born," in the sense of unique, the only one of his kind. See the note "only" at 1 John 4:9. Union with the Son gives eternal life (1 John 5:11–13). See also point 10 below. "God's son" is the title, or the name, or the designation most often used in the letter (22 times), and in many different kinds of constructions.

3. *Jesus as Messiah, God's son.* The confessions that Jesus is Messiah and that Jesus is God's son are brought together in the triple-name formula "Jesus Christ/Messiah God's son," which is found in three strategic passages in the letter: in the introduction (1 John 1:3); in the midst of the letter, in the two-part covenant commandment (3:23); and at the end (5:20). It occurs also in the covenant formulation in 2 John 3 as "Jesus Christ/Messiah, the Father's son," where God has just been referred to as Father. In a general Christian, Gnostic perspective or in an intra-Johannine progression perspective, "Jesus Christ" is taken as a single name and the formula is thus rendered "Jesus Christ, God's son." In an intra-Jewish perspective, there is good reason to interpret the meaning of the triple-name formula as "Jesus as Messiah, God's son," even if the words "Jesus Christ, God's son" are retained. Believing in the name of God's son (1 John 5:13) presumably means believing in Jesus as Messiah, God's son, and thus corresponds to the purpose statement in John 20:31: "that Jesus is Messiah, God's son." The three names are also combined in 1 John 5:6, since the demonstrative pronoun "this one/he," *houtos*, refers to God's son in 1 John 5:5, which is then made explicit with "Jesus Christ" in 1 John 5:6.

4. *Jesus as Messiah come/coming in the flesh.* The Elder summarizes the true confession in this way in 1 John 4:2, and with a slight linguistic change in 2 John 7. In a note on 1 John 4:2, I have listed various translations made from differing syntactical analyses, and likewise in point 2 of the Analysis for 1 John 4:1–6, those

Appendix 14: Jesus as Messiah, God's Son

dependent on several text-critical variants in 4:3. It is obvious that these words have always been interpreted on the basis of differing contexts and thus have been given differing meanings. The most common interpretation is based on the translation "Jesus Christ (as) come in human form."

5. *God's son is the one who came by water and blood, Jesus Messiah, not only by water, but also by blood.* The confession in 1 John 5:5 continues in v. 6 with a description of God's son. Various interpretive possibilities are discussed in Appendix 17, By water and blood. I have interpreted the phrase as a reference to Jesus' entire mission, from birth to death, with a special emphasis on Jesus' death.

6. *Jesus is the one who is born of God.* A statement like this about Jesus occurs only in 1 John 5:18, probably in connection with the usual description of the Jesus-believers who are born of God. Likewise in 1 John 5:1, the author plays with the words "beget/bear." See Appendix 11, Begotten/born of God. People as born of God are also regarded as born in the usual way. They are born "by water," i.e., born in a natural way, and born "by spirit," i.e., from above, or from God (John 3:5). The Elder's depiction of Jesus would be of the same sort. There is no clear mention of the Virgin Birth in Johannine writings. "Jesus as the one born of God" should be understood to mean the same thing as "God's son."

7. *Jesus as the true God.* This statement in 1 John 5:20 goes a bit further in describing Jesus Messiah, God's son, and bluntly indicates his divine character. It is reminiscent of Jesus as God in John 1:1, 18, and 20:28. With "the true God," the description of Jesus comes to culmination in these last lines of the letter.

8. *Jesus is the one who takes away the sins of all humanity.* He is "the savior of the world" (1 John 4:14). This is described with such concepts as "cleansing" (1 John 1:7, 9), "forgiveness" (1 John 1:9; 2:12), and "atonement" (2:2; 4:14). In 1 John 3:5, the words "take away sins" are used; in 3:8, the words "destroy the works of the devil." See the note there. Even intercession has a role to play where taking away sins is concerned (1 John 2:1; 5:16–17). Both the high priest and Moses had such an intercessory role. See the Interpretation for 1 John 2:1 and Appendix 7, Expiation and forgiveness. It is with reference to humanity's sin that Jesus' earthly work, and particularly his death, become so decisive in the Elder's way of thinking (1 John 5:6).

9. *Jesus is righteous, pure, without sin.* These descriptions of Jesus occur in connection with his taking away of sins (1 John 2:1; 3:5) and in connection with the instruction about Jesus as an example (1 John 2:29; 3:3, 8). To keep God's commandments in the renewed covenant is to live like Jesus lived (1 John 2:6). They are obliged to give their lives for the brothers, just as Jesus gave his life for them (1 John 3:16). Just as Jesus Messiah, God's son, is, so are they in this world (1 John 4:17). In this way Jesus' earthly work and particularly his death become

significant even here.

10. *Jesus is eternal life.* This is said explicitly in the closing lines of the letter (1 John 5:20), as well as implicitly in the opening lines, where what is raised for consideration in 1 John 1:1 is described in v. 2 as eternal life. Thus a perspective on Life is what frames the entire letter. It is also the central theme as the letter comes to a close (1 John 5:11–13). I have earlier interpreted what is said in 1 John 1:1 as statements about Jesus and his work on the earth, both in word and deed. The word "revealed" in 1 John 1:2 has the same meaning as it does in 3:5, 8. See the notes "the life was revealed" at 1 John 1:2 and "was revealed" at 3:5. In 1 John 5:20, the possession of eternal life is coupled with the covenant pronouncement that God's son has come and given them understanding, so that they might know the true God. It is the consequence of the coming of Messiah, God's son, into the world in the form of Jesus, summed up in the concept of "eternal life," that holds together the letter's argument. The one who has God's son has eternal life; the one who does not have the Son does not have eternal life (1 John 5:12). Perhaps the first two points in this list should be translated as confessions that Messiah is Jesus, that God's son is Jesus. See the note "Jesus is the son of God" at 1 John 4:15.

In an *intra-Jewish perspective* the confession in 1 John 4:2 is most readily understood as "Jesus as Messiah having come in the flesh." Abbreviating it to "Jesus" in 4:3 speaks in favor of an analysis like the one given above under points 1–4. It is a matter of confessing the Messiah, who is further described as "having come in the flesh." In Johannine language, the word "come" is used especially often with reference to the Messiah (John 4:25; 7:27, 31; 11:27) or to Jesus (John 1:9, 11; 3:2, 19; 5:43; etc.) with a connection to the believers' work and mission in the world. The Samaritan woman knew "that Messiah [i.e., Christ] is coming, and when he comes he will proclaim all things to us" (John 4:25). Some in Jerusalem refer to the time "when Messiah comes" (John 7:27, 31). Those who were satisfied beside the Sea of Gennesaret exclaimed, "This must be the Prophet, the one who is to come into the world" (John 6:14). Martha confessed that "Jesus is Messiah, God's son, the one who is to come into the world" (John 11:27). Jesus says several times, "I have come (into the world)," and has in mind his entire earthly work (John 5:43; 9:39; 10:10 [that they may have life]; 12:27 [with a focus on his death], 46–47; 16:28, 37). In all these passages, Messiah's/Jesus' coming into the world has to do not simply with his physical presence in the world, but with his saving and judging activity as well. He who comes has a mission to save. The formula "the one who is to come" has much in common with "the one whom God has sent," a typical description of Jesus' salvation work in the Gospel of John. See also 1 John 4:9, 10, 14.

The words "the one who is to come" (*ho erchomenos*) probably with roots in Ps 118:26 and its use in the great Jewish festivals, undoubtedly designated the savior figure expected by Jews in Jesus' day (Matt 11:13). The connection of Messiah with "the coming one" is therefore a natural one in Johannine usage. It likewise explains to a great degree the use of the present participle in 2 John 7 ("coming") and the perfect participle in 1 John 4:3 ("having come/come"). Generally speaking, the two tense-forms express the same thing: Messiah is characterized as "coming"; with the perfect, that coming is depicted as a previous event valid even now. The perfect is used in 1 John 5:20 as well.

The verb "come" occurs in 1 John 4:3 with the preposition *en*, meaning in, with, or through/by. It has to do with the means, the manner, or both. It is not a typical construction, but it occurs in the phrase "in someone's name," as in the quotation of Ps 118:26 in John 12:13—"Blessed is the one who comes in/with the name of the Lord"— and in John 5:43; it is usually interpreted there as being on someone's business, as being someone's representative. Otherwise "come in/with/through/by" occurs only in 1 John 4:2 and 5:6. In some sense, "come in the flesh" and "came by water and blood" refer to Jesus' earthly work: in 1 John 4:2 expanded to Messiah, in 5:6 as characterizing God's son. God's son and his salvific mission became visible in a human being's life and work, from birth to death, and especially through his death. This is how I have primarily interpreted 1 John 5:6. See Appendix 17, By water and blood. "Jesus as Messiah come in the flesh" can be understood in a similar way. Messiah, sent by God into the world to save the world, has come and carried out his work as a human being through Jesus' life and activity. This is the same characterization that we have in the first lines of the letter and the same content that lies in the claim in 1 John 1:2; 3:5, and 8 that Life/He/God's son "has been revealed." "Messiah come in the flesh" would quite simply mean that Messiah has come and that he has done so in and through a human being's life and work. Messiah is Jesus. In an intra-Jewish perspective, the decisive question thus becomes whether Messiah has come, whether Messiah is Jesus or not. Every spirit that confesses that Messiah has come in the figure of Jesus is from God. Both Messiah's becoming human and his salvific death, i.e., both the beginning and the end, are included within the phrase "come in the flesh," but neither one appears to be especially emphasized in 1 John 4:3.

In a *general Christian, Gnostic perspective,* the point of departure in 1 John 4:2 is "Jesus Christ who is come in the flesh." *Christos* here has lost the sense of Messiah and is seen only as an extension of the name Jesus. The emphasis thus falls not on Messiah, but on the meaning of "come in the flesh" and what those words say about a correct conception of Christ—Christology—in the letter. Confessing Jesus Christ is a traditional formula, but it is important to interpret it in the right way. The point of departure is often John 1:14 regarding the Word's having become flesh, interpreted as stressing Jesus' humanity, his humanness. The formulation in 1 John 4:2 would then be a position taken in the disputes about whether Jesus was exclusively divine or exclusively human. The interpretation is strengthened later by anti-docetic statements in Ignatius and by other Gnostic depictions of Jesus.

Ignatius of Antioch, en route to Rome at the beginning of the second century, combated Christians who denied Jesus' humanity. They claimed that Jesus "only seemed to suffer" (Ign. *Trall.* 10; Ign. *Smyrn.* 2; 4:1–2). They do not confess that the Lord was "flesh-bearing" (5:2). Against this, Ignatius insists that Jesus "truly suffered" for us so that we might be saved (Ign. *Smyrn.* 2). He "was truly born, and did eat and drink. He was truly persecuted under Pontius Pilate; he was truly crucified and died" (Ign. *Trall.* 9:1–2). Jesus is "both flesh and spirit" (Ign. *Eph.* 7:2). At the end of the second century, Irenaeus tells the story of an early Gnostic, Cerinthus, who was said to have met the disciple John in Ephesus. According to Cerinthus, the world was not created by God; Jesus was not born of a virgin; the divine Christ united with Jesus at his baptism, but left him before his death, "because he was a spiritual being" (Irenaeus, *Haer.* 1.26.1). This corresponds to the Gnostic division of reality into matter and spirit. "The flesh" is to be disparaged; the Spirit is utterly essential. A docetic or Gnostic interpretation of 1 John 4:2, however, has very little support in the letter as a whole. Outside of the Johannine letters, the phrase "Jesus Christ as come in the flesh" is interpreted solely from a materialistic point of view.

In an *intra-Johannine perspective,* according to which the letter is an exposition of specific statements in the Gospel, the point of departure once more is "Jesus Christ as come in the flesh" or "Jesus Christ come in the flesh" as an independent expression. The focus is on the interpretation of "come in the flesh." Raymond Brown rejects an interpretation that implies the incarnation. It does not say that Jesus became flesh, but that he came in the flesh. Nor does the emphasis lie on Jesus' humanity itself, but on the significance for salvation that was attributed to Jesus' humanity. The opposition denied that what Jesus was and did during his earthly life had any relationship to one's being a Christian, i.e., that it had any salvific significance. Martinus de Boer has developed this interpretation further by reading 1 John 4:2 together with 5:6; he claims that "in the flesh" is primarily a reference to Jesus' death as a model for loving one's fellow believers, which is the theme of 1 John 3:11–24 and 4:7–21. The section 4:1–6 would then be part of the argument running through 3:11—4:21. This reading, too, goes far beyond the most natural understanding of the words, even though it is more connected to the letter as a whole. It also puts the focus on the opposition in the letter much more than I do, and de Boer's suggested reading rejects the structure that takes 1 John 4:1–6 and 4:7–21 as respectively deepening the two halves of the foundational commandment in 1 John 3:23.

All these interpretations of 1 John 4:3 have their difficulties. Nevertheless, I think that the first of them corresponds best to the usual meanings of the words and is well anchored in the letter as a whole. But this view presupposes an intra-Jewish perspective. Jews who had at one time confessed Jesus as Messiah, God's son, had now left this "teaching about the Messiah" and returned to their previous faith. This is the serious background to the argument in 1 John, an argument intended to encourage and strengthen the faith of the letter's recipients. When this intra-Jewish situation no longer existed for the letter's later readers, the words took on a new meaning.

Appendix 15

God in Them and They in God

The believers' close union with God or with Jesus is often described in the Johannine writings with phrases of the type "A is in B" or "A remains in B." These phrases occur also in the reciprocal formulation, "A is/remains in B and B is/remains in A." Thus sometimes "remain in" is used and sometimes "be in." Only the word "in" occurs in both. The differences between the alternatives are seldom significant. In "remain in" there is often a nuance of permanency. Permanence is what characterizes God and what belongs to God (Dan 6:26; Wis 7:27; 1 Pet 1:25). Even the Messiah "remains forever" (John 12:34), and thus Jesus, God's son. In John 14:10 both expressions are used in parallel.

In his commentary on the Johannine letters, Raymond Brown has catalogued various examples, first for the phrase "be in" and then for the phrase "remain in." Since there is no great difference between these phrases as used in 1 John, I will consider them together. The notation "+John" following an example indicates that the corresponding combination occurs in the Gospel of John.

A. Someone Is/remains in Someone

God is/remains in them (1 John 3:24; 4:4 (?), 12, 13, 15, 16).

They are/remain in God (1 John 2:5, 6; 3:24; 4:13, 15, 16).

They remain in Jesus Christ (1 John 2:27, 28; 3:16 (?) +John).

They remain in the Son and the Father (1 John 2:24 +John).

They are in the True one, in his son Jesus Christ (1 John 5:20).

The Spirit of truth is in them (1 John 4:4 (?) +John).

Appendix 15: God in Them and They in God

B. Something Is/remains in Someone

The Father's love is not in the one who loves the world (1 John 2:15).

God's love does not remain in the one who does not love (1 John 3:17).

God's word is not in the one who does not believe (1 John 1:10).

God's word remains in the believer (1 John 2:14).

God's seed remains in the believer (1 John 3:9).

The anointing that the believers received remains in them (1 John 2:27).

The truth is not in the one who does not believe (1 John 1:8; 2:4 +John).

The truth remains in the believer (2 John 2).

There is no darkness at all in God (1 John 1:5).

There is no sin in Jesus (1 John 3:5 +John).

Eternal life is in God's son (1 John 5:11).

Eternal life does not remain in the one who does not believe (1 John 3:15).

There is no cause of stumbling in the believer (1 John 2:10).

What the believers heard from the beginning remains in them (1 John 2:24).

C. Other Similar Phrases

Someone is/remains in the light/darkness (1 John 1:7; 2:9–11).

Someone/something is in the world (1 John 4:3, 4, 17; 2:15–16 +John).

Someone remains in death (1 John 3:14).

Someone remains in love (1 John 4:16 +John).

Someone remains in the teaching about the Messiah (2 John 9).

Someone has God's testimony within himself or herself (1 John 5:10).

There is no fear in love (1 John 4:18).

The use of the verb "remain in" (*menein en*) in these phrases is entirely unique to the Johannine writings. The verb itself is used often—68 of 118 times in the New Testament—and has a broad field of meaning: remain, be, be left, stay, remain behind, dwell, rest, continue, be closely united with. The verb contains both a spatial and a temporal component. For the examples listed above, the most frequently used translation is "remain in" or "abide in," as in the metaphor of the branches in the vine (John 15:4). The use of *menein en* is common in both the letters and the Gospel, but there are marked differences. Group B above is used significantly more often in the letters, and as for Group A, the emphasis of its use in the first letter lies on the relationships between God and Jesus and the disciples.

Appendix 15: God in Them and They in God

Typical of the Gospel are such Jesus-sayings as "I am in the Father and the Father is in me" (John 14:10–11); "Remain in me, and I will remain in you" (John 15:4); and Jesus' prayer, "that as you, Father, are in me and I in you, so shall they also be in us" (John 17:21). There are three parties involved, even though "remain in" is never used of the relation between God and the disciples. The relationship between God and Jesus is described with "remain/ be in" 13 times and the relationship between Jesus and the disciples 14 times, in both cases with reciprocal formulations. Especially striking is the use of "remain in" in Jesus' discourse about the true vine, a picture of the genuine Israel, or—perhaps better—the renewed Israel (John 15:1–17).

The use of "remain in" in the letters has to do almost exclusively with the relationship between God and human beings: they remain in God and God remains in them (1 John 3:24; 4:13, 15, 16). The examples of the believers being/remaining in Jesus Christ have been questioned by some commentators—only the word "him" occurs in 1 John 2:27–28 and 3:6, and the word *en* in 1 John 5:20 can be interpreted instrumentally, "by means of." But in the main the Gospel and the letter are quite alike. Jesus is always there as mediator between God and human beings. Both documents speak in the same terms regarding the relationship between the believers, the Son, and the Father (John 14:23; 1 John 2:24). But the focus and the formulations are markedly different. Rudolf Schnackenburg claims that the relationship between the Father and the Son is primary: the Father in the Son and the Son in the Father expresses unity in word and deed between the two. This is then carried over to the relationship between Jesus and the disciples. It was then developed into a description of the relationship between God and the believers. What is remarkable, however, is that statements of the type "the Father is in the Son and the Son is in the Father" are completely absent from the letter and that the formulation "God remains in them and they remain in God" is not found in the Gospel.

The examples in Group A are the most interesting ones, especially the unique reciprocal formulations of the type "God is in us and we are in God." Groups B and C are related to the dualistic pattern in the letter, whereby people are distinguished according to what dominates their inward being and thus characterizes their lives. These formulations are not used in contemporary extra-biblical texts, even though they contain numerous parallels to the first part of the expression, namely that humanity is in God. The reciprocal formula remains characteristic for the Johannine concept of God's presence in humanity and vice versa. It is an essential part of Johannine immanence theology: the believers in God/Jesus, God/Jesus in the believers, God and Jesus in each other.

To this point, no one has identified a plausible background for the formulations of this mutual immanence between God and humanity in 1 John. Some interpreters have referred to the OT: God dwells among his people in the temple and its cultus (2 Chron 6:18); likewise according to promises for the future (Ezek 48:35). The divine wisdom has found a place in Israel's midst (Sir 24:3, 6; Wis 7:25, 27). Others have

Appendix 15: God in Them and They in God

recalled the Pauline formula "in Christ" with its probable connection to the idea of the congregation as the body of Christ. But this scarcely suffices as background. The best suggestion is the complex of ideas regarding the covenant in the OT and within Judaism, especially ideas regarding a renewed covenant. When God reestablishes Israel and renews his covenant, he will build his temple in their midst and dwell with them. He will be their God and they will be his people in truth and righteousness. He will create "a holy spirit for them" and then they will cling to his commandments with all their soul. "I will be a father to them and they will be sons to me." All of them will be called "sons of the living God." All the angels then will realize that "they are my sons and I am their father in truth and righteousness, and that I love them" (*Jub.* 1:15–25).

Conceptions of "God in them" occur in other texts. God will put his law within them—LXX has "in their mind"—and write it on their hearts. Then he will be their God and they will be his people (Jer 31:31–34). God will give them a new heart and put a new spirit in their breast. "And I will give my spirit in them" (thus the LXX). Then they shall be God's people and God will be their God (Ezek 36). God has put "the spirit of truth" in the lives of the pious in Qumran so that they do his will (1QS 3). The formulations are reminiscent of such statements in the letter as God's word in them, God's love in them, the anointing in them, the truth in them, etc. Even God's son is in them, and the Paraclete is in them, according to the Gospel. God's *sperma* in them belongs with the fact that they are begotten of God. See Appendix 11, Begotten /born of God. It is not a big step to saying "God is/remains in them." The expanded reciprocal formula, God in them and they in God, thus has been inspired by the fundamental confession of the covenant: "I will be their God and they will be my people." In a new way Yahweh is now their God and they are his people. The new union with God is expressed also with words like "they are my children and I am their father," "I love them," "they shall all know me." The old formulations, according to Edward Malatesta, have been "interiorized," i.e., God and the divine have moved in within individual persons.

An interiorization of older concepts through the renewal of the covenant is, as I see it, the best explanation for the Johannine formulas. It also explains the letter's concentration on the God-humanity relationship and the close connection with the demand for keeping God's commandments (1 John 3:24a), with the Spirit (3:24bc), and generally the close connection with God's love.

Appendix 16

God is Love

"GOD IS LOVE" MUST be the words most quoted from 1 John. Since Augustine preached on the letter in a time of internal church conflict, in the year 407 or 415, it has become one of Christendom's primary texts about love. In the New Testament, the concept occurs most in Paul and John. The former predominantly uses the noun "love" (seventy-five of 108 times), while the latter gives greater place to the verb "to love" (seventy-one of 101 times), perhaps as a way of expressing the great weight John lays on the very act of love. Viewed in terms of percentages, 1 John is the New Testament writing that has most to say about love. The noun "love" (*agapē*), occurs twenty-one times, the verb "to love" (*agapan*), thirty-one times, and the verbal adjective "beloved" (*agapētos*), ten times. Two thirds of these "love"-words are found in the section 1 John 4:7—5:4.

Similar to expressions such as "remain in," "know," and "be one with," the word "love" functions in the Johannine writings as a term of relationship, primarily between persons, and it can thus have various subjects and objects:

1. God loves human beings.
2. Human beings love God.
3. God loves Jesus.
4. Jesus loves God.
5. Jesus loves his disciples.
6. The disciples love Jesus.
7. The disciples love one another.

Frequently a mutual—reciprocal—relationship is expressed where several of these clauses are used simultaneously, e.g., Jesus loves the disciples and the disciples love Jesus. There is however a noticeable difference between the Gospel and the letter. In the Gospel, there are eleven instances of (5) and ten of (6), seven of (3) and one of (4), six of (7) and four of (1). Alternative (2) does not occur at all. In the letter, alternative (7)

Appendix 16: God is Love

dominates; if we include "love/hate one's brother/brothers/God's children," it occurs 14 times. Alternatives (1) and (2) occur twelve times, and "love" (as both noun and verb) without a clearly marked object occurs eleven times. Alternatives (3), (4), (5), and (6) do not occur at all. In addition, the formulations are more varied, especially regarding the love of God: God's love in us (six times), the love that God has in us (once), God is love (three times), and love comes from God (once). Thus the letter focuses entirely on the love between God and the Jesus-believers and on the mutual love between Jesus-believers. At the center stands God's love. The letter gives no general Christian teaching about love, even though many people try to read it that way.

There are thus a number of passages in the letter where it is not clear what the subject and object are: "the love of God/the Father" (1 John 2:5, 15; 3:17; 4:9, 12; 5:3; see the note, "the love of God" at 2:5); the noun "love" (1 John 3:16; 4:7, 10, 16, 17, 18 (three times); 5:3), and the verb "love" without an object (1 John 3:14, 18; 4:7, 8, 19). The immediate context for these passages and the letter's teaching about love in general supports the view that even here the topic is God's love for humanity, or in some instances the mutual love between brothers and sisters in the faith. An argument for this is provided also by constructions of the type "God's love has been perfected in someone" (1 John 2:5; 4:12), "God's love is in someone" (1 John 2:15), "God's love remains in someone" (1 John 3:17), "God's love is revealed in someone" (1 John 4:9). 1 John 5:3 and 2:15 have been suggested as exceptions. The letter's entire frame of reference is dominated by the fact that God is love and that this love flows out in the mutual love among those born of God. In one sense it is like a divine ellipsis with God and those who have been made divine as subject and object. Indirectly it also involves Jesus (1 John 3:16), not least through the description of God's love as his having sent his son into the world in order to save it (1 John 4:9–10, 14). This last point can also be taken as an argument that in the end, all humanity is involved.

There are many words for "to love" in Greek, e.g., *erasthai* (mostly referring to sensual, erotic love); *philein* (often referring to friendship); *stergein* (a more general term for love); and *agapan* (which especially indicates genuine appreciation and respect). These various words do, however, overlap one another in meaning. In the letters of John, only *agapan* and words derived from it are used. It is not a common word in Greek literature and to a great degree has received its content from its use in biblical texts. The sharp distinction that has sometimes been drawn between *agapē* and *erōs/eros*, however, is not supportable. In the LXX, *agapan* is also used with reference to the incestuous love between Amnon and Tamar (2 Sam 13:15), to the erotic love in Song of Songs (e.g., Song 2:4–5; 5:8), to the relationship between David and Jonathan (1 Sam 18:1, 3; 2 Sam 1:23), and to Yahweh's love for his "wife" Israel (Jer 2:2). Yet often *agapan* is connected to the love and obedience within marriage and family and within Yahweh's covenant with Israel. See below. This has a close parallel in treaty texts regarding the relation between a king and a vassal. The verb *agapan* can be used as an imperative, i.e., for admonitions to love, which *erasthai* by contrast cannot.

Appendix 16: God is Love

The words "God is love" should be compared with the Johannine expressions "God is light" (1 John 1:5) and "God is spirit" (John 4:24). These are not general philosophical definitions of God; they are instead firm declarations that God is a personal and active God. He is defined in terms of what he does and his deeds are closely bound up with the consequences they have for humanity. "God is light" proceeds from humanity's situation in darkness and sin and implies that God reveals himself to human beings, intervenes and rescues them and gives them guidance in how they should live. See the Interpretation of 1 John 1:5. "God is spirit" implies that God lives and works among human beings and through his presence in Jesus Christ provides conditions and possibilities for worshiping God "in spirit and in truth," i.e., in the sphere of activity that became reality through Jesus Christ, who is himself the truth and who imparts both spirit and truth. "God is love" implies that God completely without conditions and in full measure loves humanity in all its sin and rebellion against God, and demonstrates that by giving the world his only son (John 3:16), by sending his son to the world (1 John 4:9–10, 14), and with clearly intended consequences for humanity: cleansing from sin, salvation, eternal life. It also means that human beings receive clear instruction on how they should live (1 John 3:16), described in the letter as "to love the brothers," "to love one another." In the Gospel, Christ stands out as love's example and source (John 13:34–35; 15:12, 17). Love is anchored in the love that exists between the Father and the Son (John 15:9–10). Cf. John 14:31 and 17:23–24.

There is no admonition to love Jesus in the Johannine letters, nor any clear admonition to love God, although it can be found indirectly expressed in 1 John 2:15 and 5:2. Everything is aimed at "loving one another," at "loving one's brother." There are two directions in the outflow of divine love as described in the letter: vertical from God to humanity and horizontal from human being to human being. And the latter is limited to the Johannine community. This is the natural reading of the letter's statements regarding love between people. Many readers have reacted against such a limited interpretation, perhaps mostly because Jesus clearly incudes fellow human beings, even foreigners and enemies, in love for one's neighbor (Mark 12:33ff—see also, predating Jesus, *T. Iss.* 5:2; 7:6—Luke 10:2ff; Matt 5:44ff). But this cannot alter what the letter says. A number of readers have pointed to the example of Cain and Abel and the general formulations in 1 John 3:12–16 as evidence that the letter's concern is for humanity in general, but language usage, rhetoric, and context all speak against an interpretation that "brothers" means all fellow human beings. Many have also appealed to the absolute use of "to love"—lacking an expressed object—as a general formulation regarding all people, e.g., 1 John 4:8 and 19. But even here the context speaks against such readings. Many others want to find the double love command beneath the formulation in 1 John 4:21 and thus also love for one's neighbor. But in my view none of these attempts holds up.

The Elder is not concerned with people outside the Johannine fellowship when he writes about love. What he thinks about love within marriage and family, or about love between people in general or about Christians' love for their fellow human beings is not discussed. It is best to keep such questions open. Because God's love applies to all human beings, the Elder could certainly have formed an instruction on how Christians ought to love all peoples, but he does not do so. Love in a special ethical sense is not a theme in 1 John, but rather love as part of the salvation event in "the last day," which began with the coming of God's son.

Why then is mutual love between the Johannine Christians so important? Many are of the view that the author's words are primarily directed against the secessionists, those who had left the Johannine community. But they are more conspicuous by their absence from the letter's central section on love. Others believe that his words about love are part of his pastoral teaching. It is important for practical and ideological reasons that his readers are united and solidified. Brotherly love confirms that they are on God's side. Brotherly love strengthens the congregation's inner fellowship. I want to develop this point further in order to include a basic, fundamental argument regarding the effects of the coming of the Messiah, God's son. Mutual love is part of the renewed covenant, part of the eternal life that the addressees possess here and now. The new union between God, who is love, and those born of God (and thereby divine) have as a necessary consequence that they love one another. God's love in them excludes love for the world (1 John 2:15–17). This is why the argument for brotherly love is so intense. If it fails, then likewise fails the entire concept of the new thing that has come with Jesus the Messiah, God's son. Thus, brotherly love forms one of the core conditions in the new covenant (1 John 3:23; 4:21). Therefore mutual love is coupled both with the idea that God is in them and they in God (1 John 3:23–24; 4:12–16) and with the concept of their being born of God (1 John 4:7; 5:1–2). See Appendix 15, God in them and they in God, and Appendix 11, Begotten/born of God. Thus in one sense the instruction about love in 1 John is a way of insisting on the renewal of the covenant in contrast to Jews who did not believe in Jesus as the Messiah, God's son.

The concept of love as a commandment from God (1 John 3:23 (see Interpretation); 4:21; 5:2–3; 2 John 6) points to the fact that the most immediate background for the Johannine instruction about love is to be found in an Old Testament, Jewish tradition, paired with a conviction that Jesus is the Messiah, God's son. In *Let. Aris.* 229, love is described as a "gift of God" and as "the power of piety." And another intertestamental text reads: "The beginning of wisdom is the most sincere desire for instruction, and concern for instruction is love of her, and love of her is the keeping of her laws, and giving heed to her laws is assurance of immortality, and immortality brings one near to God" (Wis 6:17–19). God demonstrates his love for the people by promising them to send the Messiah; his love is identical with the mercy he has toward the entire world (*Ps. Sol.* 18:3–4).

The idea of God's love in the Old Testament is primarily connected with God's covenant with Israel, made visible through the Exod from Egypt (Hos 11:1). In the desert God found his beloved (Jer 2:2). The covenantal relationship is described as

Appendix 16: God is Love

love between a man and a woman within marriage (Hosea 1–3) or as love between father and son (Hos 11:1). Israel becomes God's firstborn son, his only son (Exod 4:22). Israel has no other god than Yahweh. And this "love-relationship" has its origin exclusively in God's love. It was he who first loved Israel and elected her for his very own. His love for Israel is not grounded in anything Israel has deserved, but rests entirely on God's grace (Deut 4:37; 7:7, 10; 10:14–22; Ezek 16:1–14).

In a covenant context, hatred also becomes the antonym for love (Mal 1:2). To love is to prefer one person over another. In his love God chose Israel. In the Old Testament this love is described with many words: grace, mercy, righteousness, being slow to anger and abounding in steadfast love and faithfulness, to list a few. This is clear especially from the so-called grace-formula in the Old Testament (Exod 34:6–7, etc.). See Appendix 9, A renewed covenant. On the basis of their conviction that the Messiah, God's son, has come into the world in the form of Jesus in order to renew the covenant and to give humanity eternal life, Johannine theologians gather up these many words for God's love for his people in the Old Testament, Jewish tradition into a single word: *agapē*.

There is much more to say about love, even about love in the New Testament. I have chosen in this commentary to concentrate on what is said in the Johannine writings, especially in 1 John. The theme "God is love" could fill many volumes.

Appendix 17

By Water and Blood

THE FORMULATION, "THE ONE who came through water and blood," or "with water and with blood" (1 John 5:6), is most naturally interpreted with referenced to events in Jesus' life or to happenings connected with the earthly Jesus. See notes on the passage. The first question becomes then which events or happenings the Elder has in mind. Or what the intended audience thought when they heard these words. Using abbreviated expressions or new images or visual expressions at the end of an address or a text has a special effect. The content must be filled in by the audience themselves, based on what they have already heard and based on the situation in which the words are uttered. What was expressed before the words in 1 John 5:6 is preserved in the letter as such; the situation on the other hand is quite unknown. The wisest path therefore is to first attempt to interpret "water" and "blood" from what has been said previously in the letter.

From this perspective, there can be no doubt that "blood" is a way of speaking of Jesus' death. Blood, sacrifice, cleansing from sin, and forgiveness have been mentioned already in the letter's opening and have a decisive meaning for the letter's entire argument (1 John 1:7, 9; 2:2, 12; 3:5, 8, 16; 4:10). Cleansing from sin is a presupposition in the renewal of the covenant. See Appendix 9, A renewed covenant. The fact that Jesus gave his own life for the letter's recipients provides clear guidance for how they should live (1 John 3:16). Both as atonement and as model, Jesus' death is undeniably a part of the basic argumentation in the letter.

From an intra-Jewish perspective as well, the focus on Jesus' death is understandable. In the Gospel of John, Peter reacts violently against the idea of cleansing through Jesus' death (John 13:3–10). In the Synoptics the disciples do not at all understand that the Son of Man must suffer and die (Mark 8:31–33 par), and similarly later, during the trip up to Jerusalem (Mark 10:32–34 par). Paul writes in the 50s that talk of the cross is a "stumbling block to the Jews" (1 Cor 1:23). For Jews who struggled with the question whether Jesus was the one who should come or whether they should wait for another, the interpretation of Jesus' death became important, as a historical event,

Appendix 17: By Water and Blood

as an atonement for sins, and as a model for those who wanted to live according to God's commandments. The Elder had many reasons for insisting on Jesus' death as an indispensible part of the confession of Jesus as Messiah, the Son of God. The word "blood" alludes to what was previously said about Jesus' death.

Blood can stand as a symbol for many things: violence, war, death, mortal danger, sacrifice, martyrdom, means of atonement, life, etc. But the question is whether the symbolic use of water is not even more inclusive. Within the Johannine thought-world alone it can be associated with cleansing, baptism, birth, sanctification, instruction, life, eternal life, the Spirit. The interpretation of "water" in 1 John 5:6 is what most determines the understanding of the verse. But here, the letter as a whole does not provide the same help as it does in the question about the blood. The absolutely dominant interpretation that the water has in view Jesus' baptism is placed in doubt simply because Jesus' baptism does not appear to play any role at all in the letter. Even in the Gospel, it has no particular significance. The act itself is not described; even the fact that John baptized Jesus is not mentioned (John 1:32–34). Rather, what does occur there is a heavily emphasized distinction between baptism in water and baptism in the Holy Spirit. John represents the former; Jesus represents the latter. Some commentators thus want to interpret the water as a reference to the fact that Jesus himself baptized, something mentioned several times in the Gospel of John (John 3:22, 26; 4:1–2). It is of course pointed out that it was the disciples who did the baptizing (John 4:2), and what distinguished Jesus was the baptism in the Holy Spirit. The interpretation in terms of baptism is mostly built on the basis of extra-Johannine parallels, in part Christian baptism, in part later Christological concepts. See below.

The only thing in the letter that enters into an understanding of water in 1 John 5:6 is the emphasis on Jesus' earthly life and work in its fullness: "What was there from the beginning, what we have heard, what we have seen with our eyes, what we have looked at and touched with our hands" (1 John 1:1). The word "revealed" (1 John 1:2; 3:5, 8), presumably refers to Jesus' entire life's work. See notes on the texts referred to. And through the phrase "in the flesh" (1 John 4:2), it is the earthly Jesus that is clearly in view. Messiah, the one who was to come, the one God would send into the world, is this same Jesus. From this perspective, water can function as a symbol for a part of Jesus' earthly life, his birth for example. In texts from the Near East and the contemporary Greco-Roman world, water is used as a technical term or as a familiar circumlocution for anything having to do with begetting and giving birth, for the ability to bear children and for the bearing itself. Some texts allude to semen (Prov 5:15–19; 'Abot 3:1); others to amniotic fluid (Song 4:12–15; 4 Ezra 8:8). The question then is whether "water" in John 3:5 should be interpreted in the same way. Set there in opposition to one another are natural physical birth and birth by the Spirit. The former is alluded to in the word "flesh"; the latter in the word "spirit" (John 3:6). Here too a later interpretation in terms of Christian baptism has obscured the content that lies most readily to hand in the Johannine context. The formulations in 1 John 4:2

Appendix 17: By Water and Blood

and 5:6 are reminiscent of the rhetorical figure that the Elder uses in 1 John 2:12–14, a so-called *distributio*. See the Analysis on 1 John 2:12–17, point 2. Here (as there), he first mentions the entirety, "in the flesh," and then the entirety divided into two parts, "water and blood." The latter affords him the possibility of putting special emphasis on Jesus' death. The formulation "not only A, but A and B" needs mean nothing more than that the Elder wants to set forth B as an important part of the whole. Cf., e.g., 1 John 2:2, 21; 3:18; 4:10; 2 John 5.

Raymond Brown, with accustomed thoroughness, has assembled the interpretations proposed up to the beginning of the 1980s, classifying them into four groups. My interpretation is not among those in his overview. Since it is so difficult to define content and function in 1 John 5:6 and its mention of water and blood, it is well worth mentioning here all four types of interpretation. The words "came through/with water and blood" can refer to:

1. *Jesus' baptism and Jesus' death.* This is the most common interpretation in academic commentaries and is almost always combined with various theories about the opponents as Docetists or Gnostics of some sort. Jesus' ministry, according to the Synoptics, begins with his baptism and ends with his death. This interpretational alternative corresponds also to the natural understanding of the word "came" in 1 John 5:6 as having to do with two events in Jesus' life. Blood as an abbreviated expression for Jesus' death has good support both in the letter and in other texts. See above, as well as John 19:34; Matt 23:35; 27:4, 6, 8, 24, 25; Acts 5:28; Heb 9:12, 14, 19–20. Allowing "water" to stand for Jesus' baptism is much more difficult to argue. See the argumentation above. Cerinthus' teaching about a heavenly spirit-being that inhabited Jesus at his baptism and then left him before his death is already attested in Irenaeus and has subsequently become part of the interpretive tradition. See Appendix 14, Jesus as Messiah, God's son. Support for this interpretation of water can be adduced only from outside the Johannine text.

2. *Jesus' death.* Brown, e.g., represents this type of interpretation, pointing to John 19:34–35. There it is noted that blood and water come out of Jesus' dead body, the only place in the Johannine literature, apart from 1 John 5:6, that mentions water and blood together, although in reverse order. Already Augustine had brought these two passages together. Brown's interpretation is very dependent on his construal of the opponents, who claimed that Jesus "came with water." They would not have interpreted the phrase as the divine descent into the human Jesus when he was baptized, nor as the mark of Jesus' humanity—see alternative 1 above—but as an expression of the saving significance that Jesus' incarnation had. According to them, the incarnation took place when Jesus was baptized in water and the Spirit came upon him (John 1:31–32; 3:34). Faith in the incarnation was sufficient for understanding Jesus' action as salvific. The secessionists, therefore, with reference to John 1, would have claimed that Jesus by virtue of his coming

Appendix 17: By Water and Blood

(in his baptism) was Christ, the Son of God, filled with the Spirit.

In Brown's view, the Elder had a broader conception of Jesus' saving, life-giving role. The Spirit came upon Jesus at his baptism, but the disciples received a part in the Spirit only through Jesus' death (John 7:39; 19:30, 34–35). It was Jesus' death that was life-giving. The true salvation "came through water" and took place when water flowed from Jesus' side. The water stands for the Spirit and the blood for the atoning sacrifice. And the Spirit, which the Beloved Disciple received at Golgotha (John 19:30) bore witness already in John 19:35. Consequently, in 1 John 5:6, the blood, the water, and the Spirit are all knit together with Jesus' death. This interpretation seems to me to be considerably more complicated than the one I proposed above. If water stands for the Spirit, then there are of course only two witnesses. And why is the order of blood and water reversed in 1 John 5:6? Does not the text indicate that we are dealing with two separate events in Jesus' life? Does Brown's ultra-Johannine interpretive model really do justice to the formulations in the letter?

3. *Jesus' incarnation.* "Through/with water and blood" is interpreted next as corresponding to "in the flesh" in 1 John 4:2, understood in terms of the incarnation, that Jesus truly did become a human being. The word "come" in John 1:11 and 16:28 is used of Jesus' entry into the world, and at this time the human embryo was regarded as consisting of the woman's menstrual blood and the man's semen (Wis 7:2). By the words "water and blood," the author wanted to emphasize Jesus' becoming a human being and Jesus' humanity. The opponents were understood as Docetists. Any support for this latter idea is lacking in the letter, however. See Appendix 14, Jesus as Messiah, God's son.

4. *Baptism and Eucharist.* This is an early interpretive tradition (Ambrose, Augustine, Chrysostom, etc.). Some are of the opinion that it applies to both v. 6 and v. 7, while others find it more natural to interpret v. 6 as referring to events in Jesus' life and v. 7 as referring to the sacrament. The preposition "through" in v. 6 is then interpreted as "with," which is possible, but not very likely. Jesus came with the sacrament. Most frequently appeal is made to John 3:5 as a reference to the baptism and to John 6:54–56 as a witness to the eucharist. Even John 19:34, understood in terms of the sacrament, has been adduced in favor of this interpretation. It can be viewed as the most unlikely in the first stage of the text's history. Nothing in the context calls for "through" to mean "with." Nothing in the letter prepares us for such an interpretation, and the sacrament has a disputed place in the Gospel. The fact that it later became a standard interpretation in the church is naturally reasonable.

It is completely clear that these readings are to a great degree dependent on the interpreter's view of the opponents in the letter and of the opponents' significance for the formulations in the letter. If the opponents are described as Jesus-believing Jews

Appendix 17: By Water and Blood

who have abandoned both their faith in Jesus as Messiah, the Son of God, and thereby also the Johannine community, and if the author writes in order to comfort, teach, and admonish his readers so that they might be fully assured that they possess eternal life through their faith in Jesus as Messiah, God's son, then the simplest solution is to take water and blood as symbolic expressions for Jesus' birth and Jesus' death. The same basic thought is then found both in 1 John 4:2 and 5:6, but with an additional nuancing of faith in Jesus as Messiah, God's son. In 1 John 4:2, everything hangs on a faith in the Messiah as having come in Jesus' earthly life and work. In 1 John 5:6 as well, attention is directed to Jesus' entire life, from the cradle to the grave, but with special emphasis on Jesus' death and its significance. Only if 1 John 4:2 is treated as concerned with Jesus' divinity and Jesus' humanity is there a clash with 1 John 5:6 interpreted as evidence that the opponents accept Jesus' humanity, but not his death. The fact that the author has used "in the flesh" as a reference to Jesus' entire life in 1 John 4:2 need not hinder him in 5:6 from using "through water and blood" in the same way.

In an interpretation of "water and blood" as referring to Jesus' entire activity, the Spirit in 1 John 5:6–7 takes on the same function as the Spirit of truth in John 14–16, i.e., he bears witness to the content and significance of what Jesus said and did. The disciples could not receive everything during Jesus' time on the earth. Thus there are three that bear witness: the humanity of Messiah, God's son; his death; and his spirit, which the Father sent in his name. And these three are in agreement (John 14:25–26; 15:26–27; 16:12–15). Or in other words: the testimony is the tradition about Jesus, especially that about his death, and the Spirit. The Word and the Spirit as utterly decisive for the audience's remaining in eternal life is emphasized already in 1 John 2:22–27.

The words about the water and the blood in 1 John 5:6, however, quite soon left behind their intra-Jewish context and began to live a new life in new situations. Irenaeus seems to be the first person who clearly read the words in terms of the intra-Church, Christological disputes during his own day and attributed to the opponents a great deal of significance for understanding the letter. His reading became ecclesiastical tradition, later on—quite naturally—complemented with an interpretation in terms of baptism and eucharist. The Word and the Spirit, of course, were continuously active in these sacraments. Irenaeus' exposition likewise came to determine the academic interpretative tradition for a long time. The ecclesiastical situation in the 1970s was different (ecumenical aspirations with focus on tradition and office, among other things) as is likewise the situation in our own time (inter-faith dialog all the more important, not least the relationship between Jews and Christians). This too has left its mark on academic research.

Appendix 18

Testify

THE VERB "TO TESTIFY" (*martyrein*) and the noun "testimony" (*martyria*) occur sixty-four times in the Gospel of John and the Johannine letters. This constitutes considerably more than half of all their occurrences in the New Testament. The two words almost always indicate a relationship to Jesus, either as testimony about Jesus or as Jesus' own testimony. It is completely obvious that these testimonial statements play a role in discussion among Jews about who Jesus is, that is, about whether or not he is Messiah, the Son of God. They have as their overarching goal to set Jesus forth as Messiah, God's son, so that people will believe in him and have a part in eternal life. A "judicial," general logically reasoned argument and a generally forensic situation frequently characterize the Johannine speeches, conversations, and presentations of evidence, with all their variations, sharp formulations, and disputes with Jews and with the world.

Testimonial statements are also part of the picture in problems among the believers: How can one believe without having seen? This is the disciple Thomas's question (John 20:24–29). Seeing and testifying belong together (1 John 1:1–3, 5; 4:14), as do testifying and believing (1 John 5:9–12; John 1:7; 10:22–39). What is seen and heard become traditions that are passed on by persons who simultaneously hand on and interpret their material. See Appendix 5, We in the Johannine letters, and Appendix 10, What you heard from the beginning. The basic question is how what happened once in history can be valid for all times.

In the Gospel there are many witnesses to Jesus: John the Baptist (John 1:6–8, 19–36; 3:26–30; 5:33–36; 10:41–42); the holy scriptures (5:39); Jesus' teaching (7:17), and Jesus' word (10:38; 14:11). Also the disciples who had been with him from the beginning, especially the Beloved Disciple (John 19:35; 21:24); likewise the Spirit of truth, the Helper, who comes in Jesus' place, is to testify regarding him (John 15:26). There are many human witnesses, but the Father's testimony is the most important (John 5:36–37; 8:18). It can appear in Jesus' miracles and in the Spirit's testimony and in the Father's ultimate glorifying of the Son.

Appendix 18: Testify

The letters provide a broader and more multi-dimensional use of testimonial statements, even though it is closely related to what is found in the Gospel. Those who saw with their own eyes testify to the divine life that belongs to God, but that has also become visible for them and through them for others (1 John 1:1–3). They can testify to God's having sent his own son to the world (1 John 4:14). God himself has testified of his son, of the eternal life that is now found in all who believe (1 John 5:9–12). See further the Interpretation for these verses. To the tradition's testimony regarding Jesus' entire life, especially regarding his death, is added the Spirit's testimony regarding it (1 John 5:6–8). In 3 John 3, 6, 12, reference is also made to testimony that believers can make regarding other believers. In their entirety, the testimonial statements in the letters, as in the Gospel, play a role in the intra-Jewish problem over Jesus as Messiah, God's son, and faith in him. For those who believe, but who cannot see, the Elder must also point to visible signs of what is not visible. He refers among other things to the tradition about Jesus, the Spirit's testimony through the believers and their mutual love for fellow believers.

APPENDIX 19

Sin that Leads to Death

IN 1 JOHN 5:16–17 a distinction is drawn between "mortal sin" and "sin that is not mortal" (NRSV), in the original text literally "sin to death" and "sin not to death." Even the verb, "commit a mortal sin" occurs (v. 16). Very likely in view here are sin that leads to death and sin that does not lead to death. Although the former can be understood simply as a very serious sin, that scarcely represents the complete sense of the Greek expression, and the phrase "mortal sin" likewise easily leads to thoughts of multiple "mortal sins," but the author consistently speaks only of "sin unto death" in the singular.

The Elder primarily wants to admonish his audiences to pray for a fellow believer who has committed a sin that does not lead to death, so as to give life to that person, a formulation remarkable as it stands. If the sin is such that it does not lead to death, then why would an intercessor need to give life to a sinner of this sort? It would be simpler if sin leading to death and sin not leading to death were distinguished. In that case, sin that leads to death would be a clearly defined concept. In the second case, the author is thinking only about those who have sinned "unto death." By death in these verses it is spiritual death that is in view. Death is the opposite of Life, eternal life, the concept that holds the entire letter together (1 John 1:2; 2:25; 5:11–13, 20). According to 1 John 3:15, no murderer has "eternal life abiding in him." A murderer is defined as "anyone who hates his brother."

Of course, there have always been attempts to rate and classify various sins. This was also the case in the time during which the New Testament came into being. In contemporary Judaism, one distinguished between intentional and unintentional sins. The latter could be atoned for through sacrifice (Lev 4:1–3; Num 15:22–29); the former, however, were punished in various ways (Num 15:30–31). Qumran document 1QS 8:20—29:2 contains rules regarding those who transgress the law of Moses. The one who commits an inadvertent sin is punished and tested for two years before he can be reinstated in the community. The one who commits a deliberate sin is excluded from community life and is forbidden from ever returning. No one is to have anything

Appendix 19: Sin that Leads to Death

to do with him, whether in matters of money or in any matter of communication. Even the expression "sin unto death" occurs in Jewish texts: "I am not conscious of committing any sin unto death" (*T. Iss.* 7:1). *Jubilees* 21:22 warns against committing a "sin unto death" in the presence of the Most High God. Anyone who does is delivered to the power of sin and will be uprooted from the face of the land.

Some texts distinguish sin punishable by death from other sins (Num 18:22; Deut 22:25-26; *Jub.* 33:12-18). Cf. Acts 5:1-11 and 1 Cor 5:1-13; 11:30). The phrase "unto death" can be used of physical death (John 11:4), but nothing suggests that this idea is in view in 1 John 5. The Christians in Sardis are condemned as spiritually dead (Rev 3:1). Other texts attempt to point out certain sins as especially grievous and as sins that cannot be forgiven. Sin unto death is equated with blasphemy against the Holy Spirit (Mark 3:29 par), or with denying the Son of Man on earth and being ashamed of him (Mark 8:38 par). Some interpreters define mortal sin as an intentional and permanent repudiation of the true faith in favor of old pagan belief or new false teachings.

If 1 John 5:13-21 is seen as an integrated and very important part of the letter (see chap. 12, point 6) and vv. 16-17 are read on the basis of what has been previously said in the letter, there is in my opinion only one answer to the question of what is meant with "sin unto death." The author clearly proceeds from the assumption that the letter's readers understand the expression. To commit sin unto death is to transgress against God's commandments in the renewed covenant, i.e., to deny that Jesus is Messiah, God's son, and to fail to love one's fellow believers (1 John 3:23). The author is thinking of the secessionists, the deniers, the deceivers, the murders, the false prophets, those who have Cain for their example, those led by the spirit of deceit. The descriptions in the letter are many. They have committed the sin that leads to death, i.e., they have lost eternal life, which now at the end of time has become reality through Jesus Messiah, the Son of God. They had abandoned their Messiah-faith and thereby put themselves on the side of the devil, on the side of darkness. For them, according to the author, there is no returning.

The idea is not unique to 1 John. For those who had once been enlightened there is no other remedy, according to Heb 6:1-4 and Hermas *Sim.* 6.2.1-4. No intercession can help them. Neither did Jesus pray for the world (John 17:9). Likewise the psalmist at Qumran wished to display no mercy "on all who depart from the Way" (1QS 10:20-21). See also Jer 14:11; Deut 3:26; 1 Sam 3:14, and Isa 22:14. The believers who transgressed against the fundamental commandment from God in the renewed covenant had permanently put themselves outside the fellowship with the God of the covenant. Murderers—i.e., those who hate their fellow believers—do not have eternal life abiding in them. Therefore the author says, indirectly, that no one should pray for them. According to 2 John, neither should anyone receive these false prophets into the fellowship.

The expression "sin unto death" belongs among those words that early on sprouted their own wings and left the context found in the letter. Christians' interest in sin, and others' interest as well, has always been strong. As soon as the words began to be

Appendix 19: Sin that Leads to Death

read as part of the Christian canon, a shift occurred. Sin unto death came to be generally interpreted as referring to Christians and their manner of living. It then sailed further on and settled in the secular sphere as well. Naturally enough there came to be a considerable number of interpretations of what "mortal sin" can mean.

The distinctions listed above, e.g., have often had an impact on the history of interpretation. Sin unto death is interpreted as intentional sin, or as sin punishable by death, or as unforgiveable sin. Not least, attempts have been made to define the content by designating especially grievous sins. Around the year 100, *Did.* 5:1 mentions a rather large number of them as characterizing the "way of death." At the end of the second century, Tertullian lists murder, idol-worship, unrighteousness, apostasy, adultery, and fornication. During the medieval period, one spoke of the seven so-called mortal sins: pride, greed, fornication, envy, gluttony, wrath, and sloth. Some readers have tried to escape the unforgivability that seems to be implied in the Elder's words by claiming that the text does not actually forbid intercession for those who have sinned unto death. But neither does it enjoin such intercession. They can safely leave these people in God's hands. Or one may try to find a distinction between the two words for "pray" used in the text. See the notes on v. 16. With regard to sin unto death, there is no guarantee of assured answer to prayers.

All of these attempts to highlight various types of prayer, various types of punishment, or various types of sin are contradicted by what is otherwise said in the letter. The letter's basic division of those who belong or have belonged to the Johannine fellowship into children of God and children of the devil remains valid. God's children are admonished to pray for a child of God who has committed a sin, so that individual sins do not lead to the loss of eternal life. Forgiveness and intercession according to God's will removes whatever separates a person from God. For those who "have gone over to the other side" in the final struggle between God and Satan, there is no forgiveness. See the Interpretation of 1 John 2:28—3:10, and Appendix 12, They cannot sin.

Annotated Bibliography

FIRST JOHN HAS THROUGH the ages had unusually many readers and interpreters in the church and the academy. This is obvious in the sheer number of commentaries and special studies. The most comprehensive and basic commentary is the one written by Raymond E. Brown, *The Epistles of John*, AB 30 (New York: Doubleday, 1982). After publishing a large commentary on the Gospel of John (1966, 1970), Brown worked during the latter portion of the 1970s through all the foundational literature regarding the Johannine letters and framed the results in his major hypothesis regarding the history of the Johannine tradition, which he presented in *The Community of the Beloved Disciple* (New York: Paulist, 1979). It should be obvious, especially in my Notes and Interpretation sections, that I have had much joy from the rich content of his work, even if my own overall interpretation deviates appreciably from his. To a great degree he has had influence on the commentaries that came after his. Among the researchers within Brown's "school" I have referred especially to Martinus C. de Boer, particularly his two articles, "Jesus the Baptizer: 1 John 5:5–8 and the Gospel of John," *Journal of Biblical Literature* 107/1 (1988) 87–106, and "The Death of Jesus Christ and His Coming in the Flesh (1 John 4:2)," *Novum Testamentum* 33 (1991) 326–346.

In addition to Brown there are a number of larger commentaries; among the older, e.g., is B. F. Westcott, *The Epistles of St. John: The Greek Text with Notes* (London: Macmillan, 1883; repr., Grand Rapids: Eerdmans, 1966), which deals especially with linguistic details and finds a semantically significant nuance in every variation within the text. He also provide a rich selection of material from the early church fathers. Rudolf Schnackenburg, *Die Johannesbriefe*, Herders theologische Kommentar zum Neuen Testament XIII 3 (Freiburg: Herder, 1953–; English translation, *The Johannine Epistles: Introduction and Commentary*, trans. Reginald and Ilse Fuller [New York: Crossroad, 1992]), was long a standard work within the general, gnostic interpretive tradition. Schnackenburg has a particular interest in the letters' theological content. Stephen S. Smalley, *1, 2, 3 John*, Word Biblical Commentary 51 (Waco: Word, 1984), sums up to a significant degree the English interpretive tradition, but proceeds on the assumption that the first letter is aimed against several opposition groups. Georg Strecker, *Die Johannesbriefe* (Göttingen: Vandenhoeck & Ruprecht, 1989; English translation, *The Johannine Letters: A Commentary on 1, 2, and 3 John*, Hermeneia [Minneapolis: Fortress, 1996]), belongs to the famous Meyer series, where it replaced

Rudolf Bultmann's very concise work from 1967 (also appearing in English in Hermeneia). To these larger commentaries definitely also belong the two volumes of Hans-Josef Klauck, *Der Erste Johannesbrief*, Evangelisch-katholischer Komentar zum Neuen Testament 23/1 (Zürich: Benziger, 1991) and *Der zweite und dritte Johannesbrief*, Evangelisch-katholischer Komentar zum Neuen Testament 23/2 (Zürich: Benziger, 1992), and John Painter's recent volume, *1, 2, 3 John*, Sacra Pagina 18 (Collegeville: Liturgical, 2002).

Grammatical and lexicological problems are treated as a rule with considerable thoroughness in these larger commentaries, but there are special works as well, such as, e.g., C. Haas, M. de Jonge, and J. L. Swellengrebel, *A Translator's Handbook on the Letters of John* (London: United Bible Societies, 1972) and Martin M. Culy, *1, 2, 3 John: A Handbook on the Greek Text* (Waco: Baylor University Press, 2004).

Only a handful of the smaller and medium-sized commentaries can be listed here. C. H. Dodd, *The Johannine Epistles* (London: Hodder & Stoughton, 1946), writing before the discovery of the Dead Sea Scrolls and the Nag Hammadi materials, interprets the letters primarily from the perspective of contemporary extra-biblical religious texts (*Corpus Hermeticum*). Pheme Perkins, *The Johannine Epistles* (Dublin: Veritas, 1979), on the other hand, uses the most recently discovered gnostic texts in her description of the opponents in the letters. Christian Lindskrog, *Fortolkning til Første Johannesbrev* (Copenhagen: Nordisk, 1941) can be regarded as the commentator who most cites Luther. Robert Law's well-known interpretation of 1 John, *The Tests of Life* (1885), as a collection of theological, ethical, and social tests, is taken up by John R. W. Stott in *The Epistles of John* (London: Tyndale, 1964-). One of the more recent commentaries of this length came out in 2000 in the evangelical series, Pillar New Testament Commentary: Colin G. Kruse, *The Letters of John* (Grand Rapids: Eerdmans). The same year brought forth Johannes Beutler's *Die Johannesbriefe*, Regensburger Neues Testament (Regensburg: Pustet); Beutler utilizes traditions of a renewed covenant in his exposition. In Swedish, we have Bertil Gärtner's treatment in Bo Reicke and Bertil E. Gärtner, *De katolska breven*, Tolkning av Nya testamentet 10/2 (Stockholm: Verbum, 1970), 111–309. This work is based on lectures delivered at Princeton Theological Seminary and is an expression of Gärtner's desire to bring in the study of modern problems in texts and commentaries. Thus his commentary deviates in form from the other volumes in the series.

The way in which commentators have typically framed the interpretation of the letters in a polemic toward opponents, probably most clearly seen in Brown's work, has begun to come into question. The critique can be found among other things in the views of Judith Lieu, who wrote her dissertation on the two smaller letters, *The Second and Third Epistles of John: History and Background* (Edinburgh: T. & T. Clark, 1986). Her contribution, *The Theology of the Johannine Epistles*, New Testament Theology (Cambridge: Cambridge University Press, 1991), provides an excellent introduction to the issues and the conceptual world behind the letters. See also, "What Was from the Beginning: Scripture and Tradition in the Johannine Letters," *New Testament Studies* 39 (1993) 458-477. One of her doctoral students has taken her critique of current interpretation to a further stage: Terry Griffith, *Keep Yourself from Idols: A New Look at 1 John* (Sheffield: Sheffield Academic, 2002). Griffith argues, as I do, that the opponents were Jesus-believing Jews within the Johannine community who reverted to their earlier faith. This is a very unusual point of view within the history of interpretation of these letters. It can be found in a couple commentaries from around 1800 and in a few treatments from around 1900, among others Alois Wurm, *Die Irrlehrer in ersten Johannesbrief* (Freiburg: Herder, 1903). It has begun to be discussed again in recent years (Hartmut Stegemann, Hartwig Thyen, Dietrich Rusam). For a thorough account of the entire problem surrounding the opponents, see Hansjörg Schmid, *Gegner im 1. Johannesbrief? Zu Konstruktion und Selbstreferenz im johanneischen Sinnsystem* (Stuttgart: Kohlhammer, 2002).

Treatments of a renewed covenant are important for my interpretation of the Johannine letters. There are a few monographs on the subject from recent years with reference to earlier literature: Petrus J. Gräbe, *Der neue Bund in der frühchristlichen Literatur unter Berücksichtigung der alttestamentlich-jüdischen Voraussetzungen* (Würzburg: Echter, 2001); Stanley E. Porter and Jacqueline C. R. de Roo, *The Concept of the Covenant in the Second Temple Period* (Leiden: Brill, 2003); and Adrian Schenker, *Das Neue am neuen Bund och das Alte am alten* (Göttingen: Vandenhoeck & Ruprecht, 2006). None of these deals with the Johannine letters, however. Edward Malatesta, on the other hand, does so in his dissertation on 1 John from 1978, *Interiority and Covenant* (Rome: Biblical Institute).

A fairly recent survey of research with abundant bibliographic references is found in Hans-Josef Klauck, *Die Johannesbriefe*, Erträge der Forschung 276 (Darmstadt: Wissenschaftliche Buchgesellschaft, 1991). There is also value in consulting Martin Hengel, *Die johanneische Frage* (Tübingen: Mohr, 1993), appearing also in a shorter English version, *The Johannine Question* (London: SCM, 1989).

No major work on rhetoric in the Johannine letters has yet been published, but a few articles are noted in Klauck's review of research, *Die Johannesbriefe*, 75-77, 84-87, and in Duane F. Watson and Alan J. Hauser, *Rhetorical Criticism of the Bible: A Comprehensive Bibliography with Notes on History and Method* (Leiden: Brill, 1994). A number of various structural analyses of 1 John are presented and evaluated in my article, "Första Johannesbrevet: Diskursanalyser och tolkningar," *Svensk exegetisk årsbok* 60 (1995) 141-163; English version, "First John: Discourse Analyses and Interpretation," in Stanley E. Porter and Jeffrey T. Reed, eds., *Discourse Analysis and the New Testament: Approaches and Results* (Sheffield: Sheffield Academic, 1999) 369-391. See also Jonas Holmstrand, "Is There Paraenesis in 1 John?" in James Starr and Troels Engberg-Pedersen, eds., *Early Christian Paraenesis in Context* (Berlin: de Gruyter, 2004), 405-432.

Annotated Bibliography

[Additional comment from translator.] In the process of rendering into English the many quotations from non-biblical sources throughout the commentary, I have often made use of the following collections: James H. Charlesworth, ed., *The Old Testament Pseudepigrapha*, 2 vols. (Garden City, NY: Doubleday, 1983–1985); Geza Vermes, *The Complete Dead Sea Scrolls in English*, rev. ed. (London: Penguin, 2004); Michael O. Wise, Martin G. Abegg, Jr., and Edward M. Cook, *The Dead Sea Scrolls: A New Translation* (San Francisco: HarperSanFrancisco, 2005); *The Apostolic Fathers: with an English Translation by Kirsopp Lake*, 2 vols., Loeb Classical Library (Cambridge, MA: Harvard University Press, 1950–52); *Ante-Nicene Fathers*, eds. Alexander Roberts and James Donaldson (1885–96; repr., Peabody, MA: Hendrickson, 1994); and *Nicene and Post-Nicene Fathers*, 2nd series, eds. Philip Schaff and Henry Wace (1890; repr., Peabody: Hendrickson, 1994).

Subject Index

Anointing, anoint, 53, 66, 139, 140, 142-49, 151, 153-54, 156-58, 171, 176, 184, 195, 247, 266, 299, 310, 315, 321, 339, 341

Antichrist, antichrists, xiv, 12, 52, 55, 59, 65, 66, 131, 139, 140-43, 146, 147, 150, 151-58, 171, 174, 196-202, 205-7, 252, 266, 277

Apocalyptic, eschatological, 52, 58, 59, 65, 66, 76, 127, 134, 144, 146-47, 150, 161-64, 166, 169, 171, 177, 181, 191, 197, 205, 207, 246-47, 250, 256-60, 265-68, 271, 277-79, 287, 289, 309, 312, 322, 325, 327-28

Assembly, see Church

Atonement, sacrifice of atonement, atone, 93, 94, 99, 102, 104, 176, 300, 302-3, 311-12, 334, 347-48, 354

Baptism, baptismal confession, 103, 127, 132, 135, 149, 154, 177, 226, 233-35, 246, 265-66, 269, 293, 298, 315, 319-21, 337, 348-50

"Beginning, the," xiii, 5, 19, 28, 30, 34, 35, 37, 42, 47, 50, 51, 54, 57, 60, 64, 67, 68, 73, 74, 78-80, 82, 83, 85, 97, 101, 104, 106, 110, 112-14, 120, 121, 125, 127, 128, 131, 133, 135, 136, 139, 140, 143-45, 147, 149, 150, 152, 154, 156-60, 166, 171, 174-79, 185, 195, 222, 233-34, 244-46, 252, 266-67, 286, 291, 296, 309, 314-16, 319, 321, 339, 348, 352, 359

Begotten of God, see Born of God

Beloved, 3-6, 11, 16, 20, 23-28, 36, 39, 43, 82, 106, 110, 113, 117, 159, 162, 165, 168, 179, 185, 190, 192, 196, 197, 201, 204, 208-11, 215-16, 257, 276, 285, 310, 312, 342, 345

Beloved Disciple, the, 19, 44, 111, 261, 262-63, 350, 352, 357

Blood, 42, 88, 91, 101-5, 158, 164, 173, 176, 181, 203, 223, 226-30, 233-35, 265-69, 276, 302-3, 309, 312, 318, 324, 334, 336, 347-51

Body, see Flesh

Born of God, xiv, 17, 80, 85, 93, 160, 162, 166, 169, 170, 173, 176, 177, 208, 210, 217-25, 229-33, 237, 239, 242-43, 247-48, 257, 267, 272, 299, 306, 310, 317-26, 331, 333, 334, 341, 343, 345, 348

Brother, brothers, 3, 4, 7-18, 26-44, 58, 68-69, 82, 106-7, 111-14, 116, 120-22, 131, 146, 154, 160, 167, 170, 178-81, 185-92, 197, 204-5, 209-10, 214-16, 218-19, 221-22, 232, 237, 247, 256-60, 262, 264, 268-69, 271-72, 276-77, 283-84, 285-88, 296, 311, 314, 323, 325, 329-31, 334, 343-45, 354

Brotherly love, 131, 187, 190-92, 345

Cain, 55, 166, 177-81, 185-91, 256, 329-31, 344, 355

Child, children, xv, 3, 8, 10-11, 18, 28, 34, 36, 39, 47-49, 56, 58, 60-62, 82, 87, 89, 92-93, 97, 99, 104-5, 110, 117-18, 123, 125-26, 128, 132, 135, 139-40, 146, 150, 152, 159-63, 165-74, 177, 179-80, 182, 185, 187-89, 192, 196, 199, 201, 204, 207, 218, 223-25, 229, 231-32, 238, 241, 245, 247, 249, 251, 257, 272-74, 276-77, 285-86, 292-93, 297, 306-8, 310-11, 317-21, 325-26, 328-29, 341, 343, 348, 356

Children of the devil, 152, 159-61, 167, 170, 172, 174, 177, 251, 273, 277, 311, 325-26, 329, 356

Christology, Christ, xiii-xiv, 12, 14, 18, 35, 39, 42-44, 47, 52-54, 59-60, 62-63, 65-67, 69, 76-77, 79-81, 86-87, 94, 96, 98, 101-2, 110, 114-16, 118, 120-22, 133, 135, 140-41, 143, 145-51, 153-55, 158, 161, 163, 165, 172, 174, 176-77, 191, 194, 198-99, 202-6, 213, 215-16, 218-19, 221, 224, 238, 240, 242, 247, 249, 252, 259, 264-68, 270, 275-79, 290, 295-98, 302, 305-6, 311, 314, 317, 319, 321, 323-26, 328, 332-38, 340-41, 344, 350, 357

Church, house church, congregation, xiv, 3-5, 7-11, 14-17, 23-35, 38-44, 48, 50, 52, 54-56, 61-62, 64-65, 67-69, 77, 80, 85-87, 91, 103, 111, 127, 151, 156, 193, 197, 203-4, 206, 239, 251-55, 257-59, 262, 264, 270,

Subject Index

273, 278, 283, 285, 287–89, 292–93, 300, 308, 341–42, 345, 350–51, 357

Comma Johanneum, 230–31

Command, commandment, 11, 20, 29, 36, 39, 47, 49–51, 54–55, 57–60, 64–68, 90, 92, 96, 98–99, 103, 106, 108–9, 111–24, 126, 128, 131, 135, 138, 150, 170, 173, 179, 181, 183–86, 188–89, 191, 193–95, 204, 209, 214–16, 218, 220–23, 225, 229, 231–32, 235, 247–48, 272, 275–76, 293, 304–5, 308, 310–12, 314–15, 320–21, 333–34, 337, 341, 344–45, 348, 355

Confess-deny, xiii, 18, 33, 37, 42–44, 47, 52–54, 59, 60–61, 65, 67–69, 75, 81–82, 86, 119, 135, 139, 143–44, 146–47, 150, 153, 155–56, 158, 171, 173, 195–96, 198–203, 205–6, 209, 212, 215, 220, 224, 226, 229, 231, 233–34, 239, 241, 244–46, 249, 252, 254–56, 258, 264–67, 269, 275–76, 291, 295, 298, 309, 320, 324–25, 332–37, 341, 348, 355

Confession of sin, 52, 88, 91–92, 95–96, 103–5, 123, 239, 307, 311, 315, 324, 326, 328

Confident, confidence, xv, 78, 130, 138, 166, 171–72, 174, 179, 183, 186–87, 193–94, 209, 213, 215–16, 219, 221, 235, 237–38, 246–47, 260, 323

Congregation, see Church

Conscience, 182, 193–94

Covenant, renewed covenant, xv, 6, 49, 54, 59–65, 67, 69, 80, 83–84, 86, 90–92, 102–4, 106–24, 132, 135, 137, 142–44, 148, 150, 154, 156–58, 162–65, 167, 170, 173, 175–77, 183–84, 186, 188, 193–95, 204, 206, 214–15, 217–20, 222, 231–33, 242–43, 245–49, 256–57, 268–69, 273, 275–78, 289–91, 299, 302–3, 307–13, 315–16, 319–21, 323–24, 327–28, 333–35, 341, 343, 345–47, 355, 358–59

Darkness, see Light

Death-life, 84, 98, 119, 130, 150, 158, 171, 177–78, 180, 186, 190–91, 211, 220, 241–42, 245, 267, 272, 277, 296, 354

Deceive, deceiver, 47, 52, 54–55, 59, 61, 65–69, 88, 91–92, 141, 143–44, 146, 151–52, 155, 157, 160, 174–75, 190, 197–98, 207, 324, 355

Demetrius, 4, 18, 22, 27, 29, 33–34, 36, 38–39, 43–44, 253, 271, 285–86, 288

Deny, see Confess

Desire, 11, 29, 105, 111, 126, 129–30, 134, 137–38, 183, 345

Devil, the, the Evil one, 55, 68, 103, 125, 127, 127–28, 131, 133–38, 143, 146, 152, 159–61, 165–68, 170, 172, 174, 176–80, 182, 186, 189, 197, 199–200, 202–3, 206–7, 226, 237, 239–40, 242–43, 248, 251–52, 273, 277, 311, 318, 323–26, 328–31, 334, 355–56

Diotrephes, 3, 14–18, 27, 29, 31–34, 36–44, 253, 256, 269, 285, 288

Docetism, 264, 267, 349–50

Dualism, 100, 113, 122–23, 127–28, 130, 136–37, 150, 157, 172, 176, 180, 186, 189, 190–91, 198, 200, 207, 248–50, 257, 271, 277–78, 291, 313, 328, 331, 340

Elder, the, 3–5, 8, 11, 15, 18–20, 23, 28–29, 31, 33–39, 43–44, 48–49, 56, 58, 60–62, 68, 82–86, 97, 100–101, 104–5, 118–19, 121–22, 134–37, 141, 150, 152, 154–56, 158, 163, 187–95, 197, 204–7, 214, 216–22, 227, 231–35, 245–47, 249–50, 254, 257, 260–62, 269–70, 275–76, 278–79, 286, 295, 318, 325–26, 332–34, 344–45, 347–50, 353–54, 356

Eschatological, see Apocalyptic

Essene, Essenes, see Qumran

Eternal life, xiii, xv–xvi, 30, 60, 65–66, 73, 75–76, 79, 81–86, 97–98, 100, 103, 118–19, 122, 124, 135, 137–38, 140, 144, 147, 153, 156–57, 161, 171, 173, 178, 180–81, 186–87, 190, 194, 206, 211, 218, 223–24, 228–30, 235–38, 240–43, 245–50, 257, 270–71, 273, 275–77, 296–99, 305–6, 310, 315, 320, 328, 330, 333, 335, 339, 344–46, 348, 351–56

Ethics, 96, 99, 116–17, 121, 146, 158, 251, 266

Eucharist, 154, 235, 265, 350–51

Evil one, see Devil

Example, model, xv, 17, 20, 27, 29, 31, 39–40, 44, 58–59, 99, 120, 127, 132, 135, 150, 165, 172, 176, 179, 181, 184, 186, 188–91, 194, 217, 219, 234, 244, 256, 261, 272–73, 276, 293, 302, 305, 311–12, 315, 329–30, 332, 334, 337, 344, 347–48, 350, 355

Faith, faithful, faithfulness, xiii–xiv, 3, 7–10, 12, 24, 26, 28, 30, 32, 35–40, 50, 52–54, 64–66, 68–69, 82–86, 88, 92, 97, 103, 105, 110, 112, 115–17, 122–24, 127, 135–36, 138, 152–57, 164, 167, 176, 187, 189, 191, 194, 200, 204–6, 214, 216–19, 223, 226, 228–31, 233, 235–36, 241–47, 251–52, 255–56, 258, 261, 264, 266–71, 273, 275, 277–78, 283, 285–86, 291–92, 296–99, 302, 308, 310, 319–22, 324, 327, 331, 333, 337, 343, 346, 349, 351, 353, 355, 359

False prophets, xvi, 12, 52, 69, 90–91, 141, 144, 151–52, 155, 157, 175, 196–202, 204–6, 287, 355

Father, the, 16, 18, 44, 47–51, 54–55, 57, 59–60, 62–68, 73, 76–78, 80, 85–86, 89, 95, 97,

108-9, 114-15, 118-19, 125-40, 143-44, 147, 149-50, 155-57, 159, 166, 168, 171-72, 174, 176, 182, 184, 197, 208-9, 218-19, 224, 227-28, 230-32, 239, 249, 267, 270-71, 297, 302, 305-6, 315, 318, 333, 338-40, 343-44, 351-52

Fear, 109, 209, 213, 216, 219, 221, 269, 309, 323, 339

Flesh, body, 42, 52, 59, 67-69, 80, 121, 126, 129-30, 137-38, 158, 173, 196, 198-99, 202, 205-6, 234, 252, 264-66, 268, 298, 309, 317-18, 333, 335-37, 348-51, 357

Forgiveness, 88, 92, 94-97, 102-5, 117-18, 124-27, 131, 133, 135, 176, 187-88, 193, 247, 276, 298, 300-303, 307-8, 310-12, 315, 324-28, 334, 347, 355-56

Friends, friendship, 4-6, 11, 19-21, 24-25, 28, 31, 33, 35-38, 40, 81, 129, 191, 257, 285, 300, 343

Gaius, 3-11, 14, 16-23, 27-29, 33-41, 43, 253, 257, 259, 285-86, 288

Gnosticism, xiv, 20, 32-33, 66, 86, 118, 157-58, 203, 217, 222, 233, 244, 251-52, 254, 264-66, 298, 320, 326-27, 331, 333, 336-37, 349, 357-58

God, children of, 152, 159-60, 167-68, 170, 172-73, 177, 223-24, 273, 277, 310-11, 318-21, 325-26, 329, 356

God, fellowship with, 27, 29, 33, 36, 39, 44, 60, 63-65, 67, 69, 77, 79, 83, 85, 86, 88, 90, 95-96, 100-101, 103-5, 112, 135, 147, 156-57, 173, 186-87, 202, 217, 235, 242, 247, 271, 273, 302-3, 308, 310-11, 315, 328

God, love of, 67, 100, 103-4, 106, 109, 119-20, 123, 128, 167, 173-74, 177-78, 180-81, 185-86, 188, 190-92, 195, 208, 210, 215-22, 225, 251, 278, 296-98, 302, 309-11, 331, 339, 341, 343, 345-46

God, son of, xiii-xiv, 44, 53-54, 64-65, 82, 86, 99-101, 124, 128, 136, 138, 141, 151, 155, 157, 160, 166, 175, 184, 202, 204, 206, 209, 212, 223-24, 226, 228-29, 233, 237-38, 246, 254, 256, 258, 262, 266, 268, 271, 276, 291, 302, 305, 314-15, 348, 350-52, 355

God, *sperma*/seed of, 153, 160, 166, 173, 177, 189, 247, 267, 299, 304 317-18, 320-21, 327, 339, 341

God, word of, 83, 92, 98, 100, 108, 110, 115, 119-20, 125, 128, 133, 135-36, 138, 148, 153, 177, 194, 206, 218, 226, 247, 256, 276, 305, 314-15, 321, 324, 339, 341

Hate, see Love-hate

Have God, 47, 54, 67, 143, 156, 189, 228, 271, 310

Heathen, 151, 244

Hospitality, 3, 7, 9, 13, 33, 36, 38, 41, 44, 68, 283-84

House church, see Church

Idols, 112, 137, 156-57, 238, 241-42, 244-45, 249-50, 307-9, 311-12, 356, 359

Immanence formula, 157

Incarnation, 10, 76, 86, 119, 137, 158, 164, 199, 206, 218, 246, 266, 279, 298, 337, 349-50

Insight, see Know

Intercessor, 93, 104, 138, 302-3, 308, 311, 334, 354

Itinerant, 4, 7, 9, 11-15, 17-18, 27, 29, 32-40, 42-43, 54, 60-61, 67-69, 197, 204, 258-59, 269, 271, 283-88

Johannine Christians, xiii-xv, 4-5, 8, 10-11, 13-14, 16-17, 20, 29, 33-40, 42, 44, 50, 53-54, 56, 58, 60-61, 63, 65-68, 83, 86, 96, 100, 110, 116, 128, 134, 141, 155, 158, 189, 191, 197, 210, 222, 233-35, 250-51, 254-58, 262, 264, 266-70, 288, 294, 295, 305-6, 323-25, 332, 345

Josephus, 15, 17-18, 283, 330

Joy, 3, 7-8, 22, 30, 36, 48, 55-56, 59-60, 64, 66-67, 73, 77-79, 81, 85-86, 94, 245-46, 273, 294

Jubilees, book of, 112, 151, 256, 278, 307-8, 319, 355

Know God, xiv-xv, 17, 43, 49, 67, 107-8, 112, 116-22, 128, 131-32, 135, 148, 156, 172-73, 195-96, 207-8, 210-11, 217-18, 220, 242, 247, 249, 299, 305-6, 310, 312, 315, 318

Know, have insight, 68-69, 86, 98, 100, 107, 117-18, 139, 142, 147-48, 153-54, 158, 176, 185, 187-88, 197, 206, 245, 249, 289, 297, 310

Lead astray, see Deceive

Lie, liar, 88, 90, 92, 95, 100, 102, 106, 119, 136, 139-40, 143, 145-46, 148, 150, 152, 154-55, 157, 209, 214, 224, 232, 251, 272, 291, 315, 324

Life, see Death

Light-darkness, xiv, 67, 80, 83, 88-91, 95-102, 104-7, 111-18, 121-23, 127-28, 130-31, 134-37, 150-53, 175, 180, 207, 217, 246, 249, 251, 272, 275-77, 279, 310, 315, 326, 339, 344, 355

Like God, 86, 150, 163, 165, 172, 174, 257, 277, 306, 310, 328

Subject Index

Love-hate, 111, 123, 133–34, 136, 150–51, 175, 186, 190–91, 215, 221, 272, 296, 308, 311, 330, 343, 355

Messiah, xiii–xiv, 15, 33, 37, 42–44, 47, 52–54, 60–61, 64–65, 67–69, 73, 77, 79, 81–86, 89, 97, 99–101, 105, 116, 122–24, 128, 130, 136, 138–41, 143–44, 146–47, 150–58, 160, 164, 167, 171–73, 176–77, 179–80, 184, 187, 189, 191–92, 194, 196, 198–99, 202, 204–6, 212, 215–17, 219–24, 226, 228–29, 231–35, 238, 240–43, 246–49, 251, 254, 256, 258, 261–63, 266–71, 276, 290–91, 296–98, 303, 305, 309–10, 312, 315–17, 320, 323–25, 327, 332–39, 345–46, 348–53, 355

Model, see Example

My beloved, see Beloved

Name, the, xiii, 3–4, 11, 29, 39, 69, 114–15, 126, 133, 135, 179, 184, 194, 204, 206, 222, 237–38, 241, 246–48, 275, 285, 304, 314, 333, 336

Old Testament, 58–59, 61, 67, 83, 90–91, 97–98, 108, 114, 119, 126, 128–29, 132, 137, 149–50, 153–54, 172, 174, 187, 193, 204–5, 216–17, 232, 244–45, 247, 256–57, 275, 291, 298, 300, 311–12, 319–20, 329–30, 345–46

Opponents, see Secessionists

Overcome, see Victory

Parousia, 161, 171

Philo, 10, 84, 118, 129, 137, 194, 249, 284, 330

Prayer, response to prayer, 3, 6, 22, 50, 93, 104, 115, 121, 137–38, 165, 176, 183, 186, 193–94, 221, 238–39, 241–42, 247–49, 265, 292–93, 303, 324–25, 328, 340, 354–56

Presbyter, the, see Elder

Prophets, see False prophets

Pure, purification, purify oneself, xiv–xv, 99–102, 105, 120, 122, 159, 163, 168–69, 174–77, 191, 194, 243, 246, 300, 306–7, 315, 323–24, 334

Qumran, Essene, Essenes, xv, 17, 32, 77, 83, 91, 93, 103, 112, 118, 129, 135, 137–38, 140, 143, 149–51, 157, 164, 175, 192, 197–98, 207, 244–45, 249, 251, 256, 259, 277–78, 283–85, 289–90, 298–99, 307–8, 313, 315, 320, 329, 341, 354–55

Remain in, 47–49, 53–54, 58–61, 67–68, 85, 107, 139–40, 142–50, 155–57, 159–60, 165–66, 169–71, 176–80, 184, 208–9, 211–13, 215, 219–21, 234, 239, 247, 249, 270, 272, 314, 320–21, 323, 326–27, 338–43, 351

Reveal, revelation, 36, 44, 49, 53, 63, 73–77, 80, 83–84, 89, 89, 92–94, 98–102, 105, 114, 117, 120, , 124, 127, 141, 158–60, 162–64, 166, 169, 174–75, 188, 192, 194–95, 199, 208, 210, 217–18, 227, 234–35, 239–40, 242, 249, 275–76, 278, 286, 289–91, 296–97, 302, 306, 314, 324, 335–36, 343–44, 348

Rhetoric, rhetorical, 19, 97, 122, 132, 192, 222, 232–33, 242, 244, 251, 256, 260–61, 271–72, 274, 344, 359

Righteous, righteousness, unrighteousness, 5, 69, 89–90, 92, 94, 103–5, 117, 120, 122, 159–61, 163–65, 167–78, 180, 186, 188–89, 191, 194, 207, 237, 239, 247, 265, 272, 287–88, 302, 306–7, 310, 315, 317, 320–21, 323–27, 330–32, 334, 341, 346

Save, savior, xiii, 22, 99, 128, 155, 158, 206, 208, 212, 216, 249, 265, 269, 275–77, 302, 334–37, 343

Secessionists, opponents, 32, 40, 42, 68, 87, 90–92, 96, 100, 105, 118–19, 137, 141, 155–58, 164, 169, 192, 205, 214, 216–17, 222, 226, 233–34, 244, 249, 252, 264–68, 278, 295, 326, 332, 345, 349–51, 355, 358–59

See God, 17, 43, 163, 174, 219, 271, 306

Sin, sins, xiv–xv, 18, 52, 88–97, 99–105, 112, 118, 121, 123–27, 130–31, 133, 135, 149, 158–61, 163–70, 172, 174–77, 187, 189, 192–94, 206, 208, 211, 218, 234, 237, 239, 241–44, 246–50, 252–53, 267, 272, 276, 295, 297–98, 300–303, 307–8, 310–12, 314–15, 317–18, 320–21, 323–28, 330, 332, 334, 339, 344, 347–48, 354–56

Spirit, God's Spirit, Spirit of truth, xv, 16, 63, 66, 69, 86, 89–90, 93, 116–17, 126, 138, 142–44, 146, 148–56, 158, 173, 175, 177, 179, 182, 184, 188, 193, 195–202, 204–8, 212, 215, 217, 220, 223, 226–27, 229–30, 235–36, 247, 257, 259–60, 263, 266–67, 269, 287, 290, 299, 305, 307, 309–10, 312, 315, 317–21, 334, 336–38, 341, 344, 348–53, 355

Teacher of Righteousness, 278, 289

Testaments of the Twelve Patriarchs, the, 198, 256

Testify, testimony, 3–4, 7–10, 14, 18–19, 28, 30, 32, 38, 44, 79, 83–84, 87, 102, 104, 115, 120, 128, 164, 187, 202, 208, 212, 220, 223–24, 227–31, 235–36, 266, 268, 285–87, 296, 315, 333, 339, 351–53

Truth, xv, 3–10, 12–14, 16, 18–19, 23–24, 27–30, 32, 36, 38–39, 44, 47–51, 55–56, 58–64, 66–69, 80, 83, 85, 88, 90, 92, 95, 100–102, 106, 108–9, 112, 114–16, 118–19, 121–22,

130, 136, 138–39, 142–44, 148–50, 152–54, 156–57, 161, 173, 175, 179–80, 182, 184–88, 192–93, 195–98, 200–201, 204–7, 214, 223, 227, 235, 247, 251, 257, 260, 263, 265, 272, 275–77, 286–87, 288–91, 294, 307–8, 310–11, 314–15, 320, 324, 338–39, 341, 344, 351–52

Victory, overcome, 125, 127, 131, 133, 135, 138, 151–53, 176, 196, 199, 206, 223, 225–27, 229, 231–33, 235, 248, 272–73, 300, 317, 319

Walk in the light/darkness, walk in the truth, 3, 6, 8–9, 23, 28, 47, 49, 56, 88, 90–91, 95–96, 99–101, 104–5, 107, 114, 121–23, 134, 153, 175, 275, 289, 326

Witness, witnessing, 7, 18–19, 28, 39–40, 44, 66, 73–74, 76, 79–82, 84, 87, 136, 155, 204, 215, 227, 229–30, 235–36, 253, 256, 258–60, 262, 272, 279, 286–87, 289–90, 294, 296, 350–52

World, the, xiii, 5, 12, 14, 47, 52, 76–77, 84, 90–91, 95, 98–101, 103–5, 111, 120–21, 123, 125–26, 128–31, 133–38, 141, 143–44, 146–47, 151–53, 155, 159, 162, 164, 166, 172, 175–76, 178, 180, 182, 186, 189–91, 196–202, 206–9, 211–12, 216, 218–20, 222–23, 226, 228–29, 231–32, 239–40, 248, 257, 265, 268–69, 276, 296–98, 302, 309, 315, 317–18, 328, 330–31, 334–37, 339, 343–46, 348, 350, 352–53, 355